SAINT EPHREM'S COMMENTARY ON TATIAN'S DIATESSARON

Carmel McCarthy

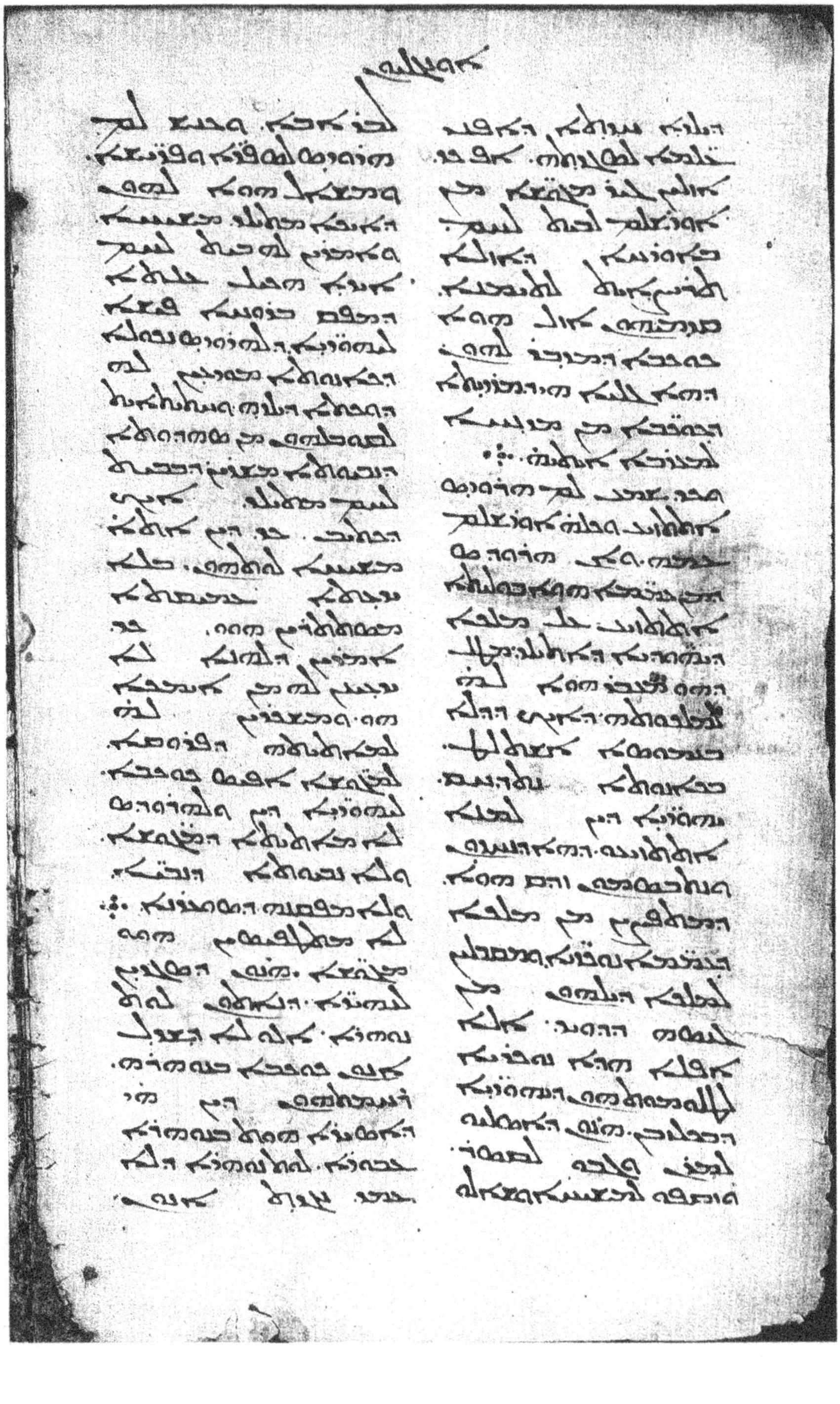

ܗ̇ܢܘܢ ܣܒܪܘ ܕܐܦ ܟܐܠܐ ܠܒܪ
ܐܟܠܩܪܨܐ ܡܛܠ ܚܣܡܐ ܕܒܗ.
ܡܢ ܣܒܪܐ ܕܠܝܬ ܐܠܗܐ ܐܝܠܝܢ
ܐܠܗܐ ܐܠܗܐ ܗ̇ܘ ܠܣܛܝܘ
ܐܘ ܪܚܝܐ ܐܚܪܝܐ
ܚܪ̈ܒܐ ܢܣܝܢ̇ܗ ܠܐܢܫܐ
ܡܪܥܬܡܬܢ ܐܝܠ ܡ̇ܢ
ܚܕܬܐ ܕܡܚܕܝܐ ܚܕ̇ܘܬܢ
ܪ̇ܐܡ ܠܟܐ
ܗ̇ܘ ܐܠܐ ܗ̇ܘ ܕܡ̇ܕܒܪ
ܚܣܡܬ̇ܟ ܡܢ ܡܕܝܢܬܐ
ܠܚ̣ܕܐܟܐ ܐܝܢ̇ܐ ܀܀
ܡܢ ܥܒܕܐ ܠܒܪ ܡܚܪ̈ܘܝܐ
ܐܝܬܘܗܝ ܗܘܐ ܠܐܝܘ̈ܢܐ
ܝܗ̣ܒ ܠܟ̇ܐܠ ܢܥ̇ܒܪ ܥܡ
ܐܟܬܠܗܝ ܟܠ ܗ̇ܘ ܕܪ̇ܗܛ
ܐܬܐ ܡܟܠ ܐܢܐܠܐ ܝܘܟܝܘ
ܘܕܠܐ ܗ̇ܘ ܡܢ ܠܒܟܝܐ ܠܒܐ
ܠܘܬ ܗ̇ܘ ܕܫܐܠ ܥܠ ܡܠܟܐ
ܝܗ̣ܒ ܐܢܐ ܐܠܐ ܗ̇ܘ
ܐܚܪ̈ܢܐ ܥܒܕܘ ܗܝܢ ܡܠܟܐ
ܘܢܒܗ̇ܘ ܐܗܡ ܪ̇ܥܐ
ܘܪܚ̇ܡ ܡܢ ܡܠܟܐ
ܢܒܗܝܐܝܐܟܝܐܘ̈ܐܡܐ
ܠܐܡܠܟ̇ ܗܠܟ̇ ܡ̇ܢ
ܠܣܒܐ ܗܕܢܝܕ ܐܠܐ
ܐܠܐ ܗ̇ܘ ܡܗܕܐ ܘܚܕܐ
ܐܠܐܠܠ ܘܗ̇ܘܬܢܡ̇ܘ
ܡܚܕܠܝܢ ܗ̇ܘܬ ܐܠܐ
ܠܐܟܢ ܘܠܕܐ ܠܨܘܡܐ
ܗܘܝܘ̈ܐ ܐܦ ܡܢ ܫܠܝܐ

Journal of Semitic Studies Supplement 2

SAINT EPHREM'S COMMENTARY ON TATIAN'S DIATESSARON

An English Translation of *Chester Beatty* Syriac MS 709 with Introduction and Notes

by

Carmel McCarthy

Published by Oxford University Press on Behalf of the University of Manchester
1993

OXFORD

UNIVERSITY PRESS

Great Clarendon Street, Oxford OX2 6DP

Oxford University Press is a department of the University of Oxford.
It furthers the University's objective of excellence in research, scholarship,
and education by publishing worldwide in

Oxford   New York

Athens Auckland Bangkok Bogotá Buenos Aires Calcutta
Cape Town Chennai Dar es Salaam Delhi Florence Hong Kong Istanbul
Karachi Kuala Lumpur Madrid Melbourne Mexico City Mumbai
Nairobi Paris São Paulo Singapore Taipei Tokyo Toronto Warsaw

with associated companies in Berlin Ibadan

Oxford is a registered trade mark of Oxford University Press
in the UK and in certain other countries

Published in the United Kingdom
by Oxford University Press, Oxford

A catalogue for this book is available from the British Library

Library of Congress Cataloguing in Publication Data
(Data available)

ISSN 0022-4480
ISBN 0-19-922163-4

Subscription information for the *Journal of Semitic Studies* is available
from

Journals Customer Services
Oxford University Press
Great Clarendon Street
Oxford OX2 6DP
UK

Journals Marketing Department
Oxford University Press
2001 Evans Road
Cary, NC 27513
USA

Printed and bound in Great Britain by
CPI Antony Rowe, Chippenham and Eastbourne

Table of Contents

PREFACE

The challenge of translating this fourth-century Commentary of Ephrem into English for a wider audience first took root through informal conversation with a colleague, Professor Kevin J. Cathcart, the person responsible for the acquisition of the additional folios of the Diatessaron Commentary, on behalf of the Trustees of the Chester Beatty Library, in 1986. I would like to acknowledge my great indebtedness to him for his enthusiasm, support and help at every stage of the venture, and in particular for generously undertaking the arduous task of reading the translation, and discussing the intricacies of Ephrem's style and syntax in some of the more difficult passages.

It has been my special privilege, as a result of this translation project, to have come to know Dom Louis Leloir, OSB, not only through continuous contact with his many publications and editions of the work of Ephrem, but also in person. His sudden death on 15 August 1992 therefore came as a shock, and I particularly wish to acknowledge my gratitude to him for his generous availability, his encouragement and the many useful suggestions he made at various stages in the course of this work. I wish to record my indebtedness too to Dr. Sebastian Brock for his initial help and advice in the undertaking of this project, and most especially for his critical and perceptive reading of the finished draft. His many helpful observations and suggestions have been incorporated into the final product.

Two of my students of Syriac, Elizabeth Barry and Edward Halton, contributed to the clarification of some selected passages from Ephrem's Commentary, and it is with pleasure that I acknowledge the particular fruits their suggestions brought to the translation. I also wish to thank the Faculty of Arts Revenue Committee of University College Dublin for its generous research grant.

It is also my pleasant duty to express gratitude to the members of my community in Baggot Street, Dublin, for their support and interest throughout the undertaking, and in particular to Sr. Cecily Murphy, RSM, for her unflagging energy in reading each draft and in offering many useful suggestions. Special thanks are due also to Dr. William Riley, both friend and colleague, who read portions of this work and offered helpful comments.

Gratitude must also be expressed to the JSS editorial board for accepting this project into the JSS Supplement Series, and in particular to Dr. John F. Healey, editor for this volume. It was a special pleasure to work again in collaboration with Dr. Healey, whose acquaintance I first made when we were both students together in Dublin, more years ago than either of us cares to remember.

Last and by no means least, I am grateful to my family and friends for the support and encouragement they gave in many and varied ways while the translation was in progress.

Dublin, 30 April 1993   Carmel McCarthy, RSM

ABBREVIATIONS

1.   Editions of Ephrem's Commentary on the Diatessaron

CSCO 137   L. Leloir, *Saint Ephrem. Commentaire de l'évangile concordant* (version arménienne), CSCO 137 (Louvain, 1953).

CSCO 145   L. Leloir, *Saint Ephrem. Commentaire de l'évangile concordant* (traduction latine), CSCO 145 (Louvain, 1954).

EC-CBM 8   L. Leloir, *Saint Ephrem: Commentaire de l'évangile concordant. Texte syriaque (MS Chester Beatty 709)*, CBM 8 (Dublin, 1963).

EC-FA   L. Leloir, *Saint Ephrem: Commentaire de l'évangile concordant.Texte syriaque (MS Chester Beatty 709), Folios Additionnels* (Leuven/Paris, 1990).

EC-SC 121   L. Leloir, *Ephrem de Nisibe, Commentaire de l'évangile concordant ou Diatessaron, traduit du syriaque et de l'arménien*, SC 121 (Paris, 1966).

2.   Other Abbreviations

BibOr	Biblica et Orientalia
C	Curetonian Manuscript of the Old Syriac Gospels
CBM	Chester Beatty Monographs
CBQ	*Catholic Biblical Quarterly*
CSCO	Corpus Scriptorum Christianorum Orientalium
EstEcl	*Estudios Eclesiásticos*
ETL	*Ephemerides theologicae lovanienses*
HTR	*Harvard Theological Review*
JBL	*Journal of Biblical Literature*
JEH	*Journal of Ecclesiastical History*
JSS	*Journal of Semitic Studies*
JTS	*Journal of Theological Studies*
LXX	Septuagint
LXX (B)	Codex Vaticanus
MT	Masoretic Text
NT	*Novum Testamentum*
NTS	*New Testament Studies*
OBO	Orbis Biblicus et Orientalis

OCA	Orientalia Christiana Analecta
OCP	*Orientalia Christiana Periodica*
RB	*Review Biblique*
S	Sinaiticus Manuscript of the Old Syriac Gospels
SC	Sources Chrétiennes
SEA	Studia Ephemeridis Augustinianum
StPapyr	*Studia Papyrologica*
SuppNT	Supplements to Novum Testamentum
VigChr	*Vigiliae Christianae*

Corrigenda to 1993 original

p. 52, l. 17	Delete 'in your womb'
p. 78, l. 20	For 'lost' read 'destroyed'
p. 93, l. 15	For 'understood him to have come from' read 'had him come out of'
p. 93, l. 16	For 'Nazareth:' read 'Nazareth.'
p. 93, l. 17	For 'leader' read 'ruler'
p. 93, ll. 17,19,26	For 'prince' read 'leader'
p. 94, l. 2	For 'prince' read 'leader'
p. 114, l. 15	For 'it is… .' read 'is it … ?'
p. 114, l. 22	For 'debt' read 'corruption [i.e. adultery]'
p. 116, n. 3	For 'Mark 9:23' read 'Matt 17:20; 21:21'
p. 117, l. 4	For 'a man, according to the justice of Moses' read 'a man justly, [according to] the precept of Moses'
p. 117, ll. 8-9	For 'sum, lose that which was not required [of him] through that [precept] of our Lord?' read 'sum, according to [the precept of] our Lord, lose that which was not required [of him]?'
p. 117, l. 24	For 'But' read 'And'
p. 117, l. 25	For 'resists' read 'sets right' and for 'He' read 'One'
p. 117, l. 26	For 'He' read 'The other'
p. 119, ll. 6-7	Italicize: '*if each one of you does not forgive his brother*'
p. 121, l. 17	For 'heaven' read 'God'
p. 123, l. 13	For 'given' read 'added'
p. 123, l. 18	For 'more will be given' read 'it will be added'
p. 123, l. 27	For 'taken, we will be given' read 'received, it will be added to us'
p. 126, n. 9	For 'Matt 8:19' read 'Matt 8:22'
p. 128, n. 13	For 'Luke 8:31' read 'Luke 8:37'
p. 133, l. 13	For 'to trangress' read 'to trangress and to sin'
p. 229, n. 13	For 'Luke 7:35-70' read 'Luke 7:35-50'
p. 321, l. 14	For 'showed [that] wood can vivify water' read 'made manifest wood that is linked with water'
p. 322, l. 31	For 'we were bought back' read ' he redeemed us'
p. 323, l. 25	For 'into him' read 'into it'
p. 326, l. 11	For 'while he' read 'while it'
p. 327, ll. 24-5	For 'watches over the faithful' read 'the faithful are guarded'
p. 331, l. 26	For 'I am going up' read 'I am going'
p. 332, l. 6	For 'I am going up' read 'I am going'

Saint Ephrem's Commentary on Tatian's Diatessaron

Introduction

Although Christianity came into being within the Roman Empire, the borders of this vast empire did not mark the boundaries of the early Church. Nor was Christianity in its first flowering confined to the language and culture of Greece. For too long Church historians have tended to look at the early Church through Western eyes, focussing only on its Graeco-Roman origins. This emphasis is understandable to a certain extent, inasmuch as the New Testament itself reflects the spread of Christianity from Jerusalem in a north-westerly direction, leaning towards the capital of the Roman Empire. And one cannot deny that most of the outstanding figures and literature of early Christian history are associated in some way with the area surrounding the Mediterranean seaboard. But it is nonetheless important to remember that another great Christian tradition existed alongside that of the Mediterranean, rooted in those ancient lands dominated by the mighty rivers of the Tigris and Euphrates.

In these lands, whose borders were in constant dispute between Roman and Persian superpowers in the third and fourth centuries, there existed, possibly even as early as the end of the first century AD,[1] a distinctive, independent branch of Christianity, ascetic in outlook and strongly influenced by Jewish ways of thought. The language of this community was Syriac, a form of Aramaic not far removed from that spoken in first-century Palestine, and the concern of this community was with the meditative, poetic and ascetical dimensions of the Christian experience rather than with its intellectual formulation. Its thought patterns and modes of expression were distinctively Semitic and in close continuity with the spiritual and cultural context from which the Gospel emerged. It even managed to retain its indigenous Syriac Bible, liturgy and

---

[1] Cf. L. W. Barnard, "The Origins and Emergence of the Church in Edessa during the First Two Centuries A. D.," *VigChr* 22 (1968), pp. 161-175, who argues that the history of the Church in Edessa can be pushed back into the first century, and that it was strongly influenced by an early Jewish-Christian Gospel tradition.

doctrine up until the early fifth century, at which point the then bishop of Edessa, Rabbula, took measures to deal with the confusion arising from the Nestorian controversy which was in full spate. Thus began the process whereby this Syriac-speaking Christianity eventually became assimilated, on a practical although not on a theological level, to Antioch and the other major centres of Greek-speaking Christianity.

The spiritual centre of this Syrian Christianity was Edessa, the capital of the small principality of Osrhoene, east of the Euphrates, a city which, in terms of its contribution to the spread of early Christianity, deserves to rank in importance alongside those of Rome, Ephesus, Alexandria and Antioch. While there is little, if anything, to link the Diatessaron specifically with Edessa with regard to its origins, some scholars hold the view that Tatian may have composed it in Edessa towards the end of the second century.[1] Whatever the uncertainty regarding where the Diatessaron was originally composed, there is no doubt whatever that it was in Edessa that Ephrem produced his Diatessaron Commentary some two hundred years later.

A brief overview, therefore, of some of the more important aspects to Ephrem's Commentary on Tatian's Diatessaron may be useful, if one is to appreciate the wider significance and richness of this gospel commentary. Exploration of the second-century Mesopotamian world into which Tatian was born will provide some context for understanding the emergence of the Diatessaron or Gospel Harmony itself. It will also prepare for the journey forward into the fourth century, into the Edessa of Ephrem's time when this Diatessaron commentary came into being. The reader will then be introduced to some of the extraordinary events surrounding the relatively recent discovery and identification of the unique Syriac *Chester Beatty* MS 709 which contains this commentary, a work which up to 1957 was thought to be irretrievably lost. The introduction will then conclude with some paragraphs outlining the main features of this English translation of the commentary.

---

[1] See Barnard, *op. cit.*, pp. 167-168, as well as the section below which examines the various opinions as to where the Diatessaron may have been composed.

1. Tatian's Diatessaron (c. 170 AD)

The Architect of the Diatessaron

Born some time between 110-120 AD in "the land of the Assyrians,"[1] Tatian was equally at home in his native Syriac culture and in the language and learning of the Greeks. We know little about Tatian except that he was a controversial figure in second-century Christianity and that he was judged to be heretical in his later years (after 170 AD). Most of our information concerning him comes from the fourth century *Ecclesiastical History* of Eusebius, Bishop of Caesarea,[2] and from various autobiographical comments that can be gleaned from Tatian's extant writings in his *Oratio ad Graecos*.[3]

Tatian was born into a decade that saw the Mesopotamian region caught up in active conflict between the warring Roman and Parthian empires. In 116 AD both Adiabene and Ctesiphon, the Parthian capital in Mesopotamia, were conquered by the Romans, while a generation later the Parthians were again rebelling. Although that region east of the Euphrates was chiefly within the Parthian sphere of cultural influence, it had already come under Greek rule during the conquests of Alexander the Great some four hundred and fifty years earlier. Thus its cultured inhabitants spoke and wrote both Syriac and Greek. Consequently, when Tatian arrived in Rome towards the middle of the second century he would have had no difficulty in communicating in the Greek language, since, as Eusebius tells us, he was "a man who in early life was trained in the learning of the Greeks and gained great distinction in it."[4] We can only surmise why Tatian should have gone to Rome in the first place. Of an enquiring mind and restless spirit, he travelled extensively, and must, at least for a time anyway, have found the principal city of the empire more stimulating and attractive than its eastern fringes.

At Rome he became a convert to Christianity and a disciple of St. Justin whom he greatly admired. Eusebius cites Tatian as a witness to the

---

[1] This is how Tatian describes his origins in the *Oratio ad Graecos*. The term "Assyria" is vague and can often mean "Syria" as well as "Assyria." Consequently, although a number of writers suggest Northern Mesopotamia, possibly in Arbela in the region of Adiabene, as Tatian's birth place, this is by no means certain.

[2] *Historia Ecclesiastica IV*. Cf. G. Bardy, ed., *Eusèbe de Césarée, Histoire Ecclésiastique, Livres I-IV. Texte Grec, Traduction et Annotation*. SC 31 (Paris, 1952).

[3] *Tatian, Oratio ad Graecos and Fragments*, edited by M. Whittaker (Oxford, 1982).

[4] *Historia Ecclesiastica IV*, 16. 7-9.

martyrdom of Justin at Rome (165 AD), using passages from the *Oratio ad Graecos*, Tatian's only extant work. Written in Greek, the *Oratio* was a forthright and vehement rejection of hellenism and a powerful apologia for Christianity, already showing indications in Tatian's personality of the extremist tendencies that were to attract him to aspects of the encratite movement soon after Justin's death. Eusebius described this treatise as "famous, ... the best and most helpful of all his writings."[1]

We also learn from Eusebius that, due to his association with the encratites, Tatian was identified as a heretic in 172 AD. He was even attributed the role of sect leader by Irenaeus and Jerome among others. It seems to have been Western sources which credited Tatian with the founding of the sect, since Syriac sources make no reference to this. Indeed Tatian's ascetic religious ideals would have been fairly typical in the Eastern Church, and, as Drijvers observes, he was "an exponent of that Syriac spiritual climate and its powerful promoter."[2] It is ironic therefore that Tatian should have been remembered in the West, not so much for his outstanding achievement in creating the Diatessaron, but for his various heretical associations.[3] Eastern Christians by contrast respected him first and foremost as Justin's disciple and author of the gospel harmony. Some centuries later, under the influence of Theodoret (423-457 AD), they too retrospectively placed him in the category of heretic. About the year 172 AD Tatian returned to the East. There has been much scholarly debate as to which place in the East Tatian returned after leaving Rome. Some argue that he returned to his home country, since Adiabene was an important centre in the late second century.[4] Nothing is known of the circumstances and date of his death.

The Diatessaron or Evangeliōn Da-Mehalletē

There are many unresolved questions surrounding the original form and language of the Diatessaron. What seems reasonably certain however is that its author was Tatian, and that, having come into use in

---

[1] *Historia Ecclesiastica* IV, 29. 7.

[2] Cf. H. J. W. Drijvers, "East of Antioch, Forces and Structures in the Development of Early Syriac Theology," pp. 1-27, *East of Antioch, Studies in Early Syriac Christianity* (London, 1984), p. 7.

[3] Cf. M. Whittaker, *Tatien*, pp. xv-xvii, and L. W. Barnard, "The Origins and Emergence of the Church in Edessa," pp. 168-169 for useful summaries of Tatian's theological tenets.

[4] Cf. A. Vööbus, *History of Asceticism in the Syrian Orient, I*, CSCO 184 (Louvain, 1958), pp. 38-39.

its Syriac form towards the end of the second century in the Edessan Church, it succeeded in maintaining its position there until its final suppression in the mid-fifth century. The Syrians called it the *Evangeliōn Da-Meḥalleṭē*, "the Gospel of the mixed," and we read in *The Doctrine of Addai*, a document whose date can be fixed around 400 AD, that "many people assembled daily and came together for prayer and for the reading of the Old Testament, and the New, the Diatessaron."[1] Its contribution to the growth and development of Syrian Christianity was due to a number of factors, not least of these being its handy size and its rather rigorous interpretation of the Christian faith along lines that would have found a favourable echo in the ascetic communities of the East.[2]

Notwithstanding its rapid success in the Syrian Orient, scholars simply do not know with any degree of certainty when, where, and in which language Tatian composed his harmony. In favour of Syriac as the original language of composition is the fact that its main circulation was in the East. If one could be sure that Tatian composed it after his return to Mesopotamia in 172, this would tilt the balance in favour of Syriac. However, in favour of Greek is the fact that the Dura Europos parchment, the only extant fragment of the Diatessaron, is written in Greek. This parchment is dated from before the fall of the Dura Europos fortress town to the Persians in 256-7 AD, and covers two verses from Matt 27:56-57 (and parallels) in fragmentary fashion.[3] The fact that the Diatessaron never fell under suspicion of heresy suggests that it might have been produced in Rome before Tatian returned home to the East. Since there is no evidence of a Syriac version of the separate gospels earlier than the Diatessaron, it might seem more logical that Tatian would have made his harmony in Rome in Greek and then taken it eastwards with him, where he would have subsequently written it in Syriac for use in the churches in the language of the ordinary people.[4]

---

[1] Cf. G. Phillips, ed. *The Doctrine of Addai the Apostle* (London, 1876), fol. 23a, p. 34.

[2] Cf. A. Vööbus, *Early Versions of the New Testament, Manuscript Studies* (Stockholm, 1954), pp. 24-25 and L. W. Barnard, "The Origins and Emergence of the Church in Edessa," pp. 168-169.

[3] It was edited by C. H. Kraeling, *A Greek Fragment of Tatian's Diatessaron from Dura, Studies and Documents*, Vol. III (London, 1935). A literal translation of the fragment shows how words and phrases from all four gospels were interwoven. Cf. B. M. Metzger, *The Text of the New Testament, Its Transmission, Corruption and Restoration* (Oxford, 1968, 2nd ed.), pp. 90-91.

[4] Kraeling argues in favour of an original Greek form of the Diatessaron (*op. cit.*, pp. 15-18). W. L. Petersen gives an excellent summary of the arguments of those in favour of Greek as the original form on pp. 40-43 of his monograph, *The Diatessaron and Ephrem Syrus as Sources of Romanos the Melodist*, CSCO 475 (Leuven, 1985).

Yet there are contemporary scholars who favour the view that Tatian wrote the Diatessaron originally in Syriac.[1] Western literature, up to the time of Victor of Capua in 541, contains practically no evidence attesting the Diatessaron's existence. Leloir notes that the West knew Tatian principally as a disciple of Justin, a disciple who subsequently became heretical, but makes no mention of his Diatessaron. Up to the time of Eusebius the situation was somewhat similar in the Greek Church; the Diatessaron was known only by hearsay. Its position in the Syriac and Graeco-Syriac churches of the East by contrast was far less complex. Ephrem regularly cited the Diatessaron text,[2] which in the mid-fourth century Edessan Church was used exclusively in the liturgy, and which, as will be seen later, formed the basis of his commentary. Leloir cautiously observes that if it were certain that the Diatessaron was composed after Tatian's return to the East, then its original language would have almost certainly been Syriac; but he hastens to add that this Mesopotamian origin, if certain, would be the only solid argument in favour of Syriac being the original language of the Diatessaron. Acknowledging that it is not possible to determine with absolute certitude whether the Diatessaron was written in the East or in the West, and whether it was written first in Syriac or Greek, Leloir concludes nevertheless that a Syriac origin is more probable.[3] W. L. Petersen also opts for Syriac as the original language in a closely argued analysis of select Diatessaronic readings.[4] He illustrates very convincingly how these readings "can be retranslated back into perfect Syriac, replete with suffix pronouns, conjunctions in the proper places, and the proper verb forms," and insists that "they *cannot* be retranslated back into Greek agreeing with any known form of the Graeco-Latin NT MS tradition."[5] Tatian's pen, he concludes, when it composed the Diatessaron, wrote in Syriac. A middle position is argued by scholars such

---

[1] Cf. R. Murray's critique of I. Ortiz de Urbina's attempt to reconstruct the Diatessaron in "Reconstructing the Diatessaron," *Heythrop Journal* 10 (1969), pp. 43-49, and L. Leloir, *Ephrem de Nisibe, Commentaire de l'évangile concordant ou Diatessaron, traduit du syriaque et de l'arménien*, SC 121 (Paris, 1966), pp. 16-17. Cf. L. W. Barnard, "The Origins and Emergence of the Church," p.169, n. 26.

[2] Although Ephrem does not mention Tatian by name, there is no doubt but that his commentary is essentially based on the Diatessaron, since its sequence and readings are in agreement with other witnesses to the Diatessaron.

[3] Cf. Leloir, EC-SC 121, p. 18.

[4] W. L. Petersen, "New Evidence for the Question of the Original Language of the Diatessaron," *Studien zum Text und zur Ethik des Neuen Testaments: Festschrift zum 80. Geburtstag von Heinrich Greeven* (Berlin, 1986), pp. 325-343.

[5] *Op. Cit.*, p. 343.

as Drijvers, who suggests that it may even be supposed that texts were written down in two versions from the very outset.[1]

Whatever the uncertainty associated with the origins of the Diatessaron, its importance as an early witness to the New Testament text is beyond doubt. If one sets aside those readings which specifically reflect Tatian's encratite tendencies,[2] one is still left with a considerable number of others which permit entry to the textual situation of the gospels immediately prior to Tatian. In addition to this, the Diatessaron's influence in the East was considerable. Given that it held pride of place in the Syriac Orient for almost three centuries, the Diatessaron has left its imprint on all the Eastern versions of the separate gospels, especially the Old Syriac, and the Armenian and Georgian versions.[3]

Scholars are agreed that Tatian's work in composing the Diatessaron was carried out with great care. This was no random collation of texts, but a careful combination of sentences and pericopae of the four gospels, following a sequence based principally on Matthew which Tatian filled out with non-Matthean material where this was imperative. Two principles in particular appear to have guided Tatian in his work: the elimination of all needless repetition of parallel passages, and an attempt to iron out divergences and contradictions in the words and order of deeds of Jesus. In an analysis of the Dura Europos fragment Metzger argues that a literal translation of the piece shows that words and phrases from all four gospels have been woven together with great care, and he suggests that Tatian possibly worked from four separate manuscripts, one of each gospel, and that as he wove phrases together from the different gospels he would cross out those phrases in the manuscripts from which he was working, according as the work progressed.[4] Otherwise, Metzger holds, it is

---

[1] Cf. Drijvers, "East of Antioch, Forces and Structures," pp. 1-27, who suggests that the Diatessaron was "probably composed after Tatian's return to the east, and most likely in a Greek and a Syriac version" (p.7). Assuming that "the Greek was the first version, based on Greek versions of the four gospels, but that the Syriac one was produced at about the same time," Drijvers asks: "But what does 'original' mean in a thoroughly bilingual situation?" (p. 7).

[2] Cf. S. P. Brock, "Early Syrian Asceticism," *Syriac Perspectives on Late Antiquity* (London, 1984), pp. 4-7; A. Vööbus, *History of Asceticism in the Syrian Orient*, pp. 40-45 and L. W. Barnard, "The Origins and Emergence of the Church," pp. 168-169.

[3] Cf. Leloir, EC-SC 121, p. 20.

[4] Cf. B. M. Metzger, *The Text of the New Testament*, pp. 90-91. In the context of a short note on Tatian appended to his main article, "A Paradigm Perplex: Luke, Matthew and Mark," *NTS* 38 (1992), pp. 15-36, F. G. Downing suggests that Tatian's procedure seems to have been to use "one scroll at a time, inserting material from it in blocks, adding from the other three any detail his current source 'omits' from 'the same' pericope" (p. 36). His argument that Tatian would have used a scroll rather than a codex because the Dura fragment is from a

difficult to understand how he was able to put together so successfully a cento of very short phrases from four separate documents.

In due course the Diatessaron was totally replaced in the Syriac-speaking Church by the separate gospels. In destroying the Diatessaron copies still in use in 200 of the 800 churches in his diocese, Theodoret, Bishop of Cyrus in upper Syria (423-457), was putting the final touches to an initiative to supplant the Diatessaron which had been gradually gaining momentum. At some time probably in the third century the Syriac-speaking Church began to feel the need for the separate gospels, and, as J. N. Birdsall notes, "sought to remedy this by a version which retained much of the honoured wording of the Diatessaron but possessed a fourfold form."[1] This fourfold form of the gospels is generally accepted to be that of the Old Syriac, accessible to us today in only two manuscripts, the Sinaiticus[2] and the Curetonian.[3]

The Diatessaron continued to be used alongside the separate gospels until the fifth century, but its demise seems to have been accelerated by a twofold initiative. The first of these is attributed to Rabbula, Bishop of Edessa (411-435 AD), who ordered the priests and deacons to see that every church should have a copy of the separate gospels. The second, already mentioned, was the more forceful approach of Theodoret. The fact that the Diatessaron was tolerated alongside the separate gospels up to Theodoret's time can probably be taken as further evidence that Tatian was not considered heretical in the East up to the fifth century.

The successful destruction of the Diatessaron in its Syriac form has meant that access to it over the centuries has been possible only through secondary and indirect sources. It is beyond the scope of this introduction to enter into the complexity of the textual transmission and interrelationship of the many forms into which the Diatessaron was

---

scroll is not conclusive, since there is no guarantee that, even if the Dura fragment was written on a scroll, Tatian would have also used a scroll in the original composition. Earlier fragments such as the John Rylands papyrus were already written in codex form, and in an article entitled "The New Testament Papyrus Manuscripts in Historical Perspective," *To Touch the Text: Biblical and Related Studies in Honour of Joseph A. Fitzmyer, S. J.*, edited by M. P. Horgan and P. J. Kobelski (New York, 1989), pp. 261-288, E. J. Epp has shown how extensively the codex form was used in the earliest Christian manuscripts of the Bible (cf. pp. 267-268).

[1] Cf. J. N. Birdsall at p. 364 of "The New Testament Text," *The Cambridge History of the Bible*, Vol.1, edited by P. R. Ackroyd and C. F. Evans (Cambridge, 1970), pp. 308-377.

[2] Cf. A. Smith Lewis, *The Old Syriac Gospels* (London, 1910).

[3] Cf. F. C. Burkitt, *Evangelion daMepharreshe. The Curetonian Version of the Four Gospels* (Cambridge, 1904).

subsequently translated.[1] Suffice it to say that, while it has been translated into many languages, including Arabic and Persian in the East, and Latin, Medieval Dutch, Old English and Old Italian in the West, undergoing various transformations and adaptations in the process, the publication of the original Syriac form of Ephrem's Commentary on the Diatessaron contained in the recently discovered *Chester Beatty* MS 709 represents a very significant development in the search for the Diatessaron text. In referring to these later translations of the Diatessaron, some New Testament scholars estimate that "all these versions with their variants cannot compare in textual value with the witness of Ephrem's commentary."[2]

2. Ephrem, Theologian, Poet and Lyre of the Holy Spirit

Early Years

Born about 306 at Nisibis or its neighbourhood on the borders of the Roman and Persian empires, Ephrem was destined to become the most celebrated Father of the Syrian Church and one of the most famous personalities of the fourth century. His father may have been pagan,[3] and his mother came from Amida, an important city on the Tigris to the north-west of Nisibis. Situated on the fringes of the Roman empire which had become Christian since 313 AD, the region was caught up into political and religious conflicts between Persia and Byzantium. It was against this background of warring factions and religious persecutions that the character of the young Ephrem was formed. He was instructed in the Christian mysteries by Bishop Jacob of Nisibis (303-338) and baptized as a young man in his twenties.[4] The greater part of his life, up to his late

---

[1] T. Baarda gives a very useful "survey of recent Diatessaron research intended for the average theologian" in an article entitled "In search of the Diatessaron Text," *Early Transmission of the Words of Jesus: Thomas, Tatian and the Text of the New Testament* (Amsterdam, 1983), pp. 65-78.

[2] Cf. K. Aland and B. Aland, *The Text of the New Testament*. Translated from the German by E. F. Rhodes (Grand Rapids/Leiden, 1987), pp. 188-189. See also B. M. Metzger, *The Text of the New Testament*, pp. 89-92, B. M. Metzger, *The Early Versions of the New Testament* (Oxford, 1977), pp. 10-36, and L. Leloir, "Le Diatessaron de Tatien et son commentaire par Ephrem," *La Venue du Messie: Messianisme et Eschatologie*, édité par E. Massaux, Recherches Bibliques 6 (Bruges, 1962), pp. 243-260.

[3] The sixth-century *Life of Ephrem* refers to Ephrem's father as pagan; however, his own writings in two passages suggest he was brought up by Christian parents.

[4] In modern Nuseybin today there still stands a baptistry, the erection of which Ephrem probably witnessed during his time there.

fifties, was spent as a deacon, serving the catechetical school at Nisibis. He became a close worker with the bishop who vigorously sought to sustain the morale of the citizens of Nisibis when under threat, especially during the sieges of 338, 346 and 350 AD. Tradition attributes to Ephrem an active part in the fierce but successful defence of Nisibis against an attack by the Persian armies in 350, but some caution is required in attempting to reconstruct Ephrem's activities at Nisibis, since some of these deeds are also attributed to Jacob of Nisibis in *The Life of Jacob*.[1] However, Ephrem does give a graphic account of the siege in one of his early works.[2]

In 363 Nisibis was ceded to the Persians and, in order to escape the persecution raging in Persia, most of the Christian population fled from Nisibis *en masse*. Ephrem went with his people and settled first at Beit-Garbaya, then at Amida, and finally went to Edessa where he spent the remaining ten years of his life. These were energetic years in which he concerned himself with many and varied activities. Tradition tells us that he first worked as a bath attendant, and that he refused advancement to high ecclesiastical office, choosing to remain a deacon to the end of his days. We also know that he was an eloquent preacher, a theologian, a prolific composer of melodies, a choir master, a poet and a famine-relief worker. He lived in a cave close to Edessa, was ascetic in his ways, dressed in the rags of the poorest class, and one biographer records that he ate no food but barley, dry pulse and occasionally vegetables and that his only drink was water.[3]

Although tradition also tells us that "he was sad at all times and did not indulge in laughter at all,"[4] this hardly rings true when one becomes familiar with his writings in their totality. There is no doubt that he would have been influenced by the context of Syrian asceticism in which he lived and would have been aware of its more extreme forms.[5] His later biographers would have been only too happy to picture him in terms of their own framework of exaggerated ascetical practices, thus retrospectively blurring the real stature of the man. The more reliable

---

[1] Cf. D. Bundy, "Jacob of Nisibis as a model for the episcopacy," *Le Muséon* 104 (1991), pp. 235-249, for a detailed study of the sources relative to our knowledge of the Jacob of Nisibis tradition.

[2] Cf. *Carmina Nisibena*, edited and translated by E. Beck, *Des Heiligen Ephraem des Syrers, Carmina Nisibena I*, CSCO 218-219 (Louvain, 1961), Hymns I-III.

[3] Cf. J. B. Segal, *Edessa, The Blessed City* (Oxford, 1970), p. 88.

[4] Cf. *Idem*.

[5] S. P. Brock gives a graphic summary of these excesses in "Early Syrian Asceticism," pp. 11-13.

accounts of Ephrem's life-style introduce us to an ascetic, but one who did not go to extremes. While he certainly practised a very strict poverty, his concern for people, especially the poor and starving, never permitted him the "luxury" of a solitary life in the desert like many of his contemporaries.[1] Leloir confirms this view in noting that if Ephrem had lived monastic life strictly speaking, it could only have been intermittently, since the extent of his activities involved him in a very active way in the service of the Church.[2]

Ephrem and Fourth-Century Edessa

When Ephrem fled from Nisibis in 363 and finally settled in Edessa, he made his home in a city with an established tradition of Christianity. Capital of the small principality of Osrhoene east of the Euphrates and situated on the great trade route to the East, Edessa became a major centre of the early Church, as important in its area as any of the great cities of the Mediterranean such as Rome, Ephesus, Alexandria or Antioch. The accounts of the correspondence between King Abgar and Jesus[3] and the Addai story[4] as testifying to the evangelization of Edessa in the first century have no historical foundation in the strict sense, but these richly embroidered legends do point towards a Christian presence in Edessa reaching back into at least the second century AD.[5] Perhaps one of the earliest clues with a solid historical basis that we possess with regard to the existence of an early Christian settlement there is contained in the narrative of the flood of Edessa, c. 201 AD.[6] This chronicle from the secular archives of Edessa notes that among the beautiful buildings destroyed by the flood waters was "the nave of the church of the Christians." In this context Segal notes that "at the beginning of the third century there was a Christian church in a prominent quarter of Edessa, but probably the

---

[1] Segal notes that Ephrem is said to have lived in one of the innumerable caves in the hillside outside Edessa, which may have given him the reputation of a hermit (cf. *op. cit.*, p. 88).

[2] Cf. Leloir, "L'Actualité du Message d'Ephrem," *Parole de L'Orient* 4 (1973) p. 62.

[3] Cf. G. Howard, ed., *The Teaching of Addai*, Texts and Translations 16 (Chico, California, 1981), pp. 6-9.

[4] Cf. *Idem*, pp. 12-15.

[5] L. W. Barnard even argues in favour of first-century origins for the history of the Church in Edessa, and maintains that it was strongly influenced by an early Jewish-Christian Gospel tradition (cf. "The Origins and Emergence of the Church in Edessa," pp. 161-175).

[6] Cf. Segal, *Edessa*, p. 24 for an English translation of the account of this event.

majority of the population was still pagan."[1] He then points out that a century later Christianity was the dominant faith of the city and the story of its evangelization had become famous throughout Christendom.

This Christian community in the fourth century would have been one in which the Diatessaron must have featured as a central liturgical text, given that this was the form of the gospels upon which Ephrem chose to compose his commentary. Even if there was already a movement in hand to introduce the fourfold form of the gospels into the Syrian liturgical tradition, there can be little doubt that the Diatessaron played a central role in Edessa.[2] The Christian community there would as yet have been relatively unified, particularly when one reflects on the major fifth-century christological controversies which lay just around the corner. These stormy controversies were to engender deep and lasting divisions in the form of later Nestorian and Monophysite communities co-existing alongside the community that had accepted the pronouncements of the church councils of Ephesus and Chalcedon.

Yet Ephrem's writings already testify to many dangers threatening his Syrian Christians, arising particularly from the influence that the doctrines of Marcion, Bardaisan and Mani were continuing to exert on the faithful, long after the respective deaths of these heretics. Here we encounter the forceful side of Ephrem's character as one fearless in speaking the truth. His arguments against the heretics are marshalled with great vehemence, even to the point of virulence: "We have not come to stir up now the mire of Bardaisan, for the foulness of Mani is quite sufficient. For behold our tongue is very eager to conclude at once, to flee from him."[3] Elsewhere of Bardaisan he wrote, "The dirt of the wiles of Bardaisan is found to speak with subtlety" and, "Pray for Bardaisan, for in his heathenism there went a Legion in his heart but our Lord in his mouth."[4] While Ephrem tried with all his might to quench the popularity of Bardaisan's songs, replacing them with his own compositions, he was not entirely successful. Forty years later Bishop Rabbula was dismayed to

---

[1] Cf. *op. cit.*, p. 62.

[2] Cf. Birdsall, "The New Testament Text," p. 364.

[3] Cf. Segal, *Edessa*, p. 90.

[4] Segal, *Edessa*, p. 36. Cf. H. J. W. Drijvers, *The Book of the Laws of Countries. Dialogue on Fate of Bardaisan of Edessa* (Assen, 1965) and H. J. W. Drijvers, *Bardaisan of Edessa* (Assen, 1966). Little in fact is known of Bardaisan. Born in Edessa about 154, he was later expelled and formed a sect. He was an able disputant and composed about 150 hymns around the themes of his religion and philosophical doctrines. Only fragments of these latter have survived, most often in the quotations of them by Ephrem. He died in 222.

discover that Bardaisan's songs had lost none of their popularity and influence at Edessa.

Thus the Christian community of Edessa was fortunate to have in Ephrem a formidable champion at a time when its basic beliefs were being challenged by various forms of heresy. It is noteworthy therefore that in later years his memory was revered by all, whether Orthodox, Nestorian or Monophysite. Even the Greeks, who rarely mention Syrian authors, honoured him, while some twenty years after his death St. Jerome in the Latin West referred to him in his catalogue of illustrious Christians in glowing terms: "Ephraim, deacon of the Church at Edessa, composed many works in the Syriac language, and became so distinguished that his writings are repeated publicly in some churches, after the reading of the Scriptures. I once read in Greek a volume by him, *On the Holy Spirit*; which someone had translated from the Syriac, and recognized even in translation, the incisive power of lofty genius."[1]

In brief, Ephrem was a prolific writer of metrical homilies and hymns in addition to his scriptural commentaries, expository sermons and polemical tracts. His works were quickly translated into Greek, Armenian, Coptic, Arabic, Ethiopic and Latin. These extensive writings fall into four main categories as follows: (i) prose works, of which the finest are his scriptural commentaries on Genesis and the Diatessaron,[2] as well as a number of controversial writings against the followers of Marcion, Bardaisan and Mani; (ii) works in artistic prose, notably the *Discourse on Our Lord* and the *Letter to Publius*; (iii) verse homilies, the most important of which is the collection of six on Faith; (iv) hymns, of which at least five hundred survive. It is upon these latter, collected together into separate cycles in the early fifth century, that his reputation as a theologian and poet principally rests.[3] The influence of Ephrem's

---

[1] Jerome, *De Viris Illustribus*, Chapter CXV. Cf. *A Select Library of Nicene and Post-Nicene Fathers of the Christian Church (Second Series)*, under the editorial supervision of H. Wace and P. Schaff (Oxford, 1892), Volume III, p. 382.

[2] For a fuller listing of Ephrem's scriptural commentaries see p. 296 of P. Yousif's article, "Exegetical Principles of St Ephraem of Nisibis," *Studia Patristica* 18,4 (Kalamazoo/Leuven, 1990), pp. 296-302. For the Old Testament these include an Armenian version on Genesis, Leviticus, Joshua, Judges and Kings, and original Syriac commentaries on Genesis, Exodus, the Minor Prophets and a part of Isaiah. From the New Testament, as well as the Diatessaron commentary, there is also one on the Letters of Paul, extant only in an Armenian version.

[3] Cf. S. P. Brock, *The Syriac Fathers on Prayer and the Spiritual Life* (Michigan, 1987), p. 31. See also Brock's excellent analysis of Ephrem's poetic qualities in the introduction to his translation of some of Ephrem's poems in *The Harp of the Spirit. Eighteen Poems of Saint Ephrem* (Second enlarged edition, San Bernardino, California, 1984), pp.5-17.

writings extended throughout Mesopotamia, Syria and indeed all of Christendom, so much so that it was not surprising to find that a number of later works in both Syriac and Greek were attributed to Ephrem, writings which scholars agree cannot have been composed by him.[1]

Ephrem died in 373. It is said that his body was buried among the graves of the destitute and criminals at his own request, but that shortly afterwards it was removed to the place of burial of the bishops of Edessa. The Armenian monks of the monastery of St. Sergius of Edessa claimed to possess his body.

Ephrem's Exegetical Style and the Syriac Orient

Perhaps one of the greatest advantages in reading Ephrem's commentary in its original Syriac lies in the fact that it permits direct entry into the earliest phase of Syrian Christianity, of which St. Ephrem is undoubtedly one of the finest representatives. This earliest phase of Syrian Christianity is, in the insightful comment of Sebastian Brock, "usually expressed in a manner much more characteristic of the Semitic - and biblical world out of which it grew."[2] Here one encounters a form of Christianity whose theological expression is as yet uninfluenced by the Greek philosophical tradition, but which uses thought forms that are in direct continuity with the Semitic world from which Christianity emerged. Syriac was the local Aramaic dialect of Edessa, the traditional birthplace of Syrian Christianity, and would have been mutually comprehensible with Galilean Aramaic. Indeed it has been suggested that the form of the Lord's Prayer used in Syrian churches today cannot be all that different from the words that Jesus himself must have uttered in first-century Galilean Aramaic.[3]

---

[1] Cf. R. Murray, *Symbols of Church and Kingdom, A Study in Early Syriac Tradition* (Cambridge, 1975), pp. 29-32 for a useful summary of this question.

[2] S. P. Brock, *The Syriac Fathers*, pp. x-xi.

[3] Cf. S. P. Brock, *The Syriac Fathers*, p. x. It is difficult to see how one could opt for one of the two traditions of the Lord's Prayer as representing what might have been the original Aramaic, all the more so since the Lukan tradition is shorter, and both forms show the tendencies of their respective redactors! Therefore, it is rather surprising to find Johannes de Moor in "The Reconstruction of the Aramaic Original of the Lord's Prayer," *The Structural Analysis of Biblical and Canaanite Poetry*, edited by W. van der Meer and J. C. de Moor, *JSOT* Supplement Series 74 (Sheffield, 1988), pp. 397-422, holding the view that "the differences between Matthew's and Luke's version of the Lord's prayer ... can be fully explained on the basis of the characteristics of Semitic Poetry" (p. 422). For a full analysis of the Aramaic dialects of this period see in particular the very thorough work of K. Beyer, *The Aramaic Language. Its Distribution and Subdivisions*, Translated from the German by

The Syriac literature of this period therefore can rightly be characterized "as the sole surviving representative of a genuinely Semitic Christianity."[1] The two major authors of the fourth century, Aphrahat and Ephrem, attest a Semitic form of Christianity, to be distinguished in many respects from the Christianity of the Greek and Latin-speaking world of the Mediterranean seaboard. Perhaps a simple way of distinguishing this form of Christianity might be to characterize its approach as being primarily symbolic and synthetic, whereas the Greek approach soon demonstrated a more philosophical and analytical character. It would have been only from the fifth century onwards, in the aftermath of the Chalcedonian and post-Chalcedonian controversies, that the Syriac-speaking Churches would have been rapidly exposed to hellenization, with the result that no subsequent authors would have escaped from Greek influence of one kind or another. Yet one must not imagine however too sharp a divide between the Semitic approach and that of Ephrem's contemporaries who wrote in Greek and Latin. When it is remembered that, by the fourth century AD, Hellenistic cultures would have been present in the middle East for over half a millennium, one could expect that no Syriac writer of Ephrem's time would have been totally unhellenized, nor would any Greek Christian writer of that time be totally unsemitized. As Brock puts it, "it was simply a matter of degree."[2]

It is therefore important to reserve the term *Syriac Orient* for specifying that earliest flowering of Syriac-speaking Christianity as yet essentially uninfluenced by either Greek or Latin thought forms. Brock is quite adamant in insisting that to the familiar pair of Greek East and Latin West there should be added a third component of Christian tradition, the Syriac Orient.[3] But he immediately adds that none of these three traditions was isolated from the others, for not only do they have common roots in the gospel message, but throughout their existence they have always

---

John F. Healey (Göttingen, 1986), pp. 34-40, as well as J. A. Fitzmyer's classification of Aramaic dialects in his work, *The Genesis Apocryphon of Qumran Cave I, A Commentary* (Rome, Second, Revised Edition 1971), pp. 22-23, n. 60 and his article on "The Languages of Palestine in the First Century AD," *CBQ* 32 (1970), pp. 501-531.

[1] S. P. Brock, "An Introduction to Syriac Studies," *Horizons in Semitic Studies: Articles for the Student*, edited by J. H. Eaton, University Semitic Study Aids 8 (University of Birmingham, 1980), pp. 4-5.

[2] *The Luminous Eye. The Spiritual World Vision of St. Ephrem* (Kalamazoo, 1992), p. 143.

[3] S. P. Brock, *The Syriac Fathers*, p. xxxiii.

interacted with one another, directly and indirectly, and often in unexpected ways.[1]

If early Syrian Christianity can indeed be described as the product of a creative and fruitful meditation upon Scripture, then the person of Ephrem is by far its most eloquent spokesperson. It is no small statement on the part of Brock to have characterized Ephrem as certainly ranking "as the finest poet in any language of the patristic period."[2] Robert Murray speaks of him in equally superlative terms as follows: "Personally I do not hesitate to evaluate Ephrem ... as the greatest poet of the patristic age, and perhaps, the only *theologian-poet* to rank beside Dante."[3] Even when Ephrem is expressing himself in prose, his poetic genius seeps through what has been termed "his involved and highly allusive Syriac."[4] It is not surprising therefore that there are some passages, even in his commentary, which are difficult to translate because they are charged with a variety of meanings which cannot be accommodated in a single English equivalent.[5]

Characteristic Themes and Imagery in the Commentary

Ephrem's exegesis is a testimony to how much both he and the Church for whom he wrote were at home in the Scriptures. The gospel text as he encounters it in the Diatessaron is his starting point, but he displays great freedom and at times unpredictability in what he chooses to

---

[1] In a paper presented to the International Conference on Patristic Studies in Oxford 1987, "From Ephrem to Romanos," *Studia Patristica* 20 (Leuven, 1989), pp. 139-151, S. P. Brock has examined this interaction in the area of poetry, by taking Ephrem and Romanos as representatives of Syria's two great literary traditions, Syriac and Greek, and, set within the framework of the fourth to the first half of the sixth century, has focussed on "the possibility (I would say probability) of the transmission of literary motifs in the other direction, from Syriac to Greek" (p. 144, the words in parentheses are Brock's). Cf also W. L. Petersen, "The Dependence of Romanos the Melodist upon the Syriac Ephrem," *Studia Patristica* 18,4 (Kalamazoo/Leuven, 1990), pp. 274-281, who argues in favour of a Syriac original for Romanos' compositions.

[2] *The Syriac Fathers*, p. xv.

[3] R. Murray, *Symbols of Church and Kingdom*, p. 31.

[4] P. Robson, "Ephrem as Poet," *Horizons in Semitic Studies: Articles for the Student*, edited by J. H. Eaton, University Semitic Study Aids 8 (University of Birmingham, 1980), p. 34: "Ephrem the Syrian... was not only a very great poet and theologian, he was the foremost wielder of an involved and allusive Syriac which *will not translate* without a host of explanatory notes."

[5] Some of his phrases are quite long, and it is usually possible to simplify them in translation without loss of meaning or emphasis. However, there are one or two places where it is not possible to do this, as for instance in V, §17a, where Ephrem illustrates how ready the Lord is to receive sinners, given how patient God was with Israel in former days in the desert.

comment on. Sometimes he quotes a lot of gospel text with brief comment. At other times he takes off and develops his reflections and theology at length, with little or no gospel text serving as the immediate basis. He has the freedom of a bird to move at will over the vast range of Scripture, and select whatever text pleases him in the execution of his task. In this sense his commentary is deeply biblical. To illustrate a particular point he can sometimes call up a wide range of texts from both New and Old Testaments. At another time he will interweave scriptural events by way of allusion and typology rather than by direct quote, thereby demonstrating the particularly Semitic nature of his thought patterns and language.

Perhaps the most distinctive and pervasive characteristic of Ephrem's literary style in the commentary is this frequent use of symbolism and parallelism. His poetic genius expressed itself in many forms of rhythmic balancing between personalities, institutions and situations, whether similar or divergent.[1] Examples abound on almost every page. For instance, in contrasting the angel's annunciation to Zechariah with that to Mary in I, §11 of the commentary, Ephrem develops a number of insights. Zechariah goes to the angel because his child is destined to be inferior to the angel, whereas it is the angel who comes to Mary, since her child will be the angel's Lord. Moreover, the angel did not go to Elizabeth, since Zechariah is the true father of John. Gabriel did not go to Joseph however since Mary alone gave birth to her first-born. In III, §17 Ephrem uses the theme of being espoused near a well of water to draw together three separate Old Testament betrothals[2] as types of the Lord's betrothal to his Church through his baptism in the Jordan waters.

In commenting on the Sermon on the Mount in VI it is not surprising to find Ephrem focussing at length on the Antitheses and related texts[3] since these already belong to this central Semitic mode of expression through parallelism.[4] Although the paragraphs devoted to the

---

[1] Cf. Leloir, EC-SC 121, p. 31.

[2] The betrothals of Rebecca (Gen 24:1-67), Rachel (Gen 29:1-21) and Zipporah (Ex 2:16-21).

[3] Cf. Matt 5:20-48 (*You have heard it said ... but I say to you*). Cf. S. P. Brock, *The Harp of the Spirit*, 1984, pp.10-13 for an examination of Ephrem's creative use of typological exegesis in his extended meditations on Scripture.

[4] Cf. C. McCarthy, "Gospel Exegesis from a Semitic Church: Ephrem's Commentary on the Sermon on the Mount," *Tradition of the Text, Studies offered to Dominique Barthélemy in Celebration of his 70th Birthday*, edited by Gerard J. Norton and Stephen Pisano, OBO 109 (Freiburg und Göttingen, 1991), pp. 103-123, especially pp. 114-117.

Antitheses are of varying length, they constitute the longest single section of his commentary on the Sermon on the Mount,[1] and develop in depth a central theme in Ephrem's writings, the creative tension between God's grace and his righteousness or justice.[2] In the development of this theme Ephrem uses a variety of images and concepts which he places in parallelism with each other. An extract from §11b illustrates this point particularly well:

> When justice had reached its perfection, then grace put forth its perfection. *An eye for an eye* is the perfection of justice but, *Whoever strikes you on the cheek, turn the other to him,* is the consummation of grace. While both continually have their tastes, he proposed them to us through the two [successive] Testaments. The first [Testament] had the killing of animals for expiation, because justice did not permit that one should die in place of another. The second [Testament] was established through the blood of a man, who through his grace gave himself on behalf of all. One therefore was the beginning, and the other the completion.

Ephrem frequently develops more than one interpretation for a given text, particularly texts that seem contradictory or ambivalent to him. A good illustration of this occurs in VIII, §14 where he quotes Matt 10:34: *Do not think that I have come to bring peace upon the earth*, and then immediately asks how this can be reconciled with Col 1:20, *He came to reconcile those things which are in heaven and those which are on earth.* His answer is nuanced. He begins by quoting two other passages from the Pauline letters which state that Christ did bring peace,[3] but then shows how different faith responses to Christ resulted in various kinds of divisions.[4] There are interesting variations offered in XIV, §7 as to why Peter wanted to build three tents on the occasion of the Transfiguration.

---

[1] §§4-15.

[2] S. P. Brock holds that this is one of the many Jewish traditions, found only outside the Bible in post-biblical literature, not attested in any other Christian source apart from Ephrem and some other early Christian Syriac writers. Cf. S. P. Brock, *The Luminous Eye,* p. 20.

[3] Eph 2:14 and Gal 6:16.

[4] There is a lengthy discussion in XV, §§9-11 on how Jesus could say "No one is good except God" to the rich man (Mark 10:18), but elsewhere refer to himself as "the good shepherd" (John 10:11). In XVIII, §15, he explores the seeming contradiction in how Jesus could say in Matt 24:36, "Not even the Son knows the day or the hour," in view of the intimate knowledge between Father and Son expressed in Matt 11:27, "No one knows the Father except the Son."

Similarly, in reflecting on Gethsemane, Ephrem suggests many different reasons as to why Jesus should have been fearful and sorrowful, to the point of asking that the chalice of suffering be removed from him (XX, §§1-7).

Although the Diatessaron commentary is essentially a prose work, it is rich in poetic imagery and metaphors. Of Jesus' birth Ephrem writes: "At his radiant birth therefore a radiant star appeared, and at his dark death there appeared a dark gloom" (II, §24). His description of the awe and amazement experienced by the angels in heaven at the sight of Jesus eating with sinners is eloquent: "Angels stand and tremble, while tax collectors recline and enjoy themselves; the watchers tremble at his greatness, while sinners eat with him"(V, §17b). There are some beautiful reflections on the richness of God's word in I, §§18-19:

Who is capable of comprehending the immensity of the possibilities of one of your utterances? What we leave behind us in [your utterance] is far greater than what we take from it ... Many are the perspectives of his word, just as many are the perspectives of those who study it ... His utterance is a tree of life, which offers you blessed fruit from every side ... The thirsty one rejoices because he can drink, but is not upset if unable to render the source dry. The well can conquer your thirst, but your thirst cannot conquer the fountain.

While best appreciated in their original Syriac formulations, Ephrem's puns and word-plays testify to a richly fertile, and at times playful, imagination. In commenting on Zechariah's disbelief in I, §13, he notes that "[God] who can close an open mouth can open a closed womb." In VII, §18 the woman who was a sinner "could scoff at the cunning thoughts of him who had been scoffing at her tears," while at the same time the Lord "was judging the secret [thoughts] of one who thought that he [the Lord] did not even know those that were manifest" (VII, §10). At the well in Samaria Jesus "asked for water, that he might give water, under the pretext of water" (XII, §16). In VII, §7 Ephrem describes the woman who had a haemorrhage as "she who had wearied physicians and she whom the physicians had wearied." The force of the interplay between the images of sleeping and waking in VI, §25 in relation to Jesus' calming of the storm is difficult to capture fully in translation: "He that was sleeping was awakened, and cast the sea into a sleep, so that by the wakefulness of the sea which was [now] sleeping, he might show forth the wakefulness of his divinity which never sleeps." After commenting on the Lord's recommendation to cut off one's hand or foot if it offends,[1] Ephrem wryly observes in VI, §7 that "Herod's right hand was Herodias, and instead of cutting it off and casting this unclean hand away, he cut off and cast away a holy head."[2] Pharaoh drowned in the waters in which he himself had drowned the infants (IV, §12).

Pithy admonitions and observations are plentiful. In VI, §18a he advises: "Nourish your soul with the fear of God, and God will nourish your body." Elsewhere, in that same paragraph, he notes that "Anxiety tortures the soul, and the money that one accumulates injures oneself." In XV, §12 there is an economy of words in the statement that "Not [all] who are living are alive, nor are [all] those who are buried dead," as also in XXI, §15: "He died to our world in his body, that we might live to his world in his body." Indeed there is a touch of humour in XIX, §13: "Our Lord's words, *As I have loved you*, can be explained, Let us die for each other; but we do not even want to live for one another!"

The key theological themes that Ephrem wrestles with are concerned essentially with the person of the Lord. The mystery of the Incarnation, the mystery of the divinity hidden in and clothed with humanity is developed at length in I, and at various other points in the commentary.[3] In commenting on the miracles of healing, Ephrem often refers to Jesus' humanity which was manifest and to his divinity which was hidden. The relationship between the Father and Son is often highlighted in reflection on the Incarnation.[4] The theme of Jesus' suffering and death is one that was dear to Ephrem too. In commenting on the Lukan beatitude, *Blessed are those who weep*,[5] he quotes Rom 8:17 to illustrate its meaning: *If one has suffered with him, one will be glorified with him* (VI, §1a). The example that Jesus gave in not fleeing from those who wanted to kill him is cited in VIII, §7, while his commentary on the passion and death of Jesus in XX-XXI attests just how central to Ephrem was the conviction that true followers of the Lord must be prepared to face suffering for his sake.[6]

---

[1] Matt 18:8.

[2] The beheading of John the Baptist, cf. Matt 14:3-11.

[3] Cf. VII, §17; XIV, §7. In this context it is worth recalling that Jacob of Nisibis, the bishop who instructed the young Ephrem into the Christian faith, had been present at the council of Nicaea in 325.

[4] Cf. XV, §§1-2; XX, §30; XXI, §29.

[5] Luke 6:21b.

[6] Cf. XXI, §§ 15, 17 and 21 in particular.

Philosophical reflections in the strict sense will not be found in Ephrem. Yet there is a recurrent wrestling on his part with a number of issues of a philosophical nature, particularly the question of freedom and freewill. In analysing the text of Matt 11:11, *The least of these [latter] who preach the kingdom of heaven is greater than [John]*, in IX, §§16-17, Ephrem concludes that John's greatness was conferred on him and was not the result of freewill, whereas, in the case of ordinary human beings, the role of their free response, their freewill, is highlighted.[1] The mystery of human freedom and freewill is illustrated too in the number of times Ephrem returns to grapple with why Judas should have betrayed the Lord.[2]

Occasionally he includes extended reflections which are more spiritual in nature, such as those contained in VII, §§3-12. In this section he has been commenting on the woman who had a haemorrhage and who touched Jesus' cloak from behind.[3] He then develops a keenly argued reflection on various kinds of touching and their spiritual benefits. Other extended reflections occur in VIII, §§3-4 in the context of the peace greeting[4] and in X, §8 in relation to the sinful woman.[5]

Ephrem could be a formidable adversary. Marcion gets dishonorable mention on a number of occasions.[6] It is not always possible to work out the precise point of contention, since the references are brief, and we only have one side of the argument. Arius is referred to by name in XII, §9 as one who contradicted the birth of the Lord. In XVIII, §3 there is a possible allusion to one of Bardaisan's tenets regarding Satan. Far more frequent are the anti-Jewish passages.[7] It is no secret that Ephrem was very anti-Jewish in his writings, and seldom lost an opportunity to express this bias.[8] The discovery of the additional folios brought to light even further anti-Jewish material, in passages absent from the Armenian version.

---

[1] Cf. VI, §§5,7; X, §2; XI, §12; XIII, §7.

[2] Cf. IX, §14; X, §§5-6; XIV, §12; XVII, §§7, 13; XX, §§12, 18-19; and particularly Ephrem's discussion of the text, *It would have been better for him if he had never been born* (Matt 26:24) in XIX, §1f.

[3] Mark 5:24-34.

[4] Luke 10:5.

[5] Luke 7:36-50.

[6] Cf. IV, §1; V, §§20b-21; VI, §27; XI, §§9, 23; XII, §7.

[7] Cf. II, §21a, 21b; III, §2-3; V, §4b; VII, §27b; VIII, §1b; XI, §26; XII, §§13-15; XIII, §§2-3; XVII, §10; XIX, §10; XX, §§3, 20, 29, 35-38; XXI, §§14, 19 and many others.

[8] Cf. R. Murray, *Symbols of the Church and Kingdom*, p. 68: "It must be confessed with sorrow that Ephrem hated the Jews. It is sad that the man who could write the magisterial Commentary on Genesis, with the command it shows of the tradition which still to a great extent united Christians and Jews, could sink to writing *Carmina Nisibena 67.*"

Reading through Ephrem's commentary one comes across a number of interesting and sometimes unusual observations. In his pen-portrait of Simon Peter in IV, §20 we learn that Peter was timid, because he was frightened at the voice of a young servant girl, and poor, because he was not able to pay his own tax, and stupid, because he did not know how to take flight after denying the Lord. In VI, §24a, the motive Ephrem attributes to the rich young man in his aspirations to follow Jesus is that "one who performs such deeds must possess much money"! In commenting on the phrase, *Are not two sparrows sold for a penny?*, he observes in a practical vein that things sold in bulk like vegetables are of lesser value.

In the early Christian centuries Edessa was a centre with a certain reputation for healing and medicinal skills.[1] Disease and illness were a source of constant anxiety and preoccupation in the ancient Near East, and the search for cures and healers is a theme recurring in the literature from these times.[2] Syrian Christians it seems devoted much of their energies to medicine, and in later centuries they were to become renowned for their role as the transmitters of Greek medical science to the East, and for their status as physicians at the Persian court.[3] Edessa's many springs and their healing properties were well known. It is interesting therefore to note how the theme of healing is a frequent one for Ephrem, in which he often contrasts the divine healing powers of the Lord with the rather powerless ones of human physicians.[4]

Another characteristic trait of Ephrem is his keen eye for nature and his readiness to see therein the reflection of the Creator.[5] In commenting on the miracle at Cana in V, §§11-12, he points out that the Lord, in creating the wine, did not go outside of creation, but instead transformed the original creation "to make it known that he was its Lord." The imagery he uses in describing nature testifies to his alert powers of observation, particularly in relation to birds,[6] and the natural phenomena such as

---

[1] Cf. Segal, *Edessa*, p. 71f.

[2] The Abgar-Addai legend has the search for healing at its centre.

[3] Cf. M. W. Dols, "Syriac into Arabic: The Transmission of Greek Medicine" in *Aram* 1 (1989),pp. 45-52.

[4] Cf. V, §23; VI, §14; VII, §§2, 7, 12, 16-17, 19, 21; X, §7a; XIII, §2f.

[5] For a fuller treatment of the relation between the Bible and nature in Ephrem's exegesis, see for example, P. Yousif, "Symbolisme christologique dans la Bible et dans la Nature chez saint Ephrem de Nisibe (De Virginitate VIII-XI et les textes parallèles)," *Parole de l'Orient* 8 (1977-1978), pp. 5-66.

[6] Cf. IV, §8c, VI, §§ 17a, 18a, VIII, §§6, 12 XI, §13 and XII, §16.

lightning and wind.[1] Linked with Ephrem's approach to nature is his insistence on trusting in divine providence. The Lord, he says, wanted his disciples "not to be dragged down by the anxiety of the world, but rather to rely on the heavenly bread, and to reflect on what is above rather than on what is on earth" (VI, §18a).

Just as one will have difficulty in finding a fully systematized theology in Ephrem, so too one will look in vain for a fully developed set of hermeneutical principles.[2] Occasionally through the commentary however Ephrem lets slip some incidental insights on his understanding of Scripture and its interpretation. The poetic images in I, §§18-19 concerning the utterances of God have already been cited above. He proposes in XII, §15 that, when interpreting a parable, "one should accept firmly the point of the comparison and the point of the parable, and not be distracted with all the parts of the comparison or by the many garments of the parable." But in VII, §22 however he tells us that:

> If there were [only] one meaning for the words [of Scripture], the first interpreter would find it, and all other listeners would have neither the toil of seeking nor the pleasure of finding. But every word of our Lord has its own image, and each image has many members, and each member possesses its own species and form. Each person hears in accordance with his capacity, and it is interpreted in accordance with what has been given him.

3. The Diatessaron Commentary - Textual Considerations

The Armenian Version

Prior to the discovery of a substantial portion of the Syriac text of Ephrem's commentary in the *Chester Beatty* MS 709 in 1957, access to this commentary was chiefly through the Armenian version,[3] and, to a much

---

[1] Cf. I, §32 and X, §13.

[2] In his article, "Exegetical Principles of St Ephraem of Nisibis," P. Yousif has set about presenting "the general shape of Ephraem's exegetical principles in a short, comprehensive and logical way" (p. 301), using the Diatessaron commentary as the most important source, but making reference also to the other extant biblical commentaries of Ephrem (cf. p. 296).

[3] For example, T. Zahn's attempt to reconstruct the Diatessaron in 1881 was based mainly on the Armenian translation of Ephrem's Commentary, a critical edition of which had been published for the first time just five years before. Cf. T. Zahn, *Tatians Diatessaron* (Leipzig, 1881).

lesser extent, either through rare Syriac fragments of the commentary,[1] or citations of Ephrem by later authors in which one could detect or infer the presence of his commentary.[2] Before the publication of the text of the Armenian version in the nineteenth century there was even doubt in some circles as to the very existence of this commentary.

The Armenian text was first published in 1836 by the Mekitarist Fathers of the Monastery of San Lazzaro at Venice[3] on the basis of the one single manuscript available to them at that time, as the second part of a four-part work comprising Ephrem's writings translated into Armenian.[4] They acquired a second manuscript sometime later,[5] and in 1876 Georg Moesinger published a revised Latin translation of the Armenian version which had been already prepared by the original editor, J. B. Aucher in 1841.[6] This revised Latin translation of Moesinger was based on both manuscripts and helped to make Ephrem's commentary available for the use of scholars not expert in the Armenian language.

It was not until 1953 however that a critical edition of the Armenian text based on both manuscripts was published by Louis Leloir.[7] The two manuscripts in question are medieval, copied in the year 1195 AD [644 of the Armenian calendar], but in separate locations, geographically distant and ideologically distinct. According to Leloir they constitute two recensions, one (A) representing a type of old Armenian, particularly in relation to scriptural citations, and the other (B), a more recent Armenian.[8] The former could be described as more faithful and the latter more harmonized, where difficult readings have been suppressed and scriptural citations adapted to the Armenian vulgate. In the following year Leloir published a Latin translation of the Armenian version to

---

[1] Cf. T. Baarda, "A Syriac Fragment of Mar Ephraem's Commentary on the Diatessaron," *NTS* 8 (1961-62), pp. 287-300.
[2] Cf. J. Rendel Harris, *Fragments of the Commentary of Ephrem Syrus upon the Diatessaron* (London, 1895); I. Ortiz de Urbina, *Vetus Evangelium Syrorum et exinde excerptum Diatessaron Tatiani*, Biblia Polyglotta Matritensia Series VI (Madrid, 1967).
[3] *Srboyn Ep'remi Matenagrowt'iwnk'* ii (Venice, 1836).
[4] MS 452 (A).
[5] MS 312 (B).
[6] Cf. J. B. Aucher, G. Moesinger, *Evangelii Concordantis Expositio, facta a Santo Ephraemo Doctore Syro* (Venice, 1876).
[7] L. Leloir, *Saint Ephrem. Commentaire de l'évangile concordant* (version arménienne), CSCO 137 (Louvain, 1953).
[8] Cf. *op. cit.*, pp. vi-viii.

accompany the critical edition, and to replace Moesinger's translation which he considered defective.[1]

To facilitate usage of the work Leloir divided the Armenian text into twenty-two "chapters," which were then further subdivided into paragraphs. He reproduced these same divisions in the Latin translation, and in due course, when called upon to edit the newly discovered manuscript of the Syriac original, he again reproduced this sense division of the material in both the Syriac edition, and its accompanying Latin translation. Because there were several passages in the Syriac with no corresponding Armenian translation,[2] he was obliged to devise even further subdivisions of paragraphs in the Syriac edition to cater for those sections which were present in the Syriac but absent from the Armenian. He himself has recognized that if the Syriac had been discovered before the Armenian he would have ordered the material differently.[3]

The Syriac Text

Up until the autumn of 1957 therefore the only route to Ephrem's Diatessaron commentary was a secondary one via the Armenian version. Given that the Syriac original was believed to be irretrievably lost, it was not surprising that there was considerable excitement and interest when a very fine vellum manuscript acquired by Sir Chester Beatty in 1956 was subsequently identified by Cyril Moss of the British Museum as containing a significant portion of the Syriac text of Ephrem's commentary. Since it was only about four years since Leloir had completed the first critical edition and translation into Latin of the Armenian version, he was invited by Sir Chester Beatty to prepare this unique Syriac manuscript for publication too. In due course the newly discovered text of *Chester Beatty MS 709* was published in Dublin in 1963, complete with a Latin translation.[4]

---

[1] L. Leloir, *Saint Ephrem, Commentaire de l'évangile concordant* (traduction latine), CSCO 145 (Louvain, 1954). According to T. Baarda this is "an entirely new and very accurate translation of the Armenian text" (cf. "In Search of the Diatessaron Text," p. 75, n. 17).

[2] This is particularly true now because of the more recently discovered additional folios; cf. L. Leloir, *Saint Ephrem: Commentaire de l'évangile concordant, texte syriaque (Manuscrit Chester Beatty 709), Folios Additionnels* (Leuven/Paris, 1990).

[3] Cf. Leloir, EC-FA, p. xi: "Si j'avais eu à éditer le texte syriaque d'abord, j'aurais souvent divisé autrement."

[4] L. Leloir, *Commentaire de l'évangile concordant. Texte syriaque (MS Chester Beatty 709).* Chester Beatty Monograph Series 8 (Dublin,1963).

But further surprises were in store. The manuscript published by Leloir in 1963 contained significant lacunae. Comprising a total of sixty-five folios, it contained two larger gaps and a number of smaller ones. The sections commenting on the end of Matthew's infancy narrative, and earliest parts of Jesus public life, including his baptism and temptations, the call of the first disciples, the wedding feast of Cana, the healing of the paralytic, the sermon on the mount, the mission discourse to the disciples and Jesus' meeting with Martha and Mary, were among the main incidents that were lacking, as well as a lengthy section commenting on part of the last supper and the beginning of the passion narrative. In 1966 Pedro Ortiz Valdivieso published a stray folio which is currently located in Barcelona,[1] containing Ephrem's commentary on the end of the Benedictus and some initial comments on Jesus' conception and birth in Matthew 2, which fits word for word at the beginning of the first significant lacuna of *Chester Beatty* MS 709. There was some debate and doubt at that point concerning the exact relationship between this stray folio and *Chester Beatty* MS 709, even though it visually represented the same type of script and continued in the same style.

But even more amazing was the acquisition in 1984 of five folios and of a further thirty-six in 1986 of this same manuscript by the trustees of the Chester Beatty Library, under the chairmanship of Kevin J. Cathcart, Professor of Near Eastern Languages at University College, Dublin.[2] These additional folios fit exactly after the Barcelona folio, and, apart from four lacunae of about a folio each and one which is slightly longer, contain the missing section mentioned above, from the end of Matthew's infancy narrative through to Jesus' meeting with Martha and Mary. They exhibit the same script and style as the Barcelona folio as well as that of *Chester Beatty* MS 709. The discovery of these forty-one folios means that approximately eighty per cent of the original codex has been reassembled,

---

[1] P. Ortiz Valdivieso, "Un neuvo fragmento siriaco del Comentario de san Efrén al Diatésaron (PPalau-Rib. 2)," *Studia Papyrologica* 5 (1966), pp. 7-17.

[2] K. J. Cathcart, "The Biblical and Other Early Christian Manuscripts of the Chester Beatty Library," *Back to the Sources, Biblical and Near Eastern Studies in honour of Dermot Ryan*, edited by K. J. Cathcart and J. F. Healey (Dublin, 1989), pp. 137-138. Plates VIII to XII (Commentary on Mt 2:1-16) on pp. 155-159 are the first reproductions of any of these folios and illustrate very beautifully the quality of *Chester Beatty* MS 709. These forty-one additional folios have now been edited by Leloir, and include a Latin literal translation, and a reproduction of Valdivieso's edition of the Barcelona folio in the appendix, cf. L. Leloir, EC-FA.

with probably less than thirty folios still to be tracked down![1] This discovery also confirmed retrospectively that the Barcelona folio was indeed part of the very same manuscript. How it and the other missing folios became detached from the original manuscript in the first place and where they are currently located remains a mystery.[2] It is to be hoped that more of these missing folios will some day be identified and their contents made available to scholars.

---

[1] Cf. Cathcart, "The Biblical and Other Early Christian Manuscripts of the Chester Beatty Library," p. 138. In outlining what is known of the history of *Chester Beatty* MS 709 prior to its acquisition by Sir Alfred Chester Beatty, Leloir refers to an inventory drawn up by Professor M. Kamil of Cairo University which listed that part of the Syriac manuscript containing Ephrem's commentary as comprising one hundred and thirty-four folios (cf. EC-FA, p. iv). Leloir believes that sometime between 1952 and 1957) there was a "dismembering" of the manuscript, and that what Sir Alfred Chester Beatty purchased was a significant but incomplete portion comprising sixty-five out of an original one hundred and thirty-four folios. An examination of *Chester Beatty* MS 709 in its present condition confirms this total. The forty-one additional folios have greatly reduced the largest lacuna in *Chester Beatty* MS 709. The other significant lacuna runs from the end of XVIII, §3 through to the beginning of XXI, §4, and contains Ephrem's comments on the last supper and the beginning of the passion narrative. A rough estimate based on the amount of material contained in the Armenian translation for this lacuna suggests that this gap covers about eighteen or nineteen folios (it is impossible to make any kind of accurate estimate because of the fact that there are differences from time to time in the length of the Syriac and Armenian texts). There are seven other small lacunae of one folio each, and one slightly longer one of probably two folios, scattered throughout the manuscript (two lacunae in I and one each in II, III, IV, VII, IX and XVI). These yield a total of nine folios which, together with the block of eighteen/nineteen folios already suggested, provide an estimate very close indeed to the inventory cited by Leloir. Thus one can say that, with the sixty-five folios of the 1958 discovery, the forty-one additional folios of recent times, and the Barcelona folio, we are now in possession of one hundred and seven folios of a manuscript which once contained one hundred and thirty-four folios (i.e., we are currently in possession of approximately eighty per cent of the total manuscript).

[2] It seems almost certain that the manuscript came from Egypt, from the Coptic Monastery of Deir es-Suriani in Wadi Natrun. The monastery, as its name suggests, was originally linked with Syrian monks. Founded in the sixth century, it was purchased in the eighth by a wealthy Syrian merchant for monks from Syria. It was several times devastated in the ninth century by Berber raiders and in the fourteenth century ravaged by a severe plague. In the sixteenth century, the monastery, then almost totally abandoned, was taken over by Coptic monks, who still occupy it. The monastery possessed a number of ancient Syriac manuscripts, the most important of which are now in the British Library. In the introduction to EC-FA (p. vi) Leloir has given an outline of the complicated series of events whereby *Chester Beatty* MS 709 found itself on the market. In 1952 the Coptic bishop of Deir es-Suriani discovered some manuscripts, about thirty in number. These were catalogued by Professor M. Kamil of Cairo University, who gave the number 31 to the manuscript containing Ephrem's Commentary. Some time later it seems that this manuscript disappeared and was replaced by another manuscript 31, with a totally different content. Meanwhile the original MS 31 must have been partially dismembered, and by 1957 a significant portion of it acquired by Sir Alfred Chester Beatty.

Contents and Age

The vellum manuscript acquired by Sir Chester Beatty in 1957 contains a total of seventy-five folios and consists of two clearly distinct sections.[1] The first ten folios reproduce an exchange of letters between Severus of Antioch and Julian of Halicarnassus relating to the corruptibility or incorruptibility of the body of Christ,[2] while the remaining sixty-five folios contain a substantial portion of Ephrem's Diatessaron Commentary. The parchment is consistently thick in this first part, whereas in the second it is sometimes thick, sometimes thin. Leloir observes that since the writing in this first part is a mixture of the Estrangela, Nestorian and Serta scripts, and contains certain distinctive orthographic features, it should be dated several centuries later than the second part, probably in the eighth or ninth century.[3] The script in the second part is Estrangela, and Leloir dates this part of the manuscript to the end of the fifth or beginning of the sixth century, at the latest. He cites certain peculiarities of script as a basis for this dating, and compares its script to that of MS Syriac Add. 12150 of the British Museum [written in Edessa in 411/412 AD] which contains writings of Clement of Rome, Titus of Bosra and Eusebius of Caesarea.[4] Valdivieso agrees with this dating, also citing MS Syriac Add. 12150, as well as three further MSS of a slighly later period.[5]

The Present State of the Manuscript

The manuscript is 25 cm. high, and 16.5 cm. wide. Each page contains two columns of 30-40 lines, about 31-33 in the first part, and 35-36

---

[1] Cf. Cathcart, "The Biblical and Other Early Christian Manuscripts of the Chester Beatty Library," pp. 137-139.

[2] This correspondence had been already edited on the basis of one manuscript from the British Museum and a second manuscript from the Vatican. Cf. *Severi Antiiulianistica*, quae ex manuscriptis Vaticanis et Brittanicis syriace edidit et latine interpretatus est A. Sanda (Beyrouth, 1931).

[3] Cf. Leloir, EC-CBM 8, p. iii.

[4] Leloir, EC-CBM 8, p. iv. He also cites other early Syriac manuscripts in support of this early dating.

[5] MS Add. 14571 which contains works of St. Ephrem, written in Edessa in 519; MS Add. 17176 written in 532 and MS Add. 14610 written in 550/551, cf. "Un neuvo fragmento siriaco del Comentario de san Efrén al Diatésaron," pp. 10-11.

in the second.[1] The manuscript is very legible in the first part, and usually so in the second part also, apart from some passages damaged by strips of parchment used to try to join the folios together. In two places in the additional folios stains have given rise to some difficulty in reading.[2] The scribes for each of the two parts are clearly different persons belonging to different centuries, but in each case it seems fairly safe to assume that there was only one hand at work in the transcription of the respective sections. In folio 18r of the commentary there is an unfortunate but interesting error on the part of the copyist. The material on this folio is quite different from its immediate context, and the simplest explanation seems to be that the scribe must have erroneously transcribed onto folio 18r a page taken either from another context or from another manuscript. The content of this extraneous material is given in a footnote to XI, §17 below. Ephrem's commentary is resumed on the back of the folio, 18v.

There are two systems of numeration of the pages in the 1957 acquisition. The top, outer edge of the folios is numbered from 1 to 75, while the inner, lower edge is numbered 1 to 10 for the first part, and 1 to 65 for the second. This is not so however in the case of the additional folios, and Leloir describes how certain of these folios were placed in an incorrect order.[3]

The Syriac and Armenian Traditions Compared

The relationship between the Syriac text of *Chester Beatty* MS 709 and the Armenian version is complex and, in view of the paucity of manuscripts, difficult to determine in any real sense of the term. However, a certain amount can be noted from examination of the three manuscripts we possess, one in Syriac and two in Armenian. In 1961-62, just before the publication of the Syriac text of *Chester Beatty* MS 709, T. Baarda compared the contents of a Syriac fragment of part of XXI, §1 with its Armenian counterpart and observed, in relation to the tradition represented by this fragment, that "the Armenian text seems to have been

---

[1] See the very fine photographic reproductions of folios 3r-5r of the Additional Folios on pp. 155-159 of Cathcart, "The Biblical and Other Early Christian Manuscripts of the Chester Beatty Library."

[2] Cf. Leloir, EC-FA, p. ix: "L'écriture est *estrangelo*, et identique à celle de la partie déjà éditée du manuscrit. Elle est généralement claire et, sauf aux folios 25ra and 34 rv, il n'y a pas de fortes taches, gênants pour la lecture et l'intelligence du texte."

[3] Cf. EC-FA, p. ix.

a very accurate one," and that "although the Armenian text stands the reliability test on the whole, in details the Syriac seems indispensable."[1]

With the publication of *Chester Beatty* MS 709 in 1963 it became possible to form some initial impressions of the relationship between the two traditions on a broader basis. In the first instance, it can be stated with some confidence that the Syriac text confirms that the Armenian translation is generally a faithful one. However, a second observation raises questions of a different nature, for at various points throughout *Chester Beatty* MS 709 up to XVIII, §3[2] there are passages in the Syriac not found in the Armenian. Then conversely, from XXI, §4 to the end, including the Prayers and the Appendix on the Evangelists, there are some lengthy passages featured in the Armenian which are absent from the Syriac. Moreover, Leloir notes that, not only does the Armenian become the *textus longior* in these latter sections, but also the differences between Armenian and Syriac in the manner of rendering scriptural quotations are less striking here than in the rest of the manuscript.[3] From this he concludes that the conditions in which the two texts were constituted cannot have been identical for all the sections, and that the Syriac text that formed the *Vorlage* for the Armenian must have represented a type of tradition different from that of *Chester Beatty* MS 709.[4]

Examination of those passages absent from the Armenian tradition may point towards some of the particular tendencies of its translator. For example, Leloir observes that some of the passages that were omitted seem to have aimed at the suppression of allusions to original sin and the corporeality of Christ's body, and that several anti-Jewish passages have either been omitted or toned down.[5] While it may be true in the case of certain passages that the translator omitted them because of their strong anti-Jewish bias, this does not account fully for all the omissions in the Armenian recension, if indeed one may call them such, since one can

---

[1] Cf. "A Syriac Fragment," p. 64. This fragment is taken from MS *Borgia Syriaca* 82 of the Museo Borgiano di Propaganda in Rome. For further details on the contents and distinctive features of this fragment, see below at XXI, §1.

[2] It is not possible to comment on the content of XVIII, §3 - XXI, §4 since the Syriac text here is missing for approximately eighteen to nineteen folios.

[3] Cf. EC-SC 121, p. 28.

[4] *Ibid.* Further details on comparisons between the two textual traditions are discussed by Leloir in both *Le Témoignage d'Ephrem sur le Diatessaron*, CSCO 227 (Louvain, 1962) and "Divergences entre l'original syriaque et la version arménienne du commentaire d'Ephrem sur le Diatessaron," *Mélanges Eugéne Tisserant*, II (Citta del Vaticano, 1964), pp. 303-331.

[5] Cf. EC-SC 121, p. 29. In the introduction to EC-FA Leloir indicates that, in the course of the forty-one folios, there are nine anti-Jewish passages which have been omitted by the Armenian translator (cf. p. x).

argue that some of them at least could be seen as interpolations into the Syriac.[1] In particular, the Syriac text is noticably longer in the commentary on the sermon on the mount (VI), where the Armenian version contains no trace of commentary on the Lord's Prayer (§16a) or on the exhortation to trust in divine providence (§18a), and neither of these rather lengthy sections are anti-Jewish in content. Moreover, the question still remains as to why some of the other anti-Jewish statements were in fact translated from the Syriac and allowed to remain untouched.

Another step forward in highlighting the need for analysis of the interrelationship between the two traditions was taken by Baarda in an examination of XVII, §10 of the commentary.[2] In confirming Leloir's view that the extra wording in the Syriac text here was not a secondary insertion, but the result of an omission on the part of the Armenian translator, or of a copyist responsible for the Syriac recension underlying the Armenian version,[3] Baarda rightly cautions against using the Armenian text of Ephrem's commentary for reconstructing the early Syriac Diatessaron. "It is a translation with its own peculiarities" he observes, and stresses the need for "a minutious commentary on the most important witness to the Syriac Diatessaron."[4]

The Integrity of the Commentary

The fact that a certain number of additions or omissions can be identified when one compares the two traditions leads naturally to questions relating to the integrity of the commentary. In other words, now that both Syriac and Armenian recensions are available, even if on a very meagre manuscript basis, it is possible to identify those sections which are additions in one recension or, when viewed from the perspective of the other recension, omissions. Of the twenty-three "additions" investigated by W. L. Petersen,[5] thirteen of these were found in the Syriac (thus, absent

---

[1] Cf. W. L. Petersen, "Some Remarks on the Integrity of Ephrem's Commentary on the Diatessaron," *Studia Patristica* 20 (1989), pp. 197-202; A. de Halleux, "L'adoration des Mages dans le commentaire syriaque du Diatessaron," *Le Muséon* 104 (1991), pp. 251-264.

[2] Cf. T. Baarda, "Mar Ephrem's Commentary on the Diatessaron, Ch. XVII:10," *Early Transmission of the Words of Jesus: Thomas, Tatian and the Text of the New Testament* (Amsterdam, 1983), pp. 289-311.

[3] Cf. Leloir, "Divergences entre l'original syriaque et la version arménienne," p. 307.

[4] Cf. "Mar Ephrem's Commentary on the Diatessaron, Ch. XVII:10," p. 311.

[5] Cf. W. L. Petersen, "Some Remarks on the Integrity of Ephrem's Commentary," pp. 199-202. The thirteen Syriac additions as listed by Petersen belong to the 1963 edition (EC-CBM 8): I, §25; I, §26; IX, 14a; X, §7a; XI, §11a; XII, §19; XII, §21; XIV, §7; XV, §17; XV, §19;

in the Armenian), and ten in the Armenian (thus, absent in the Syriac). This led Petersen to the conclusion, already hinted at by Leloir, that there must have been at least two recensions in Syriac, and that "unless Ephrem penned both of them, or one reflects Ephrem's revision of the other, then we are not only dealing with Ephrem's base text, but also with the interpolations of later scribes or a school."[1] Excluding the possibility that Ephrem revised his own work, Petersen argues that "we have at least 23 places of paragraph length where *either* the Syriac *or* the Armenian represents Ephrem's text, but not both of them."[2] While the substance of this line of reasoning is logical and attractive, it does not allow for the possibility that some of the so-called "additions" in the Syriac could well represent either deliberate omissions on the part of the Armenian translator for various motives, or indeed accidental omissions.

Thus, in those instances where the integrity of the text may be genuinely in doubt the task of determining which of the traditions is more likely to represent Ephrem's work is both difficult and delicate. To begin with, as already mentioned, the manuscript evidence is very limited. One simply cannot make absolute statements or generalizations on the basis of one Syriac and two Armenian manuscripts, and one fragment in Syriac. It is possible however to attain a certain degree of probability in identifying secondary material, using some of the methods of source criticism. For instance, interpolations are often recognizable because they clearly disrupt the continuity of a text, introducing either new or alternative ideas. One may also in some instances be able to further confirm the secondary nature of a given passage by means of a rigorous examination of the vocabulary, grammar and style of the passage, together with a study of its theological concepts, its manner of citing and interpreting the biblical text, and an analysis of its historical and polemical background. Armed with material of this kind one would then be able to compare all of this with other writings which indisputably come from Ephrem's pen. In comparing textual traditions in this way one may also be able to identify

---

XVII, §3; XVII, §10; XVIII, §1. To these one can now add the eighteen "additions" in the 1991 edition (EC-FA): II, §21b; IV, §1b; IV, §8b; V, §4b; V, §17a; V, §20a; V, §22b; VI, §1b; VI, §3a; VI, §11a; VI, §16a; VI, §18a; VI, §21b; VI, §22b; VI, §24b; VII, §27b; VIII, §1b; VIII, §9b. The ten Armenian additions as listed by Petersen are: XXI, §7; XXI, §12; XXI, §13; XXI, §15; XXI, §16; XXI, §31; XXII, §32; XXII, §2; Précis 2; Précis 3.
[1] Petersen, p. 199.
[2] *Idem*. Petersen's total of twenty-three can be increased to forty-one in the light of the eighteen further "additions" in EC-FA.

with a certain amount of confidence either an accidental loss or a misplacement of material.[1]

More difficult to accept however are conclusions based uniquely on perceived differences in theological terms or on the singular use of terms. To argue, as E. Beck does, that certain paragraphs cannot have come from Ephrem because the use of certain terms there are not in harmony with Ephrem's typical terminology in his hymns is hardly a sufficiently objective premise on which to formulate conclusions.[2] Comparing the use of language in a prose commentary with that found in what are essentially poetic compositions may not necessarily be the most reliable way of determining the authenticity of a passage, since people write differently in different genres, and they write differently for different audiences. It seems somewhat over-cautious therefore, if not even misleading, on the part of Beck to have suggested that one should use the term "The Syriac Commentary on the Diatessaron" when referring to Ephrem's commentary, on the grounds that one cannot uncritically accept its authenticity.[3]

This is not to deny that there are secondary interpolations in each of the respective recensions of the commentary, as already illustrated above. And to this debate one might also add the fact that there is an almost word for word repetition in both traditions of X, §§1-2 in XV, §19, a fact which further suggests that the work must have had a complicated pre-history to the forms in which we now have it.[4] Additional confirmation that the commentary in its present form is not uniform comes from a recent study of M.-E. Boismard.[5] As a result of his analyses of IV, §§4-16 (the

---

[1] Cf. A. de Halleux, "L'adoration des Mages," especially his concluding observations on pp. 263-264.

[2] In three separate articles, "Der syrische Diatessaronkommentar zu Jo. I 1-5," *Oriens Christianus*, 67 (1983), pp. 1-31; "Der syrische Diatessaronkommentar zu der unvergebbaren Sünde wider den Heiligen Geist übersetzt und erklärt," *ibid.*, 73 (1989), pp. 1-37; and "Der syrische Diatessaronkommentar zu der Perikope von der Samariterin am Brunnen übersetzt und erklärt," *ibid.*, 74 (1990), pp. 1-24, Beck became progressively more critical in his analyses, reaching a point in the most recent of these of suggesting that the commentary could not be attributed to Ephrem, but instead was an anonymous work: "Der Kommentar war offenbar eine anonyme (Schul)schrift, mit der man ganz frei umgehen konnte"(p. 24).

[3] "Das macht es mir unmöglich, die überlieferte Zuweisung des ganzen Kommentars an Ephräm kritiklos zu übernehmen, und ich halte dafür, dass es geratener ist, zunächst nur von dem syrischen Diatessaronkommentar zu sprechen" ("Der syrische Diatessaronkommentar zu Jo. I 1-5," p. 31).

[4] I am indebted to Sebastian Brock for drawing my attention to the repetition of material in these two passages.

[5] Cf. M.-E. Boismard, *Le Diatessaron: De Tatien à Justin* (avec la collaboration de A. Lamouille, Etudes bibliques, nouvelle série 15, Paris, 1992), especially section V entitled "La tradition syriaque," pp. 93-125.

temptations of Jesus), V, §§1-12 (the wedding at Cana) and V, §§17a-b and 21 (Jesus eats with tax collectors and sinners) Boismard has shown that there is duplication of material in the case of the first two sections, and even triplication in the third. From this he concludes that Ephrem's commentary is not homogenous, but rather the result of a fusion of two distinct commentaries, one on Tatian's Diatessaron and the other on an early harmony also known to Justin.[1] The question as to whether these two distinct commentaries could have both come from Ephrem Boismard prefers to leave to others to resolve, but he does note in passing that "ce n'est pas impossible."[2]

In view of this complexity, it must be stated however that, while it is possible to attain a certain measure of success in a critical evaluation of the integrity of the commentary using a combination of methods, drawn both from internal and external evidence,[3] it would nevertheless appear to be unduly sceptical to remove Ephrem's name totally from a commentary which Leloir has termed "la plus importante des oeuvres exégétiques d'Ephrem."[4]

4. Features of this English Translation

A Translation rather than a Paraphrase

At an early stage a choice had to be made as to whether this translation should convert the Semitic flavour and idiom of the Syriac original into a more standard English expression and thereby lose some of its intrinsic symbolism and original modes of expression in the process, or should attempt a formal equivalency, in which the skilled eye could detect the underlying turn of phrase, but which might make heavy reading for the uninitiated. The version which follows is an attempt to follow a middle route between these two poles. While trying to be as faithful as possible to the original text, it also seeks to express this in a more contemporary idiom, particularly where this facilitates the flow of a difficult or obscure passage. Words not explicitly present in the Syriac text,

---

[1] Cf. *op. cit.*, pp. 103-104, and pp. 29 ff. for details on the Pepys harmony which, he holds, is close to a harmony known to Justin.

[2] Cf. *op. cit.*, p. 103.

[3] Studies of this kind are already well under way. Cf. de Halleux, "L'adoration des Mages" and M.-E. Boismard, *Le Diatessaron: De Tatien à Justin*.

[4] Cf. Leloir, *Doctrines et Méthodes*, p. 40.

but presupposed from the context or contained in suffixes which are clear in the original but not in translation, are supplied in parentheses. Occasionally a particularly striking paranomasia will be explained in a footnote. In general it is safe to conclude that even in translation the distinctive characteristics of Ephrem still shine through, particularly his skill in drawing together biblical texts into new and imaginative syntheses.

Scriptural Citations and Allusions

There are various reasons why it is not always easy to identify the scriptural texts which Ephrem cites. The first and most obvious reason arises from the fact that we are not dealing with a commentary on a version of the gospels (such as the Old Syriac or Peshitta forms) as such, but rather on a harmony of the gospels for which we do not possess an original Syriac form. In some cases, particularly in very short citations, there appears to be no distinction between the Old Syriac, the Peshitta and the text cited by Ephrem.[1] In other cases Ephrem [rather than Tatian] seems to have abbreviated a quotation for his own reasons, so that the end result does not represent any text strictly speaking but constitutes instead a mosaic of scriptural words.[2] In yet other cases it is not possible to be certain whether Ephrem was formally quoting a text or simply citing from memory. And finally Ephrem often only alludes to or paraphrases a scriptural event. Even if one were to undertake a vast text-critical study in identifying the scriptural texts used by Ephrem one might not always succeed in achieving certainty, since Ephrem is basically commenting on a

---

[1] In a recent M.A. thesis at University College Dublin (1990), "St. Ephrem's Commentary on Tatian's Diatessaron, Chapter Five," Elizabeth Barry examined the gospel quotations attested in Ephrem's Commentary V, comparing them with both Old Syriac and Peshitta texts. In the light of the variations in Ephrem's text in V she observed "that it is difficult to draw any firm conclusions from this data, apart from noting that there tends to be a greater agreement between Ephrem and the Peshitta text, than between Ephrem and the Old Syriac" (p. 74). In an unpublished Ph. D. dissertation ("Tatian's Diatessaron and the Old Syriac Gospels: the Evidence of MS. Chester Beatty 709," Edinburgh 1969), G. A. Weir states that, on the basis of a detailed comparison of the gospel quotations in this MS with the corresponding passages in the Sinaitic and Curetonian MSS of the Old Syriac and in the Peshitta Syriac, "the Syriac Diatessaron known to Ephraem was a text of Old Syriac rather than of Peshitta, type, and that its relationship to the Sinaitic and Curetonian texts is a complex one" (Preface).

[2] Cf. W. L. Petersen, *The Diatessaron and Ephrem Syrus as Sources of Romanos the Melodist*, p. 27: "As a witness to the Diatessaron, the major drawback of the Commentary is that its citations are often difficult to separate from Ephrem's comments: where does the one end and the other begin?"

Diatessaron text and not on a Syriac form of the four separate gospels.[1] This uncertainty has necessitated a two-fold approach to biblical material in the following translation. What approximates to a recognizable scriptural citation, whether in the form of a direct quotation, or a paraphrase, or an abbreviated or expanded citation, has been placed in italics, with a footnote giving the scriptural reference. Allusions by contrast are not italicized, but the relevant scriptural reference is indicated in a footnote. A detailed text-critical analysis of each scriptural citation is clearly beyond the scope and purpose of this translation, but even a cursory examination of some of Ephrem's Gospel citations in the light of the Greek textual tradition reveals some interesting variations.[2]

In the case of identifiable scriptural citations within the Commentary, the policy for citing them devised by Leloir in the Syriac and Armenian editions has been followed here too. When a citation can be referred indiscriminately to any one of the evangelists and the text of one of them suffices in accounting for all the elements in the citation, only one evangelist is mentioned in the footnote, the first according to modern editions of the gospels (Matthew, Mark, Luke, John). If more than one evangelist must be mentioned, but not on an equal basis, the one which is featured first in the footnote is the one closest to the text cited by Ephrem, or the one which takes into account the first of the points being elaborated by Ephrem in the passage in question.

The reader will find further scriptural references attached to an appendix at the end, which gives in outline the sequence of topics in the Diatessaron Commentary. The purpose of these references is to give the general context in which the scriptural texts are quoted by Ephrem. Parallel texts are cited according to the order found in modern editions and consequently do not always reflect Ephrem's choice of one evangelist over the other. These scriptural references however do give a bird's eye view of the sequence of gospel texts Ephrem chose to comment on, a sequence with obvious implications for questions relating to the original order in Tatian's Diatessaron.

---

[1] Although Weir (*op. cit.*) argues for the existence of a pre-Tatianic Syriac Tetra-evangelion, of "western" textual complexion, which he suggests would have been the common ancestor of the Diatessaron and of the S and C texts, such a proposal would need much further research, given our lack of textual evidence for the earliest phases of the Syriac Tetraevangelion traditions.

[2] The complexity of such a text-critical task should not be underestimated. Some work has already been initiated by Leloir in his monograph, *Le Témoignage de S. Ephrem sur le Diatessaron* (1962) and in his introduction in EC-FA.

Division of the Text

The division of the text in this translation follows that of the Syriac text as edited by Leloir in 1963 and 1990, with additional paragraph headings inserted at appropriate intervals throughout to give a summary of the contents. As already indicated above, this division of the text was first based on the work Leloir had undertaken in his 1953 edition of the Armenian version, and he has retained this division in all subsequent editions of the commentary whether in Syriac, Latin or French.[1]

The Lacunae

This translation is essentially concerned with offering the contents of the Syriac *Chester Beatty* MS 709 to the English-speaking world in a form which is both readable and faithful to the original. Given that aim, the question of the various lacunae had to be resolved. Rather than leave gaps in the commentary represented by the twenty-seven or so missing folios, it was decided that the content of these as attested in the Armenian tradition would feature in the respective gaps, with a footnote at each point to alert the reader to the presence of this secondary material.[2] In this context I would like to express a special debt of gratitude to Dom Louis Leloir for his kind permission to use his Latin translation of the Armenian version as the basis for supplying the content of these lacunae. One of the special advantages of using this Latin translation is that it is very literal, even to the point of reproducing the word order. This literalness therefore was of particular benefit in an attempt to feature the underlying Syriac substratum.[3] However, while the Armenian version

---

[1] As noted above, Leloir recognizes some of the complexities which have arisen retrospectively, particularly due to the fact that the additional folios contain significantly more material than the Armenian, particularly in VI, in relation to the Sermon on the Mount.

[2] The nine lacunae occur at the following places: I, §§1-2 and §§27-31; II, §§15-20; III, §§6-15; IV, §§2-6; VII, §§25-27; IX, §§10-14; XVI, §§17-21; XVIII, §3 - XXI, §4. The content of XI, §§17-18, which in *Chester Beatty* MS 709 represents extraneous material probably due to a copyist's error, has also been supplied from the Armenian tradition.

[3] In the *Avant-Propos* to his Latin translation (CSCO 145, p. i) Leloir explains his *méthode de travail* as follows: "De cette version arménienne d'un original syriaque, il était nécessaire, m'a-t-il semblé, de viser à donner une traduction où l'élégance serait sacrifiée à l'exactitude: l'ordre des mots du texte arménien a été, dans la mesure du possible, conservé dans la traduction latine, et toute formule dure, mais fidèle, a été préférée, pourvu qu'elle demeurât intelligible, à un formule plus aisée, mais moins proche de l'expression du

contains much material which originates with Ephrem and is, generally speaking, a reasonably faithful rendering of that material, even a cursory comparison of both texts as illustrated above reveals that there are significant differences in both content and the pluses and minuses of the respective textual traditions. Therefore the filling of lacunae from the Armenian must be seen as a very limited exercise which, one hopes, will soon be made unnecessary by the discovery of the other missing folios of *Chester Beatty* MS 709.

---

traducteur arménien; dans une version qui est la traduction d'une traduction, cette règle de littéralité devait être de stricte rigueur, sous peine d'exclure presque toute possibilité de retrouver le substrat syriaque, et d'empêcher la traduction d'être un sûr instrument de travail."

TRANSLATION

I

Reflections on the Mystery of the Incarnation

§1.[1] {Why did our Lord clothe himself with our flesh?[2] So that this flesh might experience victory, and that [humanity] might know and understand the gifts [of God]. For, if God had been victorious without the flesh, what praise could one render him? Secondly, so that [our Lord] might show that, at the beginning, he experienced no jealousy towards him [who had wanted] to become God. For he in whom [our Lord] was abased is greater than he in whom he was dwelling when [Adam] was great and glorious.[3] This is why [it is written], *I have said, You shall be gods.*[4] Thus, the Word came and clothed itself with flesh, so that what cannot be grasped might be grasped through that which can be grasped,[5] and that, through that which cannot be grasped, the flesh would raise itself up against those who grasp it.[6] For it was fitting that our Lord be the haven of all good things, unto whom [people] might be gathered together, the

---

[1] The first folio of Ephrem's Commentary in *Chester Beatty* MS 709 is missing. The translation given here of §§ 1-2 is based on the Armenian version, edited and translated by Leloir (cf. CSCO 145, pp. 1-2). To facilitate recognition of where the Armenian has been used to supply for the lacunae in the Syriac, special brackets will be used at the beginning and end of the passages in question (as well as at the beginning of each paragraph within these blocks), as follows: {Why did the Lord clothe himself with our flesh ... }.

[2] The commentary opens with what is probably one of Ephrem's most typical images, that of putting on and off of clothing. His preferred way of referring to the Incarnation was through the use of these or similar words: "He clothed himself with a body/with the flesh." Through this concrete imagery Ephrem was able to present his Christian community with a cohesive picture of salvation history, following the earliest Syriac translation of "he became incarnate" of the Nicene Creed (cf. S. P. Brock, *The Luminous Eye*, p. 39).

[3] The reference here is to the First Adam before the fall. The Second Adam is superior to the First. The typology of the First Adam - Second Adam played a very significant role in early Syrian Christianity, particularly in Ephrem's writings, and cannot be fully appreciated without reference to another of his key themes, that of baptism as re-entry into Paradise. The eschatological Paradise, to which the Christian is restored through baptism, is far more glorious than the original Paradise, for Christ, the Second Adam, has definitively reversed the effects of the disobedience of the First Adam. Adam's pre-fallen state was neither mortal nor immortal, and, although he enjoyed a certain glory then, it was radically inferior to that of the Second Adam (cf. *Commentary on Genesis* and *Hymns on Paradise*).

[4] Ps 82:6.

[5] This phrase probably means: "so that what cannot be grasped (the divinity) might be grasped through that which can be grasped (humanity)."

[6] Possibly a reference to demonic forces or powers of Satan which wage war against the flesh.

end of all mysteries, towards whom they would hasten from everywhere, and the treasure of all the parables, so that everyone, lifted up [as though] on wings, might rest in him alone.

[See][1] the wisdom [of God], that, in the fall of him who fell, there fell with him the One who was destined to raise him up.[2] Because the body of Adam was in existence before his [evil] passions, [our Lord] did not assume the passions with which [Adam subsequently] clothed himself, since they were a kind of additional weakness to a healthy nature. Our Lord clothed himself therefore with a healthy nature which had lost its health, so that the original health of this nature might thereby be restored. For even though the swords of the beasts had wounded [us] severely, the remedies of the Benefactor nevertheless hastened to revive us. [Humanity] had been held by involuntary bonds undeservedly, for its wounds were undeserved. [Adam] had not sinned against Satan who struck him, just as he had not given anything to the Benefactor who healed him. Samson killed many with the jawbone of an ass,[3] but the serpent killed the entire human race through Eve. Our Lord therefore took up these [same] arms with which the adversary had been victorious, and the world condemned. He came down into the combat and, in the flesh which [he had received] from a woman, conquered the world. Conquered, the adversary was condemned.

Although the Church was hidden, the mysteries were proclaiming it, while it remained itself silent. But then, when the Church itself became manifest, it began to interpret the mysteries, its erstwhile interpreters, which were silent [from now on] because of this revelation [of the Church].

The Prologue of St John[4]

§2.   [*In the beginning was the Word.*[5] [The evangelist said this] to show that, just as the Word was with its Generator, [so] it was the

---

[1] A conjectural reconstruction, since both MSS have lacunae here.
[2] Ephrem uses the same verb, "to fall," to refer to both the fall of the First Adam and the abasement through the incarnation of the Second Adam.
[3] Cf. Judg 15:15-16.
[4] Cf. E. Beck, "Der syrische Diatessaronkommentar zu Jo. I 1-5," *Oriens Christianus* 67(1983), pp. 1-31, for a detailed study of this part of the commentary. Beck holds that the way in which certain words and phrases are used in these paragraphs is not in keeping with Ephrem's style in his hymns and sermons, which leads Beck to raise the question as to whether one can uncritically attribute the entire commentary to Ephrem.
[5] John 1:1.

companion of its Generator in every work that exists, both in itself and outside of itself}.[1] For even though a word may not yet be spoken it can have existence. Take for instance [the case] of Zechariah, who without [using his] lips spoke [a word] through writing.[2] [Our Lord is called the Word] also because those things that were hidden were revealed through him, just as it is through a word that the hidden things of the heart are made known. For Paul bears witness that the mystery of God is Christ, through whom was revealed all the hidden things of wisdom and knowledge.[3] A word however is not pronounced except by means of a form, since the nature of a word is that it is generated. He has disclosed concerning himself through this that he was not self-existent,[4] but was begotten, and that he was not the Father, but the Son. For he has said, *No one has ever seen God. The Only-Begotten One, who is from the bosom of the Father, has disclosed concerning him,*[5] and, *I went forth from the Father, I have come.*[6] If then you say that what [already] exists cannot be begotten, you accuse Scripture of falsehood, for it says [in one place] that *He was,* and says [elsewhere] that *He was begotten* from his bosom.[7]

§3.　　*In the beginning was the Word.*[8] Do not understand it as an ordinary word, or reduce it to a voice. For it was not a voice that *was in the beginning,* since, before it is sounded, [a voice] does not exist, and after it is sounded it does not exist. Therefore it was not a voice which was the likeness of his Father, nor was it the Father's voice, but his image. If your son, who is born from you, is like you, would God have begotten a voice and not God? If Elizabeth's son, who was called a voice,[9] was a man, God, who was called the Word, is God. If you say that the Word was called the Son, know that John, who was called the voice, existed in [his own] person. Likewise, God, who was called the Word, and the Word-God, is God. If you were to think that the Son is the Thought of the Father, does

---

[1] The Syriac text is extant from this point onwards, the beginning of *Chester Beatty* MS 709 in its present condition (cf. EC-CBM 8).

[2] Cf. Luke 1:63.

[3] Cf. Col 1:26-27. The reference to Paul's witness here is not a direct quotation, but an allusion to the content of these verses which indicate that "the mystery hidden for ages" is Christ.

[4] Literally, ܐ ܝܬ ܘܬ ܐ , "being, substance."

[5] John 1:18.

[6] John 16:28.

[7] Cf. John 1:18.

[8] John 1:1.

[9] Cf. Mark 1:3.

this mean that the Father thought [only] once and for all? But, if he has many thoughts, how can [the Son] be the Only-Begotten One? If he is the Thought which is within, how can he be at his right hand?

§4.   *In the beginning was the Word.*[1] The Word [in question here] then is not that which was posited subject to a beginning, but that which was above and beyond the beginning.[2] For, in the case of this [kind of word, one subject to a beginning]: because there was a time when its utterer did not exist, there was also a time when it too did not exist. But with regard to the true Word, however, there was not a time when it either existed or did not exist, or at [one] time it was not, and at [another] time it was. Rather, from all time and from eternity it was, because the One who pronounced it exists at all times and forever. The Word of the One who pronounced it is like the One who pronounced it. This is why [the evangelist] said, *In the beginning was the Word*, so that he might show that its manifestation is exalted over the entire beginning and boundary of times.

§5.   [The evangelist] said, *He was with God*,[3] and not *in* God. Therefore, through [the words] *with God*, he has shown us clearly that just as [God] was the One that [always] was, so too this *Word was with God. In the beginning was the Word*. [The evangelist] teaches us two things through this: [one] concerns his nature, and [the other] his generation.[4] But, in order not to leave the Word without an explanation, he said that this *Word was with God*. Thus, here too he proclaims two things with regard to the Word: that it is not like a human word, for it was *with him*, and concerning its essence. *And this Word was God*. [The evangelist] teaches three things: God, hypostasis and generation. *He was in the beginning with God*.[5] He is careful in his use of words lest his preaching be thought to be referring to one hypostasis [only]. *He was in the beginning with God*: He is referring, in the first place, to his generation; secondly, that he was *with him*, thirdly, that he *is God*, and fourthly, that he was always with him.

---

[1] John 1:1.
[2] Ephrem seems to be contrasting the creative word of God spoken in Genesis, which had a beginning in time, with the pre-existent Word of God.
[3] John 1:1.
[4] Note how the rest of this paragraph is poetically structured through a progression in numbers, as far as four.
[5] John 1:2.

§6.   *Everything was through him,*[1] because by means of him the works [of creation] were created, according to what the apostle [has said], *Through him he made the ages.*[2] *Apart from him there is not a single [thing].*[3] This is the same as, *Whatever came to be is in him and he is life, and that life is the light of humanity.*[4] For, because of his rising forth, the error of earlier times was dispersed. *This light was shining in the darkness, but the darkness did not apprehend it.*[5] This is like, *He came to his own and his own did not receive him.*[6]

§7.   *This light was shining in the darkness.*[7] See then what kind of darkness was against him who [was] the light of humanity, and discern the sense in which *He was shining* in it from former times. Since [the evangelist] has said, *He was shining,* you must not interpret this too naively. Because he did not say, *He is shining in the darkness,* you must discern that he has called darkness that time which preceded his divine emergence, and has shown that *He was shining in it.* Concerning this darkness, therefore, we can also understand from the Gospel when [the evangelist] says, repeating what was spoken by the prophet, *Land of Zebulun and Naphtali, the way of the sea, and beyond the Jordan river, Galilee of the Gentiles; the people who dwell in darkness have seen a light.*[8] This darkness, which he attributed to them, [was] because they were tribes which were dispersed and dwelling by the sea shore, and were far removed from the discipline and instruction of the Law. This is why he was referring to them as *the people who dwell in darkness.* [It was] concerning these that the evangelist spoke thus, when [he said], *this light,* referring to the teaching of his insight. This *darkness* of former times, which is error, *did not apprehend.*[9] He went on to proclaim the beginning of the divine plan, which is by means of the Body[10] and he commenced by

---

[1] John 1:3.
[2] Heb 1:2.
[3] John 1:3.
[4] John 1:3-4.
[5] John 1:5.
[6] John 1:11.
[7] John 1:5.
[8] Matt 4:15-16; cf. Isa 8:23; 9:1.
[9] John 1:5.
[10] Ephrem often refers to Christ's body as a symbol for the mystery of the Incarnation.

43

saying that he, whom *the darkness did not apprehend*, came into being *in the days of Herod, King of Judea*.[1]

§8. After having completed the account concerning the Word, under what form, up to what point and for what motive it lowered itself, the [evangelist] said elsewhere, *The Word itself became a body and dwelt* [2] *among us*.[3] Now, all that you hear after the completion of the account of this Word, you should not understand it in relation to the Word merely in itself, but to the Word that clothed itself with a body. Consequently, these are mixed accounts, they are divine in their entirety, and they are also human, apart from that [Word] which is the first and the beginning of everything.

The Birth of John the Baptist Foretold

§9. *In the days of Herod, King of Judea, there was a certain priest whose name was Zechariah, and his wife Elizabeth*.[4] The [statement], *They were blameless in their entire way of life*,[5] [is made] lest it be said that it was because of their wrongdoing that they had not had any children. Rather, they were continuing to hope for a miracle. *And you will have joy*;[6] not because you will have given birth, but on account of the one to whom you will have given birth. *For there is none greater among those born of women than John*.[7] *Wine and strong drink he shall not drink*,[8] like the Nazirites, sons of the promise, so that it would be known that he was of [their] family.

§10. *And you, little child, you shall be called the prophet of the Most High*,[9] since the Spirit was in the little child as well as in the old man. *You will go before the face of our Lord*,[10] taking the place of the prophets who

---

[1] Luke 1:5.

[2] On ܐ see S. P. Brock, "The Lost Old Syriac at Luke 1:35 and the earliest Syriac term for the incarnation," *Gospel Traditions in the Second Century*, edited by W. L. Petersen (Notre Dame, 1989), pp. 117-131.

[3] John 1:14.

[4] Luke 1:5.

[5] Luke 1:6.

[6] Luke 1:14.

[7] Matt 11:11; Luke 7:28.

[8] Luke 1:15; cf. Num 6:1-4.

[9] Luke 1:76.

[10] *Idem*.

had heralded his fame. *So that he might give knowledge of perfect life:*[1] so that [people] might distinguish the transitory mysteries from the truth that does not pass away. *For grace [came] through Jesus,*[2] so that a *path be prepared* for him.[3] What is this path? That he might destroy sin and render the curse void, and give knowledge of God and the promise of the resurrection, and the kingdom of heaven. Concerning this path therefore he said, *Prepare Ye.*[4] You must not leave anything in it that is opposed [to our Lord]. Prepare your ears and get your hearts ready. John, herald of the Lord of the right, was announced from the right of the altar.[5] It was at the time of worship that he was announced to show he was the end of the former worship. And it was in the middle of the sanctuary that Zechariah became dumb to show that the mysteries of the sanctuary had become silent, for he who was to fulfil these mysteries had come. Because [Zechariah] did not believe that his wife's barrenness had been healed, he was bound in his speech.

§11.   Zechariah went to the angel, that it might be seen that his child was inferior to the angel. The angel came to Mary, that it might be known that her child was the angel's Lord. The angel came to the Temple, lest it be a pretext for those who wanted to find a pretext for an alien [God].[6] The angel did not go to Elizabeth, for Zechariah was the progenitor of John. Nor did Gabriel go to Joseph, since it was Mary alone who gave birth to the First-Born. Gabriel did not go to Elizabeth, because she had a husband, but he went to Mary that he might fulfil in his [own] name[7] the symbolic place of a husband. *God has heard the voice of your prayer.*[8] If [Zechariah] had known that this was to be, he would have prayed well. But if he had not believed that this was to be, he would have made supplication poorly. [His prayer] was close to being realized; he was in doubt as to whether it would

---

[1] Luke 1:77.

[2] John 1:17.

[3] Cf. Mark 1:2-3.

[4] *Idem.*

[5] Cf. Luke 1:11 and Ps 110:1.

[6] Ephrem is alluding here to a central error of Marcion, namely his distinction between an inferior God, creator of the world and proclaimed in the Old Testament, and a superior God, elevated beyond the realm of humanity, known only to the Son, and to those to whom the Son has revealed him.

[7] A clever play on words based on the Syriac form of the name, ܠܘܐܝܪܒܓ , Gabriel.

[8] Luke 1:13. The Greek and Peshitta read a passive form: *Your prayer has been heard.* Ephrem's text here is similar to that of the Old Syriac (S), and reflects the MT of Ps 66:19, "He has given heed to the voice of my prayer."

be. Rightly then, when his request was close [to being realized], the word distanced itself from him. At an earlier stage, he had been praying for this, but when his request [was granted], he turned about and [said], *How can this be?*[1]

§12.   Thus, because his mouth expressed doubt concerning his request, his word distanced itself from him and ministered unto his will. Thus it was that when [the matter] was at a distance he prayed, but when it drew near and was [about] to be announced, he did not believe. Accordingly, as long as he continued to believe, he was also able to speak, but when he ceased believing he became silent. He believed and he spoke; *For I believed and therefore did I speak.*[2] Therefore, because he despised the word, the word afflicted him, that he might honour through his silence the word that he had despised. It was appropriate that the mouth which had said, *How can this be?*,[3] was silenced, so that he might learn that this [petition] was indeed possible. The tongue which had not been tied became bound that he might learn that it was possible for a bound womb to be untied. For he knew that he who had bound his tongue was also able to untie the womb.

§13.   It was this trial therefore that taught him who was unwilling to allow faith to teach him. He prayed that he might speak, but experienced the inability to do so. Thus did he learn that he who could close an open mouth was able to open a closed womb. Through being made silent with just reason he recognized how he had spoken unjustly. Why did the Law command, *An eye for an eye,*[4] if not so that the evildoer might learn, through the destruction of his eye, how beautiful is the handiwork he has destroyed? Thus Zechariah transgressed by means of the word and was punished by means of the word, that he might experience the imposition of the destruction [of his sight] in payment for his transgression.[5] He was [left] without a word because he thought that the word spoken to him could not be realized. By reason of the fact that he had ceased [being able to

---

[1] Luke 1:18.
[2] Ps 116:10.
[3] Luke 1:18.
[4] Exod 21:24.
[5] There is a play on words here between ܚܘܒܠܐ, "debt/transgression" and ܚܘܒܠܐ, "destruction," reinforcing the idea that it is the offending member of the body that should undergo due punishment. An allusion to Rom 1:27, "receiving in their own persons the due penalty for their error," is possibly intended here.

speak] any word that was of use, he learned that he had wrongly rendered the word of the promise void. His word had spurned the angel's word; so this word too received punishment from the angel. For, even if all the members suffer with one member,[1] nevertheless it is only right that the member which transgressed should be punished in this present case. Even if its suffering affects [all] the members, nevertheless the precise suffering should be tasted by that member itself. Such was this transgression that its punishment pressed hard upon its heels, lest something like this might happen again.

§14.   It was only fitting, therefore, [with regard to] the message which was announced to Zechariah by the angel, that he should go forth and be its herald. Because he did not believe there and then that he would be its herald through his word, he was punished, so that he might become its herald through his silence. Since the vision had appeared to him in the sanctuary, the people perceived that he had been worthy of it; but, because they saw that he was muzzled in silence, they perceived that a guard was necessary for his lips. The tongue was smitten that the mind might be admonished, for the mind has control over the bridle of the lips. Thus, because he did not set a guard for his mouth,[2] the gate of his mouth was stopped up in silence.

Because it was in the Holy of Holies that he had been addressed, the people perceived that it was good tidings that had been spoken to him there. But, since they saw that he was not speaking, they perceived that he had given a wrong response. Because the vision had appeared to him at the hour of prayer when petitions were being made, they perceived that some gift was being offered to him, but, since thanksgiving was not found on his lips, they perceived that he had not in fact accepted the gift. If Zechariah had indeed been in doubt concerning the angel's word, no one was in doubt concerning his silence. He, who had not believed in the promise [made] through the angel, [brought it about that] everyone believed in the promise because of his silence. The silence of Zechariah was both a prophet and a judge for others, so that, as though from a prophet they might learn about the promise, and, as though from a judge they might fear to spurn the promise. For [Zechariah] too, the angel was

---

[1] Cf. 1 Cor 12:26.
[2] Cf. Ps 141:3.

both a prophet and a judge; as a prophet he disclosed hidden things to him, and as a judge he meted out punishment to him.

§15.   Good tidings were sent to humanity at that time. But, because the one who first heard them doubted them, [God] placed a sign in him lest all the others might imitate him. Thus, these good tidings, which were not believed when the angel spoke them forth with his voice, were believed when Zechariah disclosed them with a sign. When Zechariah saw that everyone believed them through his own sign, he learned that he had done wrong to have doubted the angel's voice. Consequently, it was fitting that being dumb, he should cause others to hear. Because he did not believe the angel, who was a mouth for God, [the angel] made him dumb, so that he had a writing tablet instead of speech.[1]

§16.   When he heard the promise of John from the angel and did not believe, he was made dumb. But when he saw John coming forth from the womb, he began to speak. The word which had come forth from the angel passed over [Zechariah's] mouth and closed it, and reached out to [Elizabeth's] womb and opened it. Then this [word] closed once again the womb it had opened, so that it would not give birth again, and opened once more the mouth it had closed so that it would not be closed again. It was therefore fitting that the mouth which had not believed be closed, seeing that a barren womb would be opened. And it was fitting that the womb which had given birth to John be closed so as not to give birth again, in order that the only-begotten[2] be herald to the Only-Begotten. Thus, even if Zechariah was alone in his doubt, nevertheless through his doubt, he removed doubt from everyone else.

§17.   Therefore, through his lack of faith, he procured faith for everyone else. When John was born through the promise from the mouth of the living angel, his father did not believe in his spiritual birth. But when he was born from a dead womb, he believed in his bodily birth.

---

[1] Cf. Luke 1:63.

[2] The term ܝܚܝܕܐ, "only-begotten" has a wide variety of connotations in Syriac, among which any of the following could be applied to John the Baptist: "singular, individual, unique, singleminded, undivided in heart, single, celibate." In the Syriac Bible it is the term used to translate the title μονογενης in John 1:14, 18. In the fifth century and later the term came to be used as an equivalent to the Greek μοναχος in the sense of monk, and more specifically as the equivalent of a hermit or a solitary.

48

Because he did not believe in the living mouth, his mouth became dead to the word. And because he believed in a barren womb more than in the angel, his lips became sterile, without words. [The people] saw that he had become dumb, and in good faith they quickly believed, since they saw that he had done wrong in doubting. The lips, on account of their haste, had stumbled through their word, and were delivered over to silence that they might learn to slow down, and not lapse again through their haste. Because Zechariah had been in doubt about his Lord and about his own petition, it was fitting that he be made dumb, so that he would not doubt either God or his petition again.

§18.   Who is capable of comprehending the immensity of possibilities of one of your utterances? What we leave behind us in [your utterance] is far greater than what we take from it, like those who are thirsting, [when they imbibe] from a fountain. Many are the perspectives of his word, just as many are the perspectives of those who study it. [God] has fashioned his word with many beautiful forms, so that each one who studies it may consider what he likes. He has hidden in his word all kinds of treasures so that each one of us, wherever we meditate, may be enriched by it. His utterance is a tree of life, which offers you blessed fruit from every side. It is like that rock which burst forth in the desert, becoming spiritual drink to everyone from all places. *[They ate] spiritual food and drank spiritual drink.*[1]

§19.   Therefore, whoever encounters one of its riches must not think that that alone which he has found is all that is in it, but [rather] that it is this alone that he is capable of finding from the many things in it. Enriched by it, let him not think that he has impoverished it. But rather let him give thanks for its greatness, he that is unequal to it. Rejoice that you have been satiated, and do not be upset that it is richer than you. The thirsty one rejoices because he can drink, but is not upset because he is unable to render the source dry. The well can conquer your thirst, but your thirst cannot conquer the fountain. If your thirst is satiated, without the fountain running short, whenever you are thirsty, you can drink again. But if, through your being satiated, the fountain were rendered dry, your victory would be unto your misfortune. Give thanks for what you have taken away, and do not murmur over what remains and is in excess. That

---

[1] 1 Cor 10:3-4.

49

which you have taken and gone away with is your portion and that which is left over is also your heritage. That which you were not able to receive there and then because of your weakness, receive it at another time by means of your perseverance. And do not, in your impudence, attempt either to obtain in one moment that which cannot be taken up in one moment, or to desist from that which you are able to take up little by little.

§20. The fingers wrote *John* on the writing tablet, a name which signifies the need for compassion.[1] For the fingers asked for compassion on the basis of grace, in place of the lips which were closed on the basis of justice. *For God has heard the voice of your prayer.*[2] Given that the divinity had granted this [petition], and this prayer had been made, he was rightly deprived[3] of speech, since insight had been withdrawn from him. For when he had been asking a petition of God in his prayer he was a witness to prayer, that prayer could make petition, and that God was able to grant. But then, when that which he had been asking for drew near to being realized, he said, *How can this be?*[4] There happened to him there and then that which he did not want to happen, because he had spurned that which he had wished would happen. A new thing happened to him, something he did not learn, since he was found to be inexperienced in that which for a long time he was being taught. Because his ears did not hear that for which his lips were praying, his mouth, source of words, dried up, so that it could not send its drink to the ears.

§21. How could he, who was unable to cultivate fruit in his own ear, cultivate fruit in any other ear? For Zechariah was comforting men who were barren, through Abraham their father, and was consoling women who were devoid of children, through Sarah their mother, showing how he and his wife were similar to these. Abraham and Sarah were common ancestors, and were placed like a common mirror in the midst of all. The eyes of barren men and women were gazing into [this mirror] that they might be consoled, as in the case of Isaac, who, after ninety-nine years, was

---

[1] Cf. Luke 1:63. Note the pun here on ܝܘܚܢ, "John" and ܚܢܢ, "compassion."
[2] Luke 1:13.
[3] The Syriac text reads ܐܬܓܠܝ, "he was revealed," which, if read as ܐܬܓܠܙ, "he was deprived," makes more sense in the context. It seems likely that there was a scribal error here in the confusion of the two consonants, or possibly a corruption of ܐܬܓܠܝ, "he was withdrawn from."
[4] Luke 1:18.

50

outlined in it. [Zechariah] was gazing into this [mirror] through faith, but was in doubt about it on account of old age. Because he had doubted him who is able to change nature, he sought to speak but could not, that he might learn about him who is omnipotent. A sign was required for him who believed not, that through it he might believe. Therefore, [God] gave him a sign in his mouth because of the doubt in his heart, that he might know who it is that is able to render silent that nature which speaks, and who it is that is able to rejuvenate a dead womb. Only when his lips were unable to give birth to speech [did he believe that] his old age would be able to procreate a son.

§22.   *God has heard the voice of your prayer.*[1] Prayer made the petition; the divinity granted [it], but freewill spurned [it]. It was thereby revealed that prayer can ask all kinds of requests, and the divinity can bestow all kinds of gifts, but freewill can either receive or spurn all [these] things. It is not fitting however to lay {blame}[2] on those who *were blameless in their entire way of life.*[3] Because he was terrified by the angel's splendour, [Zechariah] was troubled in his tongue only, and not in his heart. This is like [the passage], *They made his spirit bitter and he spoke with his lips.*[4] Consequently the angel judged him through his mouth. If he had doubted in his heart, he would have been punished through his heart. But when these things were fulfilled, the priest too {repented}[5] of his error.

§23.   *He will turn the heart of the fathers to the sons.*[6] They had been mislead from Judaism to paganism, and had separated {themselves}[7] from the covenant of their God. Therefore he said, *He will turn* [their heart], so that they might serve the Lord of all in truth like their fathers, and, *That he might prepare for the Lord a perfect people,*[8] like Elijah, who by his zeal

---

[1] Luke 1:13.

[2] This is the first of a number of words on this folio that are difficult to decipher, due to the poor condition in which the folio has been preserved. It has been reconstructed on the basis of the Armenian (cf. CSCO 145, p.11).

[3] Luke 1:6.

[4] Ps 106:33.

[5] This word is illegible in the Syriac (cf. CSCO 145, p. 11 for its reconstruction). The priest in question of course is Zechariah.

[6] Luke 1:17.

[7] This word in the Syriac is unclear (cf. CSCO 145, p. 12 for its reconstruction).

[8] Luke 1:17.

{brought back}[1] many to the fear of his Lord. If they say that this is something that is about to come to pass, [let them see] that fathers are not divided against their sons, nor sons against their fathers, nor do they adore idols.

§24.   *Elizabeth hid herself* [2] because of Zechariah's grief. Or alternatively, she *hid herself*, because she was ashamed {on account of the fact that she had resumed intercourse; so it was}[3] because of her old age that *Elizabeth hid herself*. But see, [Moses] did not write in relation to Sarah that she hid herself, when at the age of ninety she carried Isaac, nor with regard to Rebecca who was pregnant with twins. *Elizabeth hid herself for five months*,[4] until her infant would be sufficiently formed in his members to exult before his Lord,[5] and because Mary was about to receive the annunciation.

The Birth of Jesus Foretold

§25.   [The words], *In the sixth month*,[6] are reckoned in relation to Elizabeth's pregnancy. *The angel was sent to a virgin*,[7] and he said to her, *Behold in your virginity*[8]*you will conceive in your womb and bear a son, and you shall call his name Jesus*.[9] He was speaking about him who was to appear in the Body.[10] He did not say to her, "That name which is called Jesus," but, *You shall call his name*. This shows that this name is of the economy which is through the Body, since Jesus in Hebrew means Saviour. For [the angel] said, *You shall call his name Jesus*, that is Saviour, *for he shall save his people from sins*.[11] This name therefore refers not to his nature but to his deeds.

---

[1] The Syriac word here is unclear, and the translation has been reconstructed from the Armenian version(cf. CSCO 145, p. 12).

[2] Luke 1:24.

[3] The Syriac text here is unclear (cf. CSCO 145, p. 12 for the reconstructed text).

[4] Luke 1:24.

[5] Cf. Luke 1:41.

[6] Luke 1:26.

[7] Luke 1:26-27. This citation and the commentary which follows until the citation of Luke 1:32 are missing from the Armenian version.

[8] This word is not attested in the Greek, nor by the Peshitta version; unfortunately this section of Luke is not extant in the Old Syriac. The addition could reflect the influence of Tatian, given his encratite views.

[9] Luke 1:31.

[10] This is one of Ephrem's typical ways of referring to the mystery of the Incarnation.

[11] Matt 1:21.

Mary said to him, *How can this be, since no man has known me?* [1] He said to her, *The Holy Spirit will come, and the power of the Most High will overshadow[2] you.*[3] Why did he not mention the Father's name but instead, the name of his Power and the name of the Holy Spirit? Because it was fitting that the Architect of the works [of creation] should come and raise up the house that had fallen, and that the hovering Spirit should sanctify the buildings that were unclean. Thus, if the Progenitor entrusted the judgement that is to come to his [Son], it is clear that he accomplished the creation of humanity and its restoration through him as well. He was the live coal which had come to kindle the briars and thorns.[4] He dwelt in the womb and cleansed it and sanctified the place of the birthpangs and the curses.[5] The flame which Moses saw was moistening the bush[6] and distilling the fat lest it be inflamed. The likeness of refined gold could be seen in the bush, entering into the fire but without being consumed. This happened so that it might make known that living fire which was to come at the end, watering and moistening the womb of the virgin, and clothing it like the fire that [enveloped] the bush.

The Lord will give him the throne of David.[7] This [recalls the prophecy], *The sceptre will not depart until he comes.*[8] When the angel instructed her that all things are easy for God to accomplish,[9] since, in the case of *Elizabeth, your kinswoman,*[10] [God] has also given her conception in her old age, Mary replied, "If it is thus for her, *Behold I am the servant of God; let it be to me as you have said.*"[11] From what the angel said to Mary, namely, *Elizabeth, your kinswoman,* it could be supposed that Mary was from the house of Levi; nevertheless up to this, the prophecy was established within the framework[12] of the husbands. The family of David continued as far as Joseph who had espoused her, and [the birth of] her child was [reckoned] through the framework of the men, for the sake of

---

[1] Luke 1:34. Note change of subject.
[2] See note on §8 above in relation to S. P. Brock's discussion of the lost Old Syriac at Luke 1:35 and the earliest Syriac term for the incarnation.
[3] Luke 1:35.
[4] Cf. Gen 3:18; Isa 9:17-19.
[5] Cf. Gen 3:16.
[6] Cf. Exod 3:2-3.
[7] Luke 1:32.
[8] Gen 49:10.
[9] Cf. Luke 1:37.
[10] Luke 1:36.
[11] Luke 1:38.
[12] The word used here and in the next sentence is ܛܘܦܣܐ , "type" or "typology."

the family of David. {It is in Christ that}[1] the seed and family [of David] are brought to completion. Scripture is silent [about Mary's genealogy] since it is the generations of men that it numbers and reckons. If Scripture had been accustomed to indicate the family [line] through the mothers, it would be in order for one to seek the family of Mary. But, lest [the words], *Elizabeth, your kinswoman*, were to show that Mary was also from the house of Levi, take note that [the evangelist] has said [elsewhere], concerning Joseph and Mary, that *They were both of the house of David*.[2] The angel did not say to Mary that Elizabeth was her sister, but, *Elizabeth, your kinswoman*.

§26.   If Mary had been from another tribe, it would have been a lie [to have said], *From the house of David*. For the angel said, *The Lord will give him the throne of his father, David*.[3] He is the son of Mary, however, and not the son of Joseph. He did not appear in the body from any other lineage, except from David. For [the prophet] said, *There will come forth a shoot from the stock of Jesse, and a scion will blossom from his root*.[4] Zechariah also testified [to this] when he said, *He has raised up for us a horn of salvation in the house of David, his son*.[5] In like manner also the apostle said, *Our Lord Jesus Christ came from Mary, from the seed of the house of David*.[6] He wrote to Timothy as well, *Remember Jesus Christ, he who rose from the dead, he who came from the seed of the house of David*.[7] In the letter of the Romans he said, *It was promised beforehand in*

---

[1] The first part of this sentence is supplied from the Armenian version (CSCO 145, p. 13), since the Syriac text is corrupt here.

[2] Cf. Luke 2:4. Neither the Greek nor Peshitta texts say that *both* were of David's house, but that Joseph "was of the house and lineage of David." Ephrem's text however agrees with the Old Syriac (S). Cf. Leloir, *Le Témoignage d'Ephrem*, for a discussion of the sources which reflect the view that Mary and Joseph were both descendants of David (cf. Ephrem's commentary on 2 Tim 2:8, Aphrahat, and various citations from later Diatessaronic traditions), pp. 84-88.

[3] Luke 1:32.

[4] Isa 11:1.

[5] Luke 1:69. Ephrem's text has "son," whereas the Greek , Old Syriac (S) and Peshitta read "servant."

[6] A citation from the apocryphal third letter of Paul to the Corinthians (3 Cor 5), written about 190-206 A. D. Cf. K. Pink, "Die pseudo-paulinischen Briefe I," *Biblica* 6 (1925), pp. 68-91. Pink, having outlined the letter's origins and dissemination in third century in the earlier part of his study, refers to its presence in the Syrian Church on pp. 74-75, and gives a Latin reconstruction of the Greek text on pp. 81-89. His version of the extract quoted by Ephrem reads as follows: "quod dominus noster Iesus Christus ex Maria natus est ex semine David" (p. 85).

[7] 2 Tim 2:8. The Greek text is much shorter: "Remember Jesus Christ, risen from the dead, descended from David."

the Holy Scriptures, concerning his Son, who appeared in the flesh from the seed of the house of David.[1] And in the letter of the Hebrews he also said, It was known beforehand and revealed that our Lord would spring from Judah, from a tribe concerning whose priesthood Moses had nothing to say.[2] [This text] shows convincingly that Mary was not from the tribe of Levi, but from the house of Judah. In the Acts it is written, He swore an oath to David, I will set one of your descendants upon my own throne.[3] However, we find the tribes of Judah and Levi mixed up together through Aaron, who married {the sister of Nahshon},[4] prince of the house of Judah, and through the priest Jehoiada who married the daughter of King Jehoram of the house of David.[5] Even if the angel's word made reference to the close kinship of Elizabeth and Mary, these tribes were also [already] intermarrying with each other.[6] Moreover, [the words], Elizabeth, your kinswoman,[7] were spoken with reference to Israel, for both of these were of [that] people.

Matthew wrote concerning the genealogy of Mary, from whom our Lord was born. This was why he began with, From David and from Abraham, according as the promise indicated. Not to you and to your descendants as though unto many, but to you and to your descendant, which descendant is Christ.[8] Luke however [was concerned] only with Joseph, husband of Mary, and [went back] as far as Adam who is from God,[9] so that he might teach that he, who in the beginning created Adam, established the Temple.[10] Adam therefore was from [ ][11] and Joseph was from the house of David, For they were both from the house of David.[12] The evangelist Luke was expressing himself carefully when he said, Our Lord began to be, as it were, just considered to be the son of Joseph.[13] Luke

---

[1] Rom 1:2-3.
[2] Heb 7:14.
[3] Cf. Acts 2:30; Ps 132:11.
[4] Cf. Exod 6:23. Part of the Syriac text is corrupt here and the reconstruction is based on the Armenian version (cf. CSCO 145, p. 13).
[5] Cf. 2 Chr 22:11.
[6] The Armenian version does not contain the remainder of §26, from this point onwards.
[7] Luke 1:36.
[8] Gal 3:16.
[9] Cf. Luke 3:38.
[10] The Syriac text for this phrase is unclear, due to the poor condition of this folio. Consequently, the translation given here is approximate.
[11] It is not possible to determine what the underlying word here is, since there is no parallel in the Armenian version.
[12] Luke 2:4.
[13] Luke 3:23.

did not mention Mary, for he did not record her genealogy, in order to show that he, who was worthy to be a minister unto the [divine] economy and be called the husband of Mary, was of the family of David, since it was not fitting that he be from a stock other than that from which his mother Mary came.

The Visitation

§27. *Mary went up therefore* [1] to Elizabeth to learn whether it was true, and also lest she be in doubt about herself. Moreover, *Mary went up* to Elizabeth, who was less important than she, just as our Lord [came] to John. *Why should he do this to me that the mother of my Lord should come to me?*[2] Mary saw that others were priding themselves in the gift [of God]. She too praised him, *From henceforth all generations will account me blessed.*[3] {While John was yet in the loins of Zechariah, as Levi had been in Abraham's loins, he was already serving this same Lord and awaiting him, flower of the month of Areg[4] silently announcing the grape which was crushed in the midst of Jerusalem. Just as the flower precedes the beginning of the blood of the grape[5] by five months, so too John was conceived in advance so that he might be the adoring herald of the adorable conception. *Blessed is she who believed that there would be a fulfilment of all these words which were spoken to her by the Lord.*[6]

§28. {When she had revealed to [Elizabeth] what [the angel] has spoken to her in secret, and that he had called her blessed because she had believed in the realization of the prophecy and the teaching which she had heard, then Mary gently brought forth the fruit of what she had heard from the angel and Elizabeth, *My soul bless the Lord.*[7] To that which [Elizabeth] had said, *Blessed is she who has believed,*[8] [Mary replied], *From*

---

[1] Luke 1:39.

[2] Luke 1:43.

[3] Luke 1:48. From this point in §27 until midway in §31 one folio of *Chester Beatty* MS 709 is missing. Its contents have been supplied from the Armenian version (cf. CSCO 145, pp. 14-16).

[4] The eighth month of the Armenian calendar, corresponding approximately to March/April. See below at XX, §15 for further reference to the month of Areg.

[5] The process of crushing the grapes in the winepress.

[6] Luke 1:45.

[7] Luke 1:46.

[8] Luke 1:45.

henceforth all generations will call me blessed.[1] It was then that Mary began to preach the new kingdom. *She returned home after three months,*[2] lest the Lord [whom she was carrying] be in service before his servant. She returned to her husband to clarify [the matter], for if she had become pregnant through human fruit, it would have been appropriate for her to flee from her husband.

§29.   [Elizabeth conceived in the month of Sahmi,[3] the time when Zechariah had completed the days of his service of the ministry. The annunciation was made to Mary on the tenth day of the month of Areg, just as [it was made] to Zechariah on the tenth day of the month of Hori,[4] *Behold it is her sixth month.*[5] But the Law prescribes that on the tenth day of the month of Areg the [paschal] lamb is to be closed up.[6] According to the same computation the Lamb of truth was closed up in the womb of the virgin at the time when the light was reigning. In this way he showed that he had come to cover Adam's nudity. He was born on the sixth day of the month of Kaloc,[7] according to Greek computation, at the time when the light begins to conquer, to show that Satan was condemned and that Adam had conquered in him who conquers everything.

§30.   [John *jumped for joy*[8] to announce concerning his [future] preaching. The infant of the barren woman exulted before the infant of the virgin. He sought out his mother's tongue, and [desired] to pronounce a prophecy concerning [the Lord]. Therefore Elizabeth's conception was kept hidden from Mary for six months, until the infant would have limbs sufficiently formed to exult before the Lord with his jumping, and become

---

[1] Luke 1:48.

[2] Cf. Luke 1:56. A paraphrase rather than a citation?

[3] The third month of the Armenian calendar, corresponding approximately to October. The Armenian months are not coterminous with the Syriac/Julian ones. For further details on some of the computations referred to in this paragraph see S. P. Brock's translation of Ephrem's *Commentary on Exodus,* XII. 2-3 in *The Luminous Eye* (Kalamazoo, 1992), pp. 108-9; *Idem,* "Passover, Annunciation and Epiclesis," *NT* 24 (1982), pp. 222-33.

[4] The second month of the Armenian calendar, corresponding approximately to September.

[5] Luke 1:36.

[6] Cf. Exod 12:3.

[7] The fifth month of the Armenian calendar, running from December 9 - January 7, the nativity date in the Greek tradition being Jan 6th. Cf. J. F. Coakley, "Typology and the birth of Christ on 6 Jan," *V Symposium Syriacum,* edited by R. Lavenant, OCA 236 (Rome, 1990), pp. 247-256, and A. de Halleux, "Le comput éphremien du cycle de la Nativité," *The Four Gospels: Festschrift F. Neirynck,* Bibliotheca ETL 100 (Leuven, 1992), pp. 2369-2382.

[8] Luke 1:41.

a witness to Mary through his exultation. Moreover, that *He exulted in the womb of his mother*,[1] was not of himself, nor because of his five months, but so that the [divine] gifts might show themselves in the barren womb which was now carrying him. [It was also] so that the other womb, that of the virgin, would know the great gifts [given to Elizabeth] and that the [two] soils might believe in the seeds they had received through the word of Gabriel, cultivator of both [terrains]. Since John could not cry out in his exultation and render witness to his Lord, [his mother] began to say, *You are blessed among women, and blessed is the fruit of your womb.*[2] Our Lord prepared his herald in a dead womb, to show that he came after a dead Adam. He vivified Elizabeth's womb first, and then vivified the soil of Adam through his body.

The Birth of John the Baptist

§31.   {The elderly Elizabeth gave birth to the last of the prophets, and Mary, a young girl, to the Lord of the angels. The daughter of Aaron gave birth to *the voice in the desert*,[3] and the daughter of king David to the Word of the heavenly king. The wife of the priest gave birth to *the angel of his face*,[4] but the daughter of David to the strong God of the earth. The barren one gave birth to him who remits sins, but the virgin gave birth to him who takes them away.[5] Elizabeth gave birth to him who reconciled people through repentance, but Mary gave birth to him who purified the lands of uncleanness. The elder one lit a lamp in the house of Jacob, his father, for this [lamp] itself was John;[6] while the younger one [lit] *the Sun of Justice*[7] for all the nations. The angel announced to Zechariah, so that the slain one would proclaim the crucified one, and that the hated one [would proclaim] the envied one. He who was to baptize with water [would proclaim] him who would baptize *with fire and with the Holy Spirit*,[8] and the light which was not obscure [would proclaim] *the Sun of*

---

1 *Idem.*
2 Luke 1:42.
3 Isa 40:3; Matt 3:3.
4 Cf. Isa 63:9.
5 Cf. John 1:29.
6 Cf. John 5:35.
7 Mal 3:20.
8 Matt 3:11.

Justice.}[1] [The one] filled with the Spirit [would proclaim] concerning him who gives the Spirit; the priest calling with the trumpet [would proclaim] concerning the one who is to come at the [sound of] the trumpet at the end; the voice [would proclaim] concerning the Word, and the one who saw the dove [would proclaim] concerning him upon whom the dove rested, like the lightning before the thunder.

§32.   *The rising [of the sun] from on high*[2] [refers] to the star of the Magi. *And to those who dwell in darkness*[3] [refers] either to those who were slow in understanding concerning his rising forth, or to Israel which was in darkness. The Magi however enlightened them. It is for this reason that [he adds], *So that he will guide our feet in the way of peace.*[4] *To those who dwell in the shadows*[5] [refers] to the ingenuity of the Chaldeans or to the idolatry of the Gentiles.

---

[1] The Barcelona folio takes up at this point in §31 and continues into the next section. For the text of this folio see P. Ortiz Valdivieso, "Un nuevo fragmento siriaco del Comentario de san Efrén al Diatésaron (PPalau-Rib 2)", *StPapyr* 5 (1966) 7-17 and L. Leloir, EC-FA, pp. 145-157.
[2] Luke 1:78.
[3] Luke 1:79.
[4] *Idem.*
[5] *Idem.*

II

The Conception and Birth of Jesus

§1.   *The birth of the Messiah took place as follows. When Mary had been betrothed to Joseph, she was found to be pregnant.*[1] The evangelist did not say this without reflection, for the pagans in their stories fantasize that their gods have been subjected to shameful seductions and the procreation of sons [in a way] which is not in accord with nature. Consequently, lest you too, in hearing about Mary, might think that her [case] was like that of the pagans, [the evangelist] added that *she was pregnant through the Holy Spirit.*[2] He was not born as a result of conjugal intercourse. Through her holy conception therefore an entrance was [made possible] for chastity, that it might dwell in all bodies.

[The fact] that she was [first] betrothed and carried a man's name, and then after that became pregnant, [was] on account of the genealogy of kings, since it was impossible that a child, who had been enrolled among the kings [as] son of David, be enrolled in his mother's name. Alternatively, [it was] because of the minds of wicked men, who were falsely accusing her in the name of adultery. This was why she was entrusted to a chaste man, who, when he saw that she was pregnant, took care of her who was about to give birth. He did not drive her out of his house, but lived with her. Associating himself with her calumny, he was a witness before everyone on her behalf, that he who was to be born of her was not conceived through adultery but through the movement of the Spirit.

§2.   [Mary] gave birth without [the assistance of] a man. Just as in the beginning Eve was born of Adam without intercourse, so too [in the case of] Joseph and Mary, his virgin and spouse. Eve gave birth to the murderer,[3] but Mary gave birth to the Life-Giver.[4] The former gave birth to him who shed the blood of his brother, but the latter to him whose blood was shed by his brothers. The former saw him who was trembling

---

[1] Matt 1:18.

[2] *Idem.*

[3] Gen 4:1 records the birth of Cain, who later murdered Abel.

[4] This is one of the words Syriac typically uses for Saviour [ܡܚܝܢܐ]. The other is ܦܪܘܩܐ.

60

and fleeing[1] because of the curse of the earth, the latter [saw] him who bore the curse *and nailed it on his cross*.[2] The virgin's conception teaches that he, who begot Adam without intercourse from the virgin earth, also fashioned the Second Adam without intercourse in the virgin's womb. Whereas the First [Adam] returned back into the womb of his mother,[3] [it was] by means of the Second [Adam], who did not return back into the womb of his mother, that the former, who had been buried in the womb of his mother, was brought back [from it].

§3.　　　Mary was trying to convince Joseph that her conception was from the Spirit, but he did not accept [it] because it was an unwonted thing. When he saw however that her countenance was serene, although her womb was heavy, *he was not willing to put her to shame, being a just man*,[4] but neither [was he willing] to receive her as husband, for he thought that she had had intercourse with another man. In his uprightness therefore he judged that he should not take her, but also that he should not denounce her. Therefore, *the angel appeared to him and said, Joseph, son of David*.[5] It was a wonderful thing that [the angel] also called him, *Son of David*, to remind him of David, the head of his ancestors, to whom God had made a promise that from his descendants[6] according to the flesh he would raise up the Messiah. *Do not be afraid to take Mary your spouse, because what is in her is from the Holy Spirit*.[7] If you are in doubt as to whether the virgin's conception was without intercourse, listen to Isaiah who said, *Behold the virgin will conceive*,[8] and to Daniel, *A stone was cut off, but not with [human] hands*.[9] This is not like that [other passage], *Look at the mountain and the well*;[10] since that [passage implies] a man and woman, whereas here it is [written], *Not with [human] hands*. Just as Adam fills the role of father and mother for Eve, so too does Mary for our Lord.

---

[1] Cf. Gen 4:10-14.

[2] Col 2:14.

[3] That is, the earth.

[4] Matt 1:19.

[5] Matt 1:20.

[6] Literally, "From the fruit of his belly." Cf. Ps 132:11.

[7] Matt 1:20.

[8] Isa 7:14; Matt 1:22-23.

[9] Dan 2:34,45.

[10] Isa 51:1. The following verse refers these images of mountain and well to Abraham and Sarah respectively (cf. Isa 51:2).

§4. *Joseph, because he was a just man, was not willing to denounce Mary.*[1] His justice was in opposition[2] to that of the law, *For your hand shall throw [stones] against her first,*[3] since *he sought to divorce her in secret.*[4] For Joseph saw that [this] conception was unusual, and that the event was out of the ordinary in relation to the way of women, and the conception of married women. Consequently, these things were suggesting to him that he recognize that this matter was from God. For at no time did he see any licentious plot in it. Indeed, it was impossible that he should disbelieve Mary, since she had many testimonies [in her favour]. These were the silence of Zechariah, Elizabeth's conception, the angel's annunciation, John's exultation and the prophecy of his fathers; all these were crying forth concerning the virgin's conception, along with the others. Accordingly, *he thought* that in justice *he should divorce her quietly.*[5] For, if he had known that her conception was not from the Holy Spirit, it would have been unjust not to have denounced her.

§5. He understood that this was a wonderful deed of God. But nevertheless, since it was not credible for others, he considered it [an act of] righteousness that she be divorced.[6] [This was] in accordance with his reasoning, lest perhaps that deed [of God] might suffer some accusation if they cohabited with each other. He thought [that he should divorce her] all the more so, "Lest this be a sin for me that I be called father of her divine child." He was afraid to live with her lest he destroy that name of "Son of the Virgin." The angel said to him, therefore, *Do not be afraid to take Mary.*[7] [The evangelist] also wrote, *He lived with her chastely,*[8] et cetera.[9] This was why, [it is said], they killed Zechariah because he accepted Mary as

---

[1] Matt 1:19.

[2] The Barcelona folio ends at this point, and the remainder of the sentence forms the first line of the forty-one additional folios. These folios are edited by L. Leloir in EC-FA.

[3] Cf. Deut 17:5,7; 22:23-24.

[4] Matt 1:19.

[5] *Idem.*

[6] Cf. Matt 1:19-20.

[7] Matt 1:20.

[8] Matt 1:25.

[9] After this short quote Ephrem has ܘܫܪܟܐ , "and the rest" or "et cetera." This method of abbreviating a scriptural quotation occurs occasionally throughout the commentary, varying from time to time with the form ܥܡ ܫܪܟܐ , "with the rest" or "cum ceteris." Sometimes the point of the quotation in question can only fully be grasped when the fuller (non cited) text is taken into account.

a virgin, for the virgins used to gather together into one place.[1] Or, when the infants were being killed and his son, [who] was at his hand, was being demanded from him. Because he made [John] flee to the desert, they killed him on the altar, as our Lord had said.[2]

§6.   Because there are those who dare to say that Mary [cohabited] with Joseph after she bore the Redeemer, [we reply], "How would it have been possible for her who was the home of the indwelling of the Spirit, whom the divine power overshadowed,[3] that she be joined to a mortal being, and give birth filled with birthpangs, in the image of the primeval curse?"[4] If *Mary was blessed of women,*[5] she would have been exempt from the curse from the beginning, and from the bearing of children in birthpangs and curses. It would be impossible therefore to call one who gave birth with these birthpangs blessed. If the animals in the ark were restrained because of Noah, it was fitting that the prophetess in whom Emmanuel dwelt should not turn to marriage. Noah's animals [were restrained] of necessity, but she however through her own [free] will. Just as she gave birth purely, so also she remained holy.

§7.   If the sons of Aaron died because they offered up an alien fire,[6] how much more so should she have suffered. If wine merchants who mix water with wine have punishment laid upon them, how much more should retribution have been decreed in this case. If, from the [fact] that some are called brothers of our Lord, people think that these are sons of Mary, take note that he was called son of Joseph, not just by Jews only, but by Mary his mother too. *For I and your father have been seeking you, with much anxiety.*[7] If the angel commanded Joseph to take Mary into his care,[8] [this was] so that he would [thereby] eliminate any suspicion from her calumniators, and especially so that he might protect her lest those, who

---

[1] According to Leloir, this is an allusion to Zechariah's death based on apocryphal Eastern traditions (cf. EC-SC 121, p. 68, n. 3). See also R. W. Cowley, "The 'Blood of Zechariah' (Mt 23:35) in Ethiopian Exegetical Tradition," *Studia Patristica* 18.1 (1985), pp. 293-302.
[2] Cf. Matt 23:35.
[3] Cf. Luke 1:35.
[4] Cf. Gen 3:16.
[5] Luke 1:42.
[6] Lev 10:1-2.
[7] Luke 2:48.
[8] Cf. Matt 1:20.

were scandalized [in thinking] that it was from the angel[1] that she was pregnant, might kill her. It was a great source of scandal to them that a virgin should give birth, because they were convinced that through her giving birth their city would be destroyed, and that their kingdom, priesthood and prophecy would be abolished. It was for this reason too that they also killed the prophet [Isaiah] who announced these things, that a virgin would give birth to a child.[2]

§8.   The virgin gave birth to her First-Born, but the signs of her virginity remained. He begot us too through baptism and made us first-born [children] by his [free] gift. For there is neither older nor younger in the womb of baptism, since we are all first-born in faith.[3] For it is about us that [Scripture] is fulfilled, *Every first-born that opens the womb is holy unto the Lord.*[4] While we are [still] corrupt in [our] sins baptism conceives us, and when we are sanctified from evil it gives birth to us from its inner depths.[5]

§9.   *He lived with her chastely until she gave birth to her First-Born.*[6] [This] word is spoken after its companion: [first] *He took her,*[7] and then, *He lived with her chastely.*[8] It is [to be] understood as follows: *He lived with her chastely, and he took her.*[9] That is, *he took her,* because he was called "her husband" after her conception. Another interpretation of *He lived with her chastely* is that desire did not rise up in his consciousness at the sight of her. *Until she gave birth to her First-Born* means that, on the birth of her First-Born, people were convinced that this conception was not a human [matter], but that this birth was divine.

---

[1] The Syriac text reads ܡܠܟܐ , "king" here, most likely a spelling mistake for ܡܠܐܟܐ, "angel," which is the rendering in the Armenian version.

[2] Cf. Isa 7:14.

[3] Cf. Heb 12:23.

[4] Num 8:16-18; Luke 2:23.

[5] Literally, "From its intestines."

[6] Matt 1:25. Note how the text here differs from the Greek, "He did not know her until she had borne a son." Leloir lists this reading as one of those most probably of Tatianic origin, not that Tatian would necessarily have been its author, but "Tatianic" in the sense that it was a reading that may have existed in the tradition before him, which was then adopted by him and crystallized in the Diatessaron (cf. *Le Témoignage d'Éphrem*, p. 237).

[7] Matt 1:24.

[8] Matt 1:25.

[9] Matt 1:25 and 1:24; an inversion of the two texts is to be understood. Cf. A. Vööbus, *Early Syriac Asceticism*, p. 42, in relation to Tatian's attempts to avoid reference to Joseph as Mary's husband.

§10. A further [interpretation] of *He lived with her chastely until she gave birth to her First-Born* is that this holiness[1] was of necessity, even though they both willingly shared in it. But the holiness they observed after the birth of our Lord was of their own freewill.

§11. [The evangelist] defined [the nature of] this necessity, and showed us concerning its limit, that it was *until*. *He lived with her chastely until she gave birth to her First-Born.* [Should it be deduced] from this therefore that he did not live with her chastely after she had given birth, since it is indicated *until*? But *until* is not the [end] limit. For he said, *The Lord said to my Lord, Sit on my right, until I put your enemies under your feet.*[2] Therefore, when his enemies were put beneath his feet, did he stand up? Another [interpretation] of *He lived with her chastely* [follows]. Is not marriage pure, according to the testimony of the apostle, *[The fruit of] their womb is pure*?[3] But, if one were to say, "See, the brothers of our Lord are named in the gospel!," [I would reply], "Because our Lord entrusted his mother Mary to John,[4] it is clear that these are not her sons, nor is [Joseph] her husband." For how could he who said, *Honour your father and your mother*,[5] have separated Mary from her sons, and entrusted her to John [instead]?

The Census

§12. *They were enrolled, each one in his own city*,[6] since Israel was dispersed and Judah [was] in captivity. Because these testimonies which are in the royal archives are true, [the evangelist] said that his birth took place in the days of Augustus.[7] Why then did *this first census* [8] take place when our Lord was about to be born? Because it is written, *The sceptre will not depart from Judah nor the interpreter from between his feet, until he*

---

[1] For a discussion of the technical sense of marital continence associated with this term see S. P. Brock, *The Luminous Eye* (Kalamazoo, 1992), pp. 133-34.

[2] Ps 110:1.

[3] Heb 13:4.

[4] Cf. John 19:27.

[5] Mark 10:19.

[6] Luke 2:3.

[7] Cf. Luke 2:1.

[8] Luke 2:2.

comes,[1] so that it would be known that when he was to spring forth, there would be a census. For, at the time when he was born, the Gentiles would be ruling over this people which had formerly been reigning over itself, so that it might be fulfilled that *the Gentiles will hope in him.*[2] He came therefore because that sceptre and interpreter had departed.

The Angels' Message

§13.   *Today there is born to you a Life-Giver.*[3] [The angel] did not say, "There is born a man, who will be a life-giver, or who will be a messiah," but rather, *Today there is born to you a Life-Giver, who is*; not "who is to become," but, *Who is the Lord, the Messiah.*

§14.   Thus, as peace began to be [established], the angels proclaimed, *Glory in the highest and peace on earth.*[4] When lower beings received [peace] from superior beings, *they cried, Glory on earth and peace in the heavens.*[5] At that time when the divinity came down [and] was clothed in humanity, the angels cried, *Peace on earth.* And at the time when that humanity ascended in order to be absorbed into the divinity and sit on the right, - *Peace in heaven,* - the infants were crying forth before him, *Hosanna in the highest.*[6] Hence, the apostle also learned that one should say, *He made peace by the blood of his cross [for] that which is in heaven and on earth.*[7]

§15.[8]   {A further [interpretation]: The angels were crying forth, *Glory in the highest and peace on earth,* and the children, *Peace in heaven and glory on earth,*[9] to show that, just as the grace of his mercy gave joy to sinners on earth, so too their repentance gave joy to the angels in heaven.[10] *Glory to God!* [came] from freewill; *peace* and reconciliation [were] for those against whom he was angry, and *hope* and remission

---

[1] Gen 49:10.
[2] Isa 11:10.
[3] Luke 2:11.
[4] Luke 2:14.
[5] Luke 19:38.
[6] Matt 21:9.
[7] Col 1:20.
[8] One folio of *Chester Beatty* MS 709 is missing at this point. The translation given here for §§15-20 is supplied from the Armenian version (cf. CSCO 145, pp. 23-25).
[9] Luke 19:38.
[10] Cf. Luke 15:7-10.

[were] for the guilty. If the angels began with the shepherds, [it was] so that none of those who were living in the wilderness might be deprived [of grace], but rather that, saved, they might find peace in the joyful news of the true Shepherd. *Glory to God in the highest and peace on earth*; not to the animals or beasts, but, *Good hope for human beings.*

Simeon

§16. {*Now you may dismiss your servant*,[1] said [Simeon], because he had received the consolation of his people and had held on to Israel's goal. *Now you may dismiss your servant in peace*, like the Law and the priesthood. The words of Simeon, *You may dismiss your servant in peace*, apply to the Law. Simeon and Moses dismissed [it], but *in peace*. The dismissal of the Law was not done in enmity, but he made it rest in charity and peace. [Simeon] also said, *Behold my eyes have seen your mercy, which you have prepared before all the nations.*[2] [This corresponds] to what [the prophet] said, *All the nations were waiting for him.*[3] When he said, *Behold he is for the fall and the rising,*[4] this too is [like] what [the prophet] said, *Behold I am laying in Zion a stumbling-block; the one who believes in it will not be confounded.*[5] Alternatively, [one may understand] *for the fall and the rising* of the people and the Gentiles, or *for the fall* of iniquity, and *for the rising* of justice.

§17. {[Simeon] also said, *In a sign of contradiction, and in your soul itself,*[6] for many heretics have expressed different opinions on this matter. Some say that he assumed a body incapable of suffering, and others that he did not accomplish his role as guide in a true body. Some say of [his] body that it was terrestial, while others say that it was celestial. Some affirm [that he existed] before the world, while others say that his beginning was in Mary. [Simeon] said likewise, *You will remove the sword.*[7] [The sword],

---

[1] Luke 2:29.
[2] Luke 2:30-31.
[3] Isa 11:10.
[4] Luke 2:34.
[5] Isa 28:16.
[6] Luke 2:34-35.
[7] Cf. Luke 2:35. The verb is used here in a second person, causative sense, "You will remove the sword." In the citation of this same text at XXI, §27, the Syriac text likewise reads, ܚܪܒܐ ܬܥܒܪܝܗ̇, "You will remove the sword." In his discussion of the text of Luke 2:35 at II, §17 in *Le Témoignage d'Ephrem*, pp. 92-93, Leloir also refers to a citation of Ephrem by Ishodad in which the Syriac verb is also in the second person, causative form

which was protecting Paradise because of Eve,[1] was removed by Mary. Alternatively, *You will remove the sword*, that is, a denial.[2] For the Greek says clearly, *The inner thoughts of a great number will be revealed*,[3] that is, the thoughts of those who had doubted. For he said, *You will remove the sword*. Indeed, you too will doubt, because *she thought that he was the gardener*.[4] [Mary] was in wonderment at his birth, it is said, and at his conception, and she recounted to others how she had conceived, and indeed how she had given birth; and those who had doubted it were comforted by the wonderment of her word.

The Star and the Magi[5]

§18.   [The star appeared because the prophets had disappeared. The star hastened in order to explain who he was towards whom the prophets'

(ܕܥܠܟܪܣ ܢܝܚܬܐ). According to this rendering of Luke 2:35 Mary is seen to take an active role as the antitype of Eve, in removing from the gates of Paradise the sword which was placed there as a result of Eve's disobedience. See also R. Murray, "The Lance which Re-opened Paradise, a Mysterious Reading in the Early Syriac Fathers," *OCP* 39 (1973), pp. 224-34, 491.

[1] Cf. Gen 3:24.

[2] See below at XXI, §27 for a similar interpretation of Luke 2:35, in which the term "a denial" also features. It is difficult to identify the precise meaning implied by the use of this term.

[3] Luke 2:35. This is the first of five instances in the commentary in which Ephrem refers to "the Greek." It is a disputed question as to what precisely he means in using the term "Greek" here and in the other passages (cf. V, §2; X, §14; XV, §19; XIX, §17). While it is not impossible, it hardly seems likely that he had direct knowledge of the Gospels in Greek, since there is insufficient evidence to show that he was proficient in the Greek language. It is probably most prudent therefore to follow Leloir's view that Ephrem, without actually knowing Greek, was aware of a certain number of readings which differed from those of the Diatessaron, and which were accessible to him through a Syriac translation of the separate Gospels in the Edessan Church. He would have referred to these as representing "the Greek," to distinguish them from the Diatessaron (cf. Leloir, *Témoignage d'Éphrem sur le Diatessaron*, p. 73 and EC-SC 121, pp. 29-30).

[4] John 20:15. Ephrem's writings attest a confusion or "fusion" between Mary, Mother of Jesus, and Mary Magdalene. See V, §5 and XXI, §27 below for further instances. In *Symbols of the Church*, R. Murray notes that this "fusion" is not a peculiarity of Ephrem, but is found in other Syrian witnesses (p. 146). He traces the development of this "fusion" from the earlier Judaeo-Christian and Gnostic fields (cf. *Gospel of Thomas* and *Gospel of Philip*) into the Syriac tradition (pp. 329-335) and suggests that "Syriac tradition, starting from Judaeo-Christian ideas, many of which received unacceptable expression at the hands of the Gnostics, gradually purified its beliefs with the help of typology, till the sharing of the name of Mary by our Lady and Magdalen came to have a purely symbolic significance and to be quite innocent" (pp. 333-334). Cf. also L. Leloir, EC-SC 121, p. 75, n. 3 for a useful summary of R. Murray's conclusions.

[5] Cf. A. de Halleux, "L'adoration des Mages dans le commentaire syriaque du Diatessaron," *Le Muséon* 104 (1991), pp. 251-264, for a detailed analysis of II, §§18-25, in which he puts forward the hypothesis that this section contains two misplacements and two lacunae.

words were hastening. Just as the sun hastened from the West towards the East for Hezekiah,[1] so too the star hastened from the East towards the West because of the infant in the manger.

§19.   {The former indicated Israel through the sign of the sun, while the latter came to confound the people by the gifts which they were bringing. The Magi came with their signs, like the prophets, and they testified to his birth. [This was] so that, when he appeared, he would not be taken for a stranger, but [rather] all creatures would know about his birth. Zechariah was struck dumb and Elizabeth conceived, so that all the regions would understand and know about his [coming].

§20.   {But this star was in control of its course; it ascended and descended as though there were no link holding it, because it had power over the spaces}[2] in the air, as though not fixed in the firmament. When it hid itself[3] [this was] lest [the Magi] come directly to Bethlehem. [God] hid it from them to test Israel, so that [the Magi] would come to Jerusalem in order that the scribes might declare concerning his birth, and so that they would receive trustworthy evidence from the prophets and the priests. [This was] lest they might think that there was any power other than that which was dwelling [as] his presence in Jerusalem. In a similar manner, the elders received of the spirit which was in Moses lest they might think that there was another spirit.

§21a.   The Eastern [people] therefore were illuminated by the star, but Israel was rendered blind by the sun which had become dark. Thus, the East adored the Messiah first, just as [Zechariah] had said, *The East will show forth light from on high.*[4] After the star had brought them to the Sun, it stood over its appointed place and disclosed him, and [thus] completed its journey, like John, the voice that was proclaiming the Word. When [the Word] was heard, and became incarnate and was seen, the voice which had been preparing the way cried out, *He must increase and I must decrease.*[5]

---

[1] Cf. 2 Kgs 20:8-11; Isa 38:7-8.
[2] The Syriac resumes at this point after the lacuna of one folio.
[3] Cf. Matt 2:9-10.
[4] Luke 1:78.
[5] John 3:30.

§21b.[1] *The Magi came from the East to Jerusalem, saying, Where is the king of the Jews who has been born, whose star we have seen. We have come to adore him?*[2] Those who rely on astrology say, "See, the star disclosed concerning his birth." But, if it disclosed concerning the birth of a king, as they say, why then did the stars, which follow their own course in accordance with [their] law, not also disclose the place of his birth? Especially [that] of him who was born of a virgin, who had not had intercourse? For this was more exalted than the artifice of astrologers,[3] and loftier than the reasonings of humanity. A lofty star, which encompasses many peoples in its light, was not able to show the place of the manger. But [the star of the Magi] not [only] made known Bethlehem, but even disclosed the manger in which the child was lain. This showed convincingly that [the star of the Magi] was lower down on the surface of the earth, and not one of those which had held the course of the heavens from eternity. It was a new [star], disclosing a new birth which would convert worlds to the worship of it. So, when the Magi went forth from Jerusalem to Bethlehem on the way which went directly to the South, the star which was leading them went before them,[4] [although] it is clear that [normally] the course of the stars is from East to West.[5]

When Herod heard, he was disturbed and all Jerusalem with him.[6] If Herod, who was of the Gentiles, was of necessity disturbed concerning the king of the Jews who was born, given that he was extending his kingdom, and was consequently ruling against the Law, he was justly repelled. But, in the case of the Jews, why should they have been disturbed? It would have been fitting that they should have rejoiced

---

[1] This rather lengthy paragraph is not found in the Armenian version, and, according to de Halleux, has been incorrectly inserted here, interrupting the flow of II, §21a and 21c (*op. cit.*, p. 252).

[2] Matt 2:1-2.

[3] The Syriac text reads ܗܝܡܢ , "he believed," which does not make sense in the context. If the components of this word are divided in two [ܗܝ ܡܢ], then a comparison, parallel with the second half of the sentence is possible, as translated above. Leloir edits and translates it as one word, "to believe" (cf. EC-FA, pp. 10-11), but with reluctance, aware that in so doing he has chosen the *lectio difficilior* (cf. "Le Commentaire de Ephrem sur le Diatessaron. Réflexions et Suggestions," *The Four Gospels: Festschrift F. Neirynck* (Leuven, 1992), pp. 2359-2367.

[4] Cf. Matt 2:9.

[5] There are interesting parallels in St. John Chrysostom's homilies on the Adoration of the Magi for these two reasons as to why one should distinguish the star of the Magi from ordinary stars, namely, that it was located on a lower level of the firmament, and its course was from north to south, rather than the normal east-west movement. For a fuller discussion of these parallels, see de Halleux, *op. cit.*, pp. 262-263.

[6] Matt 2:3.

and have been glad to be set free from the king of foreign Gentiles, and receive their own king from the stock of David. But this was not untypical of the continual ingratitude of the Jews - these [Jews] who rejected our Lord and preferred Caesar,[1] who crucified the Messiah and asked for Barabbas.[2]

Herod gathered the scribes and pharisees and was inquiring of them where the Messiah was to be born. They were saying to him, Bethlehem.[3] What reason, therefore, by way of excuse, remains for the Jews? For they revealed the place of his birth to Herod, one crafty in relation to uprightness, and, against themselves indeed, affirmed from the testimony of prophecy, "He is to be born *in Bethlehem*, as it is written."[4] When the Messiah came to them however, they took refuge in a profound ignorance and said, *As for this man, we do not know where he is from,*[5] and they were defaming the coming of the Redeemer. The star persuaded the Magi, but neither the arrival of the Magi, nor the prophecy of the prophets, nor the outcome of the event [persuaded] either the Jews or Herod.

§21c.[6] The Magi, who worship the luminaries, would not have been persuaded to go towards the light, if the star had not enticed them with its light. Their love, which was bound to a transitory light, led them towards the Light which does not set.

§22. Herod, who in a waking vision deceived the Magi with his cunning, was deceived by a dream in sleep. For it was revealed to them in a dream *that they should not go back to him.*[7] Even if the Magi in their vigilance had praised [Herod] who did not [appear to be] jealous of him, for he had said, *I too will go and worship him,*[8] in their sleep they despised him who had deceived them so that he might kill him. Through the fact that it was revealed to them in a dream that they should not go back to him, they saw his corrupt cunning as in a mirror. He, who thought that he had deceived the mind of the wakeful, was himself deceived by sleepers.

---

[1] Cf. John 19:15.
[2] Cf. Matt 27:20-26.
[3] Matt 2:4-5.
[4] Mic 5:1.
[5] John 9:29.
[6] The Armenian version resumes at this point, after the omission of §21b.
[7] Matt 2:12.
[8] Matt 2:8.

§23.   Herod thought that he had fooled them when he saw that they believed him. But he was the one who was fooled by them through a dream. Thus, he that had fooled[1] was in fact the one who was deceived. At what point? When the Magi became aware through a dream that he had indeed been deceiving them, when he said, *I will go and worship him*.[2] For, in like manner, a sign was given with reference to Hezekiah which was to proclaim to creatures that, through the sun's turning back, they would know who it was that would bring back from death to life.[3] So too, when a sign was given through the Magi, that sign was proclaimed to all creatures because of the Magi. Through the star, which was obedient supernaturally[4] to human beings, [God] was opening up a way before them, [so that] they might learn about God, who was obedient to humanity, so that he might open up a path for his kingdom. Just as *the sun became dark* at his death[5] so that creatures might become aware of his death, so too the star that was resplendent became dark, so that the world might become aware of his birth, [that] it was resplendent.

§24.   At his radiant birth therefore a radiant star appeared, and at his dark death there appeared a dark gloom.[6] Just as Hezekiah was delivered from open death by means of a sign, these too were delivered from a hidden death by means of a sign. The Lord of the star appeared in his own person to the two who were travelling with him along the road, but his identity was hidden from them.[7] His star too was like this, for its light appeared to all humanity while its pathway was hidden from all humanity. As for the [Magi] however, *When they saw the star, they rejoiced*.[8] They were not in fact persuaded by the witness of the Jews nor by the writings of the prophets. They, who had not been instructed in them,

---

[1] The Syriac reads ܐܬܛܥܝ, "he was fooled," probably a scribal error through assimilation to the use of this form in the preceding phrase.

[2] *Idem.*

[3] Cf. 2 Kgs 20:8-11; Isa 38:7-8. According to de Halleux's hypothesis, this comparison between the star of the Magi and the sun's turning back in Hezekiah's time constitutes the second misplacement in this section (part of II, §23 and all of §24). He suggests that this material might have been contained in one page of the size of *Chester Beatty* MS 709 which may have been accidentally detached and later incorrectly inserted at this point in the archetype of both Syriac and Armenian recensions (cf. *op. cit.*, pp. 252-253).

[4] Literally, "not according to its nature."

[5] Cf. Luke 23:45.

[6] Cf. Matt 27:45.

[7] Cf. Luke 24:13-16.

[8] Matt 2:10. The end of this paragraph is also missing from the Armenian.

nevertheless rejoiced at the sight of the star that was guiding them. They entered Bethlehem, but did not inquire of any of the inhabitants of Bethlehem concerning [the child's] domicile.

§25.   *They opened their treasures and offered him gifts, gold* for his humanity, *myrrh* for his death, and *frankincense* for his divinity.[1] Another [explanation] is *gold*, as for a king, *frankincense*, as for God, and *myrrh* for one to be embalmed. Or another [is] *gold*, because worship of gold comes back to its Lord, and *myrrh and frankincense*, because these disclose the Physician who was to heal Adam's fracture. He, who revealed to the [Magi] that *they should not go back to Herod*,[2] [also] revealed to [Joseph and Mary] that they should leave, for in their departure they would be fulfilling two [prophecies], *Out of Egypt I have called my son*,[3] and, *Rachel is weeping; this too fulfils what Jeremiah the prophet spoke*,[4] cum ceteris.[5]

---

[1] Matt 2:11. Three interpretations of the gifts are given, the first and third following what was probably the sequence in Tatian, and also preserved in the Peshitta: gold, myrrh and frankincense. The second interpretation follows the order of the Greek text, and represents a tradition also attested in Irenaeus, although in a different sequence: "... myrrhum quidem quod ipse erat, qui pro mortali humano genere moreretur et sepelitur: aurum vero, quoniam Rex 'cujus regni finis non est'; thus vero, quoniam Deus, qui et 'notus in Judaea factus est', et manifestus eis, qui non quaerebant eum" (*Against Heresies*, III, 9. 2, ed. J. P. Migne, *Patres Graeci* 7, Paris, 1859, pp. 870-871).

[2] Matt 2:12.

[3] Hos 11:1; Matt 2:15.

[4] Jer 31:15; Matt 2:18.

[5] See the note above at II, § 5 for comment on this type of indication of scriptural abbreviation.

III

Herod fooled by the Magi

§1.   *When Herod saw that the Magi had mocked him, he was furious, so he sent and slaughtered the young children.*[1] But you, evil Herod, did you not hear that this star was the herald of a king to be born? Why did you not realize that, if [the star] were from heaven, you would not be able to overcome this reality? Because [Herod] cut off infants-in-arms from those who loved them, he was punished through his three sons and his wife, and he himself died a bitter death.[2]

§2.   *When he saw that the Magi had mocked him, he was furious.*[3] Oh Israel, blind because you do not understand, and deaf because you do not hear! You have not yet woken up to the voice of Isaiah who said, *The Lord God will give you a sign.*[4] If [this sign] were to have been given through another man, he would have said so. But it was given to you through him who [was] from the virgin. Indeed it was for all of you. [A sign] was given to Moses, so that he alone might be persuaded, as though by a mystery;[5] and also to Gideon,[6] and to Hezekiah.[7] It was given to these individually, but in your case, was it not a clear event that was sent to you by the Magi, together with an accurate explanation of the allegories that are in your Law? How did you not recognize the time of redemption, and [not] believe in the birth of [the child of] a virgin? Or, perhaps you are [still] sitting with your king in a stupor, hoping that the Magi will come back to you again and expound concerning him a second time?

§3.   Was it not sufficient that foreigners should have come and woken you up so that you might perceive that [the Messiah] was born? Or rather, [did you not] share in the project of your murderous king, a second

---

[1] Matt 2:16.

[2] Cf. Acts 12:23.

[3] Matt 2:16. The sequence in the Armenian version differs slightly from that of the Syriac at this point. §§6-7 in the Syriac appear before §§2-5 in the Armenian. The sequence followed throughout this translation is that of the Syriac.

[4] Isa 7:14.

[5] Cf. Exod 3:1-6.

[6] Cf. Judg 6:17-21.

[7] Cf. 2 Kgs 20:8-11; Isa 38:7-8.

Pharaoh, a seed of Canaan, an Ashkelonite?[1] Indeed, when Saul heard that the priests had helped David unwittingly, he had them brought to him and he slew them.[2] It was fitting for you too that innocent blood be hung about your neck,[3] as was Saul's case. But the Son of David escaped from your hands amidst the Gentiles. David was persecuted by Saul, just as the Son was by Herod. The priests were slain because of David, and the infants because of our Lord. Abiathar escaped from the priests,[4] as John did from the infants. In [the person of] Abiathar the priesthood of the house of Eli was brought to an end, and in John the prophecy of the sons of Jacob was terminated.

§4.   Herod did not know how he might investigate the matter since he was blinded by jealousy, and consequently was not able to. Just as he had inquired concerning one saying of Micah, so too he inquired about a saying of Isaiah. For [the child's] lineage, his mother, his town and his time of birth were [already] known. His family was to be from the house of David, as Jacob had said,[5] and his mother a virgin, as Isaiah had said,[6] his town, Bethlehem, as Micah had said, and his time of birth as the Magi had said. It was through the census of the Romans that [Herod] learned that they had enrolled Jesus as son of Joseph, [through] those who had discovered it. But, even though he knew all these things, he was not able to recognize him because he was intoxicated with jealousy. He was like Saul, who, when it was in the hollow of his hand [to have] a drink of David's blood for which he was thirsting, did not recognize that David was within his grasp.[7] Solomon however knew how to judge and discern in the case of the infant son of the prostitute.[8] Delilah also knew how to investigate and extract the hidden secret from Samson's heart.[9]

§5.   But in Pharaoh's case by contrast, because the lineage, mother, and date of birth of the redeemer that was born to the Hebrews was not known [to him], he killed the young children to ensure that the Single One who

---

[1] Cf. Josh 13:3.
[2] Cf. 1 Sam 22:6-19.
[3] That is, "That you be held responsible for shedding innocent blood." Cf. Matt 27:25.
[4] Cf. 1 Sam 22:20.
[5] Cf. Gen 49:10.
[6] Cf Isa 7:14.
[7] Cf. 1 Sam 24 and 26.
[8] Cf. 1 Kgs 3:16-28.
[9] Cf. Judg 16:4-21.

was being sought out by him would be killed along with the many [others].[1] Just as Saul ought to have known through many [signs] that he was not able for David's power, so too Herod was not able for the power of the Son of David. But hatred, instead of knowing or learning, precipitates the doing of iniquity. These are indeed sons of the Evil One who thought, "I am able to kill Moses, destroy David, and crucify the Son of David." Cain too [was] his disciple, who thought he was able to deceive God in saying, *Am I my brother's keeper?*[2] Likewise Gehazi in the case of Elisha,[3] and Iscariot in the case of our Lord.

The Massacre of the Infants

§6.   The infants who were slain fulfilled two functions:[4] they were witnesses to the righteous who were slain, and accusers of the murderers. For, if [the latter] had dragged [the Lord] to perdition because he had unhesitatingly said, *I am God*, why did they kill the innocents before these could become his heralds? *A voice was heard in Ramah, Rachel who was weeping for her children.*[5] If Bethlehem was [a city] of Judah, the son of Leah, why was *Rachel weeping for her children who are not?*[6] [It was because they no longer existed, that they might be killed for the Messiah. [Rachel was weeping] because the Redeemer would not be born from her children, since Leah was the figurehead for the earlier people and Rachel the figurehead of the Church. *But the barren one has given birth, and the sons of the widow have become more numerous than those of the married woman.*[7] Or alternatively, because the tribe of Benjamin[8] was close to the tribe of Judah, for it is written, *Rachel died on the way to Ephrath, which is Bethlehem.*[9] Similarly Moses, when he blessed Benjamin, said of him, *He will dwell between his shoulders.*[10] The

---

[1] Cf. Exod 1:15-22.

[2] Gen 4:9.

[3] Cf. 2 Kgs 5:20-27.

[4] Literally: they were in two shapes/forms.

[5] Matt 2:18; Jer 31:15.

[6] There is a lacuna here of two folios, at the end of the first five of the additional forty-one folios. The translation given here is reconstructed on the basis of the Armenian version (cf. CSCO 145, pp. 28-33).

[7] Isa 54:1.

[8] Benjamin was a son of Rachel, cf. Gen 35:16-18.

[9] Gen 35:19.

[10] Deut 33:12.

dwelling-place[1] in fact was established in Jerusalem, which is in the inheritance of Benjamin.[2] Samuel too, on anointing Saul as king of Israel, gave him a sign: *You will meet three men at Zelzah, near Rachel's tomb, in the territory of Benjamin.*[3]

§7.   {*Rachel weeping for her children.* Alas, weep Rachel! Not like that first lamentation, when the enemies came and drew near to your children, but weep over those who, having been killed, were thrown out into the public places, not by foreigners, but by the sons of their father, Jacob. However, constrain your voice from weeping, for the recompense for your tears has been written down for the benefit of those who were born with the Son of David, at the time when he himself was born. They are to become the heralds of his joyful message at the time of the visitation. They are to receive a special place in the Jerusalem on high, our mother, whom we have confessed, who appeared to Moses on the mountain.[4] They have inherited it. Hold firm, and receive the consolation which comes to you from your chosen son, Saul, that is, Paul, your consoler, and the reward of your tears and your sorrows.

"Out of Egypt I Have Called My Son"

§8.   {Because Israel, symbolically called "son" since Egypt,[5] had lost its sonship through having worshipped Baal and offered incense to idols, John gave them [a title] which suited them, *Race of vipers.*[6] Because these had lost that title of sonship, which had been poured over them through grace in the days of Moses, they received from John a name which was congruent with their deeds.

§9.   {After the Lord went down into the land of the Egyptians and had returned from there, the evangelist said, *Now the true word spoken by the prophet is accomplished.* He said, *I will call my son out of Egypt.*[7] He also

---

[1] A reference to the Ark of the Covenant, and, at a later stage, to the Temple.

[2] Cf. Josh 18:28.

[3] 1 Sam 10:2.

[4] This appearing of the heavenly Jerusalem to Moses on the mountain seems to be based on the text of Exod 24:10, which describes how Moses and the elders saw "the God of Israel, and there was under his feet as it were a pavement of sapphire stone, like the very heaven for clearness."

[5] Cf. Hos 11:1; Matt 2:15.

[6] Matt 3:7.

[7] Matt 2:15; Hos 11:1.

said, *He will be called a Nazarene*,[1] because in Hebrew *nezer* [2] means a "sceptre" and the prophet calls him a "Nazarene" because he is the son of the sceptre. Because he was brought up in Nazareth, the evangelist notes that this is like that [other prophecy], *He will be called a Nazarene.*

The prophecy was in John but the mysteries of the prophecy were in the Lord of John, just as the priesthood was in the son of Zechariah, and the kingdom and the priesthood were in the Son of Mary. *The Law* [came] *through Moses*, with the sign of the lamb and many other symbols: Amaleck, the waters rendered sweet, the brazen serpent, but *the truth* of [these things came] *through Jesus, our Lord.*[3] The baptism of John was higher than the Law, but inferior to [the baptism] of the Messiah, because no one baptized in the name [of the Trinity] before the time of his exaltation.

John went off into the desert, not to become wild there, but to render tame in the desert the wildness of the inhabited [land]. For passion, which causes trouble like a wild beast when in the midst of an inhabited [land] at peace, calms down and becomes tame when it goes off to the desert. Be convinced of this from the example of Herod's passion. It was fierce in the midst of the inhabited [land] at peace, and burned illegitimately for his brother's wife, to the extent that [Herod] lost the mild and gentle John,[4] who [had lived] peacefully in the desert, and had made no use of marriage, even though allowed him by the Law. *The Word became flesh and lived among us*,[5] that is the Word of God, through the flesh which he assumed, lived *among us*. He did not say, "near us" but *among us*, to show clearly that it was for our sake that he clothed himself with our flesh, in accordance with what he said, *My flesh is food.*[6]

The Identity and Role of John the Baptist

§10.   {*The Jews sent to John and said to him, Who are you? He confessed and said, I am not the Messiah. They said to him, Are you Elijah? He said, No.*[7] But our Lord called him Elijah, as Scripture attests.[8]

---

[1] Matt 2:23; Isa 11:1; 53:2.

[2] The more accurate spelling for this would be *neṣer* [cf. נֵצֶר].

[3] John 1:17. Cf. Exod 12; 17:8-16; 15:22-25; Num 21:4-9.

[4] Cf. Matt 14:1-11.

[5] John 1:14.

[6] John 6:55.

[7] John 1:19-21.

[8] Cf. Matt 11:14; 17:12-13.

However, when they interrogated him, he said, "I am not Elijah." But Scripture does not say that John came in the body of Elijah, but, *In the power and the spirit of Elijah.*[1] Elijah, who was taken up into the heavens, did not return to them, just as it was not David who later became king, but Zerubbabel.[2] The pharisees however did not ask John, "Have you come in the spirit of Elijah?" but, "*Are you Elijah* himself?" That is why he said to them, *No.* Why should he have needed to be Elijah himself, if the actions of Elijah were to be found present in John? Elisha intervened and stood between John and Elijah, lest John be judged by them, since Elijah was taken up in a sacred chariot,[3] whereas his head was carried away on a dish by a corrupt young girl.[4]

§11.   {If they wished to make John a liar, Elisha, whose trustworthiness is acceptable to them, reproves and reduces them to silence. For they believe that Elisha received a double portion of the spirit of his master.[5] But for that to happen, was it necessary that Elisha be taken away to the heavens twice and in two different chariots, in order to see the highest heavens? Accepting that he was given the power of Elijah, together with his actions, this was not for all his actions, but for similar actions, according as was deemed useful. If he had not received a double portion, the abundance which he received would not have been apparent.

§12.   {Those who were sent to ask our Lord, *By what power do you do that?*,[6] were those same ones who had been sent to John. But, since [John] had not come to teach rebels, he did not show them [what they asked]. These were not people willing to learn the truth about John, but were interrogating him abruptly, "*Who are you*, who do these things?" Therefore he did not reply to them as people seeking instruction, but as rebels. To all they had asked, no matter how they had put it, he said, *I am not the Messiah, nor Elijah, nor the prophet, but the voice,*[7] lest [he call himself] either John or a man, although he was a prophet, and [another] Elijah and a messiah. But for those who were interrogating him he was none of these. Just as our Lord had said to certain people, *I am not a*

---

[1] Luke 1:17.
[2] Cf. Hag 2:20-23; Zech 3:6-10.
[3] Cf. 1 Kgs 2:11-12.
[4] Cf. Matt 14:11.
[5] Cf. 2 Kgs 2:9-11.
[6] Matt 21:23.
[7] Cf. John 1:20-23.

judge,[1] even though he was a judge, and to others, *I am not one who does good*,[2] even though he was one who did good.

§13.　{Just as the crowing of the cock, herald of the dawn, strikes the ear, so too the candle which has been lit strikes the eye. Likewise, writing and the voice are interlinked. The candle and the cock are but one, just like John and Elijah. By its crowing the cock compels us to listen. It is thus an image of the voice which wakens us. The candle in being lit is a symbol of the light of him who illumines us. Both dissipate the darkness. They are the image of the Father and the Son, in that they dispel evil. They are also the image of the prophets and the apostles, for in the case of both, the Sun has taken over.

§14.　{Take note that the candle shows that [the fire] burning in [John's] mouth was the image of Elijah, who burned evil ones with his tongue and overwhelmed them with thirst, [depriving them] of water by the ardour of his word.[3] The cock, which sings in the silence of the night, is a type for John who was preaching in the silence of the desert. But, when the candle is lit in the evening, the cock is no longer heard, for it sings only in the morning. In John the voice of the morning and the candle of the evening meet symbolically, so that he might testify to the return of Elijah.

§15.　{The voice was that of John, but the word which expressed itself through the voice was our Lord. The voice wakened them up, the voice cried out and assembled them, but the Word distributed his gifts to them. The punishment he announced was in proportion to their sins}.[4] They had acted somewhat wickedly, and God had punished a little. *He will cut down the branches of the forest with an axe*,[5] Isaiah said; [he spoke] of the *branches*, not of the root. When the measure of their sins was complete, John came and took up the roots of their trees. *For the axe is laid to the roots of the trees*,[6] [the roots] which Isaiah had left [untouched]. When will this be, if not at the rising forth of the True One, who was designated by

---

[1] Cf. Luke 12:14.
[2] Cf. Matt 19:17.
[3] Cf. 2 Kgs 1:2-17; 1 Kgs 17:1-18:46.
[4] End of the lacuna. *Chester Beatty* MS 709 takes up again at this point.
[5] Isa 10:34.
[6] Matt 3:10.

the [image of] the staff and the shoot, and upon whom rests the Spirit, who is referred to as being septiform.[1]

The Finding of Jesus in the Temple[2]

§16. *I and your father were seeking you in anxiety.*[3] To this he replied, *It is fitting for me that I should be [in] my father's house.*[4] They were seeking him out of fear lest they had killed him. For this is what they, along with Herod their prince, had wanted to do to him when he was two years old.

John the Baptist's Life-style

§17. *John was dressed in a tunic of camel-hair,*[5] because our holy sheep was not yet shorn. *From these stones God is able to raise up sons to Abraham,*[6] that is, from those who worship stones and wood, in accordance with [what is written], *I have appointed you as the father of many nations.*[7] John kept himself from all sins because he was to baptize him who was without sins. "Do not be amazed, John, that you should baptize me, for I have yet to receive a baptism of anointing from a woman." *She has done this for my burial,*[8] for his death was called a baptism. Eliezar had given Rebecca as a bride at the well of water.[9] Jacob [did likewise] for Rachel at the well of water,[10] and Moses [too] for Zipporah at the well of water.[11] All of these therefore were types of our Lord, who betrothed his Church through John's baptism.[12] Just as Eliezar introduced Rebecca to Isaac, his master, when he came to meet her in the

---

[1] Cf. Isa 11:1-2.
[2] The location of this episode in a sequence dealing with of John's early ministry appears out of its logical place, even though attested here in both Syriac and Armenian traditions. In his translation in EC-SC 121, p. 85, Leloir places it before §8, which begins the ministry of John the Baptist.
[3] Luke 2:48.
[4] Luke 2:49.
[5] Matt 3:4.
[6] Matt 3:9.
[7] Gen 17:4.
[8] John 12:7.
[9] Cf. Gen 24:1-67.
[10] Gen 29:1-20.
[11] Cf. Exod 2:16-21.
[12] Cf. Eph 5:22-23.

field, so too John introduced our Redeemer from the Jordan, *Behold the Lamb of God, who takes away the sin of the world.*[1]

---

[1] John 1:29.

IV

The Baptism of Jesus by John

§1a. *Jesus was about thirty years,*[1] when he came to be baptized. This [was a cause of] confusion for Marcion. For, if he had not assumed a body, why should he have approached baptism. A divine nature does not need to be baptized. Does not the fact that he was thirty years old also disclose his humanity?

§1b.[2] *I must needs be baptized by you.*[3] He did not make this response by way of contention, but rather that he might show forth the virtue of his Lord. For, if [John] *was not worthy* to carry *his sandals,*[4] how much more [unworthy] was he that he should actually baptize him. *Everyone is blessed by one more excellent than oneself.*[5] John's reluctance therefore was appropriate, and his obedience too was fitting. Just as it was not proper that he baptize one more excellent than he, so too it was not right that he enter into dispute concerning the command of his Lord. It was not so that John might fill in something that was [still] needed by our Lord that he was considered worthy to baptize him, but rather [the Lord] came to be baptized because he was clothed with the guilty Adam.

   If John was proclaiming *a baptism of repentance*[6] and baptizing sinners, and [if] it was written concerning our Lord that *sin was not found in him,*[7] it was therefore evident that it was not because he was in need like sinners that he approached the baptism of penitents. For John also testified, for it was in fear and supplication that he had said to his Lord, *It is fitting for me that I be baptized by you.*[8] *Permit that we may fulfil all justice now,*[9] [referring to] that which is in the Law. For, since there was also a curse on those who were transgressing the Law in minor matters, and since no one can fulfil all the justice that is in the Law, and escape

---

[1] Luke 3:23.
[2] §1b is absent from the Armenian tradition.
[3] Matt 3:14.
[4] Matt 3:11.
[5] Heb 7:7.
[6] Mark 1:4; Luke 3:3.
[7] 1 Pet 2:22.
[8] Matt 3:14.
[9] Matt 3:15.

from the curse,[1] therefore he who fulfils justice came to undo the curse and abolish sin.

§1c. *Permit that we may fulfil justice now*,[2] since liberators and kings receive [both] the anointing and the Law from the priests. Just as he clothed himself with a [human] body and appeared as in need, so too he drew near to baptism to testify to the truth [of his humanity], especially that through his baptism he might mark an ending for that [of John], for he had baptized once again those who had been baptized by John. He showed that [John's baptism] had served up until his time only, since true baptism, which purifies from the evil of the Law, was revealed through him.

§2. [The Lord said], *Permit that now*,[3] {lest he [give the impression of] entering into his sheep-fold like a robber. It was also to confound the pharisees, who were showing contempt for and despising the baptism of John. To honour yet again the humility of his herald he said, *Whoever humbles himself shall be exalted*.[4] Because John had confessed, *I am not worthy to untie the throngs of his sandals*,[5] our Lord took John's right hand and placed it on his head [saying], *Permit that we may fulfil justice now*; for John was the heel of the Law. *The Law and the Prophets [reached] as far as John*,[6] but the Messiah is the beginning of the New Testament. Through baptism [the Lord] assumed the justice of the Old [Testament] in order to receive the perfection of the anointing and to give it fully and in its entirety to his disciples. For he put an end to John's baptism and the Law at the same time. He was baptized in justice, because he was sinless, but he baptized in grace because [all others] were sinners. Through his justice he dispensed from the Law and through his baptism he abolished baptism.

§3. {A further [interpretation of] *That we may fulfil all justice*. John was at the gate of the sheep-fold where the Israelite flock was gathered together in unity. [The Lord] entered into the flock not by his power but by

---

[1] Cf. Gal 3:10.
[2] Matt 3:15.
[3] There is a lacuna of one folio at this point in the additional folios of *Chester Beatty* MS 709. The translation given here is based on the Armenian version (cf. CSCO 145, pp. 35-36).
[4] Matt 23:12; Luke 14:11; 18:14.
[5] John 1:27; Mark 1:7.
[6] Luke 16:16.

his justice. The Spirit which rested on him during his baptism attested that he was the shepherd, for he had received the prophecy and priesthood through John. He had [already] received the kingdom of the house of David through being born *of the house of David*.[1] He received the priesthood of the house of Levi through a second birth, by the baptism of the son of Aaron. Whoever believes that his second birth was in the world cannot doubt that, through his later birth by John's baptism, [the Lord] received the priesthood of John. Although many were baptized on that day, the Spirit descended and rested on one person only, so that he might be distinguished from everyone else by a sign, he who was indistinguishable in appearance from all other men. Because the Spirit had come down [on him] at his baptism, the Spirit was given through his baptism.

The Temptations of Jesus[2]

§4.   {*At that time the Holy Spirit led him out into the wilderness, to be tempted by Satan.*[3] Why did Satan not tempt him up to his thirtieth year? Because a definite sign of his divinity had not [yet] been given from heaven. He appeared modest like others, and he had not received any striking homage in the midst of his people. [Satan] refrained from tempting [him] until the beginning of this event. But when he heard, *Now, behold the Lamb of God is coming, and this is he who takes away the sins of the world*,[4] he was greatly astounded. However, he waited until he was baptized to see if he would be baptized as though in need [of it].

§5.   {When he saw, from the splendour of the light which appeared on the water,[5] and the voice which came from heaven, that he who fulfils every need had gone down into the water, and that he had not come there

---

[1] Luke 2:4.

[2] Cf. M.-E. Boismard, *Le Diatessaron: De Tatien à Justin* (avec la collaboration de A. Lamouille, Etudes bibliques, nouvelle série 15, Paris, 1992). In a chapter in this work entitled "La tradition syriaque," pp. 93-125, the author analyses IV, §§4-16 (the temptations of Jesus), V, §§1-12 (the wedding at Cana) and V, §§17a-b and 21 (Jesus eating with tax collectors and sinners) and proposes a hypothesis that these sections of the commentary illustrate that Ephrem's commentary is not homogenous, but rather the result of a fusion of two distinct commentaries, one on Tatian's Diatessaron and the other on an early harmony also known to Justin. See the Introduction (section 3) above on the question of the integrity of the commentary.

[3] Mark 1:12-13; Matt 4:1.

[4] John 1:29.

[5] See other ancient authors (Justin, Epiphanus, Jacob of Sarug) for this tradition.

to baptism as though he were someone in need, [Satan] reflected and said to himself, "As long as I have not tested him by combat through temptation I will not be able to identify him." But it was not fitting that the Benefactor should resist the will of him who had come to tempt him. For, not knowing how to tempt him, he did not dare approach him. Therefore it was not until our Lord was prepared for [and] disposed towards the impact of combat, and had clothed himself with the power of the Spirit to go out to fight, that [Satan] approached him to tempt him.

§6. {*The Holy Spirit led him out into the wilderness, to be tempted by Satan.* Because of his gentleness he did not want to resist him lest those who heard it said, "He was not able to hold firm in combat against [Satan], therefore he was unwilling to go out to meet his tempter," might be discouraged. [He acted thus] especially to prevent apostates from saying that the Spirit is inferior to the Son. For if the Spirit had only led him out to the conflict of combat, [and] not to honour and tranquillity, how could the mind not be inclined towards the opinions of the adversaries in examining this?}[1] But if the Spirit is inferior to the Son, how then was authority given to the Spirit for his expulsion [into the desert]? For in leading him out [the Spirit] appears as master. [The phrase], *The Spirit led him out into the desert to be tempted,* is [like] *No one is able to enter the house of a strong man in order to plunder his property unless he first binds the strong man and then plunders his property.*[2] Thus [the Lord] bound the strong one and conquered him in his own dwelling, and then began his preaching. He opened up the path of fasting for us so that we might conquer [Satan's] wiles through it.

§7. *After forty [days], during which he was fasting, he was hungry.*[3] [This was] in order that, through his victory over the enemy, he might expose his defeat before all people. He taught us[4] [thus] through his words that it is for the utterance of the Lord that we should hunger. Why then does [Scripture] not indicate concerning Moses or Elijah, that they were hungry, but it is written concerning our Lord that he was hungry? [This was] so that [Scripture] might confound those who say that he did not assume a body, and give a pretext to Satan to draw near to him for his

---

[1] The Syriac text in *Chester Beatty* MS 709 resumes at this point.
[2] Matt 12:29.
[3] Matt 4:2.
[4] The Syriac text reads the singular suffix here, "me."

testing, in saying to him, *Say to the stones that they become bread.*[1] But [our Lord] did not do this, lest he give the evildoer the object of his desire. But, in the case of the swine, he gave him as he demanded, not in order to do his will, but for the sake of the signs that he was to work there. For no one would go out to him from the region of the Gadarenes unless he performed a miracle.[2]

§8a.   Since [Satan] was not confounded by the first temptation, *He brought him out and set him on the pinnacle of the temple.*[3] Indeed up to this moment the place still remains [although] the temple was later destroyed, just as [our Lord] had said, *A stone will not be left upon a stone.*[4] That spot where he stood has been preserved as a sign.

§8b.[5]   *He set him up on the pinnacle of the temple,* to make him suppose that he who was a man could become God, by means of the godly house,[6] just as he had [once] made Adam suppose that he could become God, by means of that tree.[7] *He brought him up to the mountain,*[8] as though he were in need.[9] *To you will I give the kingdoms, if you will adore me.*[10] When he changed his [mode of] cunning, he did not change the True One with it. In the beginning God made him, and, when complete, he was in need and a worshipper.[11] But he became blind in the arrogance of his worship, because of all that he had acquired, and for this reason he was punished all the more. Because [Satan] did not recognize the One who knew him intimately, our Lord addressed him by his name, *Satan.*[12] But he did not know how he should address [our Lord].

---

[1] Matt 4:3.

[2] Cf. Mark 5:1-20.

[3] Matt 4:5; Luke 4:9.

[4] Matt 24:2.

[5] §8b is absent from the Armenian tradition.

[6] "The godly house" refers to the temple where the temptation is situated. It stands in parallelism with "that tree" in the garden, which was the means through which Adam was tempted.

[7] Cf. Gen 3:5.

[8] Matt 4:8.

[9] The word ܟܢܝܫܐ, "indigent/needy" is difficult to render in English. It refers to the incomplete or needy condition of humanity. Its meaning here might be paraphrased, "as though he were a mere human."

[10] Matt 4:9.

[11] Cf. Heb 1:6, "Let all God's angels worship him."

[12] Matt 4:10.

§8c.   Therefore he said to him, *Fall down from here, for it is written,* *They will guard you lest you stumble.*[1] O tempter, if it is concerning him that the psalm is fulfilled, is it not also written there, *With his wings, that* *he may deliver you.*[2] It is not possible for a bird to fall, for the air beneath its wings is like the earth. Is it not also written, *You will tread on the* *serpent and the basilisk?*[3] But [Satan] only studied those [passages] from Scripture which were convenient to him and omitted those which were harmful to him. The heretics are like this too. They appropriate from Scripture those [passages] which suit their erroneous teaching,[4] and omit those that refute their errors, thereby demonstrating that they are disciples of this master.

§9.   Furthermore, *He brought him up to a mountain and said to him,* *All these are my kingdoms.*[5] [The heretics] are truly mistaken in this and think that he is a supreme being. For, as I said, they omit those [words] which are harmful and appropriate the rest. When he says, *These are* *mine*, they make him a supreme being. But it is not from these that we learn truth. By that through which they think they conquer, they are all the more vanquished. Consequently, because he said after this, *To me* *have they been handed over,*[6] they should understand that the creator of these is another person, and not the one to whom they are handed over. That he said, *I have power over them,*[7] is not that he has authority by nature, apart from what these have chosen [to give him]. For [the apostle] has said, *You are the servants of the one to whom you entrust yourselves* *to obey*, et cetera.[8]

§10.   *Fall down, adore me.*[9] [This was] so that the pride of him who from the beginning wished to be God might be known. The body of our Lord warns all flesh, that if one enters into combat unarmed, he will be vanquished. For [the Lord] first clothed himself with the armour of

---

[1] Luke 4:9-11.
[2] Ps 91:12.
[3] Ps 91:13.
[4] Literally, "their stumbling-blocks."
[5] Matt 4:8-9.
[6] Luke 4:6.
[7] *Idem*.
[8] Rom 6:16. See the note above at II, § 5 for comment on this type of indication of scriptural abbreviation.
[9] Matt 4:9.

fasting, and then entered into the conflict. Solid armour is required against him who shoots trained arrows. *Command that these stones become bread.*[1] He shot the arrow which teaches satisfaction, that it might stir up hunger pangs and lead [him] into temptation. [Satan] however did not dominate through hunger, because that hunger was itself clothed with its fast as with a breast-plate. This hunger turned about and shot the arrows of its satisfaction against him, to teach him, the teacher of external satisfaction, that there is also an inner satisfaction which cannot be seen, *Not on bread alone, but on every utterance that comes from the mouth of God.*[2] Through that with which he had come to tempt, he was tempted; through that with which he had come to teach, he was refuted. *If you are the Son of God, command that these stones become bread.*[3] Now, the mouth of the Evil One gave a pledge [of assurance] that, since he is God, he is able to turn stones to bread.

Reflections on the Temptations

§11.   Our Lord therefore instructed [Satan] by and through his own word. If God can transform stones to bread, learn O tempter, that God can also satisfy without bread! If he can transform a stone into food, he can also transform hunger into satiety. For one who can transform a substance which is not edible into food, it is not difficult to transform the nature of hunger into satiety. It was not that he should satisfy it with something else, but he can turn the very substance of hunger into satiety, just as the tempter [ordered] that he make the substance of stone into bread. On this mountain therefore our Lord trod underfoot the desires of the tempter, and cast them down below, so that the peoples who were [formerly] trampled upon by them might trample upon them [in turn]. In their place he brought forth all good things, so that these [goods] that had been trampled upon by all might reign over all.

§12.   Just as Pharoah was drowned in those very waters in which he had drowned the infants,[4] so too David removed Goliath's head with that very sword with which he had destroyed many.[5] Moses divided the waters

---

1 Matt 4:3.
2 Matt 4:4; Deut 8:3.
3 Matt 4:3.
4 Cf. Exod 1:22; 14:23-28.
5 Cf. 1 Sam 17:1-51.

through the symbol of the cross,[1] while David laid Goliath low through the symbol of the stone. Our Lord condemned Satan by the word of his mouth when the latter was tempting him. Pharaoh was drowned by the waters with which he had drowned [others]. Goliath too was slain by the sword with which he had slain others. The Evil One was vanquished by the body which he was [trying to] destoy, and was rebuked that he was not a divine being. Through the symbol of the three immersions with which he was baptized the Life-Giver was tempted [three times]. *Command that these stones become bread*,[2] this refers to the source of nourishment of children. Secondly, *the kingdoms and their glory I will give you*,[3] this refers to the promise of the Law. Thirdly, *Fall down from here*,[4] this refers to the descent of death. But [the Lord] was not perturbed by any one of these. When [Satan] was flattering him, he did not tremble,[5] and when he was frightening him, he was not agitated, but continued along his [own] pathway, fulfilling the will of his Father.

§13.   All these [things] that [Satan] had proposed to the Living One were not a [source of] anguish to him. He gives us relief in our own anguish, and we all receive refreshment from his passion. What could he fear, he who knew that it was not possible for him to be harmed? From time to time fear is born in us because we truly know that it is possible for us to be harmed.

Those who pronounce him defiled through his birth do not know, because they are in error. They are unable to learn because they are haughty, just as they are also without fear, because they are unrepentant. This world into which he came is no different from the womb, for all defilements are in it. He also entered into Sheol, which is repugnant and unclean beyond all else. But [since] in particular it is said concerning the body that they are temples of the divinity,[6] it was therefore not unclean for God to dwell in his temples. Because he wanted to kill death and destroy

---

[1] Exod 14:16.

[2] Matt 4:3.

[3] Luke 4:6-7.

[4] Luke 4:9.

[5] MS 709 is ambiguous for the verb here, since its middle consonant lacks a diacritical point. Leloir has opted for the form ܚܕܝ, which is unattested in Syriac, and translates in Latin *gavisus est*, as though from the root ܚܕܐ, "to rejoice" (cf. EC-FA, pp. 30-31). However, if one reads ܚܙܝ, "to tremble" (poorly attested in Syriac), one gets a sense in keeping with the context, and parallel to the next part of the sentence.

[6] Cf. 1 Cor 3:16-17.

its traces, he began with the roots of the matter. For where the body is, there too is death, and the root of the body is the womb. There it begins to be formed, and it is there that death begins in it unto its corruption. How many women in fact are there, whose infants die in the month in which they are conceived, or perish in the second or third, or in any one of the remaining months? If death begins then from the womb, and comes to completion in Sheol, how could he, who is the hunter of death, not begin to walk with it from the womb until its end in Sheol, its stronghold?

§14.   Take note therefore how the Living One sought to refute death in every kind of way. He was an embryo, and while in the womb [death] was not able to destroy him. [He was] an infant and while growing up, it was not able to disfigure him. [He was] a child and during his education it was not able to confuse him. [He was] a young man, and with its lustful desires it was not able to lead him into error. [He was] instructed, and with its wiles, it was not able to overpower him. [He was] a teacher, and because of his intelligence, it was not able to refute him. [He was] vigilant, and with its commands, it was not able to turn him aside [from his purpose]. [He was] strong, and in killing him, it was not able to frighten him. [He was] a corpse and in the custody of the tomb, it was not able to hold him. He was not ill, because he was a healer. He did not go astray, because he was a shepherd. He did not commit error, because he was a teacher. He did not stumble, because he was the light. This is the perfect way that the Messiah opened up for his Church, from the beginning through conception until the completion of the resurrection.

§15.   If the Church therefore is his body, as Paul his witness has said,[1] then believe that his Church has journeyed through all this without corruption. Just as, by the condemnation of the one body of Adam, all bodies died and continue to die,[2] so too, through the victory of this one body of the Messiah his entire Church lived and continues to live. So, just as [it was] because these bodies themselves have sinned and are themselves dying, that the earth, their mother, was also accursed,[3] so too, because of this body, which is the Church without corruption,[4] its earth is blessed from the beginning. The earth of the temple is the body of Mary, in

---

[1] Cf. Eph 1:23.
[2] Cf. Rom 5:12-21.
[3] Cf. Gen 3:17-19.
[4] Cf. Eph 5:25-27.

whom it was sown. Observe too the envoy who, with a clear voice, came to sow it in her hearing. He began the sowing of the seed thus, *Peace be with you, blessed among women.*[1] Elizabeth, a second voice, sealed it, *You are blessed among women.*[2] [This was] so that it might be made known that, because the first mother was cursed, this second mother was therefore addressed with blessed names.

§16. *[Satan] withdrew from him for a time,*[3] for he was preparing himself, through the calumny and envy of the scribes, to render [the Lord's] victory useless. But, just as [Satan] was condemned in the beginning, he was also condemned at the end, for [the Lord] was all the more victorious through his death. [He said], *Get behind me,*[4] because he was angry with [Satan] since he was lying without measure when he said, *The kingdoms are mine.*[5] But this was irreverent, *For God has dominion over the kingdom of mankind, and to whom he wishes he gives it.*[6] Thus did he rebuke his arrogance with his utterance, so that he was no longer able to stand up against his word. [This was] so that he might manifest his own true dominion and instruct those obedient to him that it is from the True Giver [only] that they receive all good things. *The angels came and were ministering to him;*[7] that he might give us a type, that after baptism we enter into temptations, and after temptations, [we enter] then the kingdom of heaven.

The Calling of the First Disciples

§17. When the disciples of John heard him, as he was speaking about our Lord, they abandoned their master and went after our Lord. For the voice was not able to hold on to the disciples for itself, but sent them on unto the Word.[8] It was fitting that, when the light of the sun appeared, the light of the lantern should fade away.[9] John remained on only for this, that his baptism be put to an end by the baptism of our Lord. Then he died,

---

[1] Luke 1:28. Elizabeth's statement of Luke 1:42 is placed on Gabriel's lips here.
[2] Luke 1:42.
[3] Luke 4:13.
[4] Matt 4:10.
[5] Luke 4:6.
[6] Dan 4:14ff.
[7] Matt 4:11.
[8] Cf. John 1:35-37.
[9] Cf. John 5:35.

so that he might also be first among the dead, and a herald, just as he was a sign of Sheol in the womb of his mother.

§18.   *We have found the Messiah.*[1] This reveals that his fame was spread about, and had come from the time of the Magi.[2] It was renewed by means of John who had baptized him, and by the witness of the Spirit. Then he became solitary once again during his fast of forty days. This was why the elect were thirsting after news of him. These were his instruments, just as he had said, *You were chosen by me before the world.*[3] He chose the Galileans, a people without learning, whom the prophets described as *dwelling in darkness,*[4] since these had seen the light, so that he might put the doctors of the Law to shame. *For he chose the foolish of the world, so that he might put the wise to shame through them.*[5]

§19.   *Can anything good come out of Nazareth?*[6] Now it was written that he would be born from the house of David[7] and in his own Bethlehem.[8] But [Nathaniel] however understood him to have come from Galilee, and to have sprung from Nazareth: *Can anything good come out of Nazareth?* Even though the prophet had said that a leader and prince would rise forth from Bethlehem. Nathaniel had heard that he was from Nazareth, and therefore asked whether it was possible that a good prince could come out of Nazareth, [for this was] something that had not been written. Consequently, when our Lord saw him, he gave a good testimony on his behalf, that he was not like the scribes who were acting deceitfully in relation to the [Scripture] readings, attempting to make their interpretations follow their own will, *This is an Israelite scribe in whom no guile has been seen.*[9] For, before he knew [the Lord], he was asking whether Nazareth could produce a prince, like Bethlehem. When he saw with his own eyes, he was no longer an objector as were his companions, and no longer a questioner like the others. But he confessed that he was the Messiah, and perceived that [those prophecies] concerning both

---

[1] John 1:41.
[2] Cf. Matt 2:1-6.
[3] Cf. John 15:16, 19.
[4] Cf. Isa 9:1.
[5] 1 Cor 1:27.
[6] John 1:46.
[7] Cf. 2 Sam 7:12; John 7:42.
[8] Cf. Mic 5:1; Matt 2:5-6.
[9] John 1:46.

Bethlehem and Nazareth were fulfilled in him: *From Bethlehem will come forth a prince,*[1] and, *A light has arisen over Galilee, for the people that were walking in darkness have seen the light.*[2]

§20.   There came to him fishers[3] of fish and they became fishers of people; as it is written, *Behold, I am sending forth hunters. And they will hunt them from every mountain and from every high place.*[4] But, if he had sent forth wise men, [people would have said] that they had either persuaded them to take hold of them, or that they had led them astray to grasp hold of them. If [he had sent forth] rich men, again [people would have said] that they had either stirred them up by feeding them or had bribed them, and [so] gained authority over them. If he [had sent forth] powerful men, again [people would have said] that they had either stunned them by their force, or had constrained them by their violence.

But the apostles possessed none of these things. Through [the example of] Simon he helped them all understand. He was timid, because he was frightened at the voice of a young servant girl.[5] He was poor, because he was not able to pay his own tax, a half stater,[6] and [he said], *I have neither gold nor silver.*[7] He was stupid, for when he denied [our Lord] he did not know how to take flight astutely. These fishermen went forth then and were victorious over the strong, the rich and the wise. [This was] a great miracle, for, although weak, they attracted the strong not by force but by their teaching. Although poor, they taught the rich, and although unlearned, they made the wise and clever their disciples. The wisdom of the world yielded place to that wisdom which is itself the wisdom of wisdoms.

---

[1] Mic 5:1.
[2] Cf. Isa 8:23-9:1.
[3] Syriac uses the same word [ܨܝܕܐ] for "fisherman" and "hunter."
[4] Jer 16:16.
[5] Cf. Matt 26:69-72.
[6] Cf. Matt 17:27.
[7] Acts 3:6.

V

The Wedding Feast of Cana

§1.   *There was a wedding feast in Cana.*[1] When our Lord came there, *his mother said to him, There is no wine here. He said to her, What is that to me and to you, Woman? My hour has not yet come.*[2] This means, "Shall I impose myself on them? Rather, let them perceive themselves that the wine has run short, and let them all ask to drink." [He said this] so that his gift might increase in their eyes. She had constrained him urgently, so on account of this he instructed her. An alternative [interpretation] of *My hour has not yet come*[3] is that it could refer to the hour of his death. Since they were intoxicated, perhaps he might have escaped from suffering, if he had forced his gift upon them. But as yet this was [only] the beginning of his Gospel.

§2.   It was because Mary thought that the occasion of his miracles would be a source of glory and honour to him among the crowds that [he said], *My hour has not yet come.*[4] "For it is not as you think." He wanted to put an end to her [way] of thinking, since she was convinced that he would perform a miracle. *For she kept all these things in her mind,*[5] and *Whatever he says to you, do.*[6] For she saw that the wine had run short, and understood that his journey to the house of the wedding feast was not in vain. In Greek [the evangelist] has written that *he was reclining and the wine ran short.*[7] When his mother spoke to him, he said to her, *My hour has not yet come.*[8] That [meant] however, "Yes indeed, it has come!" She learned from him therefore that he was about to perform a sign there. When he reprimanded her because she was in doubt about him, *she said to the servants, Whatever my son tells you, do.*[9]

---

1 John 2:1. See the note at IV, §4 above in relation to Boismard's analysis of V, §§1-12.
2 John 2:3-4.
3 John 2:4.
4 *Idem.*
5 Luke 2:51.
6 John 2:5.
7 This is the second of five instances in the commentary in which Ephrem refers to "the Greek." See above at II, §17 for comment on Ephrem's use of this term.
8 John 2:4.
9 John 2:5.

§3.   Alternatively, it is said that [Mary] feared greatly that, on his arrival, those in charge of the feast would be required to offer wine. "They are spurning you, since it is because of you they are a source of ridicule. What you have done is an insult to the people, because they perceive that you have come just when their wine ran short."

§4a.   *She said to him, My son, there is no wine here. He said to her, What is that to me and to you, Woman?*[1] What was wrong with what she said? She was in great doubt concerning his word, because there was no wine there. Wherefore [the response], *What is that to me and to you, Woman?* For she had perceived that he was about to perform a miracle, according to what he had said to her. [This can be seen] from what she said to the servants, *Whatever my son tells you, do.*[2]

§4b.[3]   He took care therefore, wherever he was, to be on the alert lest he give a pretext for lack of faith on the part of the Jews. Thus, when he was invited to the feast, he did not say to his disciples that they should pour the water into the jars, but rather that the servants of the feast should. So too, when he came to raising Lazarus to life, he did not command his disciples that they should open the tomb, but rather that the Jews should.[4]

§4c.   An alternative [interpretation] of *My hour has not yet come* is that after the victory in the desert when he laid the enemy low, he entered, like a conqueror, to effect a victory at the wedding feast.

§5.   Mary hastened to be a servant of his will therefore instead of the apostles, but since it was not her place either to give orders or to anticipate his word, he reproved her for having been hasty. *My hour has not come,* that is, they will ask to drink and they will all become aware that the wine had run short, and thereafter will be the miracle. Thus, after his victory over Sheol, when she saw it, she wished to express affection for him like a mother.[5] He entrusted Mary, who had followed [him] to the cross, to John

---

[1] John 2:3-4.
[2] John 2:5.
[3] §4b is absent from the Armenian version.
[4] Cf. John 11:35.
[5] Cf. John 20:16-17. Ephrem appears to confuse Mary, the mother of Jesus with Mary Magdalene here. See II, §17 above and XXI, §27 below for similar types of "fusion" or

there, saying, *Woman, behold your son, and, Young Man, behold your mother*.[1] He restrained her again from drawing near to him, because he said, "From henceforth, John is your son."

Reflections on the Wedding Feast and its Miracle

§6. Why then did our Lord change the nature [of water] in the first of his signs? Was it not to show that the divinity, which had changed nature in the depths of the jars, was that same [divinity] which had changed nature in the womb of the virgin? At the completion of his signs he opened the tomb to show that the greed of death had no hold over him. He sealed and confirmed these two uncertainties, that of his birth and of his death. For these waters, with regard to their nature, were transformed into the [fruit of the] vine, but without the stone jars [themselves] undergoing change in their nature inwardly. This was a symbol of his body which was wondrously conceived in a woman, and, without a man, miraculously formed within the virgin.

§7. He made wine from water therefore, in order to give proof concerning how his conception and his birth took place. He summoned *six water jars*[2] as witness to the unique virgin who had given birth to him. The water jars conceived in a novel way, not in keeping with their custom, and gave birth to wine. But they did not continue to give birth. Similarly the virgin conceived and gave birth to Emmanuel, and she did not give birth again. The giving birth by the jars was from smallness to greatness, and from paucity to abundance; from water indeed to good wine. In her case, however, it was from greatness to weakness and from glory to ignominy. Those jars were for the purification of the Jews,[3] but our Lord poured his teaching into them, so that he might make it known that he was coming through the path of the Law and the Prophets to transform all things by his teaching, just as he had [transformed] water into wine.

---

confusion, and the note on John 20:15 at II, §17 above for comment on this "fusion" of the two Marys.
[1] John 19:26-27.
[2] John 2:6.
[3] Cf. John 2:6.

97

§8. *For everyone brings forth good wine first and then a lesser wine.*[1] [This was] so that he might make known that the former things were shadows. *For the Law was given through Moses, but truth and grace through Jesus.*[2] The [earthly] bridegroom invited the [heavenly] bridegroom.[3] The Lord of the wedding-feast-to-come went to the house of the wedding feast. He was invited to be seated, he who had established[4] worlds in his kingdom, and he bestowed on them a wedding gift in which they found joy. His greatness did not shrink away from their poverty. For see, there was not [enough] ordinary wine for the guests, and if he had not poured even a little of his riches abundantly upon them, they would have risen up from there, thirsting and sad.

§9. He invited them in turn to his wedding feast, but they declined.[5] As often as he increased his partaking in their banquets,[6] so often did their souls shrink back from his table, just as their fathers [shrank] from the manna.[7] Angels ate food from the table of Abraham and Lot,[8] and our Lord ate and drank with them, and did not shrink back. These others invited him and he went unto them. He invited them, but they did not come to his wedding feast. They called him, and he did not decline. He called them but they refused his meal. He honoured the guests, but they despised the guests. He delighted his table guests, but they killed his servants.[9] He filled up the void at the feast, but they rendered sterile all that he had established for them. He made them cheerful with good wine, but they exasperated him and provoked him to anger. Instead of good wine, they gave him vinegar and gall.[10]

§10. He had been invited as a guest, but he did not come with the guests. They came in advance of him to consume the ordinary wine first, so that he might then come and bring his good wine with him. He was

---

[1] John 2:10.
[2] John 1:17.
[3] Cf. John 2:2.
[4] Literally, "He who had caused worlds to be seated" [ܐ ܕܡ ܩܘܡ ܠܥܠ]. There is a play on words here which is difficult to capture effectively in translation.
[5] Cf. Matt 22:1-10.
[6] Cf. Luke 7:34-47; John 2:1-11.
[7] Cf. Num 11:6.
[8] Cf. Gen 18:1-8.
[9] Cf. Matt 22:1-6.
[10] Cf. Matt 27:34.

invited with them, while not being different from them in appearance. He performed a wonderful sign there, that he might be distinguished from them, inasmuch as he was not the same as them in his nature. His miracle distinguished him who was not different from them in his appearance. While his appearance proclaimed that he was like them, his miracle would teach them that he was greater than they. In silence he made water into wine, so that his divine silence would fashion joyful heralds for him, to give his joyful tidings to the table guests in joy. Of its nature wine is a cause of joy. Because he made it effortlessly with his command, and because it was also more excellent than any other wine in its taste, they were searching out its Lord, therefore, on account of its excellence, and also on account of its joy.

§11.   He came back victorious from the contest. The banqueting room received him on the third day, rejoicing. [This was] in order to show that there is joy for the conquerors after the contest, and to show that even if he was invited as a stranger, nevertheless he was seen to be the Lord of the wedding feast. This was because he filled the void of the banquet by his word which fills every void. [This was also] to show that he was not manifesting another creation, nor that he was using the old [order] as it was, since it was not water instead of wine that he gave them to drink. But when he created the wine, instead of going outside of creation, he created it from water which had [already] been created.

§12.   He was not therefore introducing an alien creation, but was transforming the original creation, so that, through having transformed it, he would make it known that he was its Lord. Because he did not alienate it, we must know that it is not to be despised. Indeed these same created entities will be renewed at the end. For that will, which changed ordinary water effortlessly into excellent wine, is capable of transforming all created entities to tastes which are beyond description, at the end of time. [This was too] that he might show, when he transformed their vileness into something pleasant, that they are not vile by their nature, but rather that in his nature their creator is wise. For he knew that they must needs be created, for the purposes of testing and correction, so that through them the innocent might be tested and crowned, and through them the foolish might be corrected, and obtain some benefit. He, who commanded the consuming fire, and instead of consuming [them], it was embracing

[them],[1] this is he who, at the end, will command those [things] which are destructive, and they will become beneficial; and [he will command] those things which afflict so that they become bearers of joy. First of all, therefore, he accustomed the mouth to the taste of his wine, that he might seduce and entice those who listen to the taste of his sweet teaching.

"The Times are Accomplished"

§13.   *The times are accomplished,*[2] which were completed from generation to generation. First of all, from Adam to Noah, with the covenant which those of the family of Seth established, when they were separating themselves from the family of Cain.[3] The other [covenant] from Noah to Abraham [was] that they must not eat blood, *I have given you everything as green plants, but you shall not eat blood.*[4] From Abraham to Moses, [it was] through circumcision, but without the Law,[5] and from Moses until [Christ's] appearance, [it was] with the Law. *[The times] are accomplished,* for there is no further change.

§14.   It is also said that [they offered] the freewill offering [in] the first period [from] Abel up until the time of Noah, *He will bring us relief through his sacrifices.*[6] The other [sacrifice] was on the altar which Noah [built] on the mountains of Kardu,[7] and one was Abraham's on the mountain of the Amorites.[8] Another [was] Jacob's in Bethel,[9] and another Joshua's in Cisjordan.[10] Another was at Shiloh, which was the location of the tabernacle,[11] and [another] was that of Solomon, who first [established] the tabernacle which is in Jerusalem.[12] But this one is the Messiah's, which he established in his Church until the end [of time], which, like these, will not undergo change again. This is why *the times are*

---

[1] Cf. Dan 3:49-50.

[2] Mark 1:15. The verb is in the plural here, as in *Codex Bezae.*

[3] Cf. Gen 4:25-5:8.

[4] Gen 9:3-4.

[5] Cf. Gen 17:9-14,23-27.

[6] Cf. Gen 5:29.

[7] In the Peshitta (as in the Palestinian and Babylonian Targums) the ark landed on Mt Kardu, rather than on Ararat.

[8] Cf. Gen 22:1-18. The Peshitta has "land of the Amorites" instead of "land of Moriah" (cf. LXX at 2 Chron 3:1).

[9] Cf. Gen 28:10-22.

[10] Cf. Josh 8:30-31.

[11] Cf. 1 Sam 1:3,21.

[12] Cf. 1 Kgs 8:62-64.

accomplished, for from henceforth the kingdom of heaven is proclaimed.[1]
Or alternatively, *The times are accomplished,* that is, the times of Israel.

The Baptism of the Disciples

§15.   *The disciples were baptizing,*[2] because they [themselves] had been baptized. They would not have been able to baptize others if they [themselves] had not been baptized. The meaning of this therefore is that *the one who has bathed does not need anything [further].*[3] If you wish, [you can understand] from this that they were baptized with water. And if not, take note that he said to them, *You are cleansed because of my word which I have spoken with you.*[4] Accept that this word was baptism for them, since baptism is rendered holy by this same word. Just as John was rendered holy by the commandment he had received, so too he rendered holy that baptism, which had been entrusted [to him].

§16.   Moreover, [some] say that, when he gave them his body, this was a baptism for them. For, if they had baptized or were baptized, but without possessing faith in his body and blood, [how] could he have first said to them, *If you do not eat and drink you will not have life?*[5] When these were angry, *he said to the twelve, Do you too wish to go away? Simon said to him, We believe and we know.*[6] In what did they believe, if not in that which those [others] were unable to believe - that is to say, they were not even [able] to listen to it.

The Call of Matthew

§17a.[7]   *When he had crossed over, he saw a certain man, sitting at the tax office, and his name was Matthew.*[8] He saw the soul of the apostle in the mire, floating about in the darkness of the raging waters of the adversary. It was in need of the right hand of our Saviour to rescue him. Our Lord

---

1 Mark 1:15. Note that the verb is in the plural here.
2 John 4:2.
3 John 13:10.
4 John 15:3.
5 John 6:53.
6 John 6:67-69.
7 §17a is absent from the Armenian version. See the note at IV, §4 above in relation to Boismard's analysis of V, §§17a-b and 21.
8 Matt 9:9.

called him, and, even though he did not show him a sign or a miracle, *he rose and followed him*.[1] But the priests and the scribes were not converted, although they had witnessed many signs. It was appropriate for Matthew, together with the twelve apostles, to be judging the twelve tribes of the house of Israel.[2] *Our Lord came and sat at table in his house, and the tax collectors and sinners came and sat at table with him*.[3] The sick were with the healer, and those who were in the darkness of error [came] to *the Sun of Righteousness*.[4] Although Matthew was not as yet a disciple, he was [already] his apostle. As a bird [is used as a decoy] to capture its companion, thus did Matthew [serve as a decoy] for the tax collectors and sinners, his companions. He made them partners in the kingdom of heaven. The pharisees were furious when they saw that they were sitting at table with our Lord.[5] It was not because they had any respect for our Lord, he in whom they did not believe; it was rather that they might justify themselves. If our Saviour had been a [mere] human being, even in that case, it would not have been right for them to be furious.

How could *the Sun of Righteousness* be dimmed through association with sinners? For, if this same Sun was drying up the mud, without being polluted itself by its reek, how much more then, this Healer of Souls, who was calling sinners to repentance?[6] If God in the desert did not turn away his face from the sons of Israel when they were sinning and doing evil, but sent them down manna from heaven,[7] and brought forth water from the rock for them,[8] and quails from the sea,[9] and a pillar of fire by night, and the protection of a cloud by day[10] - he was not taken away from them - but was with them while they were sinning, and assisting them even though they were doing evil, how much more will our Lord receive sinners who repent sincerely unto repentance?

---

[1] *Idem.*
[2] Cf. Matt 19:28.
[3] Matt 9:10.
[4] Mal 3:20.
[5] Cf. Matt 9:11.
[6] Cf. Luke 5:32.
[7] Cf. Ps 78:24; Neh 9:15.
[8] Cf. Exod 17:6; Num 20:8-11.
[9] Cf. Exod 16:13; Num 11:31-32.
[10] Cf. Exod 13:21-22; Deut 1:33; Ps 78:14.

§17b.   He chose James,[1] the tax collector, so that his companions might be encouraged to come with him. He saw the sinners and he invited them to recline with him. This was a wonderful sight: angels stand and tremble, while tax collectors recline and enjoy themselves. The watchers[2] tremble at his greatness, while sinners eat with him. The scribes choke with jealousy, while the tax collectors exult because of his mercy. The heavenly beings saw [this sight] and were in wonderment. The underworld [saw] and was amazed. Satan [saw] and was tormented, while death [saw] and was brought low. The scribes [saw] and were incensed, while the pharisees [saw] and were troubled. There [was] joy in the heavens and rejoicing among the angels, because rebels were being reconciled and the rebellious subdued; sinners were chastened and tax collectors justified. He did not decline the cross of ignominy when his friends were prevailing on him, nor did he decline the company of tax collectors when his enemies were mocking him. But he despised mockery, and spurned praise, and through both of these he was effecting a remedy for humanity.

The Miraculous Catch of Fish

§18.   *We have been toiling all night.*[3] [This refers] symbolically to the prophets. His teaching came down from on high on the world, which stands by way of parable for the sea. *The two boats*[4] [represent] circumcision and uncircumcision. *They made a sign to their companions.*[5] [This refers] symbolically to the seventy-two, for these [disciples] were too few in number for the catch and the harvest.

The Healing of a Paralytic

§19.   *Our Lord saw the faith of these [people]. He said to him, Your sins are forgiven you.*[6] See what the faith of some accomplishes for someone else. For he did not demand faith of [the paralytic], since he was [like] a building that was in ruins. He was not referring to [the man] himself, just

---

1 In keeping with the Tatianic reading of Mark 2:14, Ephrem speaks of James, the tax collector, instead of Levi.
2 A term for "angels."
3 Luke 5:5.
4 Luke 5:2,7.
5 Luke 5:7.
6 Matt 9:2.

as he did not demand [faith] from the only son, but from his father.[1] Nor from the little girl either, but from her mother, *Even the whelps are satisfied.*[2] Therefore let us take care of the consolidation of our souls, since this is our edifice, so that we may not be paralysed, like him who was paralysed in his sins. The Word, which rules over all, took hold of him and purified and healed him. It purified him of his sin which was hidden, and healed his flesh which was visible. He [the Lord] was believed by means of what was visible, as also in the case of what was hidden; for he is God, too, in a hidden manner, and a human person in a visible manner, seeing that, because of his humanity which was external it was evident that he was a human person, and because of his greatness which was internal it was believed that he was God.

§20a.[3] *Your sins are forgiven you.*[4] These people were saying: "That he should say, *Your sins are forgiven you*, it is easy for anyone to say this; but that he should say, *Rise, take up your bed,*[5] is amazing." When *he perceived their thoughts, he said, Why are you planning evil in your hearts?*[6]

§20b. *Your sins are forgiven you.*[7] Which sins did he forgive him? Those sins which were committed against him [Jesus]. How [then] was he alien to the Law? For what did human beings owe him - either him or his Father - people who do not accept any activity on his part, either in [regard to] nature or in [regard to] the Law? But, [if the Marcionites were right], in the case of sins committed against the God of the Law, how could Jesus forgive them, if he had no relationship to him [the God of the Law]? Or, is this [not, rather,] evident that he is the Son [of the God of the Law]? Because the paralytic had committed sin through his body, he was punished through it, according to [the Marcionite] Jesus'[8] teaching. What

---

[1] Cf. Luke 9:38; Mark 9:23-24.

[2] Matt 15:27.

[3] §20a is absent from the Armenian version.

[4] Matt 9:2.

[5] Matt 9:6.

[6] Matt 9:4.

[7] Matt 9:2.

[8] The name of Jesus used here, ܢܘܣܝ, is based on a transliteration from the Greek, a form used by the Syriac-speaking Marcionites, but not preserved elsewhere in extant Syriac literature. The usual form, ܝܫܘܥ, is based on a transliteration from the Hebrew. This and the next paragraph are anti-Marcionite polemic.

do [the words], *Your sins are forgiven you*, imply if not that he was infirm and paralysed on account of his sins? Why would he have forgiven them, if the paralytic was not guilty before him? Or what use to him would it have been that *your sins are forgiven you*? For, if they were not forgiven him, they would not have injured him. But [the Lord] delivered him once and for all from punishment unto compassion.

Jesus Eats with Sinners

§21.   Following upon this [is the text], *Why do the pharisees and scribes say, murmuring the while, that you eat and drink with tax collectors?* [1] Our Lord replied unto these, *The healthy do not need the doctor, but rather those who are sick. For I have not come to call the righteous.*[2] This can be believed without any doubt whatever. Even if in Israel there were healthy and just people, the toil of Jesus[3] would not have been alien to that of the Law, he that laboured among people and healed and justified them. And if they were Gentiles, there too, in all kinds of ways, both healthy and just people were found in the world of the Creator. With regard to [the fact] that these were not in need that he come at that moment, [he said], *For the healthy are not in need of the doctor*, nor the just [in need] of grace.

Discussion on Fasting

§22a.   During the entire period that our Lord was in the midst of the world, he compared it to a bridal chamber, and himself to the bridegroom. *For the bridal guests cannot fast while the bridegroom is with them.*[4]

§22b.[5] *The bridal guests cannot fast.* He called his disciples *bridal guests* because they are members of the Church, and ministers of the feast, and heralds who invite those who sit at table.

---

[1] Luke 5:30.
[2] Luke 5:32-33.
[3] Ephrem again uses the Marcionite form of the name here, ܝܫܘ.
[4] Mark 2:19.
[5] §22b is absent from the Armenian version.

Picking Corn on the Sabbath

§23.   *Behold your disciples are doing what is not lawful to do on the Sabbath.*[1] But our Lord had instructed them in advance, and trained them in the truth of the just, so that, whenever he dispensed from the Law fully, they would not be alarmed. His Father too had dispensed from [Sabbaths], to show that [the Sabbath] was of his own making, and he was continuing [to dispense from] it, that he might show that these were discerning remedies, proposed by the skilled physician for the pain [which stretches] from the sole of the foot to the head.[2] *They were rubbing the ears of corn and eating.*[3] That is, they depicted a parable there, for the Law does not permit one to eat the first fruits until they were offered on the altar.[4] But these took the first fruits [reserved for] the chief priests before the harvest. The pharisees did not perceive that they should accuse the disciples over this, but [rather] that they were breaking the Sabbath.

§24.   Our Lord put forward the clear example of David, who was not accused either over this,[5] as he was over something else.[6] It was not permissible, he said, for David to eat [the holy bread] since he was not a priest. However, he was a priest, because he was a temple of the Spirit. Because they did not yet understand this, he openly proved them wrong with regard to their own [position]: *The priests were defiling the Sabbath in the temple, and they were not guilty of sin.*[7] Another element is depicted for us there. Before David was persecuted, he was not permitted to approach the holy things. But after he was persecuted, he partook of them with authority. So too, in the case of our Lord. After he was persecuted he shared his body among his disciples, and his blood among those who believed in him. *The Sabbath was created for the sake of human beings,*[8] since it means rest, after six days. This is why it is *for the sake of human beings.* This is why it was named thus. The Sabbath was

---

[1] Matt 12:2.
[2] Cf. Isa 1:5-6.
[3] Luke 6:1.
[4] Cf. Exod 23:19; 34:26.
[5] Cf. 1 Sam 21:1-7.
[6] Cf. 2 Sam 12:7-15.
[7] Matt 12:5.
[8] Mark 2:27.

106

not established for God, but *for human beings*. This is why he who bestowed it is its Lord.[1]

---

[1] Mark 2:28.

VI

The Beatitudes

§1a.   When our Lord gave the beatitudes he was looking specifically at his disciples. *He lifted his eyes towards them,[1]and began to speak, Blessed are the poor in their spirit.[2] The poor* [are those] who become poor of their own volition, and lest they become exalted by this poverty, he said, *Blessed are the lowly.[3] Moses was lowlier than the sons of his generation.[4] Whom shall I look at and where shall I dwell except in the lowly in spirit?[5] Remember, O Lord, David, and his lowliness.[6] Learn of me for I am gentle and lowly, and you shall find rest for your souls.[7]*

Blessed are those who mourn,[8] those who lament[9] because of their sins. Just as, in the case of those who rejoice in their debt, *Weeping and gnashing of teeth[10]* is reserved for them. *Blessed are those who hunger and thirst for justice.[11]* This is like [the text], *Hungering, but not for bread, and thirsting, but not for water, but rather for listening unto the utterance of the Lord.[12] Blessed are those who weep.[13]* This means that *if one has suffered with him, one will also be glorified with him.[14]*

Blessed are the merciful,[15] for, if one is moved unto mercy over one's neighbour, there will be mercy upon him. *Blessed are the pure in their heart, for they will see God.[16]* This is like what the prophet was

---

[1] Luke 6:20.

[2] Matt 5:3.

[3] Matt 5:5.

[4] Num 12:3.

[5] Isa 66:2.

[6] Ps 132:1.

[7] Matt 11:29.

[8] Matt 5:4. These lines on the mourning beatitude are absent from the Armenian version.

[9] The form ܡܬܬܢܚܝܢ comes from the verb ܐܢܚ, "to groan, lament," rather than from the verb ܢܚ, "to rest," which would require the form ܡܬܬܢܚܝܢ.

[10] Matt 8:12.

[11] Matt 5:6.

[12] Amos 8:11.

[13] Luke 6:21b. In the Armenian version these lines on the Lukan beatitude of weeping occur after the comments on "the pure in heart."

[14] Rom 8:17.

[15] Matt 5:7. These lines on the mercy beatitude are also absent from the Armenian version.

[16] Matt 5:8.

asking for in prayer, *A pure heart create in me, O God.*[1] Therefore, those whose hearts are pure *will see God*, like Moses.[2] Just as the pure eye is able to behold the dazzling light of the sun, so too the pure soul can receive the vision of its Lord.

Blessed are the makers of peace for they will be called sons of God,[3] because they love peace like him. When the angels were proclaiming good tidings, they said, *Glory to God in the highest and peace on earth.*[4] *He reconciled through the blood of his cross that which is in heaven and [that which is] upon earth.*[5] When he sent his disciples forth he said to them, *Into whatever house you enter, you shall first say, Peace be upon the house.*[6] *Those who make peace* are thus called *Sons of God.* This is like, *Those who are led by the Spirit of God are indeed the sons of God.*[7]

Blessed are those who are persecuted for the sake of righteousness.[8] This is like, *They will persecute you and hand you over.*[9] *Those who wish to live in the justice of Jesus Christ will indeed be persecuted.*[10] It was for this reason too that the apostles, when they had been treated with contempt, *were rejoicing, that they were counted worthy to suffer contempt for his name's sake.*[11] [This was] as he had commanded them, *As for you, therefore, rejoice in that day, be exalted and leap for joy!* [12]

§1b.[13] *Blessed are you when they will revile and persecute you for my sake.*[14] *For my sake* is to be understood with regard to all the beatitudes. For what advantage would it be to the one *poor in spirit*, unless he believes. Or, to the one *who mourns*, if he does not do this for the sake of

---

[1] Ps 51:12.
[2] Cf. Num 12:8.
[3] Matt 5:9.
[4] Luke 2:14.
[5] Col 1:20.
[6] Luke 10:5.
[7] Rom 8:14.
[8] Matt 5:10.
[9] Luke 21:12.
[10] 2 Tim 3:12.
[11] Acts 5:41.
[12] Cf. Luke 6:23. Ephrem's citation of Luke 6:23 attests an additional verb, "be exalted," between "rejoice" and "leap for joy." One could ask whether this represents his own interpretative addition or was intended as a part of the quote from Tatian? No variants of this kind are recorded in the standard critical editions.
[13] §1b is absent from the Armenian version.
[14] Matt 5:11.

our Lord; or, to *the lowly*, if it is not for the sake of our Lord that he makes himself lowly; or, to *the one who hungers and thirsts for justice*, if it is not for the sake of the one who commanded that he do this. Or, to the one *who is pure in his heart*, if it is not for the sake of the fear of God that he becomes pure. *For my sake* therefore extends to all the beatitudes. For no acquisition of glory can be of any advantage unless acquired for the sake of our Lord. *They will see your good deeds and glorify your Father who is in heaven.*[1]

The Woes

§2.   *Woe to you, rich ones.*[2] He did not become silent [after this] lest it remain [applicable] to all [who are rich]. This is like when he said, *Blessed are the poor*, he then added, *in their spirit*, so that it would not apply to all [poor]. Thus, when he said, *Woe to you, rich ones*, this [referred] to those for whom this was their only desire. The beatitudes were not promised as honorary titles, but are [realized] only for those who live[3] them. Anyone can acquire a title, and under any pretext. But the action implied by the title is close to one who is unwilling that an outstanding title should emerge in his regard. He promised each beatitude therefore for a corresponding action, and each gift for each one who realizes the action. A reward [is proclaimed] together with the labour, recompense together with the action, and punishment with the transgression. Just as, through the association of the sun with the eye, all that is visible between heaven and earth can be seen, so too, the Life-Giver is the light of the living. When he unites himself with intelligence, he raises it up to the heights and shows hidden things to it; and he brings it down to the depths and reveals secret things to it. Therefore, *You are the light of the world*[4] and, *You are the salt of creation.*[5]

---

[1] Matt 5:16.
[2] Luke 6:24.
[3] Literally, "who do them."
[4] Matt 5:14.
[5] Matt 5:13.

Jesus fulfils the Law

§3a.[1]   So that the disciples would not think that the perfect commands which our Lord was introducing were to dispense from the Law, he first said to them, "If you hear that I am setting forth perfection, do not imagine that I am abolishing the Law. Indeed I am fulfilling it." *For I have not come to abolish, but to fulfil.*[2] For the scribe who completes a child's education does not engage in contention [that he should remain with] an instructor, nor does a father wish that his son should always be a child. Or a nurse, that her infant should always ask for milk. Milk is appropriate in its time. But when a child has grown strong, he no longer needs milk.

§3b.   He said to the scribes and pharisees who were rising up and seeking a pretext [for accusation], *I have not come to abolish the Torah and the Prophets, but to fulfil them.*[3] This was fulfilment with regard to what was lacking. He made it known what kind of fulfilment this was: *Behold we are going up to Jerusalem so that everything written concerning me may be fulfilled.*[4] With regard to those things that were lacking [the apostle] said, *The former things have passed away.*[5] Concerning those things which have entered into fullness, and are absorbed into growth, and renewed unto excellence, he said, *It is easier for heaven and earth to pass away than that one of the signs of the Torah be dropped,*[6] and, *Whoever relaxes one of the commands of* the New Testament.[7]

The Antitheses

§4.   *Whoever strikes you on your cheek, turn the other to him.*[8] For someone to uphold *a blow for a blow*[9] is [now] deficient in that he has upheld justice in the time of grace.[10] *If your righteousness does not exceed that of the scribes you will not enter the kingdom of heaven.*[11] For it was

---

[1] §3a is absent from the Armenian version.
[2] Matt 5:17.
[3] Cf. Matt 5:17.
[4] Luke 18:31.
[5] 2 Cor 5:17.
[6] Luke 16:17.
[7] Matt 5:19.
[8] Luke 6:29; Matt 5:39.
[9] Exod 21:24.
[10] That is, at a time when grace has superceded justice.
[11] Matt 5:20.

said to them, *You shall not kill,*[1] but to you, *You shall not be angry.*[2] To them, *You shall not commit adultery,*[3] to you, *You shall not have evil desires.*[4] To them, *A blow for a blow;* but here however, *Whoever strikes you, turn the other to him.* He teaches [this] in another way, *When you are offering your gift, leave it and go, be reconciled,*[5] lest anyone might think that justice can be disregarded because of the offering, or that a [penalty] not be required of the one offending against it.

Unless your righteousness exceeds that of the scribes and the pharisees.[6] The Law commands, *You shall not glean the gleanings of your plot, and you shall not shake your olive trees a second time, and you shall not glean your vineyard, but it shall be for the poor.*[7] These are [addressed] to those under the Law. What, then, shall we say to those who are in Christ, to those to whom our Lord said, *If your righteousness does not exceed that of the scribes and pharisees, you shall not enter the kingdom of heaven?*[8]

§5.   *You have heard it said, You shall not kill. For the one who kills will be liable to judgement. But as for me, I tell you that whoever calls his brother, Fool.*[9] Indeed, this [epithet] is among the most base that one can indulge in against humanity. The untutored person is able to discern the course of the years, the wise person, however, the course of the mind. He wished therefore to introduce the full-grown to the company of the full-grown, that is, the perfect to the company of angels. In the presence of our Lord, the innocent are like the guilty. Consequently, each of these should consider the other in like manner. [God] gave freewill so that human beings might be in his likeness, that they might voluntarily acquire that which God possesses by nature. Take note that [Christ], who, even if he possessed it by nature, nevertheless conducted himself according to freewill.

---

[1] Exod 20:13; Deut 5:17.
[2] Matt 5:22.
[3] Exod 20:14.
[4] Matt 5:28.
[5] Matt 5:23-24.
[6] Matt 5:20.
[7] Lev 19:9-10.
[8] Matt 5:20.
[9] Matt 5:21-22.

§6.   *You have heard it said, You shall not commit adultery. But I say to you, that whoever looks and lusts after [a woman] has committed adultery.*[1] Because there were those who loved possessions, and those who loved luxury and evil words, our Lord said, *If your hand or your foot.* [2] If I have spoken to you even with regard to the limbs [of your body], how can you have regard for possessions or luxury or for words which are easy to cut off? For if, by the cutting off of a limb, you put an end to the desire for abuse and cursing that is in you, why then do you not cut off your tongue? For it is necessary thus to learn the solution of all pains from one of your limbs. Or concede that you have acted wickedly, or that you have not listened well, or that you have cut off the limb badly. Or, that you have understood the command foolishly. With that which you did not cut off, you accuse yourself that you have cut it off very badly. For you were afraid of the pain, and you preferred to break the commandment rather than lose your limb.

§7.   Let us therefore see if blasphemies cease through the cutting off of the tongue? And if they cease, whether those who do not cut it off do very badly? Or, if they do not cease, whether those who cut it off have understood badly? Or, how could our Lord have commanded that those limbs be cut off, with the result that the body perishes in their being cut off, but without the propensity towards evil being uprooted? It is not the good limbs which the divinity has fashioned that should be cut off, but the evil thoughts which freewill has fashioned. Our Lord also showed to what extent we should have to struggle even in this way, lest we be vanquished. This is [like], *Tear your hearts, and not your robes.*[3] The riches of that rich man were his right eye, and it caused him to stumble. But he did not pluck it out, nor cast it aside.[4] The right hand of Herod was Herodias, and instead of cutting it off and casting this unclean hand away, he cut off and cast away a holy head.[5]

§8.   Simon cut off and cast away all the limbs of the old man lest they be a stumbling block to him. *Behold, we have abandoned everything.*[6]

---

[1] Matt 5:27-28.
[2] Matt 18:8.
[3] Joel 2:13.
[4] Luke 12:16-21.
[5] Cf. Matt 14:3-11.
[6] Matt 19:27.

When you hear [the word] *everything* know that they did not leave an eye, or an ear, or a nose of the old man which they did not cut off or cast away. The eye is lust, which [is sparked off] by means of the eye; the ear is calumny, and so on. Paul understood from this, *Put to death [therefore] your members, which are fornication,* et cetera.[1] The right eye however is also love. For it is through love that [a man] desires a woman whom he has seen. It is because of this and for this reason, that this subject matter enters into the centre. The hand is [the instrument] of sustenance, and the foot a support. But the Patron[2] however did not speak about the tongue, since there are not two tongues in the body. Moreover, the tongue would not be willing to speak concerning the cutting off of the tongue. However, by its silence, it becomes the tongue's opponent, and has also spoken against it.

§9.   *Whoever calls his brother, Fool, or Madman.*[3] Take note therefore that it is not as you sow that you will receive retribution. For, if you say of an adulterer that he is an adulterer, there will be no reward for you for this, nor will he receive a retribution more than he is deserving of. But, if it is discovered that what you have said about him is not in him, he will profit twice as much on what he has, whereas that [Scripture passage] will come to rest on you, *In accordance with what he wanted to befall his brother it will be done to him.*[4] That justice which you were in a hurry to administer unto him for his debt will not be tardy in repaying you in accordance with what you have lent.

§10.   Thus, the homicide of the accused reverts back upon the one who accuses. So too, the adultery of the calumniated reverts back upon the one who calumniates. The idolatry of the Assembly [of Israel] has been called an adultery. It was not inappropriate that this calumny should have been called adultery, for this too is a [form] of fornication away from the truth. Examine these [teachings] therefore and see that they are all one. It happens at times that Satan casts an evil deed on a person by means of one of his members and knocks him over. It also happens that by the mouth of

---

[1] Col 3:5. See the note above at II, § 5 for comment on this type of indication of scriptural abbreviation.
[2] The term "Patron" or "Advocate" is yet another title applied to Christ by Ephrem. John 14:16 speaks of the Spirit as "another Advocate."
[3] Matt 5:22.
[4] Luke 6:31,38.

others he casts one of the evil names upon him deceitfully and renders him odious, inciting the calumniators to calumny and the hearers to believe it.

§11a.[1] *Do not covet.*[2] But the Law commands that you must not commit adultery.[3] *Do not fornicate,*[4] and, *Go, take a wife, an adultress and a fornicator.*[5] Our Lord however has said, *Do not covet.* If therefore there is nothing alien in [that which is] contrary to and a violation of the Law, how can that which is alien be designated in the command which is the perfecter of the Law? For adultery and fornication are contrary to the Law. The [command], *Do not covet* [therefore] is the perfection of the Law.

§11b. *An eye for an eye, but I say to you, Do not resist the evil one.*[6] When the times marked out for the growing-up period were completed, then solid food was proclaimed.[7] First of all the times of restraint were appointed, because it was right to separate in the first instance from evil things. When justice had reached its perfection, then grace put forth its perfection. *An eye for an eye* is the perfection of justice but, *Whoever strikes you on the cheek, turn the other to him,*[8] is the consummation of grace. While both continually have their tastes,[9] he proposed them to us through the two [successive] Testaments. The first [Testament] had the killing of animals for expiation, because justice did not permit that one should die in place of another. The second [Testament] was established through the blood of a man, who through his grace gave himself on behalf of all.[10] One therefore was the beginning, and the other the completion. He however in whom are both the end and the beginning, he it is who is perfect. In the case of those who do not understand, the beginning and the

---

[1] §11a is absent from the Armenian version.
[2] Cf. Matt 5:27. The Greek text of Matt 5:27 begins with "Do not commit adultery," which in Syriac would require the verbal form, ܬܓܘܪ ܠܐ (cf. Peshitta). However, in the three instances in which Matt 5:27 is quoted in this paragraph the verb used is ܪܓ, "to covet, to lust after," and the form is ܬܪܓ ܠܐ.
[3] Cf. Exod 20:14; Deut 5:18.
[4] Deut 24:18.
[5] Hos 1:2; 3:1.
[6] Matt 5:38-39.
[7] Cf. Heb 5:14.
[8] Luke 6:29.
[9] "Tastes" here refers to "meanings."
[10] Cf. Heb 9:11-14.

end are alienated, one from the other. In the study of them, however, they are one.

§12.   Therefore, this [principle of] *a blow for a blow*[1] has indeed been transformed, and, if [you strive] for perfection, *Whoever strikes you, turn to him the other*.[2] We know the first [Testament] in its root as water, but, following this observance, *Whoever strikes you on your cheek*, we drink as wine. One therefore was made for us lest we err and enter into estrangement, while the other was made for us as a help, lest we turn aside and engage in that which passes away. It was baptized as though with water which had become wine, and similarly [in the case of] all of the [new precepts].

At all times let us seek what is helpful to us, while distancing ourselves at the same time from the injury of others. With us is something which we do not reckon for ourselves. Everything should be reckoned by us [according to Christ's words] *For my sake*. It was *for my sake* that we were commanded to love those who hate us, and not for their sake.

§13.   Our Lord came into the world, and, as with infants, he enticed them with bodily gifts. He did not engage in any of the afflictions that the ancients inflicted on the people. When he attracted them, he brought them to him by means of visible healings. He began by mixing spiritual healings into them as follows, *If you believe*.[3] Because he was more perfect than all the teachers, when that which was growing measure by measure, and coming by means of the ancients, reached him, it yielded its fruit, mature in taste. [When] he was struck on the cheek,[4] he exemplified the deed with the commandment, and taught, *Whoever strikes you, turn the other to him*.[5]

§14.   Thus Moses led [the people] up from the level of iniquity and established [them] at the level of justice, "Do not strike your neighbour unjustly. If he strikes you, seek [vengeance] for yourself, but justly."[6] But

---

[1] Cf. Exod 21:24; Lev 24:20.
[2] Luke 6:29.
[3] Mark 9:23.
[4] Cf. John 18:22.
[5] Luke 6:29.
[6] Cf. Exod 21:12-14; Lev 24:17-19.

our Lord led [you] up from the level of justice and established [you] on the level of grace so that you would not seek [vengeance] from the one *who strikes you on your cheek*.[1] But [instead], *Turn the other to him*.[2] For why should the one who strikes a man, according to the justice of Moses,[3] lose that which he was taught, *Do not strike unjustly*? For, even if he receives retribution through being avenged, he is nevertheless not guilty, for he has not done evil. Why should one who, on account of adding interest to the capital sum, lose that which was not required [of him] through that [precept] of our Lord? Because he forgave, is not the recompense of the first blow of necessity kept for him, because he was struck? And the recompense of the second blow is his, even if he was not struck, since he turned [the other cheek].

§15.   Thus [the Lord] delivered from evil, as did Moses, but he did much more than Moses. Whoever avenges himself loses greatly. He did not wish that those loving things advantageous would be despoiled secretly, but through his patience taught them that glory which patience can acquire. How many were the vindicators [of patience], because it did not seek vengeance for itself. Indeed, when he was nailed to the cross, the luminary bodies by their becoming darkened became his vindicators.[4] See then, that even if these expressions seem to be at variance with one another, they are nevertheless bound together in virtue of gain. Let us begin with the first level. There is a gain for the one who does not strike his neighbour unjustly. There is an advantage for the one who does not seek to avenge himself in justice against the one afflicting him. But there is victory for the one who through grace resists a blow for a blow.[5] He has not done evil, and consequently is not guilty. He has not avenged himself, and consequently he will receive recompense. He gave more [than required], and consequently he will be crowned.

---

[1] Luke 6:29.
[2] *Idem*.
[3] Literally, "justly, in that of Moses."
[4] Cf. Luke 23:44.
[5] Cf. Luke 6:29; Matt 5:39.

The Lord's Prayer

§16a.[1] *One of his disciples said to our Lord, Teach us how to pray.*[2] *H e said to them, When you pray, thus shall you say, Our Father, who is in heaven.*[3] Let the one who calls God "Father" do what is worthy of God's children. For how can one who is a slave of sin call God, Father? Then he added, *Who is in heaven*, because we also have fathers on earth; but these are according to nature. He, however, is the Lord of nature, *To those who received him, he gave them the power to become sons of God.*[4] *Who is in heaven* also [means] that he who is everywhere is neither far removed from earth nor confined to heaven. But it was because those things which are on earth are corporeal, and those in heaven are spiritual, that he said, *It is in heaven* that our Father is.

May your name be made holy![5] [*Your name*] which is holy, even if no one acknowledges it to be so. But his name is [actually] blasphemed by those who conduct themselves in an evil way. But it is made holy and glorified by those who fulfil his will. This is [like], *That they may see your deeds and glorify your Father who is in heaven.*[6] *May your kingdom come,*[7] which indicates, as a consequence of it, *May your will be done as in heaven.*[8] As the angels fulfil your will, *so too on earth*, may you have sanctifiers. *Give us our constant bread of the day.*[9] For see, he has said, *Seek ye the kingdom of God and these things over and above will be given to you as well.*[10] He said *of the day* to teach us poverty [in relation to the things] of the world, so that it would suffice for our need only, lest, when we be anxious for a time, we might withdraw from godly intimacy. Therefore this *bread of the day* indicates necessity. He does not however give us bread alone, but clothing too, and other things, as he has said, *Your Father knows what your needs are before you ask him.*[11]

---

[1] This lengthy section in §16a is not attested in the Armenian version.
[2] Luke 11:1.
[3] Luke 11:1-2; Matt 6:9.
[4] John 1:12.
[5] Matt 6:9.
[6] Matt 5:16.
[7] Matt 6:10; Luke 11:2.
[8] Matt 6:10.
[9] Luke 11:3.
[10] Matt 6:33.
[11] Matt 6:8,32.

Forgive us our debts as we [forgive] our debtors.[1] Forgive people's offences and you will be forgiven offences against God. Give little and take much, as he has said in another place, *The one who has been forgiven much.*[2] [Because] he did not have pity on his fellow-servant, *his lord commanded* that the debt be exacted without mercy. He taught, *Thus will your Father who is in heaven do to you,* if each one of you does not forgive his brother.[3]

Lead us not into temptation, but free us from the Evil One.[4] A reward however is prepared for those who undergo temptations, for the Spirit is near at hand, as he has said, *But the flesh is weak,*[5] lest [temptation] might gain victory over the endurance of the soul, through the weakness of the body. Consequently he said, *Lead us not into temptation,*[6] lest, being unable to bear temptation, we might lose all fear of God.

"When You Fast"

§16b. *When you fast, wash your face and anoint your head.*[7] First of all, so as not to curry favour with people, in the hope that one's fast might be a source of glory. Secondly, he taught that through a secret fast one will please the Hidden Recompenser. *Lest it be known that you are fasting,*[8] lest the praise of those who know that it is a fast take away the reward of one's fast. *The Father then who sees in secret will recompense you.*[9] *Wash your face and anoint your head.*[10] For the word of God is inviting you to [this] mystery. The one who anoints his head is perfumed with knowledge [of God]. The countenance of the soul of the one who washes his face is purified from filth. Receive this command then within your members, and wash the countenance of your soul from the filth of iniquity. Anoint your head with holiness, so that you may be a partner of the Messiah.

---

[1] Matt 6:12.
[2] Luke 7:47.
[3] Cf. Matt 18:35; 6:15.
[4] Matt 6:13; Luke 11:4.
[5] Matt 26:41.
[6] *Idem.*
[7] Matt 6:17.
[8] Matt 6:18.
[9] Matt 6:17.
[10] *Idem.*

Integrity of Heart

§17. *If the light in you is darkness.*[1] This means that if you sin in almsgiving, which is enlightenment - that is, that which justifies - how much more in the case of the sin which is obscurity. Adultery and blasphemy have one dimension: they are causes of sin. Almsgiving however has two dimensions. If it is given for reasons of human glory, it is rendered sinful. But if the hand that gives is stretched out to a person in need, while one's mind [is turned] towards God, a reward will be presented. This is like, *Wherever your treasure is, there too will be your heart.*[2]

Trust in Divine Providence

§18a.[3] He also said, *Do not be anxious about your life, what you are going to eat, nor about your bodies, what you are going to wear.*[4] If anyone says, "See, these material things are needed also by those who fear God,[5] we cannot live without them," our Redeemer said this in relation to these thoughts, *Do not be anxious about your life, what you are going to eat, nor about your bodies, what you are going to wear. Life is of more value than food, and the body than clothing.*[6] Therefore we should not honour food and clothing more than these spiritual things. For anxiety tortures the soul, and the money that one accumulates injures oneself. For the body is covered, but the soul is without a body, so how can food be of service to it? If food is serviceable to the body, of what service is food to the soul, which is neither mortal nor visible and which is without a body? Take note that, when the soul goes out of the body, we clothe the body. But we do not give provisions to the soul without a body.

Just as our Lord was persecuted, and was hungry and thirsty, and in his actions was drawn into both contempt of them and honour of them, so too he wanted to convince his disciples about this fact, lest they be dragged down by the anxiety of the world. He wanted them to rely instead on the heavenly bread, and to reflect on what is above rather than on what

---

[1] Matt 6:23.

[2] Matt 6:21; Luke 12:34.

[3] This lengthy section on "Trust in Divine Providence" in §18a is also absent from the Armenian version.

[4] Matt 6:25.

[5] "Those who fear God" probably refers to some category of proselytes.

[6] Matt 6:25.

is on earth. So he provided them with this example, *Look at the birds of heaven*,[1] and, *Consider the ravens: they do not sow nor reap*.[2] If these, which fly in the air and are not concerned with sowing, are given food from God, how much more the human person, who both honours and subdues all that is on the earth. Thus the [divine] providence which is over him is greater than everything else which is under his power.

If the example of the birds does not convince you, how can you not be anxious so as *to add one cubit to the height of the body*?[3] *Look at the lilies, they neither spin nor weave, for not even Solomon was clothed like them*.[4] When he spoke about food, he included the example about birds which need to be fed. When he spoke about clothing he made mention of the lilies, whose beauty exceeded the clothing of Solomon's kingship. How much more do you exceed the birds in both value and honour! The grass does not move about like birds after food, but remains standing in its place, yet God gives it growth.[5] If it is even to this extent that the providence of God submits itself, why should you then, rational beings, be in doubt and anxious? *You, therefore, must seek the kingdom of heaven, and these things over and above will be given to you as well*.[6]

Nourish your soul with the fear of God, and God will nourish [your] body. Do these things, so that what you yourself are unable [to procure] may be given you by God. Take note of this, if God does not give the rain and the wind, it avails you naught, even if you are anxious. Obey God therefore, and creation will obey your needs. If God nourished Israel for forty years in the desert, while they were murmuring and disbelieving, and effortlessly preserved their sandals and clothing,[7] how much more so, in the case of believers?

Do not be anxious about tomorrow, for tomorrow will be anxious for itself. Sufficient for the day is its evil.[8] The evil which he spoke of is not that *of the day*, but of anxiety. For the example [he gave] of anxiety is [to be] without faith. If then the smallness of our faith does not convince that we should not be anxious for one day, we will have anxiety. But let us give that which belongs to tomorrow to God. This is [like], *Give us*

---

[1] Matt 6:26.
[2] Luke 12:24.
[3] Matt 6:27.
[4] Matt 6:28-29.
[5] Cf. Matt 6:30.
[6] Matt 6:33.
[7] Cf. Deut 8:3-4.
[8] Matt 6:34.

constant bread of the day.[1] *Who is there that, when his son asks him for bread, would offer him a stone?* cum ceteris[2]

If you who are evil can discern good gifts for your children,[3] how much oftener is the Father weighed down [by repeated requests]? Moreover, he proclaims [similarly], with regard to his Son, for it is a fact that *he delivered him over even unto death.*[4] God, who was weighed down by all these generations, did not hold his anger against humanity, but caused his redemption to shine out for them. He rewarded with life immortal those who were worthy of torments. He turned back those who were straying, and *he was found by those who were not seeking him, and showed himself to those who did not ask [anything] from him.*[5] If he gave eternal life to those who did not ask [anything] from him, how much more so to those who do ask him!

"Do Not Judge"

§18b.   *Do not judge,* that is, unjustly, *so that you may not be judged,*[6] with regard to injustice. *With the judgement that you judge shall you be judged.*[7] This is [like], *Forgive and it will be forgiven you.*[8] For once someone has judged in accordance with justice, he should forgive in accordance with grace, so that, when he [himself] is judged in accordance with justice, he may be worthy of forgiveness through grace. Alternatively, it was on account of the judges, those who seek [vengeance] for themselves, that he said, *Do not condemn.*[9] That is, do not seek [vengeance] for yourselves. Or, *Do not judge,* from appearances and opinion and then condemn, but admonish and advise.

---

[1] Luke 11:3.
[2] Matt 7:9. See the note above at II, § 5 for comment on this type of indication of scriptural abbreviation.
[3] Matt 7:11.
[4] Rom 8:32.
[5] Cf. Rom 10:20.
[6] Matt 7:1; Luke 6:37.
[7] Matt 7:2.
[8] Luke 6:37.
[9] *Idem.*

"To the One Who Has, More Will Be Given"

§19.   *To the one who has, it will be given, and from him who has not, even what he has will be taken from him.*[1] This is like, *Let the one who has ears listen.*[2] This is for those who have spiritual ears within the bodily ears, so that they may listen to his spiritual words. He was increasing his teaching over and above what they already [possessed]. But with regard to those who thought they possessed it, he took away that which they already possessed so that *what they see, they will not see.*[3]

    For why is it that *the heart of the people has become hardened and they have blocked up their ears lest they hear, and they have closed their eyes, lest they see with their eyes, and hear with their ears, and repent and be forgiven?*[4] How can one who is not worthy of what he possesses hope to receive what he does not possess? For there will be given to him who is worthy of what he possesses that which he does not possess. But, if he is not worthy, even *that which he actually possesses will be taken away from him.*[5] Grace is given to human beings in accordance with their power to receive it, so that the one who receives it may rest content in the promise of a similar [grace]. *For to the one who has more will be given,*[6] so that he may increase in it.

§20.   At present, anything that befits us will be increased in us, but if it does not [befit us], it will certainly not be increased. Thus, the spirit of wisdom will not be given to one who is foolish of mind, lest the light be diminished through such a one. But the Holy Spirit, revealer of mysteries, will be given to the intelligent mind, so that wisdom which blossoms forth may flourish in it, and the word which renders joyful may abound. We are borrowers; let us become absolvers of debts. If we acknowledge what we have taken, we will be given over and above what we have received. If however we become defrauders, let us not doubt that he does not have with him those things we have received. If we defraud what we have received while in possession of it, it will remain with him. But if we

---

[1] Luke 8:18.
[2] Matt 11:15.
[3] Mark 4:12.
[4] Matt 13:15. This scriptural quote is absent from the Armenian version.
[5] Luke 8:18.
[6] Matt 13:12.

give thanks and believe concerning what he possesses, then it will be ours [too].

To the one who has, it will be given him.[1] To Paul, who possessed the righteousness of the Law, was added the faith of the Life-Giver. Whoever does not even possess justice, since he is a transgressor of the Law, *even that which he has will be taken away from him.*[2] For the course of the Law reached up as far as John the Baptist. Furthermore, *the one, who has* that which he has, [possesses] the hope of forgiveness of sins.

"Do Not Give What Is Holy to the Dogs"

§21a.   *Do not give what is holy to the dogs.*[3] For, just as one who does not announce his Gospel is guilty of sinning, since he does not keep the commandment,[4] so too, is he who throws what is holy to the dogs. Even if the dogs do not eat what is holy, and the swine do not have need of the pearls, this kind of person is an accomplice of *the one who hid his master's money.*[5] One did not produce an increase, and the other did not conserve.

§21b.[6] *Do not give what is holy to the dogs, and do not cast pearls before swine.*[7] If a person persists in sins, and wallows in evil deeds like a pig in the mud, or if another impudently fights against the fear of God like a dog, in response to this [the Lord] commanded that you must not profane holiness by the tongue of the wicked. If they repent however they will be accepted.

The crowds were astonished at his teaching. For he was teaching like one with authority and not like their scribes and the pharisees.[8] For these were giving them earthly advice, as in the Law. But our Lord however promised the kingdom of heaven to his disciples. When the crowds heard the splendid teachings of our Redeemer, they recognized that those of Moses were shadows, and that our Lord [was] *the Sun of*

---

[1] Matt 13:12; Luke 8:18.
[2] *Idem.*
[3] Matt 7:6.
[4] Cf. Mark 16:15.
[5] Matt 25:18.
[6] §21b is absent from the Armenian version.
[7] Matt 7:6.
[8] Matt 7:28-29.

Righteousness.[1] For he gave health of body and healing of soul to humanity.

The Healing of the Centurion's Servant

§22a. [The centurion] came to him, with the elders, and was asking him to save his child.[2] When [the Lord] agreed to go, he said to him, *Lord, do not trouble yourself.*[3]

§22b.[4] This was a marvel that, even before the healing of his child, he set himself on an upright course and anticipated the deed through his faith, *I am not worthy that you should enter beneath my roof,*[5] like John who said, *I am not worthy to loosen the straps of his sandals.*[6] John was a prophet, however, and sent from God, but this man [believed] although no one had spoken to him, and it was not as yet preached that our Lord was God. These deeds of our Redeemer enlightened him that God had come to a human dwelling. *I am not worthy that you should enter my house.* "I am not capable of receiving *the Sun of Righteousness* in its entirety, a little radiance from it is sufficient for me to remove sickness, as it does for the darkness."[7] *When our Lord heard this he marvelled at him.*[8] God marvelled at a human being. *He said to those who were near him, Amen, I say to you, not even in anyone among the house of Israel have I found this kind of faith.*[9] This was to confound those who did not believe in him *like this foreigner.*[10] For [the centurion] had brought them, and he came so that they would be advocates[11] on his behalf. But they were found to be reproached by him because they did not possess his faith.[12] To show that the centurion's faith was the first of the faith of the

---

[1] Mal 3:20.

[2] Cf. Luke 7:2-4.

[3] Luke 7:6. This centre portion of §22, from the end of this quote from Luke 7:6 to the beginning of the quote from Luke 7:9 is absent from the Armenian version.

[4] §22b is absent from the Armenian version.

[5] Luke 7:6.

[6] Luke 3:16.

[7] The next few sentences are present in both traditions.

[8] Luke 7:9.

[9] *Idem.*

[10] Luke 17:18.

[11] MS 709 reads ܪܟܠܐ, "advocates" (which is also the reading of the Armenian version). In the printed edition (EC-FA, p. 82) Leloir has opted for ܪܟܠܐ, "sons."

[12] The remainder of §22 is absent from the Armenian version.

Gentiles, he said, "Do not imagine that this faith can be limited to the centurion." For, *he saw and believed.*[1] *Many will believe who have not seen.*[2] *Many will come from the East and from the West and will sit at table with Abraham, Isaac and Jacob in the kingdom of heaven,* cum ceteris.[3]

The Raising of the Widow's Son

§23.   The virgin's son met the widow's son. He became like a sponge for her tears, and as life for the death of her son. Death turned about in its den, and turned its back on the victorious one.[4]

On Following Jesus

§24a.   *The foxes have their dens but the Son of Man does not have a place upon which to rest his head.*[5] That is, there was no rest for his head nor dwelling-place for his divinity. *In whom shall I dwell if not in the lowly of spirit,* et cetera.[6] Perhaps, on seeing the dead raised to life, and the blind having [their eyes] opened, this [would-be disciple] imagined that one who [performed] such deeds would possess much money, [so] he said to him, *I will come after you.*[7] This is why [Jesus replied], *The foxes have their dens.* As for him, he had no possessions whatsoever; but the fox had its dwelling.

§24b.[8]   *Leave the dead to bury their dead.*[9] By this means he made it known that the father of this disciple too was a sinner, in that he said, *their dead.* Because our Lord had first seen him allowing himself to be caught up in the anxiety of inheritance, he prevented him in the first instance from burying his father, in order that he might prevent the death of his soul.

---

[1] Cf. John 20:8.

[2] John 20:29.

[3] Matt 8:11. See the note above at II, § 5 for comment on this type of indication of scriptural abbreviation.

[4] Cf. Luke 7:11-15.

[5] Matt 8:20.

[6] Isa 66:2. See the note above at II, § 5 for comment on this type of indication of scriptural abbreviation.

[7] Matt 8:19.

[8] §24b is absent from the Armenian version.

[9] Matt 8:19.

The Calming of the Storm

§25.   He that was sleeping was awakened, and cast the sea into a sleep, so that by the wakefulness of the sea which was [now] sleeping, he might show forth the wakefulness of his divinity which never sleeps. *He rebuked the wind and it became still.*[1] What is this power? Or what is this goodness of Jesus?[2] For see, by force he subjected that which was not his. By means of the wind of the sea, and by the spirits and demons that he silenced, our Lord showed that he was the Son of the Creator.

The Gadarene Demoniac

§26.   The Gadarenes had established a ruling for themselves that they would not venture forth nor view the signs of our Lord. Consequently he drowned their swine, so that they would have to venture forth against their will. Legion, which had been chastened, is a symbol of the world, whose tumultuousness is chastened by the One who raises all to life. If [the demons] could not enter the swine before they received the order, how much more was this so, in the case of the Image of God! [This was] so that these [people], who denied that [the Lord] could cast out [a demon] from one and make it enter others, might listen and experience fear. [It was also] so that they might know who it was that had preserved them secretly from the demons, that it was he who had commanded [the demons] to enter the swine and not the man. It was he, concerning whom they had said, *It is by Beelzebub that he casts out.*[3] He engaged in battle against Satan on the mountain and against Legion, the chief of his force.[4] *When they entered into the swine, at that very moment he drowned them,*[5] so that the force of the Merciful One who was keeping watch over this man might be known. *They were begging him not to send them out of [that] region and not to send them to Gehenna.*[6] He who said, *Go into the fire which is prepared for the evil one,*[7] how could he have cast out

---

[1] Luke 8:24.
[2] Ephrem again uses the Marcionite form of the name here, ܝܫܘ.
[3] Luke 11:15.
[4] Cf. Mark 5:13.
[5] Luke 8:33; cf. Mark 5:13.
[6] Luke 8:31.
[7] Matt 25:41.

[demons] by Beelzebub and promised him Gehenna? This [word] is a witness, *Lest he send them go Gehenna.*[1]

§27.   The Gadarenes drove out from their region the One who was able to drive out the demons from their region. Since the inhabitants of the region feared him, lest he cause the demons to enter them, *he sent that man away, Go! Proclaim!*[2] Alas for them, because from now on, the devils, who have been driven out from every side, will be entering into them. For they did not give him who banishes demons entry among them. Therefore, the ills of those who did not give the One who heals entry among them increased greatly. *They were begging him to go away out of their midst.*[3] If he, the Good One, had been the son of [Marcion's] alien [god], how could he have drowned the swine who were unclean to the Creator, and have obeyed the will of the demons, and have imposed a loss on the owner of the herd? And how could the demons have known their torturer?

---

[1] Luke 8:31.
[2] Luke 8:38-39.
[3] Luke 8:31.

VII

The Woman with a Haemorrhage

§1. Glory to you, hidden offspring of Being, because your healing was proclaimed through the hidden suffering of her that was afflicted.[1] By means of a woman whom they could see, they were enabled to see the divinity which cannot be seen. Through the Son's own healing his divinity became known, and through the afflicted woman's being healed her faith was made manifest. She caused him to be proclaimed, and indeed she was proclaimed with him. For truth was being proclaimed together with its heralds. If she was a witness to his divinity, he in turn was a witness to her faith.

§2. She poured faith on him by way of remuneration, and he bestowed healing on her as the payment of her remuneration. Since the woman's faith had become public, her healing too was being proclaimed in public. Because his power had become resplendent, and had magnified the Son, the physicians were put to shame with regard to their remedies. It became manifest how much faith surpasses the [healing] art, and how much hidden power surpasses visible remedies. Before her thoughts [were revealed] he already knew, even though they were imagining that he did not know her appearance. Nor did our Lord allow to be harmed those who were seeking a reason to harm, in that he had asked [who touched him]. He may have given the impression of not knowing, through asking who touched him,[2] but he was aware nonetheless of the hidden [realities], since he only healed the one whom he knew believed in him. First of all, he saw the woman's hidden faith, and then he gave her a visible healing. If he could thus see a faith that was not visible, how much more was he capable of seeing humanity that was visible.

Reflections on Physical and Spiritual Touching

§3. Although our Lord was presenting himself for the sake of expediency as though uninformed about matters that were evident,

---

[1] Cf. Mark 5:25-34; Luke 8:43-48; Matt 9:20-34.
[2] Cf. Mark 5:31; Luke 8:45.

nevertheless he revealed his foreknowledge yet again, that he was also aware of secret matters. How then [did he do this]? Was it not when Simon said, *People are pressing in and approaching you, and you say, Who has touched me?* [1] Thus, if Simon was showing our Lord that everyone was touching him, our Lord too was showing Simon that [only] one of all these had [really] touched him. Even if all of these were touching him of necessity because of the crowd, yet only one touched him of necessity at that moment because of suffering. Simon wanted to show our Lord how many people were touching him, but our Lord however wanted to show Simon the faith that had touched him.

§4.   Know therefore, that, while many had touched him, only one was being sought out of the many who had touched him. If all of them had touched him, and from these only one was being sought out, it was clear that he was aware of all those who were pressing in on him, for indeed not one of all these could escape his notice. Even if all these were indiscriminately touching him, only one of all these was being sought distinctly. It was clear that he knew them all just as he knew [this] one person, since he knew in her distinctness one who was not [distinctly] known among all of them. Many were those who at that moment were touching him, but they were touching him as a [mere] human being. Accordingly, the one who had touched him as God was being sought out, so that those who had been touching him as a human being might be reproved. He separated out from among them the one who had touched him along with all of them, and placed her in their midst, that he might teach all of them that he knew how each one of them had touched him.

§5.   Therefore, whoever touched him bodily perceived but a bodily sensation, but whoever touched him spiritually was able to enter into contact with an intangible divinity by means of a tangible humanity. Whoever touched him as a human being encountered the sensation of humanity, but whoever touched him as God encountered a treasury of healing for his pain.

§6.   If the afflicted woman had been healed and had gone away secretly, apart from the fact that the miracle would have been hidden from

---

[1] Luke 8:45. The reading here is the longer one (+ *and you say, Who has touched me*). Cf. Nestle-Aland's critical apparatus, p. 184 for the textual witnesses to the longer reading.

many people, she too would have remained spiritually sick, although bodily healed. Even if she believed that he was a righteous man because he had healed her, she would have doubted that he was God, because he would not have been aware [of her]. In fact, there were people who were touching the righteous and they were being healed, but these righteous did not know which among those who had touched them were healed. So that the mind[1] of the one who had been healed in her body might not be sick, he took care also with regard to the healing of her mind, since it was for the sake of the healing of minds that he also drew near to the healing of bodies. This is why [he asked], *Who touched my garments?*[2] He revealed that someone had definitely touched him, but he did not wish to reveal who it was that had touched him. It was not that he wished to deceive, he who, by means of this very [word], was seeking to denounce deceitfulness. Nor was it that he might avoid professing the truth. Indeed, it was [precisely] that people might profess the truth that he did this.

§7.   Why therefore did our Lord not reveal who had touched him? Because it was fitting that one who is healed should become a witness to the Physician, and that one who has been healed might bear witness in public to that power which has healed in secret. [The Lord] was in no hurry to bear witness to himself while he was present in the midst of his enemies, but waited for his work to become his herald.[3] His patience was encouraging his friends and denouncing his enemies. For it was through his patience that he brought the woman into the midst [of the crowd]. His friends and his enemies saw her and knew that it was she who had wearied the physicians, and she whom the physicians had wearied too. A power was sent forth therefore which emanated from him. It touched the unclean womb but was not ashamed. Similarly, his divinity was not ashamed to dwell in the pure womb. Whether within the Law, or outside the Law, the virgin was purer than she who was rendered unclean because of the flow of her blood. His enemies were being denounced because [their] freewill was very wrongly disobedient to him to whom the unrestrained flow of blood in nature was obedient.

---

[1] The Syriac word ܪ݂ܥܝܢܐ is difficult to render satisfactorily here. It can mean "mind," "intellect," "conscience," "heart" or "spirit," depending on the context. It is the wellspring of motivation and reflection, and contains a thinking dimension.
[2] Mark 5:30.
[3] Cf. John 5:31,36; 10:25.

§8.   His friends therefore were being strengthened by his humanity, while his enemies were being denounced by his divinity. His friends learned that, just as his power, which had touched the afflicted womb, touched it unto the womb's own advantage, so too, in like manner, his divinity which was dwelling in humanity was joined with humanity for the advantage of the latter. His enemies however were seeking *a stone that would give rise to stumbling against it*,[1] for [they were saying], "How can this [man] be one who keeps the Law,[2] since a woman unclean according to the Law, has touched him and he did not shrink from her?" It was not apparent to those who had closed their eyes with their [own] hands how that power, by which unclean things are purified, was not itself made unclean by their uncleanness. For, if the power of fire can purify unclean things, while it does not itself become unclean by them, how much more can the power of the divinity purify, while it does not itself become defiled by anything? For fire does not need purification since there is nothing that can pollute it. If there is room between impure and pure things, one breath of wind and one ray of sunshine strengthens them and mixes them together, so that it becomes clear that only that which defiles the norms of freedom is unclean.

§9.   Why then did our Lord say, *Who touched me?*[3] [It was] so that she who had become aware of her healing might know that he too was aware of her faith. By means of her restored health she knew that he was the Physician of everyone, and by his question she knew that he was the One who searches everyone, *when she saw that even this was not hidden from him*.[4] She saw therefore that even this was not hidden from him, since she had indeed thought to herself that she would be able to hide it from him. Consequently, our Lord showed her that nothing was hidden from him, lest she go away from him deceived. She learned through this therefore that he healed visible afflictions. Moreover, she learned that he was also aware of hidden realities. She believed that he, who healed bodily afflictions and probed the hidden realities of the mind, is the Lord of the body and Judge of the mind.

Wherefore, as though for the Lord of the body, she subdued the body with its passions, and as though for the Judge of the mind, she

---

[1] 1 Pet 2:8.
[2] Literally, "A son of the law."
[3] Luke 8:45.
[4] Luke 8:47.

refined the mind and its reflections. For she was afraid to commit any offence, since she believed that he could see her, he who saw her when *she touched his cloak from behind him*.[1] And she was afraid to transgress, even in thought, for she knew that nothing was hidden from him concerning whom she had testified: *For this too is not hidden from him*.[2]

§10. If [the woman] then, once cured, had withdrawn from him in secret, our Lord would have deprived[3] [her] of a crown of victory. For it was fitting that the faith, which had shone forth brightly in this agony which was hidden, be publicly crowned. Consequently, he wove an eloquent crown for her, in that he said to her, *Go in peace*.[4] The peace he gave therefore was the crown of her victory. But, so that it be known who the Lord of this crown was, when he said, *Go in peace*, he did not end here, but also added, *Your faith has saved you*,[5] so that it would be known thus that the peace which his mouth wove was the crown with which he crowned her faith, *Your faith has saved you*. For, if it was faith that restored her to life, it is clear that it was also her faith that he crowned with a crown. This is why he cried out, *Who touched my garments?*[6] so that all the people might know who it was that had touched more than anyone else. Just as she had chosen to honour him more than anyone else, firstly [by approaching] from behind, and secondly, in that *she touched the fringe of his cloak*,[7] it was likewise fitting that she be honoured before all of these, she who had chosen to honour [him] more than all these.

§11. *I know that someone has touched me.*[8] Why did he not bring into the middle by force the one who had touched him? Because he wished to teach concerning freedom of speech in relation to faith, for faith was stealing in secret and boasting its theft in public. Because he let go of his treasure in the presence of faith he was teaching faith to steal. Because he praised it after its theft he was enticing it to boast over its theft. For it stole

---

[1] Mark 5:27.
[2] Cf. Luke 8:47.
[3] Read ܢܟܣ, "deprived", in line with the Armenian version, and probably also MS 709, in place of ܓܠܐ, "revealed" in the the edition (EC-FA, p. 94). In the Latin translation on p. 95 however Leloir translates according to the Armenian!
[4] Mark 5:34.
[5] Matt 9:22.
[6] Mark 5:30.
[7] Matt 9:20; Luke 8:44.
[8] Luke 8:46.

and grew rich. It got caught out and was praised. This was in order to show how impoverished an abased faith can become when it does not steal, and how it is thrown into confusion when it is not taken in the act. Thus, Rachel was praised on account of the idol she stole, and was crowned on account of the falsehood which she devised.[1] Michal too, by means of her falsehood, sheltered David, and because of her deceit was invited to the reward of his kingship.[2] A marvel to hear about then! That while all robberies bring robbers into shame, the theft of faith is praised in front of everyone!

§12.   *Who touched me?* The Lord of the treasure was seeking the one who had stolen his treasure, so that he might reproach and confound through her those who were unwilling to steal his treasure, even though his treasure was given over to all humanity. Those who were lazy in their faith were tormented by poverty, while those whose faith was diligent were hastening to seek it out openly, and were in a hurry to steal it in secret. *Who touched me, for power has gone forth from me?*[3] Would not he, who knew that power had gone forth from him, know upon whom the power which had gone forth from him had rested? Or why would his power have been divided against him? Or his healing stolen without his [consent]? But, because there are roots which give helpful [remedies] without being aware of this, our Lord wished to show the one receiving [healing] that he was aware of what he was giving. He showed that it was not like a medicine, which by its nature heals all who take it, but rather he was healing with discernment and willingly all those who love him.

Elijah's Faith and the Law

§13.   This power then went forth from the glorious divinity. He healed the unclean womb of her who was impure according to the Law, that he might show that the divinity does not abhor anything with which faith is associated. Indeed faith is a tree upon which divine gifts rest. For, [in the case of] uncleanness which comes from the Law, when faith of the will is associated with it, even if uncleanness sets apart and renders impure, nevertheless faith sanctifies and unites. Even if the Law selects and rejects,

---

[1] Cf. Gen 31:19-35.
[2] Cf. 1 Sam 19:11-17.
[3] Luke 8:45-46.

nevertheless the will renders equal and reconciles. Even if the Law commands and separates, nevertheless Elijah believed and sanctified, not in contention with the Law, but by making peace with the Law. Elijah was not rebuking the Law, that it be necessary that food be declared clean, but the Law was instructing Elijah that it was not necessary that food be defiled.

For Elijah was not in opposition with regard to the Law, nor was the Law found to be an adversary of the legislator. Elijah knew what the weakness of the Law was, and accordingly did not conduct himself in relation to the Law as a sick person. The Law knew what was the will of him who had established the Law, and so dispensed or bound in accordance with his will. Even if Elijah received his nourishment from impure crows, nevertheless he observed all that he had received from God's mouth.[1] But their fathers, although they received to drink in the desert from the mouth of the pure rock,[2] nonetheless they were not willing to observe that which they received from the mouth of God. While Elijah was being nourished purely by impure crows, he was nonetheless being sustained spiritually by the pure divinity. But, in the case of their fathers, although their bodies were being nourished with the food of angels, their spirits were being brought up on the worship of a calf.[3]

§14.   When Elijah said, *I alone am left as a prophet unto the Lord*,[4] he was not calumniating the just, because they were no [longer] to be found, but rather he was denouncing sinners, because they had done away with [the just]. He did not wish it to be, therefore, that he alone be found just, and for this reason, he could not be found by them for three years,[5] for he had discovered that they were not worthy of being visited by God.[6] If the greed of the prophets of Baal was rejoicing that those eating with them at Jezabel's table were multiplying,[7] the persecution of the prophets of truth

---

[1] Cf. 1 Kgs 17:4-6.
[2] Cf. Num 20:7-11.
[3] Cf. Exod 32:1-35.
[4] 1 Kgs 18:22.
[5] Cf. 1 Kgs 18:1.
[6] Literally, "because he had found concerning them that they were not found by God."
[7] Cf. 1 Kgs 18:19.

grew white-haired[1] at those who were submitting their necks to the sword with them.[2]

Why Jesus Healed a Womb

§15.   It is fitting therefore that, in relation to these present words, we give thanks for the former words, and be silent. For this account was not our intention, but because of their tenderness these words call forth to their companions to come with them. What has been our intention then is this: *Who touched me? For I know that a power has gone forth from me.*[3] The evangelist has written [elsewhere], *A power went forth from him, and healed everyone.*[4] On one occasion only our Lord acknowledged that a power had gone forth from him. Why did he say [this] on only one occasion, if not because he had not encountered an uncleanness like this one on any other occasion? A distinct gift therefore went forth from him unto a known impurity. Our Lord knew indeed that he had come forth from a womb, and he also knew those who did not believe that he had come forth from the womb. Consequently, he sent forth his power into an unclean womb, that perhaps by means of an unclean [womb] they might believe in his own coming forth from a pure womb.

§16.   *Who touched me? For a power has gone forth from me.*[5] In no [other] place is there a detail such as this reported about our Physician. This is because in no other place did our Physician encounter an affliction such as this. For this affliction had been presented to many physicians, yet only one Physician encountered this affliction [to heal it]. For many [physicians] had encountered and wearied her. But only one encountered her, who was able to give her rest from the toil of many [physicians]. The art of healing encountered a shameful affliction, but added pain after pain

---

[1] This is a difficult passage to translate and interpret. The verb in Syriac is from the root ܚܘܪ, "to become white, to grow white-haired" (a root in which the middle radicle is consonantal). Leloir's translation ("was provoking to envy") is possibly influenced by the fact that the Armenian takes the verb from the hollow verb ܚܙܐ, "to see." Cf. EC-FA, p. 101, and p. xix. In EC-SC 121, p. 147, Leloir translates: "...ainsi la persécution des vrais prophètes excitait la jalousie de ceux qui voulaient soumettre avec eux leur cou au glaive."

[2] Cf. 1 Kgs 18:4,13.

[3] Luke 8:45-46.

[4] Luke 6:19.

[5] Luke 8:45-46.

to it. The more they came, the worse [the affliction] got.[1] The fringe of [the Lord's] cloak touched her[2] and uprooted this suffering from its root. *She perceived within herself that she was healed of her affliction.*[3]

§17.   Whereas the art [of healing] clothed with all our [practical] wisdom was reduced to silence, the divinity clothed with garments was proclaimed. He clothed himself in the body and came down to humanity, so that humanity might despoil him. He revealed his divinity through signs, so that faith in his humanity alone could not be explained. He revealed his humanity that the higher beings might believe that he was a lower being, and he revealed his divinity so that the lower beings would accept that he was a higher being. He assumed a human body so that humanity might be able to accede to divinity, and he revealed his divinity so that his humanity might not be trampled under foot.

The Sinful Woman and the Woman with a Haemorrhage

§18.   The hands of the sinful woman were stretched out over his feet, that they might receive a gift from his divinity.[4] Our Lord therefore showed his humanity so that the sinful woman might approach him. He also revealed his divinity in order that the pharisee might be found guilty by him. Consequently, the sinful woman could scoff at the cunning thoughts of him who had been scoffing at her tears. She, through her love, brought into the open the tears that were hidden in the depths of her eyes, and [the Lord], because of her courage, brought into the open the thoughts that were hidden in the pharisee. The sinful woman thought he was like God. Her faith was witness [to this]. Simon thought he was [merely] like a man. What he had worked out in his mind showed [this]. Our Lord therefore, standing in the middle, worked out a parable between the two of them, so that the sinful woman might be encouraged through his pronouncing the parable, and the pharisee might be denounced through the explanation of the parable.

But now, likewise, we are in the middle; and like Solomon we have fallen between women. But, even if we have fallen between women like Solomon, we are not, like Solomon, wounded by women. For these

---

[1] Cf. Mark 5:26.
[2] Cf. Matt 9:20.
[3] Mark 5:29.
[4] Cf. Luke 7:38,44-46.

Gentile women were turning Solomon aside from the fear of God to their idols by means of their allurements.[1] We place the faith of the Gentile women above the heroic exploits of the Hebrew women. For the latter, through the wholeness of their bodies, rendered Solomon's healthy faith sick, while the former, through their being healed, restore our ailing faith to health. Who therefore would not [wish] to be healed [by such faith]?

Physicians and the Physician

§19.   Her faith [was evident] in the flow of blood which had flowed for twelve years,[2] and, in an instant, as in the twinkling of an eye, it was held back. For many years many physicians had been examining [it]. For the many years of these physicians many were her expenses that were dissipated abroad. But, in the one instant of our Physician, her scattered thoughts were gathered together into one faith. For, while the earthly physicians were treating her, she was paying them earthly expenses.[3] But, when the heavenly Physician appeared before her, she presented a heavenly faith to him. Earthly gifts[4] were abandoned to the terrestrial beings on the earth, while the spiritual gift was raised up with spiritual beings to the heights.

§20.   These physicians were indeed provoking this affliction with their remedies, as though [it were] a wild beast. Therefore [the affliction] dispersed them with their remedies to all sides like a ferocious beast. While they were all hastening to flee from it, a swift power emerged from his cloak, grabbed hold of it, bound it fast, and was renowned through it. That [affliction], through which many had been brought into ridicule, was brought into ridicule by one. One Physician alone became renowned through the affliction which had been rendered famous by many physicans. For, while the hand of this [woman] had been giving much by way of fees, her affliction had not received the least healing. But when her hand was stretched forth empty, then her womb was filled with healing. As long as her hand was full of tangible fees, it was void of hidden faith. But when her hand was emptied of tangible fees, then she was filled with invisible faith. She gave fees that were tangible, but she did not receive

---

[1] Cf. 1 Kgs 11:1-40.
[2] Cf. Matt 9:20.
[3] Cf. Mark 5:26.
[4] Literally, "The gifts of the daughters of the earth."

any tangible healing. But when she gave a public expression of faith, she received a hidden healing. Although she had been paying fees confidently, she did not experience the reward of her fees, confidently [paid]. But when she gave a fee which was stolen, she received [in return] a hidden healing for his price.

§21.   These physicians were adding pain after pain to her, but without her being healed. [These] physicians were deceiving the minds of everyone by cunning persuasion, lest [their] healing art be reproached by anyone. But, because this [woman] had deceived the mind of all of them, our Lord persisted with astute questions, *Who touched me?*, so that faith might be highly esteemed by everyone, publicly. Those, who had not been capable of healing even one woman with their remedies, were now healing many minds through [their] defence. But our Lord, who was capable of healing every [illness], was not willing to show himself capable of defending himself with even one response. [This was] not because he did not know what defence to use, but because he already knew those who would say, *If you bear witness unto yourself, your witness is not true.*[1] Therefore, while his power had healed [the woman], his tongue did not convince these people. However, while his tongue remained silent over this, his deed was resounding about it, as though through a trumpet. His silence therefore laid [their] arrogance low, and his truth was being proclaimed both by his question and by his deed.

§22.   If there were [only] one meaning for the words [of Scripture], the first interpreter would find it, and all other listeners would have neither the toil of seeking nor the pleasure of finding. But every word of our Lord has its own image, and each image has many members, and each member possesses its own species and form. Each person hears in accordance with his capacity, and it is interpreted in accordance with what has been given to him.

§23.   One person therefore came to meet her and healed her, she who had gone forth to meet many who had not healed her. One person healed her as though in an offhand way when his face was turned the other way, so that those who had been attending to her with great diligence, but had not healed her, might be proved to be in the wrong. *The weakness of God*

---

[1] John 8:13.

is stronger than human beings.[1] Even if the human face of our Lord was capable of looking from only one side, his inner divinity was all eyes that could see on all sides.

When Faith Comes to Fruition

§24.   [The Lord] therefore sealed off the diseased flow of blood from her womb and the proclamation of her healing burst forth from her mouth. She drew near to his divinity and was healed by it, while his divinity drew near to her and was proclaimed by her. The rock in the desert issued forth purifying waters for the twelve tribes of the people,[2] while this [woman] issued forth blood for twelve years,[3] [blood] which polluted all the members of her body. The rock was split by the staff [of Moses], which was a sign of our Life-Giver, and the flow of blood was sealed off by *the outer garment of the clothing*[4] of our Physician. A hard staff then split that [rock], but a soft clothing sealed off [the flow of blood]. Even if the staff was hard to all outward appearances, nevertheless, the humility of the cross was hidden in it. Even if the clothing appeared outwardly soft, nevertheless a vehement force went forth from it. Such was this husbandry, that even before the seed had fallen from the hand [of the sower], the earth had [already] received much from the abundance of the seed. While this seed was in the storehouse of its owners it was resting, but when it was sown in the earth, it was constraining it to bring forth its investment quickly, and to return the capital sum it had received with interest. Such is this powerful seed: while it is hidden in his storehouse it gathers a harvest unto itself; while it is within the hand of its sower, as in the twinkling of an eye, learned harvests are reaped from within a discerning earth unto a perceptive seed.

§25.   *For a power has gone forth from me.*[5] He was indeed provoking them with this [word], those degenerate husbandmen who were leaving their seed idle in [their] storehouses,[6] that they might be confirmed in their faith in him. He also gave a pledge of his truth, for each one of the

---

[1] 1 Cor 1:25.
[2] Cf. Exod 17:5-6.
[3] Cf. Matt 9:20.
[4] Matt 9:20.
[5] Luke 8:46.
[6] Cf. Matt 25:24-30.

other seeds that had been sown had yielded a hundredfold to him in its time.[1] There are seeds that yield their harvest after [some] time, and there are others that [yield it] at the end. There are yet[2] {others that are sown and harvested at the same time. When [the Lord] said, *He will receive sevenfold at that time,*[3] these are [the seeds] which yield a harvest in a short time. And when he said, *Then the king will say to those who are on his right,*[4] these are the seeds which yield a harvest at the end. But when [a woman] *approached him from behind as far as the fringe of his garment,*[5] this was the seed which, when scattered, yielded a large quantity of fruits. To the grains of wheat which were sown in the heart of the earth were joined weeds from the thorns hidden in it, which grew up with them.[6] To faith, which remains hidden in the brave and daring soul, is joined the divine power which grows up with it.

The Woman with a Haemorrhage and the Daughter of Jairus

§26.   {When the woman with a haemorrhage learned that [the Lord] had said to the leader [of the synagogue], *Believe, and your daughter will live,*[7] she thought to herself that he who could bring back the soul of a little girl of twelve into her body would also be able to take away an illness of twelve years and expel it from the body. When she heard him say, *Believe firmly and your daughter will live,* this [woman] reflected, "I can give the faith he requires as the price." The healing came forth from his mouth and he negotiated as its price the faith expressed by the [woman's] mouth. He gave a clear healing and demanded a clear price. The healing which came forth from his lips could be heard publicly, and he required from the lips a faith openly [professed]. Although [the woman] had professed before everyone, they did not believe her, especially since her pains were hidden. When [the Lord] opened the eyes of the blind man, they called him a madman,[8] and when he restored Lazarus to life, [certain

---

[1] Cf. Luke 8:8.
[2] There is a lacuna here in *Chester Beatty* MS 709. The translation given here is based on the Armenian version, cf. CSCO 145, pp. 76-77.
[3] Mark 10:30.
[4] Matt 25:34.
[5] Luke 8:44.
[6] Cf. Matt 13:24-30.
[7] Luke 8:50.
[8] Cf. John 10:20.

people], even among those who had seen for themselves, did not believe.[1] This is why he restored the little girl of twelve years to life. He who was able to put the continued vitality of twelve years in the body back into its place was also able to arrest and banish from its place a flow of blood which had continued for twelve years. He who was able to alleviate one [illness] was also able to banish another. He who was able to vivify all the dead members of this little girl was also able to heal the [woman's] womb.

§27a. {When [the woman] had been healed, our Lord said, *Who touched me?* [2] so that she could confess her healing before everyone. So also [in the case of the little girl] he said, *She is sleeping,*[3] so that [the spectators] might testify that she was dead, and then, on seeing her restored to life, these scorners would be converted into believers. The witness [given] by them concerning the death of the little girl and her restoration to life performed by [the Lord] was a witness in anticipation of his death, so that those who would see that he was alive [again] would not deny it. [The Lord] therefore confronted them with this alternative: if they were to say that [the little girl] had been sleeping, they would be glorifying him against their will, since he had known that she was sleeping even before he had seen her, while the spectators had judged and affirmed that she was dead. Or, if they were to say that she was not sleeping [but was dead], her [restored] vitality would convince them that he was the one who had restored her to life. If they were to say that she was sleeping, the knowledge [of the Lord] would be proof to them that he was God. As soon as they would have rejected one [of the two alternatives] he could [then] confound them by both. If she had remained prostrate in a deep sleep how could she have been awakened by his voice only? *He directed that she be given food to eat,*[4] to show that she had recovered her health at the same time as her vitality},[5] not like the sick, who recover little by little.

From that time onward therefore they were even more confounded, for those who had doubted concerning [the woman] who had been healed were proved in the wrong through [the little girl] who had been raised to life.[6] Even if the healing of the womb was hidden,

---

[1] Cf. John 11:46.
[2] Luke 8:45.
[3] Matt 9:24.
[4] Luke 8:55.
[5] *Chester Beatty* MS 709 resumes at this point.
[6] Cf. Luke 8:40-42, 49-56.

nevertheless the raising to life of the [little girl's] body was in public. Accordingly, that [done] in secret was believed because of that [done] in public. While fearful,[1] *[she came up] from behind to the fringe of his cloak.*[2] If this [woman] was fearful and trembling in approaching his garment, how much more so is it fitting to be fearful when we approach to receive his body and blood, for this is the pledge of our life.

§27b.[3]   Why then did our Lord command those who were being healed to remain silent and say [nothing],[4] but in another place commanded the one that was healed to proclaim his healing?[5] This [instance], in which he said that they remain silent, [was] so that he might teach his disciples, lest they become puffed up on account of the healings they were effecting, and lest they boast or become exalted because they were being seen by people.[6] Because he was God, and was drawing them towards faith, he was doing this in the sight of everyone so that the darkness of error might be driven away by the light of his miracles. He was [teaching][7] the disciples therefore that they were [simply] human beings. [ ][8] He advised, *Do not let your right hand know what it is doing,*[9] lest the fact that he was God give rise to vain boasting. Furthermore [he taught them this] too, so that he might reprove the lack of faith of the Jews, for those who were healed did not comply when he commanded them to remain silent, but proclaimed him,[10] lest the grace which was in them be hidden. For the Jews, on seeing the signs, doubted and did not believe. Moreover, he commanded the leper who was cleansed to tell no one,[11] because the priests were envious of our Redeemer and were making little of the power of his signs. He commanded him to go *to the priests* and to offer *the gift* as [prescribed] in the Law.[12] He was to remain silent and not to say that [the Lord] had healed him lest the priests in their envy [ ][13] our Lord, and tell lies about

---

[1] Her fear is expressed at the end of the episode only, cf. Mark 5:33 and Luke 8.47.

[2] Mark 5:27; Luke 8:44; Matt 9:20.

[3] This section is absent from the Armenian version.

[4] Cf. Mark 1:44; 5:43; 7:36.

[5] Cf. Mark 5:19.

[6] Cf. Matt 6:1,5,16; 23:5.

[7] The Syriac text is damaged here, and the verb supplied is conjectural.

[8] It is not possible to reconstruct the next sentence with any confidence since the text is in a poor condition: "He was commanding [ ] weak [ ] and a soul which was full of defect [ ]."

[9] Matt 6:3.

[10] Cf. Mark 1:45; 7:36-37.

[11] Cf. Mark 1:40-44.

[12] Cf. Mark 1:44; Matt 8:4; Luke 5:14.

[13] The text is damaged here, and it is not possible to conjecture the missing word.

the miracle, saying that he had not been cleansed. This is divine wisdom, that when he was healing the body he also cured the souls of those who [could] see, and he was warning them in advance against the cunning of those who would deny [him].

VIII

Jesus Sends Forth his Disciples

§1a. *He sent them two by two, in his likeness,*[1] that is, preaching without a salary, as he had done. This is like, *You have freely received, give freely.*[2] *In his likeness* also [means] that they should preach the truth, and perform his signs, and suffer *in his likeness.* They were to depict him in themselves as in an image. *You shall not go into the paths of the pagans and you shall not enter into the town of the Samaritans, but go to the sheep that have strayed away from Israel.*[3]

§1b.[4] For he kept the promise which was with Abraham, especially that he might confute the cunning of the Jews, lest they say that they crucified [the Lord] because he associated with the Gentiles. He therefore restrained his disciples, lest they preach to the Gentiles. After they had crucified him, he commanded his disciples, *Go out into the whole world and proclaim my Gospel to the whole of creation and baptize all the Gentiles.*[5]

§1c. When the apostles saw that [the Israelites] were not being converted, they said to them, *From now on we will turn towards the Gentiles.*[6] [He also said], *Behold I am sending you forth like lambs among the wolves,*[7] to show that as long as the shepherd was with them they would not be harmed. To encourage them, [he said], *He who receives you, receives me.*[8] *You shall not possess gold;*[9] lest there be found a Judas among them. For [gold] also deprived Achar of life,[10] and clothed Gehazi

---

[1] Luke 10:1. It is difficult to know whether the words "in his likeness" constituted part of the scriptural text for Ephrem. Could it be some adaptation of the original [Greek] text, "before his face," which is usually rendered in modern translations as "before him" or "ahead of him"?

[2] Matt 10:8.

[3] Matt 10:5-6.

[4] Paragraph §1b is absent from the Armenian version.

[5] Matt 28:19.

[6] Acts 13:46.

[7] Luke 10:3.

[8] Matt 10:40.

[9] Matt 10:9.

[10] Cf. Josh 7:1-26. The MT form of this proper name in Josh 7:1 is "Achan," but in the LXX (B) the form is "Achar." The MT of 1 Chr 2:7 also reads "Achar." There is a play on words in Syriac between the verb ܥܟܪ (it deprived) and the proper name, ܥܟܪ, "Achar."

with leprosy,[1] and led all the people in the desert into sin.[2] He forbade them money lest they be considered merchants and not heralds.

§2.   *The staff*[3] [is] a symbol of simplicity and a sign of humility. That it was not a rod was because they were not setting out like Moses to pastor a rebellious flock.[4] See then, how, when the flock was incensed against its pastor, the rod was abandoned, and the sword taken up.[5] But here, with the flocks dwelling in peace, the rod was abandoned, and the staff adopted. Also, *no shoes*,[6] that they might become poor, but *sandals*,[7] so that there might thereby be [an opportunity for] reward for those who [nevertheless] honoured them. Indeed, [chosen] from all of that people, he exalted them and conferred the likeness of Moses on them, in this sense that, as Moses was carrying the bones of the just, [the apostles] were carrying the Body that justifies all bodies. If Moses, through the three names of the house of Abraham, reconciled God with the sinful people, how much more would [the apostles] purify the entire race of the house of Adam, [through] the three names of the divinity?

The Power of the Peace Greeting

§3.   *To the house into which you enter, say first of all, Peace!*,[8] so that, in the first instance, [the Lord] himself may enter and stay there, as he did with Mary,[9] and then they [themselves] may stay there as disciples. This greeting is his mystery in the world, and through it enmity is eliminated, war abated, and people mutually recognize one another. The effect of this greeting was hidden in the veil of error, even if it was prefigured in the mystery of the resurrection of the dead, which creation [symbolizes] with the coming of the light, and with the appearance of the dawn, which puts the night to flight. When people begin to give [this greeting] to one another and receive it from one another, [they do so] that it may heal the one who gives it and bless the one who receives it. But, in the case of those

---

[1] Cf. 2 Kgs 5:20-27.
[2] Cf. Exod 32:1-35.
[3] Mark 6:8.
[4] Cf. Exod 4:17.
[5] Cf. Exod 32:25-28.
[6] Matt 10:10.
[7] Mark 6:9.
[8] Luke 10:5; Matt 10:12.
[9] Cf. Luke 10:38-42.

who receive it in word only, and whose spirit is not sealed by his members, the [greeting] flies over them like the light, and departs from them, like rays of the sun from the world.

§4. This is the greeting which is proclaimed by name. It is hidden in power, disclosed by knowledge, handed down in a symbol, and is abundant and sufficient for each person. This is why our Lord sent it forth with his disciples as a precursor, so that it would make peace and prepare [the way] before them, while clothed with the clear voice of the apostles, his labourers. It was being sown in all houses so that it might gather in [all] its members, and was creeping secretly into all those who listened to it, to separate out all its kindred. It was dwelling in them, but making known those who were strangers to it, by passing over them.

[This greeting] therefore was never-failing, [springing forth] from the apostles, its wellsprings, in order that it might disclose that the treasure of him who sent it is without shortage. Accordingly, it did not depart from those who received it, that it might disclose that the promise of its Giver is true and trustworthy. It was present in those who gave it and in those who received it, without being either diminished or divided, thus disclosing concerning the essence of the Father, that it is present to all things and is in all things. It proclaimed concerning the mission of the Son, that he is present to all things entirely, and that his final end is with the Father. Because it is in the likeness [of the Father], it has not ceased to proclaim and is not tired of disclosing until parables are brought to an end by certitude, until images are determined by the truth, and shadows are put to flight by the body itself, and all symbols are measured and come to an end by the true representations.

§5. Wherefore we are sending forth the word [as] a coagulum amidst his listeners, his kinsfolk, so that they might be set apart by it and be gathered together unto it; that they might be set apart from divisive interaction and be associated with companionship which gathers together. It is fitting therefore that he whose crown is great should also [have undergone] a severe contest. Should this be achieved, the agony will be [considered] small when compared with the glory of victory. Error must not craftily plot to enter among us through our own weapons, since it changes its appearance to all colours and transforms its flavour into all kinds of distinctions.[1] For we are Christians, Jews in secret, circumcised in the Spirit, and blessed through a [new] birth, anointed by the blood of [the Messiah], redeemed in [his] name, and in full health through [his] healing.

When Ill Received

§6.   *Shake off the dust of your feet,*[2] to show that he will require vengeance of those [who receive the disciples poorly]. For [the disciples] will cast back onto these that very dust which adhered to them from the path; they will return it back onto them, so that these might learn that those who pass through their paths will return by them. Since these received the dust of the just, they will merit the vengeance of the just, unless they repent. For they were defiled by their dust only, not by their mire. *For Sodom there will be ease,*[3] because the angels who went [there] did not perform a sign in Sodom, but made Sodom itself a sign for creation.[4] These others however did see signs, *The blind, whose [eyes] were opened.*[5] But the angels in Sodom however rendered blind even those who could see. It will therefore *be more tolerable for Sodom,* [a town] which did all these evil deeds. The judgement of the city which does not receive his disciples will be more severe than that of [Sodom]. For Sodom sinned against angels, but [the city] which does not receive the disciples rejects God himself, *Whoever rejects you indeed rejects me.*[6] *Be as innocent as doves,*[7] so that they may acquire the simplicity of doves, but not their dumbness nor their silliness; and [acquire] *the astuteness of serpents,* but not their evil. Therefore, *be innocent in face of doves and astute in face of serpents.*[8] *Be on your guard against people,* not against those *who will deliver you over,* but against those *who come to you in sheep's clothing, but within are ravenous wolves.*[9]

---

[1] Cf. 2 Cor 11:14.
[2] Matt 10:14.
[3] Cf. Matt 10:15.
[4] Cf. Gen 19:1-29.
[5] Matt 11:5.
[6] Luke 10:16.
[7] Matt 10:16.
[8] *Idem.*
[9] Matt 7:15.

§7.   *Move away from whatever town you are not received in to another, and if they persecute you in that one, flee to [yet] another.*[1] [The Lord] did not extend this [word] to everyone, but to his disciples only, because it was the beginning of the new preaching, and these men were few in number. Lest [enemies] should band together against them and uproot their memory from the earth, and lest his Gospel be suppressed from the Gentiles, and his teaching from creation, he said to them, *If they persecute you in that place, go to another.*[2] If they had not moved away when Stephen was stoned, they would not perhaps have escaped torture.[3] But, if [the Lord] had extended this word to every generation, who would have borne witness[4] for the sake of his name? But to show that he did not exempt his disciples from this, take good note of how he again strengthened[5] them not to be alarmed when [persecution] should reach them, according to the example that he gave them in his own person. For he did not flee from his slayers, nor move away from his crucifiers. But he said to them openly, *If they have persecuted me, they will persecute you too.*[6]

§8.   *Do not fear those who kill the body, for they cannot kill the soul.*[7] We can see that, in the case of those to whom it was said that they should move away, each one of them became a sacrifice of praise in his own person, as a witness to all the Gentiles. Or, [he said this] because of the great power he had given them when he chose them. For at that time it was fitting, lest they become too familiar with [this] power. Consequently, when he was with them, but [people] had not received them,[8] they said to him, *Do you wish us to say a word, so that fire may come down from heaven and devour them?* [9] He therefore instructed them in humility and said, *If they persecute you in that city, go to another.*[10]

---

[1] Luke 10:10; Matt 10:23.
[2] Matt 10:23.
[3] That is, if the disciples had not left Jerusalem.
[4] To bear witness in this context has the meaning of undergoing martyrdom.
[5] Literally, "equipped."
[6] John 15:20.
[7] Matt 10:28.
[8] Cf. Luke 9:52-53.
[9] Luke 9:54.
[10] Matt 10:23.

§9a.   Because the disciples were thinking that he had said, "You must not go into the midst of the Samaritans and the pagans,"[1] and, *If they banish you from this one, flee to another,*[2] [they said], "Should the cities come to an end what will we do?" He comforted them and said to them, *Amen, I say to you, you will not be able to complete them all until I come to you.*[3] This referred to his coming to them after the resurrection.

§9b.[4]   [He said this] to persuade them that, as long as he was with them, not one of them would suffer on his account. This was in accordance with what he had said when he was praying, *While I was with them, I was keeping watch over them,*[5] and from henceforth, *If the Jews persecute you, do not be afraid.*[6] So that he might make them acquire endurance he said, *The disciple is not greater than his master.*[7] *If they have persecuted me, they will persecute you too.*[8] *If they call the master of the house Beelzebub, what will they call the sons of the house?* [9]

§9c.   *You will not be able to complete all the cities before I come to you.*[10] [This means] that he sent them to those cities to which he himself was about to go. Or [alternatively], *You will not be able to complete* [means] because his power will come to them after the three days of his resurrection, for this [will be] his coming. Even though he had said to them that they would be banished out of many cities, and that he would then appear to them, he did not do this, however, but anticipated their timidity by appearing to them after his resurrection. He appeared to them and comforted them, and he renewed them by his breathing [upon them].[11]

---

[1] Cf. Matt 10:5.
[2] Matt 10:23.
[3] *Idem.*
[4] §9b is not present in the Armenian version.
[5] John 17:12.
[6] Cf. Matt 10:19,26; John 15:20.
[7] Matt 10:24; John 15:20.
[8] John 15:20.
[9] Matt 10:25.
[10] Matt 10:23.
[11] Cf. John 20:19-23.

Whom One Should Fear

§10.   *Whatever I say to you in darkness, you shall speak forth in light.*[1]
That is, "Let what I say to you in secret be proclaimed at the top of your
voice." For he explained, *Whatever you hear in your ears, proclaim it on
the rooftops.*[2] Perhaps he was referring to the people [of Israel] as the
darkness and to the Gentiles as the light. [He also said to them], *Do not fear
those who kill the body,*[3] to show that human beings have power over the
body only, while God's power extends to the soul, which he can cast into
Gehenna. If you say, "How can the soul perish in Gehenna, since neither
power nor death have dominion over it?," and if you also ask concerning
the body, "How can it perish, given that there will be *worms and gnashing
of teeth* there?,"[4] this saying here illuminates this. For not only does the
soul, which itself is immortal, not die, but neither does the body die, since
it remains on without corruption. [The words], *He who destroys the body,*
refer to that temporal death.[5] If the body perished entirely in Gehenna it
would not be [there], for Gehenna torments those who are living, but
without the destruction of the corruptible [bodies].

§11.   Since many people fear corruption and shrink from this death,
our Lord wished to make use of this word, *One should fear much more
him who could destroy both soul and body in Gehenna.*[6] For the soul does
not return to mortality, just as God does not turn back on his gift, nor is
the true promise of the resurrection of the body ever revoked. *Do not fear,*
for the soul does not die. If it were mortal, however, it would be
appropriate to fear. Therefore, we ought [not] to be fearful concerning our
body which is perishable, since it is not the soul but God who is able to
repair its corruption. If it is he who fashions the body which is corruptible,
it is he too who can restore to life the soul which he created from nothing.
For God does not restore the mortal body to life by the immortal soul, but
by his own power. *Do not fear those who kill* your life in this world, since
they cannot kill your life in the world to come.[7] [This he said] because his

---

[1] Matt 10:27.
[2] *Idem.*
[3] Matt 10:28.
[4] Cf. Mark 9:48; Matt 8:12.
[5] Matt 10:28.
[6] *Idem.*
[7] The literal Syriac translation of "this world" and "the world to come" in this passage is
"down here" and "above."

disciples had heard, and were about to hear again from the Sadducees and from others that *there was no resurrection of the dead.*[1]

Two Sparrows Sold for a Penny

§12.   *Two sparrows are sold for a penny.*[2] Two [sparrows] and not one. [This was] because he wanted to show the worthlessness of a sparrow. Those things of greater value are sold singly, while those with lesser value are sold in bulk, such as vegetables. *But not one of these falls to the earth without your Father.*[3] If these sparrows, which are of little value, and are but shadows, are not captured - and he did not say, "without God," but, *without your Father* - how much more is the solicitude of the Father for little things an example for us of the providence of his great love for us?

"I Will Acknowledge Him Before My Father"

§13.   The [words], *I will acknowledge him before the Father*[4] are [like], *Come, blessed of my Father,*[5] and [the words], *I will deny him* [6] are [like], *I do not know you.*[7] They are not hidden from him, but he will not acknowledge them [as his]. For see how indeed he knows them, because he rejects them and does not receive them.

"I Have Not Come to Bring Peace"

§14.   *Do not think that I have come to bring peace upon the earth.*[8] How is this [to be understood] in relation to all those [other words], *He came to reconcile those things which are in heaven and those which are on earth?*[9] For he was proclaiming peace, as the apostle has said, *For he is our peace,*[10] and, *Peace is unto those who received him.*[11] But [from another viewpoint] he did not bring peace, in that those who believed

---

[1] Cf. Matt 22:23; Acts 4:1-2; 23:6-8.
[2] Matt 10:29.
[3] *Idem.*
[4] Matt 10:32.
[5] Matt 25:34.
[6] Matt 10:33.
[7] Luke 13:25,27.
[8] Matt 10:34.
[9] Col 1:20.
[10] Eph 2:14.
[11] Cf. Gal 6:16.

were separated from those who did not believe, *For I have come in order to separate a man from his father.*[1] [He was referring to] the separation of minds, since even in faith itself all do not think alike. One person worships [God] in a certain way, and by comparison another does it differently.

[He said], *But the sword,*[2] so that he might cut off harmful love from their souls with it, and shoot the healing arrows of his love into it [instead]. *Whoever wishes to find his life will lose it.*[3] How should this be understood, since the loss and the finding refer to one [and the same] person? The one who confesses [God] before his persecutors will lose his life, but will find it [again] with God. For he has said, *Whoever loses his life for my sake will find it.*[4] Whoever loses his life for his sake therefore will, of necessity, find it again, since God, for whose sake it was lost, takes care that it will be found [again]. For his hand is capable of attaining everything and his arm is strong to rescue from every [evil]. He humbled his love for everyone more than everything, so that the love of the Lord of all might be made greater than everything, *Whoever does not love me more than his life,* et cetera.[5]

Martha and Mary

§15.   *Mary came and sat at his feet.*[6] This was as though she were sitting upon firm ground at the feet of him who had forgiven the sinful woman her sins.[7] For she had put on a crown in order to enter into the kingdom of the First-Born. *She had chosen the better portion,* the Benefactor, the Messiah himself alone, as it is said, *It will never be taken away from her.*[8] Martha's love was more fervent than Mary's, for before he had arrived there, she was ready to serve him, *Do you not care for me, that you should tell my sister to help me?*[9] When he came to raise Lazarus to life, she ran and came out first.[10]

---

[1] Matt 10:35.
[2] Matt 10:34.
[3] Matt 16:25; 10:39.
[4] *Idem.*
[5] Luke 14:26. See the note above at II, § 5 for comment on this type of indication of scriptural abbreviation.
[6] Luke 10:39.
[7] Cf. Luke 7:38.
[8] Luke 10:42.
[9] Luke 10:40.
[10] Cf. John 11:20.

IX

John the Baptist's Question

§1. *Are you he that is to come, or should we await another?*[1] It was not that [John] had been in doubt concerning him. For he had prepared the way in the wilderness, and did not hesitate to exult with joy in the womb, and, at the moment of [Jesus'] baptism, did not grasp glory for himself: *It is fitting for me that you should baptize me,*[2] and, *Behold the Lamb of God,*[3] and, *He takes away the sin of the world,*[4] and, *I am not worthy to untie the straps of his sandals.*[5] How could he, who had proclaimed all these things in public, [now] change position and be in doubt about him? [Especially] after the testimony of the Spirit, *who came down in the form of a dove,*[6] and after the voice, *which came from heaven, This is my Son and my Beloved?*[7]

Let us say, rather, that what was spoken by the prophets was [spoken] by them for the sake of those who needed to hear [it]. For our Lord had also said, *It is for the sake of the crowd that I am saying these things, so that they may believe.*[8] So likewise, in the case of John, when he saw that it was drawing close to when he was to leave the world, and that he would precede the Saviour among the dead, just as by his birth he had preceded him among the living, he took care not to allow his disciples go astray and be scattered, *like a flock without a shepherd.*[9]

§2. [John] sent them to him, not to interrogate him, but rather that [the Lord] might confirm those former things that [John] had proclaimed to them. John was directing the minds of his disciples towards [the Lord]. When other disciples of his *had heard him speaking*[10] about our Lord, and had seen him, they left John without sadness and followed [Jesus]. Just as

---

[1] Matt 11:3.
[2] Matt 3:14.
[3] John 1:29,36.
[4] John 1:29.
[5] John 1:27; Mark 1:7.
[6] Luke 3:22.
[7] Matt 3:17.
[8] John 11:42.
[9] Cf. Matt 9:36.
[10] Cf. John 1:37.

[John] had shown his [good] will with regard to the baptism, in that he did not seek redress regarding the priesthood of his father's house, so here in this context he wished to hand over to his disciples a treasury which could not be robbed. Therefore he sent them forth in such a way that, having seen [Jesus'] miracles, they might be confirmed in their faith in him.

Jesus said to them, *Go and make known to John, not what you have heard, but what you have seen. For behold, the blind see, and the lame walk.*[1] That is, "If these deeds which I am doing do not testify to the words of John, then his statements are untrue. But since they are true, you must not go after a voice, but instead, be obedient to the deed."

Jesus' Reply to John's Question

§3.   Thus, [the Lord] began with those things which appeared to be of lesser importance, even though, in the case of the miracles, little and great are of equal worth. *The blind see and the lame walk, lepers are cleansed and the deaf hear.*[2] Finally, as a seal upon all these, he introduced *the dead are raised up,*[3] which is the most important of the good deeds of the Only-Begotten. This was a dissolution and an abolition of the evil deeds that Adam had introduced into the world.

Along with these, you should learn this: *Blessed is he who is not scandalized on account of me.*[4] Through these [words] he gave a sure pledge to the disciples of John lest they be scandalized on his account. Others have said that it was concerning John that [the Lord] had said, *Blessed is he if he is not scandalized on account of me.* We would maintain however that, because these former things were said with reference to the person of John, then, of necessity, in this case likewise, when [the Lord] pronounced the beatitude, it was spoken about the person of John too. It was not that he was in doubt over John that he had said this, but it was in order to warn the disciples of John.

It was not because John was lacking in his faith that [the Lord] sent back [a reply] to him thus, for those things which follow afterwards testify [to this]. [The Lord] did not make any response to the [question] which John had sent to him earlier on, but, *after those messengers of John had*

---

[1] Matt 11:4-5.
[2] Matt 11:5.
[3] *Idem.*
[4] Matt 11:6.

155

departed, he began to speak to the crowds concerning John.[1] [Jesus] did not wish to proclaim [John's] glory in the presence of the disciples of John, lest it be thought that, while extolling their master in their presence, he was [in fact] interrogating them at length.

John is More than the Prophets

§4.   *What did you go out to the desert to see? A reed shaken by the wind?*[2] This could mean that John was afraid of afflictions, and was bending to every wind, at one time saying, *Behold the Lamb of God,*[3] and at another inquiring, *Are you he that is to come, or should we await another?*[4] *Or a man clothed in soft garments,*[5] that is, a man of rank? But the first [passage] is explained by means of this second one, since John was not dressed *in soft garments.* Indeed the Scriptures attest concerning him that *he was clothed in a rough garment of camel-hair.*[6] So too, in the case of the reed. It is not [to be understood] literally. For he believed, and did not doubt. He was not like a hollow reed, and he was not dressed *in soft garments. Such men [live] in the palaces of kings*[7] and not in the desert. *Indeed he is a prophet, and more than the prophets.*[8] For the prophets foretold concerning the coming of the king, whereas John alone was worthy to say, "This is he concerning whom the prophets foretold." If, therefore, *he is more than the prophets,* he is not *a reed which is shaken by the wind.*

§5.   John, seeing that he had completed the course of his life, handed over his flock to the Chief Shepherd. This was like his Lord who, when dying, handed over his flock to the chief pastor whose mouth had confessed him and whose tears were a pledge. [Thus] did the Shepherd make known to his flock his care for it. [The Lord] did not finally hand over his little flock to its pastor until he had received genuine pledges. He received the threefold [confession] that [Simon] had professed as

---

[1] Luke 7:24.
[2] Matt 11:7.
[3] John 1:29,36.
[4] Matt 11:3.
[5] Luke 7:25.
[6] Matt 3:4.
[7] Matt 11:8.
[8] Matt 11:9.

trustworthy pledges for the three [denials].[1] Therefore, when his Master said [to him], *Do you love me?*,[2] our Lord was wanting to receive from him his true love, so that, after having given the pledge of his love, [Simon] might receive [Jesus'] sheep as a flock. When [the Lord] saw that his mouth was confessing, and that his tears were a seal, he gave him the reward reserved for pastors, namely, death, since this is the crown of victory of the pastors, and their shepherds. [The Lord] was not able to give Simon the allotted portion of death until he had received from him [the pledge of] his love. For, in like manner, our Lord would not have given his life for his little flock if it had not been on account of his love for it.[3]

§6.   John perceived, therefore, by means of the Spirit which was upon him, when it was that our Lord [could exercise] the power of healing. For while our Lord possessed this power at all times, those who wished to be healed did not possess faith in him at all times. Consequently [John] sent [his disciples] to him at the moment when all these were receiving proof that he was the true [Messiah].[4] Consequently, he who sent showed that he was committing his little flock into the hand which rules over all, so that this flock might be comforted and this shepherd show his strength. Our Lord testified that John had not been in doubt [when he said], *This man is greater than the prophets*.[5] If John *is greater than the prophets*, how great must his honour be, since prophecy is an exalted rank among human beings? Perhaps it was because of his priesthood [that the Lord spoke thus]? But there were [other] priests. Or, because of his righteousness? But there were [other] righteous men.

No One Was Greater than John

§7.   What then was this greatness by which he surpassed *all those born of women*? Was it not [what the prophet said], *Behold I am sending my angel before you*?[6] He was not called angel by name only, but also because of his manner of life. If you examine carefully, his honour was not inferior to that of the angels, for he disdained all worldly things, and was

---

[1] Cf. John 21:15-17. The text is very succinct here in its allusion to the parallelism between Simon Peter's threefold denial and his threefold profession of faith.
[2] John 21:17.
[3] Cf. John 10:11,15.
[4] Literally, "the proof of his truth."
[5] Cf. Matt 11:9.
[6] Mal 3:1; Matt 11:10.

attentive to those of heaven. If you say that one of the twelve prophets was called *My Angel*,[1] well, he was [only] named thus by his parents, just as all other names [are usually given]. The name [given] by one's parents is one thing, but the honour [given] by God as a reward for one's actions is quite another. If [you say] he was named *My Angel* by his parents by supernal dispensation, we will not dispute this. But [the Lord] bore witness concerning John, *There is none among those born of women greater than he*.[2] If anyone becomes a holy man, he is glorified, and if anyone becomes just, he is honoured; and if anyone becomes strong and wise, he is worthy of a [further] degree of glory. Now, if all these were to be assembled together and dwell simultaneously in the one person, they could not be compared with one who loves God and is known by him. For whoever is like this surpasses human beings and stands in the category of angels.

§8.   *But he who is least in the kingdom of heaven is greater than he*.[3] Again, those who do not understand say that the least of the faithful in the kingdom of heaven is greater than John. But let us not speak thus about John, the holy one of God. For, whoever dishonours the king's attendant refuses honour to the king himself, and whoever despises the priest shows contempt for his Lord. [The Lord] wanted to proclaim his marvellous grace through what he had said concerning John's greatness, since he has prepared these good things for his chosen ones. For, even if it is to this degree that John is great and famous, nevertheless, compared with the least in the kingdom, his honour is less. [This is] in accordance with what the apostle has said, *We know only a little, and partially, and we prophesy only a little and partially*.[4] He also said, *We see as in a mirror*,[5] and, *When perfection comes, that which was imperfect will come to an end*.[6]

§9.   John was great, because he recognized [him] and said, *Behold the Lamb of God*.[7] But this greatness, when [compared] to the glory that is to be revealed to those who are worthy, is but a tiny taste. [The words of the Lord] do not mean that, when John would have departed [from this life],

---

[1] Malachi means "My Angel" or "My Messenger."
[2] Matt 11:11; Luke 7:28.
[3] Matt 11:11.
[4] 1 Cor 13:9.
[5] 1 Cor 13:12.
[6] 1 Cor 13:10.
[7] John 1:29,36.

then the least in the kingdom would be greater than he. [They mean] rather that all the great and wonderful things of here below, when compared with those good things of up above, appear in their weakness, and are found to be as nothing. This is [why he said], *The least in the kingdom of heaven is greater than he.*[1]

§10. Others say that, if *there is none among those born of women like John*, what about the fact that our Lord was born, and our Lord is [obviously] greater than John? But, our Lord was not speaking of himself, or comparing himself with those to whom he was referring. For he was the son of a virgin and not the son of a marriage union. Therefore, *the least in the kingdom* is neither Jesus nor any other person[2] {specifically designated. It is a general formula extending to everyone. Yet others think that it was spoken with regard to Elijah.

§11. {Rather, let us say that John was found worthy of the great gifts of this world,[3] prophecy, priesthood and justice. [The Lord] said, "This praiseworthy, great, beneficent and just man, whom the heavenly Father has sent you, and who is greater than [everyone] because of his knowledge and faith, is less important than the least in the kingdom." Yet [others] say that, in order to snatch [John] out of prison, [the Lord] spoke of the prophecy of the prophets, *There is none among those born of women greater than John.*[4] He calls *those born of women* the prophets, in saying, *The Law and the Prophets were until John.*[5] Therefore John is greater than Moses and the prophets. From this it is clear that the Law is in need of the New Testament, since he who is greater than the prophets said [to the Lord], *It is fitting for me [to be baptized].*[6]

§12. {[John] is great also because he was conceived through a gift, born through miracles, foretold the Life-Giver and because he baptized for the remission of sins. For he who was preaching the remissions of sins was loosening the bonds of the Law, avenger of sins. This is why *there is none*

---

[1] Matt 11:11.
[2] There is a lacuna of one folio here in *Chester Beatty* MS 709. The above rendering is based on the Armenian version, cf. CSCO 145, pp. 90-91.
[3] Literally, "of here below."
[4] Matt 11:11; Luke 7:28.
[5] Luke 16:16.
[6] Matt 3:14.

among those born of women greater than he,[1] because he preached the remission of the punishment through which the Law showed itself. When he who was greater than the prophets came, he loosened [the bonds of the Law] to inaugurate through grace that which was greater [than the Law]. John loosened [the bonds of] the Law and our Lord loosened [the bonds of] the death of John.

See how we are delivered from two sentences, one of nature and the other of legislation. Faith precedes us and patience follows us, so that patience can accomplish what faith has promised. Good things were contained in the mouth of Elijah, for his mouth was the gate of good things. Likewise John's mouth effected binding and loosening. It corrected sins through remission and sanctified the waters unto expiation. Moses led the people as far as the Jordan, while the Law led the human race as far as the baptism of John.

§13.   {If *there is none among those born of women greater than John,* who came before the face [of the Lord], how much greater are those whose feet [the Lord] washed, and upon whom he breathed his Spirit? If John was great because he baptized [the Lord], how much greater was he *who rested on his breast*?[2] He even honoured the place and number [of the apostles] through Judas, the traitor whom he washed. Since John was greater than everyone who was born because he baptized [the Lord], the apostles were even greater than he because [the Lord] washed their feet.[3] Therefore, *it would have been better* for Judas *not to have been born,*[4] because he had acted wickedly towards him who had made him greater than John. [John] was greater than [everyone] born, but the least who was to take the place of Judas was greater than he. Just as this latter person inherited the throne of the former, so too [he inherited] his washing. *If there is a son of peace there,* he said, *otherwise your greeting will return upon yourselves.*[5]

§14.   {Thus he said, *There is none born of women,*[6] to show that he was speaking of [John's] predecessors. For he had already made reference to [his] predecessors, to the prophets, the heralds and the preachers. But he

---

[1] Matt 11:11.
[2] Cf. John 13:23-25; 21:20.
[3] Cf. John 13:1-15.
[4] Matt 26:24.
[5] Luke 10:6; Matt 10:13.
[6] Matt 11:11.

revealed in the case of the latter heralds, who were baptizing in the Spirit, that they were greater than he who had baptized with water. *He must increase and I must decrease.*}[1] Our Lord therefore was honoured by his apostles, for *it was not by measure*[2] *that he [God] gave to his Son.*[3] Just as Moses was greater than everyone else, so too the apostles [were greater] than everyone else. If John was honoured for having prepared [the way] before the face of our Lord,[4] how much greater [will it be for] those whom our Lord served and before whom he prepared the way? *Know that they have hated me before you.*[5] All that he taught in the world he first accomplished [himself]. They will indeed do and *observe all that I have commanded you.*[6] If John was honoured for having prepared [the way] for his humble coming, how much more will the apostles be honoured, who went forth and prepared paths before his great coming?

§14a.[7] *There is none [greater] among those born of women.*[8] With regard to the prophets, he was more eminent than they, although born of a woman. He is less than those born of the Spirit, concerning whom the evangelist has said, *To those who received him he gave them the power to become sons of God.*[9] For John [preached] a baptism of repentance, but these a baptism for the remission of sins.

§15.   John is great, therefore, because he baptized [the Lord]. For, if *the prophets desired to see with their own eyes,*[10] and [if] the privilege of

---

[1] John 3:30. *Chester Beatty* MS 709 resumes at this point.

[2] The Armenian reading, "by measure" [cf. ܟܕܘܒܬܐ], is followed here, in preference to the Syriac, "of necessity / by pretext" [ܒܥܠܬܐ], since the latter seems to be a textual corruption. Cf. Leloir, EC-CBM 8, p. 29.

[3] This is also the Old Syriac (C) reading [ܕܠܐ ܗܘܐ ܓܝܪ ܒܟܝܠܬܐ ܝܗܒ ܐܝܟ ܐܠܒܪܗ] of John 3:34. The reading of S in the Old Syriac differs slightly from that of C in that it does not read "to his Son" at the end of v. 34, but at the beginning of v. 35 ("For God the Father did not give by measure, but to his Son [whom] he loves, and he gave everything into his hands"). Leloir lists the reading "his Son" in place of "the Spirit" in this text of Ephrem among those which are possibly "Tatianic," not in the sense that Tatian would have necessarily been their author, but that they were crystallized in the Diatessaron and influenced later writings (cf. *Témoignage*, p. 237 f.).

[4] Cf. Mal 3:1; Matt 11:10.

[5] John 15:18.

[6] Matt 28:20.

[7] This section is missing from the Armenian translation.

[8] Matt 11:11; Luke 7:28.

[9] John 1:12.

[10] Cf. Matt 13:17.

seeing with their own eyes was granted to the apostles, how much greater then is the one who actually baptized him. For each one hears [this] word according as he wishes. [The Lord] did say that [John] was more eminent than the prophets, and he called the prophets *born of women. The least of these latter who preach the kingdom of heaven is greater than he.*[1] But, [if] John is great through the baptism [of the Lord], the least of those chosen for apostleship is greater than he. This greatness that John received, which was greater than that of the prophets, [came] not from his [own] freewill but from him who made him great.[2] The *least* of humanity, if willing to enter[3] the kingdom of heaven, is *greater than he. For everyone will receive his reward in accordance with his labour.*[4]

It may be that the apostles were great by reason of [their] having been chosen, and the prophets through those things which were required [of them]. Let it be apparent, nonetheless, who it is that has toiled much. This is not something hidden, for it is through this that a person gains distinction and recognition, namely: that one person has worked more than another.[5] Indeed it is in this that greatness consists, even if there is one who is senior to him in rank.

§16.   The human mind hastily concluded that there was none greater than John the Baptist, not even in the kingdom. [The Lord therefore] resolved it for them with one of those [words] that are Scripture. For, if you make him greater than his predecessors because he baptized our Lord, he would be greater too than those after him. If greatness on earth were to render one great in heaven, what greatness was there to be seen therefore in the case of John? Would not the crown of the cross have been greater? For, even in this world [today], people continue to be crucified.

Inquire then as to what was John's greatness with which our Lord honoured him. See, a door will be opened to you to allow you to understand that he was speaking of the relation between being chosen and freewill. Even though [John] was great because he was chosen, yet one who

---

[1] Matt 11:11.

[2] According to Ephrem, John's greatness seems to have consisted in his having been chosen, rather than in any free choice exercised by John. "The least in the kingdom" by contrast must exercise some degree of freewill in following the Lord to attain to greatness. He develops this idea further in §§16-17.

[3] Read ܠܡܥܠ, "to enter" in line with the Armenian version, in place of ܠܡܠܐܐ, "to labour" in the Syriac.

[4] 1 Cor 3:8.

[5] These comments may contain an allusion to the parables of either Matt 20:1-16 or 25:14-30.

toils more than he is greater than he. That which rendered John greater than those who came before him, is [the same as] that which rendered him greater than those who came after him. Through that which rendered him greater than those who came both before and after him, he is inferior to those who are great through their free choice, to the extent that they exercise [it]. It is not because of his deeds that John is inferior. But rather, this election to prophecy or to the kingdom, which renders great down here, is inferior to the election of freewill which renders great in the kingdom. The honour of one who is chosen for the kingdom through [the exercise of] his own will is greater than that of one who is chosen by a different will. Wherefore he said, *Amen, I say to you, there is none greater among those born of women than John.*[1] John was not great because of his [own] deeds. The greatness associated with the kingdom of heaven is [the greatness] of deeds.

§17.   Since the listeners were astonished and disappointed, [the Lord] comforted them, [telling them] that their having been chosen was greater than that of [John]. For once chosen, they thought that their greatness in heaven would be in accordance with their having been chosen down here. They were saying, *Who will be greatest in the kingdom?* [2] Our Lord put this being chosen that they were talking about to one side, and introduced that of freewill: *Whoever humbles himself.*[3] So that he might put it aside all the more, [he indicated that], even if Simon were great through his having been chosen, the other disciple whose name is not even spoken, [the one] *who rested on his breast*, [was also great].[4] He, who had acquired two names, one Simon, the other Cephas, had need of [this freedom]. Moreover, [in the case of] the disciple whose blessedness was increased, was it not increased because of his deeds?[5] But, in that parable of the vineyard, [are the words], *The last shall be first*,[6] [to be understood] by reason of their deeds or because of grace? For, when he reveals his grace, his justice perishes, *The first shall be last*.[7]

---

[1] Matt 11:11; Luke 7:28.
[2] Matt 18:1.
[3] Matt 18:4.
[4] Cf. John 13:23.
[5] Cf. Matt 25:21.
[6] Matt 20:16.
[7] *Idem*.

X

The Chalice of Jesus

§1.[1]   When two [of the apostles] came in order to choose places for themselves, as though first among their companions, our Lord said to them, *Are you able to drink the chalice that I am about to drink?* [2] [He said this] to show that [such places] must indeed be bought at a price. *Like me:*[3] *Wherefore God has also elevated and exalted him.*[4] There is no one who has humbled himself more, according to his nature, than our Lord, for he was of divine origin.[5] After they had learned that [such a place] could only be bought through deeds, he said, "Now that you have learned that it is through deeds that this [place] can be acquired, there are perhaps those who have run, or who will run, swifter than you. However, in the Father's design, the one who excels all others in his running performance is [already] designated, and his [place] is prepared for him."

Because they had come so as to take possession of an election not accompanied by deeds, our Lord thrust it aside from him, and showed that he did not have the power to spare them from distress; just as [when he also said], *As for that hour, no one knows it,*[6] so that no one would question him concerning it. *It is not yours to know the time or the seasons.*[7] He came therefore and explained it to them all, while they were agitated. *Whoever wishes to be your master, let him become your servant.*[8] This is how all are to have authority. Thus did our Lord place the request of the sons of Zebedee as a crown in [their] midst, so that whoever was victorious in his combat might be crowned with it.

§2.   The apostle also built upon this [foundation] when he said, *He will examine the thoughts of [our] hearts, and so each one of us will*

---

[1] The main contents of X, §1, together with the first sentence of §2, are present in the second half of XV, §19 in a slightly shorter form.

[2] Matt 20:22.

[3] *Idem.*

[4] Phil 2:9.

[5] This sentence is not present in the parallel passage of XV, §19.

[6] Matt 24:36.

[7] Acts 1:7. The next three sentences are not present in the parallel passage of XV, §19.

[8] Matt 20:26-27.

receive glory from God.[1] Balaam too was chosen for prophecy, and the sons of Eli for the priesthood, and Jeroboam for the kingdom. This is why [he said], *Lest I myself be rejected.*[2] Thus [Paul] came forward and taught that it is of little consequence that all these instances of being chosen [derive] from a higher constraint; what is of greater importance is that which [derives] from freewill. That you might know that it is thus, [take the case of] him who spoke *with the tongue of angels.*[3] This was not a choice coming from himself, but from God. But that one should love another person, this choice comes from oneself, and accordingly, this path is greater and more eminent than the other. For it is not for a person to know *prophecy and mysteries.* It is not for a person to *transpose mountains.*[4] [Or], *If I feed the poor with all that I possess,*[5] as Annias and his wife did, but without love,[6] or, *If I deliver over my body*[7] as [did] Iscariot.

To show that the choices he put forward are useless without love, and that those [based] on freewill only [are of benefit], he [said], *Love the Lord your God. This is the greatest commandment.*[8] Moreover, [the text] *he who fed the poor* [is] in accordance with the righteousness of the Pharisees, and, *I hand over my body to be burned,* [is] like the fifty men who were calling upon Elijah, without sincerity: *Prophet of God, the king has said, Go down!* [9] They were wailing before God on behalf of him who had sent them, and were handing over their bodies, as though in great distress, that they might be burned in the fire of God, but without the love of God within them. Similarly, with regard to the house of Koreh, for it was not because of zeal for the service of God that they were burned.[10] In the days of Shadrach and Meshach,[11] there were many who were desirous of falling into the fire, so that they too might share a similar experience. And, in the days of Abraham, some fed the poor, in the hope that angels might approach and bless them.

---

[1] 1 Cor 4:5. The introduction to this scriptural text which brings the section which is paralleled in XV, §19 to an end is also absent.
[2] 1 Cor 9:27.
[3] 1 Cor 13:1.
[4] 1 Cor 13:2.
[5] Cf. 1 Cor 13:3.
[6] Cf. Acts 5:1-10.
[7] 1 Cor 13:3.
[8] Matt 22:37-38.
[9] 2 Kgs 1:11.
[10] Cf. Num 16:1-35.
[11] Cf. Dan 3:21-97.

§3.   People imitate those who do good deeds, therefore, not out of love for these good deeds, but because of their utility. For Balaam also flattered [God], in that he had seven altars built because he had heard concerning these ancient ones that, with regard to the sacrifices they had offered to him, their prayers were accepted.[1] The king of Moab took note of Jephthah. But, because it was his first-born,[2] and a human being rather than an animal that he killed, God took pity on him, since it was in affliction that he did it and not through love. In the case of Jephthah, if it had been one of his servants who had been first to encounter him, he would have killed him. But, in order that people would not engage in the sacrifice of their fellow human beings, he caused his own daughter to meet him, so that others would be afraid, lest they offer human beings by vow to God.[3]

In the case of what happened with Abraham,[4] this occurred because of [the words], *Now, I have made known*,[5] because they were sacrificing their children. When their children die, they should not get frenzied [with grief], but rejoice. For see, Abraham had many [children] in place of one, because he offered up his son in joy. It was for this reason that God opened many doors, so that people might become his friends, like Abraham his friend, and like all his other friends. To the extent that we perform deeds [like] theirs, we must needs become like them.

The Sin that Cannot Be Forgiven[6]

§4.   *Neither here nor beyond will it be forgiven him.*[7] Now our Lord forgave many people their sins freely, and indeed his baptism forgives freely the debts of those who believe.[8] But neither our Lord, however, nor his baptism, could forgive this [sin] in this world, nor could his mercy, which hides in the midst of many good things, and covers over evil things unto the end. For our Lord has not said that [such a sin] will be requited by

---

[1] Cf. Num 22:2-24:25.

[2] Cf. 2 Kgs 3:27.

[3] Cf. Judg 11:29-40.

[4] Cf. Gen 22:1-18.

[5] Cf. Peshitta at Gen 22:12.

[6] Cf. E. Beck, "Der syrische Diatessaronkommentar zu der unvergebbaren Sünde wider den Heiligen Geist übersetzt und erklärt," *Oriens Christianus* 73 (1989), pp. 1-37.

[7] Matt 12:32.

[8] It is worth noting how Ephrem uses "debts" and "sins" interchageably here in this sentence, when compared with the variation in the Lord's Prayer in Matt 6:12 ("debts") and Luke 11:4 ("sins").

compensation, but that it will not be freely forgiven. In other words, even if one were to do all kinds of good deeds and be complete in every kind of righteousness, there is no way that this [sin] can be freely forgiven him. [God] will require its retribution in Gehenna. Even David gave his righteousenss by way of compensation for the homicide which he had committed. With confidence then [I say], "There is no sin that has resisted nor will resist repentance, except this one." But this sin does not prevent that a person might be justified eventually.[1] When one will have made retribution in Gehenna, [God] will reward him for this in the kingdom. Paul for instance did not blaspheme in this way. There are many who persecute, but they do not blaspheme in this way.

§5.   The [words] that he said, *He will be guilty of an eternal sin,*[2] mean that it will certainly not be forgiven. Take note then of the explanation which is added to the statement, *But he will be a debtor.* [3] That for which a person is in debt must assuredly be repaid. It will certainly not be remitted him. Our Lord made a distinction between retribution and forgiveness. Perhaps then this scar will not become clean. For he did not say that he will be a sinner, or an evildoer, or an unjust person, but that *he will be a debtor.* You can polish silver and cleanse it with water, and without the use of fire. But only with fire can you really purify it. Likewise, *He will not be forgiven, neither here nor beyond.*[4]

Perhaps this word envisages only the latter time and does not refer to today? They saw him clothed with a body, and yet many were in doubt concerning him. But they had nothing upon which to base an idea, in the case of the Spirit. This is why [he said], *Whoever says a word against the Son of Man will be forgiven. But whoever [speaks] against the Spirit will not be forgiven; neither in this world nor in the next will he be forgiven.*[5] Perhaps two retributions are being spoken of, namely, he will be smitten here, and tormented there? Not all transgressors will receive retribution here. But those who have blasphemed will be punished both

---

1 The Syriac word here, ܟ̄ܐ ܚܝ̈ܢܐ ܕܐܘܬ̄ܐ, "by other things" might be a corruption of ܟ̄ܐ ܚܝ̈ ܕܐܘܬ̄ܐ, "at the end," which would fit the context better.

2 Mark 3:29.

3 The word ܚܝܒ means both "to be guilty" and "to be in debt." Ephrem develops his exegesis here through the imagery of being in debt.

4 Matt 12:32.

5 *Idem.*

167

here and hereafter, as in the case of Iscariot, all of *whose entrails were poured out.*[1]

§6.   See, Peter shows that this happened to [Judas] as though through the anger [of God].[2] But this was applicable only to those blasphemers at that time. Those who do so today are not aware that they are blaspheming. Repentance therefore is possible for every one alive. But [in the case of] the one who is incapable of it, *it would have been better for him if he had not been born.*[3]

All sinners then can obtain forgiveness through repentance, whether they have sinned with knowledge, or without knowledge. Our Lord will not say, "He will not obtain mercy," but, *It will not be forgiven him.*[4] For it can happen that when one has made retribution for one's debt here, one may obtain mercy in the other world. If the judge does not forgive, he shows how great is the fault of the transgressor. But if he forgives through mercy, he shows how great is the grace of the Good One, of him in whom the fullness [of grace] dwells. It is not that [God] does not forgive them if they repent, but rather it is Satan who does not allow them repent of this blasphemy. *It was while I was not aware that I did these things.*[5] Therefore, it is concerning those who do know that he said, *It will not be forgiven them.* Judas Iscariot testified that the remorse of his soul was not accepted.

Because they had made [the Lord] into an associate with demons,[6] he divided their lot for them among the demons. There is no expiation for a demon, either in this world or in the one to come. For the demon said, *You are the Holy One of God.*[7] But these others said, *There is an unclean spirit in him.*[8] It is fitting therefore that these be cursed more than demons. In all sins there must needs be some kind of corresponding blasphemy. But with this kind of blasphemy there is impudence with knowledge. For they know that [God has decreed], concerning those who [blaspheme] knowingly, that it will not be forgiven them. For these Jews had decided to reject, not anyone who would have called him a demon,

---

[1] Acts 1:18.
[2] Cf. Acts 1:16-20.
[3] Matt 26:24.
[4] Matt 12:32.
[5] 1 Tim 1:13.
[6] Cf. Matt 10:25.
[7] Mark 1:24.
[8] Mark 3:30.

but whomsoever would have called him Messiah. [This was] so that you would know that this blasphemy was unnecessary. Consequently this blasphemy is also beyond forgiveness.

The Blind and Dumb Demoniac

§7.   *They brought a man who was dumb and blind and possessed of a demon to him.*[1] A symbol of the people was depicted in him, as Isaiah said, *The heart of this people has become dull, and their ears heavy and they have covered their eyes, lest they see with their eyes and hear with their ears.*, et cetera.[2] *He healed him, and he could see and hear*[3] is a symbol of those who believed in him.

§7a.[4]   *They brought a man who was dumb and blind and possessed of a demon to him. He healed him, and he could see and hear. The crowds, therefore, when they saw this, were amazed.*[5] *But the scribes and the pharisees were saying, This is through Beelzebub, the prince of demons.*[6] There are various powers in the medicines of physicians. One, for instance, can totally purify; another can totally consume. One can strengthen, another can close [a wound], and yet another can burn, and another appease. But the heavenly medicine, which was sent from the Father, was everything to everyone. It opened the [eyes of] the blind, cleansed lepers, raised the dead to life, calmed the seas, and drove out demons. But the pharisees attributed these things to the prince of demons, so that, according to their word, the demon would be driving out the demon, and this sin would be forgiven! How could a demon open [the eyes of] the blind, or cleanse a leper, or raise the dead to life? This was a wonder, that the crowds believed, whereas the scribes and the teachers doubted. Is not this [the fulfilment of the words], *That the blind may see and those who see become blind?*[7]

---

1 Matt 12:22.

2 Isa 6:10; Matt 13:15. See the note above at II, § 5 for comment on this type of indication of scriptural abbreviation.

3 Matt 12:22.

4 This section is missing from the Armenian translation.

5 Matt 12:23.

6 Matt 12:24.

7 John 9:39.

The Sinful Woman

§8. *If this man were a prophet, he would know that she is a sinner.*[1] But you, Simon, who knew her, how could you have allowed her admission to your table? But you also did not know from this that he was God, nor were you able to restrain the hidden will which brought along this [woman]. *A creditor had two debtors; one of five hundred, and the other fifty,*[2] [this was] to show clearly that he had recorded the debt of both according to this [reckoning]. *He said to Simon the Pharisee, I came into your house. You gave me no water for my feet.*[3] It was appropriate that he had not given him water, so that the tearful petition, which the sinful woman had prepared for him to justify her, would not be in vain. Fire did not heat the water for the ablution, for the tears of the sinful woman were boiling hot through her own love. She offered tearful supplication to him who had given her an enviable gift. His humanity was washed by her tears and was refreshed, while his divinity granted redemption there and then for the price [of her tears]. Only his humanity was capable of being washed, whereas his divinity [alone] could expiate the sins which were not visible. Through her tears she washed the dust which was on his feet, while he, through his words, cleansed the scars which were on her flesh. She cleansed him with her impure tears, while he cleansed her with his holy words. He was cleansed of dust, and in return he cleansed her of iniquity. His feet were washed with tears, while his word granted forgiveness of sins.

§9. *You did not kiss me, but she has not ceased kissing my feet from the moment she entered. Wherefore her many sins are forgiven her. The one who is forgiven little loves little.*[4] He firmly established through this that, with regard to his physical members, they are [one] body and are corporeal. She moistened and dried and anointed [them]. Let penitents weep, therefore, and let sinners do penance, so that they may perhaps reach and enter the open door. Let those who love life humble themselves, because a closed door is promised to those who do nothing in their combat, and have not sought a good recompense for themselves.

---

[1] Luke 7:39.
[2] Luke 7:41.
[3] Luke 7:44.
[4] Luke 7:45,47.

§10.   The tears of the sinful woman flowed down and washed the places in which the five hundred denarii of her debts were inscribed. This was because her neediness impelled her unto shame, for she had seen him, who did not reproach the needy when they kept begging, but spurned the rich because they were ashamed [of him]. This is why [the Lord] raised his voice in pity for those in need of pity, and he opened his mouth in forgiveness for the needy. He praised those who honoured him through their loving solicitude for him, but reproached those who invited him, for their neglect of love towards him. He brought the faith of this [woman] out into the open with praise, but unmasked the thoughts of [Simon] with reproach. He was a physican to her that believed, for it is he who heals everyone. He was judging the secret [thoughts] of one who thought that he [the Lord] did not even know those that were manifest.

"The Harvest Is Great"

§11.   *The harvest is great but the workers are few.*[1] *The harvest* [consists] of those who are prepared to believe, and *the workers* are the apostles. He gave them instruments suitable for the harvest: the cleansing of lepers, the healing of bodies and the raising of the dead.

Satan Fallen from Heaven

§12.   He that fell, as though from the heavens, thought that he would hide himself on earth, but the blood and water that flowed from the side of the Life-Giver upon [the earth] did not permit him.[2] [Satan], flying through the air, was expelled from it through the stretching out of the arms [of the Crucified One]. When he fled to his stronghold, there too [the Lord] humbled him, *A thousand will fall at your side,* et cetera.[3] He set out for his house of refuge, but [the Lord] drove him from there too, when he freed those who were captives, and brought out those who were bound. [Satan] had feared this too, and therefore he persuaded those who crucified [the Lord] to say, *Come down from the cross, so that we may see and*

---

[1] Matt 9:37.
[2] Cf. John 19:34.
[3] Ps 91:7. See the note above at II, § 5 for comment on this type of indication of scriptural abbreviation.

believe,[1] so that, through these things, he might perhaps be able to dwell in his stronghold, as though in freedom.

§13.   *I was looking at Satan, who fell like lightning from the heavens.*[2] It was not that he was [actually] in them. Nor [was he in them] when he said, *I will place my throne above the stars*.[3] But he fell from his greatness and his dominion. *I was looking at Satan, who fell like lightning from the heavens*. He did not therefore fall from heaven; for lightning does not fall from heaven, since it is the clouds which engender it. Why then did he say, *From the heavens*? This was because it was as though it were from *the heavens*, like lightning which comes suddenly. For in one instant Satan fell beneath the victory of the cross. After ordinary people had been anointed, and sent forth by reason of their mission, and were highly successful in an instant, through miracles of [healing] those in pain, and sickness and evil spirits, it was affirmed that Satan suddenly fell from his dominion, like lightning from the clouds. For, just as lightning goes forth and does not return to its place, so too did Satan fall and did not again hold sway over his dominion. *Behold, I am giving you dominion*.[4]

Because justice had driven the serpent against the heel,[5] grace raised up the heel by means of the cross, so that it might be superior to the serpent, as though through dominion. This is what is shown by what follows after this, *And all the power of the enemy*,[6] which was trodden under foot by the cross. And, *Behold I am giving you dominion to trample upon serpents and scorpions*[7] because [the Lord] has removed the error which was reigning through the serpent. [This was] so that the truth of him who gave dominion over the serpents to be trodden under foot might reign, that is, over their counsels. For Mary's foot crushed [the serpent] which had struck Eve in her heel.[8]

---

1 Matt 27:40; Mark 15:30,32.
2 Luke 10:18.
3 Isa 14:13.
4 Luke 10:19.
5 Cf. Gen 3:15.
6 Luke 10:19.
7 *Idem*.
8 Cf. Gen 3:15.

The Gospel Revealed to the Simple

§14. [With regard to] this [text], *I give thanks to you, Father, who [is] in heaven*, the Greek has: *I give thanks to you, God, Father, Lord of heaven and earth*, and, *Because you have hidden [it] from the wise and revealed [it] to mere children.*[1] It is because the wise dispute against faith, and do not accept the simple things, that it is hidden from them. *For no one knows the Father except the Son.*[2] Who can know the intellect except the word which goes forth from it? It is he, [the Father], who is above all minds, and all minds are moved by him, and it is under [him] that they find motion. If it were through sight and hearing that there is knowledge, it must needs be that all who saw our Lord would have known [him]. *But they, if they had known him, would not have crucified him,*[3] and, *Father, forgive them, for they do not know.*[4] The sun and moon, the roots and rocks appear as good things, but they are not known.

§15. The Son therefore is the thought of the Father. Consequently, whoever finds the tree rejoices in its fruit. *For no one knows the Father except the Son.*[5] [This was] as though he wished to unite the knowledge of both of them, one to the other. He was recognized then as God because of his will, and he was recognized as Son because of his work. Those who blaspheme with regard to the Spirit say that it is written, *No one knows the Father except the Son, and no one [knows] the Son, except the Father.*[6] Because of this, [they say] that [the Lord] made it known that the Spirit does not know [him]. But, when he said, *No one knows what is in a human being, except the Spirit within him, so too that which is in God,*[7] does this mean that the Son does not know [the Father]? *Come to me, [all you who are] weary, and who carry burdens, and I will give you rest.*[8] Many were running after him because a word of rest had been dropped into their ears.

---

[1] Matt 11:25. This is the third of five instances in the commentary in which Ephrem refers to "the Greek." See above at II, §17 for comment on Ephrem's use of this term.

[2] Matt 11:27.

[3] 1 Cor 2:8.

[4] Luke 23:34.

[5] Matt 11:27.

[6] *Idem.*

[7] 1 Cor 2:11.

[8] Matt 11:28.

Hating One's Self

§16.   Lest any might become disciples of his teaching too readily, he said to them, *Whoever does not hate his own soul cannot be my disciple. For who is there who would build a tower, who would not first reckon his expenses?* et cetera.[1] For it is not through words that one becomes a disciple, but rather through deeds. This is why *The path of life is narrow and difficult.*[2] This refers to those who live according to the flesh.

---

[1] Luke 14:26. See the note above at II, § 5 for comment on this type of indication of scriptural abbreviation.
[2] Cf. Matt 7:13-14.

XI

The Sign of Jonah

§1.   *This evil generation is seeking a sign, but a sign will not be given it, except the sign of the prophet Jonah. For, just as Jonah was three days in the depths of the sea, so too will the Son of Man be in the heart of the earth.*[1] In saying [this], our Lord was concerned not so much with the number of three days, but rather with the healing of their ills and the raising of their dead. After these signs which are beyond description, and these testimonies which do not deceive, the blind who could not see said, *We wish to see a sign from you.*[2] He left aside his witnesses, the kings and prophets, and turned to the Ninevites. These did not recognize any kind of sign from Jonah, but, at the end, they will judge those who, after having seen many signs, denied the author of these signs.[3] For Jonah had decreed destruction on the Ninevites. He had cast fear upon them and sowed a stupor among them, and they presented him with a sheaf of contrition of spirit and the fruits of repentance.[4] [Thus] were the Gentiles chosen and the uncircumcised drew near [to God]. Pagans received life and sinners repented, to the confusion of the circumcised. These therefore will judge the apostates who did not believe.

§2.   *Therefore, a sign will not be given it, except the sign of the prophet Jonah.*[5] The sign of Jonah served the Ninevites in two ways. If they had spurned it, they would have gone down to Sheol alive like [Jonah]. But they were raised from the dead like him because they repented. Just as in the case of our Lord, who was set *for the fall and the rising [of many],*[6] [people] either lived through his being killed, or died through his death. *The men of Nineveh.*[7] [With these words] he compelled [this generation] in the end. *They were asking him for a sign from heaven,*[8] [for instance] thunder, as in the case of Samuel.[9] He

---

1 Matt 12:39-40; Luke 11:29.
2 Matt 12:38.
3 Cf. Matt 12:41.
4 Cf. Jon 3:1-10.
5 Matt 12:39.
6 Luke 2:34.
7 Matt 12:41.
8 Mark 8:11; Luke 11:16.

revealed a proclamation that was coming up from the depths, which they[1] were asking to hear from on high. Because they heard from on high and did not believe, it came up as though from the depths. Jonah, after he went up [from within the fish], was a negative sign to the Ninevites, for he proclaimed the destruction of their city. Thus too were the disciples, after the resurrection of our Lord.

§3. *Thus will the Son of Man be in the heart of the earth,*[2] in order to make known to them in advance that it was not they who would be able to kill him. For the symbol of his death had been depicted in Jonah a thousand years earlier. Where Abel had been killed, was not there the mouth of the earth, the earth which *opened its mouth and received the blood of your brother*?[3] Where our Lord was buried, was not there the heart of the earth? *The Son of Man will be in the heart of the earth, just as Jonah was in the fish.*[4] Just as Jonah was not in any way decomposed in it, neither was our Lord in the depths of Sheol. *You did not abandon my soul in Sheol, and you did not allow your Holy One to see destruction.*[5] Just as [Jonah] went up from the sea and proclaimed to the Ninevites, who repented and lived, so too our Lord, after having raised his body from Sheol, sent his disciples into the midst of the Gentiles, who were completely converted and received life in its fullness. Three days therefore are reckoned in relation to the descent and the rising from the dead of both of them.

§4. *The Queen of the South will condemn it,*[6] for she is a type of the Church. Just as she came to Solomon, so too the Church [came] to our Lord, and just as she condemned [this generation], so too will the Church. If she, who wished to see wisdom which passes away, and a king who was corruptible, was judging the synagogue, how much more the Church, which [desires to see] a king who does not pass away, and wisdom which

---

[9] Cf. 1 Sam 7:10; 12:18.
[1] The Syriac text reads a second person plural pronoun here: "which you were asking to hear."
[2] Matt 12:40.
[3] Gen 4:11.
[4] Matt 12:40.
[5] Ps 16:10.
[6] Matt 12:42.

does not go astray. *For if we suffer with him, we will also be glorified with him.*[1]

The Unclean Spirit

§5.   *Therefore, when the unclean spirit goes out of a person.*[2] He said this to them because they were seeking a sign from him. He presented this example to them: "Of what advantage is it to you if you are healed for a moment, but do not believe? For, if you are still in doubt after you are healed, something worse than the original pain may befall you." As [in] the example which he put before them, *The [evil] spirit went and brought seven of his companions, and he came; and the final [state] of that man was worse than the first. Thus will it be for this generation.*[3] This is similar to the healing of Mary Magdalene, of whom it is written that *he cast out seven demons* from her.[4] This is why he brought this deed before them as an example of the subject that he was expounding [to them]. For in this same passage [the evangelist] spoke concerning the women who were with him, *Those who were healed of unclean spirits, Mary Magdalene, she from whom he drove out seven demons, and Johanna, the wife of the steward of Herod, and Susanna,* cum ceteris.[5] *His final [state] was worse,* because the Messiah will not come again in his body to heal grievous pain freely and without requiring faith.

§6.   *Therefore, when the unclean spirit goes out of a person.*[6] [The Lord] was comparing Israel to a madman possessed by a spirit, and himself to the likeness of a physician, *For he knew Israel,* et cetera.[7] Because he was a physician for his people he made his preaching spring forth in them, and he fulfilled the words of the prophets through signs and wonders, when [he said], *If you do not believe in me, believe in my works.*[8] Because he poured out his grace among them, idolatry fled before him, and their

---

[1] Rom 8:17.
[2] Matt 12:43.
[3] Matt 12:45.
[4] Luke 8:2.
[5] Luke 8:2-3. See the note above at II, § 5 for comment on this type of indication of scriptural abbreviation.
[6] Matt 12:43.
[7] Cf. Deut 32:10. See the note above at II, § 5 for comment on this type of indication of scriptural abbreviation.
[8] John 10:38.

paganism took off into the Gentiles. And it was as if they, when the time was fulfilled, were healed of the illness of error. Their idolatry betook itself far from the rays of the Life-Giver, and through the constraint of his miracles the people's paganism deserted them. But it was not by their will that they spurned it. For, when [the Lord] gave them over to their freewill, so that it might shine forth of its own accord after his ascension, they reverted back to their former way of life. Therefore [he said], *Seven of its companions; and the last [state] was worse than the first*,[1] because the fullness of error remained with them.

§7.   Moreover, through the figure of a man, [Christ] was attributing the unclean spirit to Israel.[2] When they were dwelling in Egypt, they had an evil spirit in them, while in service to Pharaoh. But, when [God] sent them a deliverer to lead them out, the evil spirit fled from them, and they were healed. *For he sent his word, and healed them and delivered them from destruction*.[3] He led them across the sea so that they would be cleansed, but they were unwilling. He led them into fire, but they were not purified, as the apostle attests.[4] *The spirit*, therefore, which *departed from them, wandered about waterless places* - that is, among the Gentiles - *that it might find a resting place, but it did not find any*.[5] For the Gentiles also heard the voice of him who said, *All who are thirsty, come to the waters*;[6] and also, *The Gentiles will hope in him*,[7] and, *I have given you as a covenant for the people and a light for the Gentiles*.[8] Because *the desert* of the Gentiles had become pools of water,[9] the [evil spirit] did not find rest among the Gentiles. Wherefore, *I will go back to my former house*,[10] this [spirit] and its seven companions, and so it entered and took up residence among this people, according to the number of days of the week, and did away with all its religious observance.

---

[1] Matt 12:45.

[2] This is a difficult phrase to translate, even if the general meaning is clear: Israel is being designated through the image of a person possessed by an unclean spirit, as already indicated at the beginning of §6 above.

[3] Ps 107:20.

[4] Cf. 1 Cor 10:1-5.

[5] Matt 12:43.

[6] Isa 55:1.

[7] Isa 11:10.

[8] Isa 42:6; cf. Isa 49:6.

[9] Cf. Ps 107:35.

[10] Matt 12:44.

§8.   The seven spirits dwelling in [this people] were those concerning whom Jeremiah said, *She lamented and gave birth to seven*.[1] Her womb was swollen, for [Israel] bore a calf in the desert,[2] the two calves of Jeroboam[3] and the four-faced image of Manasseh.[4] *The sun set*,[5] because they were dwelling in darkness, without the light of prophecy. *[It will be] night for you, without vision, and it will be dark for you, without dawn*.[6] *For, when it goes out of a man, it goes about wandering;*[7] this it does quite by nature. He rendered this judgement with regard to [the people]: *Thus will it be for this generation*.[8] That is, in the days of the prophets the evil spirit had gone out from them, [that spirit] which was sin itself. [God] had taken a section from among them and placed them in Babylon. The prophets too attest that he took away sin from them, *For a man of one hundred years will die as a youth, and he who sins at a hundred years will be cursed*.[9] [The evil spirit] rejected them again in the days of our Lord, for it found them full of envy toward their Saviour. But this [time] their evil deed was worse than the former one. They requited the prophets with slaughter, and hung Christ on the cross. Consequently they were thrown away like a vessel for which there was no use.

Jesus' True Relatives

§9.   *Blessed the womb which bore you and the breasts which suckled you*.[10] Marcion said, "They were indeed tempting him, as to whether he was [really] born." Similarly in the case of [the words], *Behold, your mother and your brothers are seeking you*.[11] What was the purpose of the appearance of his body and his nourishment? [Marcion] said, "That he might hide his greatness and make them believe that he was corporeal, because they were not capable of [grasping] it." But why should he have denied his birth? For if, through denying this, he wished to show them that he was not [really] born, he would not have gone on and made

---

[1] Jer 15:9.
[2] Cf. Exod 32:1-35.
[3] Cf. 1 Kgs 12:26-32.
[4] Cf. 2 Chr 33:7 (Peshitta).
[5] Jer 15:9.
[6] Mic 3:6.
[7] Matt 12:43.
[8] Matt 12:45.
[9] Isa 65:20.
[10] Luke 11:27.
[11] Mark 3:32.

179

himself a brother of his disciples who were born.[1] If, from what he denied above, he refuted the idea that he was not born, then it must be believed, from what he said here, that he was born. Even if [hypothetically] kinship would have been blotted out by his denial of his mother, nevertheless through the acknowledgment of his brothers, the lineage of his paternal ancestry was made known. Moreover, even if he showed that he did not have parents because he did not recognize either his mother or his brothers, nevertheless he did say, *No one is good, except one only*.[2] Therefore, are not he and the Holy Spirit, and the chosen angels good? For he said, *Why do you call me good*,[3] which was something he did not say above, namely, "Why do you call me conceived and born"?

§10.   *Blessed is the womb that bore you*.[4] He took blessedness from the one who bore him and gave it to those who were worshipping him. It was with Mary for a certain time, but it would be with those who worshipped him for eternity. *Blessed are those who hear the word of God and keep it*.[5]

Jesus Teaches Through Parables

§11.   *Let the one who has ears listen*.[6] The one who had [ears] did listen, for this voice penetrated every ear because of its goodness. But those ears attend to whatever they wish because of their freedom. There are certain others who attend to [his voice], but do not act upon what this attentiveness requires. Therefore [the Lord] hid from the body what is difficult for the eyes to perceive, but what is easy for the mind to perceive he revealed and made manifest. The sight of [his divinity] was too difficult for the eyes, but his message was easy for the ears. They were censured, not because they were unable to perceive his divinity, but because they did not accept the word of his divinity. There are words therefore which, although sown in the hearing, have roots which do not [bear] fruit. And there are those whose roots grow and produce fruit. For three grains of wheat fell in three sets of listeners, but did not produce fruit.

---

[1] Cf. Matt 12:49-50.
[2] Mark 10:17.
[3] *Idem.*
[4] Luke 11:27.
[5] Luke 11:28.
[6] Mark 4:9.

§11a.[1] *I am speaking to them in parables, so that what they see they will not see, and what they hear they will not hear.*[2] He also said to the disciples, *You have eyes, but you do not see.*[3] This word was pronounced in their midst, referring to those who, of their own freewill, did not wish to see or hear, and it applied to anyone with a similar [outlook]. *This is fulfilled*, et cetera.[4] [was pronounced] with regard to one who persists in his audacity. The scribes persisted. The disciples were like them, but did not persist however. Therefore he said of those who persisted, *This is fulfilled in their regard.*

§12.   *Behold, the sower went out to sow his seed, and as he sowed it, some of it fell on the edge of the path, and some of it on the rock, and some of it amongst thorns, and some of it on fertile ground.*[5] If there was only one sower, and only one ground, how could four separate categories within the crop appear in that [ground] which was cultivated and fertile? How could this be, given that [the ground] was one in its nature and in its cultivation, and that it had received a pure seed from a holy hand? How then did three different categories appear in its growth, *Thirty, and sixty and one hundredfold*,[6] and [why], *To the one who has, it shall be given to him*?[7] Why did [the sower] cast [the seed] on the path where it was *trampled under foot*, and the birds snatched it away?[8] And why did the sower sow his seed in the thorny ground, in that which was fertile, [in that] which produced much briars, and upon rocky ground? The sower is one, and he scattered his seed evenly without exception of person; each ground then shows its love accordingly, through its fruit. [He said this] to show through his word that his Gospel does not justify by force, without the accord of freewill. [Nevertheless] he did not shut out sterile ears from the seed of his pure words.

---

[1] §11a is missing from the Armenian translation.
[2] Matt 13:13; Mark 4:11-12.
[3] Cf. Mark 4:13.
[4] Cf. Matt 13:14. See the note above at II, § 5 for comment on this type of indication of scriptural abbreviation.
[5] Luke 8:5-8.
[6] Mark 4:8.
[7] Matt 13:12.
[8] Cf. Luke 8:5.

§13.   *For it fell on the edge of the path.*[1] This is an image of the ungrateful soul, like the one who [received] one talent despised the goodness of him who gave it.[2] Because [this ground] was tardy[3] in receiving its seed, it became a public highway for all evil. Consequently, there was no place in its ground for the Teacher to penetrate into it like a labourer, break up its hardness and sow [his seed] there. [The Lord] described the evil one in the imagery of a bird who snaches it away.[4] He made known thus that [the evil one] does not snatch away forcefully from the heart the teaching which is entrusted to it. For behold, in the imagery he has revealed, the voice of the Gospel stands at the door of the ears, like the grain of wheat on the surface of the ground, which has not hidden in its womb the seed which fell upon it. For the birds were not permitted to penetrate [the earth] in search of the seed, which the earth had hidden under its wings.

§14.   *That which [fell] on the rock.*[5] The Good [Lord] has thus revealed his mercy, for even though the hardness [of the ground] had not yet been cultivated, he did not withhold its seed from it. [This ground] represents those who turn away from his teaching, like those who said, *This word is hard, who can listen to it?*[6] And [it is] like Judas, who heard his word and flourished through his signs, but was without fruit at the moment of testing.

§15.   The thorny ground, with the seed it had received, gave its strength to briars and thorns.[7] The Teacher showed his love in that he cast his seed boldly into a ground boasting the toil of an alien, even while thorns predominated in the ground. He poured his own [seed] upon it abundantly however, so that it would be without an excuse.

§16.   The rich man drew near to our Lord joyfully, saying, *These things have I done from my youth.*[8] Our Lord purified him and gave him a seed

---

[1] Matt 13:19.

[2] Cf. Matt 25:24-30.

[3] Leloir recommends that the negative particle which occurs here in the Syriac be omitted, as in the Armenian (cf. EC-CBM 8, p. 63).

[4] Cf. Matt 13:19.

[5] Matt 13:20.

[6] John 6:60.

[7] Cf. Matt 13:22.

[8] Mark 10:20.

that was bare, *If you wish to become perfect, sell all you possess.*[1] When [the rich man] saw that the perfection of the seed had reached him in order to free him from all the thorns suffocating him, *he was sad,*[2] on account of his riches, which were thorns hindering him.

§17.[3]   {The good and rich soil represents the souls which act according to the truth, like those who were called and have left everything they possessed to follow him. *Thirty, sixty, and one hundred*[4] correspond to the ages [of life]: childhood, youth and old age. Although there is only one ground and one seed, nevertheless [the Lord] harvests a [different] amount according to the length [of life], since some have more roots than others. The Good [Lord] showed his mercy notwithstanding, because, when they came to receive a different recompense according to the roots, the last received a recompense equal to that of the first.

---

[1] Matt 19:21; Luke 18:22.

[2] Luke 18:23.

[3] At this point in *Chester Beatty* MS 709, at the beginning of folio 18r, there appears to be a copyist's error, since this section has no continuity with the context which either precedes or follows it. Leloir suggests that a scribe must have erroneously transcribed onto folio 18r a page taken either from another context or from another manuscript (cf. EC-CBM 8, p. 65). Ephrem's commentary is resumed on the back of the folio, 18v. The contents of folio 18r are included in this footnote, while the portion of Ephrem's commentary omitted through the error is supplied from the Armenian version (cf. CSCO 145, pp. 109-110).

... he taught. But between those who accept and those who do not accept, and not with regard to the natures which are alien, one to another, but with regard to the wills of those doubting over the Lord of the wine. They banished his teaching however from their minds. [From] that [teaching] then, namely, that new wine is not put into torn wineskins, we learn whether, with regard to our nature, he was speaking of that which is alien to his teaching, or with regard to our wills which do not obey his commandment. If he had said this about our will, he was not revealing concerning what is alien, and if he was clarifying with regard to nature, there is no possibility that his wine would be placed in us, but rather because this demonstration is from the world. What is alien therefore originated in what was before him, and consented to him, because it was similar and an example to him. New wine for his teaching, and new skins [are] the ears which listen to him. This new thing therefore which he came and found, and into which he poured his wine, was it sent from an alien god, or did it come down with him? For whatever he found was old, and if, after he came, he did a new thing, then antiquity had already accepted that which is now new, so that, behold it is [now] changed. Know from the testimony which he brought, that it is not when new wine is poured into torn wineskins that he accomplishes these new things, but when a new thing meets a new thing and becomes a partner with it. They were attesting through this, without wishing it, that there was a new thing before his coming. "He that has ears, let him hear" (Mark 4:9). He put forth our Gospel, but they denied it. From that which is theirs, we will show whether this is [Christ's]. Children are the fruit of marriage. Wherefore, he was offering them in his arms to his Father, that he might show that he was the Son, and he was also loving tenderly those who were sons like him.

[4] Mark 4:8.

183

§18. {Even if the will, which received the sowing of good things with joy, was itself wholly good, nevertheless the good and rich soil produced in different ways, *thirty, sixty,* and *one hundredfold.* He showed that each part of the ground [gives fruit] according to its capacity and with joy, like those who [had received] *five talents* and [gained] *ten, each one according to his capacity.*[1] The one who makes a return of one hundred seems to possess the perfection of being chosen, since he has received the seal of a death offered in witness for God. Those who make a return of sixty are those who were called, and who delivered up their bodies to painful tortures for their God, but did not achieve death for their Lord; nevertheless they remained good up to the end. Thirty is the daily measure of the good soil. [It refers to] those who were chosen for the following [of Christ], but on whom times of persecution did not fall. They are nevertheless crowned through their good works, just as a piece of earth is crowned by its fruit. But they were not called to martrydom and to give witness to their faith}.[2] With regard to the [text], *But he did not know, because the earth was bearing fruit itself,*[3] it was not that he did not know, but rather, because he had not toiled for its growth.

§19. *Lord, you sowed good seed in your field. Where have the tares [come] from? He said to them, An enemy has done this.*[4] This was not of [the sower's doing]. If one of us is engaged in this [activity], let us ask him whether what he sowed in his portion of it was good. If this was so, let him tell us how one portion of it was sown and another was to be sown. And, if he poured forth [seed] in what was bad, well then, either he himself sowed [it] among the tares, or an evil one [sowed it] in his own [portion].[5]

§20. *Or again, the kingdom of heaven is like a grain, which is the smallest of all herbs.*[6] This was on account of how small the proclamation was at the beginning. Likewise this [text]: *Do not fear, little flock.*[7] When it

---

[1] Cf. Matt 25:14-30.

[2] *Chester Beatty* MS 709 resumes with the commentary on the parables at this point.

[3] Cf. Mark 4:27-28.

[4] Matt 13:27-28.

[5] This passage is difficult to translate. What is given above is an attempt to make sense of it (cf. also Leloir, EC-SC 121, p. 206, n. 3).

[6] Matt 13:31-32.

[7] Luke 12:32.

had grown, it was greater than all the herbs,[1] because his Gospel had reigned to the ends [of the earth]. *Their Gospel went forth into all the earth.*[2] *The winged creatures come and dwell in its branches;*[3] the Gentiles who wearied themselves over their idols will come to rest in faith. *Come to me, all you who are weary.*[4] If our Lord had not been born of a woman, nor sprung from a virgin, nor suffered, it would have been fitting for us to compare his soul to a winged creature, which had come down from heaven, and whose body had come with him. But, to show that he had truly assumed a body, he compared himself to a grain which was sown in the earth, and which received its body from the earth, that [body] upon which the winged creature rested. *John the Baptist attested, I saw the Spirit in the bodily form of a dove, coming down and resting upon him.*[5]

§21.   Again, he compared it to *leaven, which was hidden in the flour.*[6] The [leaven] works on it silently to transform it into its likeness. It is not overcome by the force of the mass [of dough], but rather draws all of it towards itself by the power which is hidden in it. His Gospel too is like this. [As] the leaven in the mass [of dough, so too] is his body in the mass of the house of Adam.

§22.   Again, *it is like a net which is cast into the sea, and gathers together [fish] of every kind.*[7] When he said, *of every kind,* understand [this] as "of every language." Again, after this choosing [of fish] from the sea, that is, from the world, there is another choosing of them, which is frightening. When they had drawn [the net] onto the shore of the sea, *they took the fish which were good, and cast out those that were inferior.*[8] The fish which enter into his net are the people who are [drawing near] to faith in him. The good [fish] represent those who have set about becoming perfect in his Gospel, while the inferior ones are those whom the Church has rejected from its midst, on account of their apostasy.

---

[1] Matt 13:32.
[2] Rom 10:18; cf. Ps 19:5.
[3] Matt 13:32.
[4] Matt 11:28.
[5] John 1:32; Luke 3:22.
[6] Cf. Matt 13:33.
[7] Matt 13:47.
[8] Matt 13:48.

Jesus in Nazareth

§23.   *After these things, he came to his town and was teaching them in their synagogues.*[1] Was there not another people, or another land apart from that of the Jews? But, in order that Marcion's lie be refuted, [the evangelist] said after this, *He entered the synagogue as was his custom, on the Sabbath day.*[2] What was the custom of him who had come just now? He had come to Galilee, and had begun to teach, not outside of the synagogue, but within it. Since the matter was known through their cultic service, he [came] to talk to them about their God. Otherwise it would have been in order for him to proclaim to them outside their synagogue. He therefore entered Bethsaida[3] among the Jews. [The evangelist] does not indicate that they said anything to him other than, *Physician, heal yourself.*[4] *They seized him and brought him out to the side of the mountain.*[5] It is not likely that the word they had spoken was leading them to anger.[6] For, if he had been speaking to them concerning the Creator, and [if] this was why they had given him the response, *They seized him that they might cast him down,*[7] why then did [the evangelist] not record in other places that it was like this too? That the people of the town hated him, there is this testimony: *A prophet is not accepted in his own town.*[8]

§24.   For Anathoth did not receive Jeremiah,[9] nor the Tishbites Elijah, nor Abelmeholah Elisha, nor Ramah Samuel,[10] nor the synagogue Moses, nor Israel our Lord. Elijah accordingly despised their wives,[11] and Elisha their men.[12] They were called *lacking in faith* to their shame.[13] But [the

---

[1] Matt 13:54; Luke 4:15.

[2] Luke 4:16.

[3] Ephrem incorrectly refers to Bethsaida here instead of Nazareth.

[4] Luke 4:23.

[5] Luke 4:29.

[6] It is not clear who "they" are. It may refer to the Marcionites, and "the word they had spoken" could refer to their belief that the Lord would have angered the Jews in placing their inferior God in opposition to the supreme God, whom Jesus had come to reveal to humanity.

[7] Luke 4:29.

[8] Luke 4:24.

[9] Cf. Jer 11:21.

[10] Cf. 1 Sam 8:1-22.

[11] Cf. 1 Kgs 17:17-24.

[12] Cf. 2 Kgs 5:1-14.

[13] Cf. Matt 6:30; 8:26; 17:17.

Lord] honoured the Arameans more than these.[1] This is why *they were filled with anger*.[2] The reason for this was as follows: *Physican, heal yourself*,[3] that is, "Save yourself from us, instead of seeking to heal [us]!" Although they were in need of healing, he was not able to heal them because of their lack [of faith]. By reason of their freewill, *they were casting him down*,[4] but because of his divinity he did not fall. Audacity was casting him down, but the submissive air received him on its wings, and he did not fall, so that through this he might perhaps procure faith for those who did not believe. Perhaps [it was] on this account that *the Galileans received him*.[5] From the moment when they saw him *passing through their midst*,[6] they did not dare do anything more to him. This was his first healing, that of the right hand which was ill.[7] Consequently, through the influence of the Prince of the Left, the Nazarenes were murmuring against him, envious of the healing of this Right [hand], which was established in the solemn mystery, and released unto every divine use.

§25.   *A prophet is not received in his own town*,[8] that is, in his own people. Elijah was from Tishbi, and [Scripture] does not say that Elijah was not received in Tishbi, but in all Israel.[9] If this is not so, let it be proved that the inhabitants of Tishbi persecuted him, and the Israelites received him. But who [received him], if not the widow from Zarephath, of the Gentiles?[10] *There were many widows*, not at Tishbi, but *in the house of Israel. But he was not sent to any of these*. Likewise, in the case of *lepers*, not in the town of Elisha, but *in the house of Israel*.[11] [The Lord] underlined thus that *he was not able to reveal miracles*, not only in Nazareth, but *in the house of Israel*.[12]

---

[1] This statement is interesting in the light of Ephrem's Syrian (= Aramean) origins.
[2] Luke 4:28.
[3] Luke 4:23.
[4] Luke 4:29.
[5] John 4:45.
[6] Cf. Luke 4:30.
[7] Cf. Luke 6:6-10.
[8] Luke 4:24.
[9] Cf. 1 Kgs 19:10,14.
[10] 1 Kgs 17:7-24.
[11] Luke 4:25-27.
[12] Mark 6:5.

§26.   The people of Nazareth saw that he despised all the land of Israel in its entirety, and that he honoured the Gentiles without measure. On this account, *they arose, took hold of him and cast him out*,[1] like people *burning with zeal* for the descendants of Abraham, saying that God had honoured these more than all the Gentiles. On this occasion of Nazareth, therefore, our Lord proposed two examples to distinguish the people [of Israel] from the Gentiles.[2] Just as on the occasion of the temple, he revealed another temple, which was his body,[3] and on the occasion of the fields, [he revealed] the harvest of humanity in Samaria.[4] All the people in fact were of the race of the prophet and the tribes were his brothers.

§27.   The centurion honoured him and [the Lord] marvelled at him.[5] The Canaanite woman honoured him, and he was amazed at her.[6] One person [honoured him] like Naaman[7] and another like the widow from Zarephath.[8] Elijah fled to the territory of the Gentiles.[9] But our Lord forbade his disciples to salute the Gentiles.[10] He received the Canaanite woman with difficulty. Our Lord showed through these things that his Gospel would spread throughout the Gentiles. Our Lord give himself up to be cast down, because the Evil One thought that it was on account of fear that he did not throw himself from *the pinnacle of the temple*.[11] But when they cast him down and he did not fall,[12] the Evil One himself fell from his kingship.[13] It was like when [the Lord] did not change stones to bread, so as not to give in to the desire of the Evildoer.[14] But he perfomed [a miracle] in the desert with bread,[15] and in Cana, with wine.[16]

---

[1] Luke 4:29.
[2] The examples of Elijah being sent to the widow of Zarephath, and the healing of Naaman the Syrian (cf. Luke 4:25-27).
[3] Cf. John 2:19-21.
[4] Cf. John 4:35.
[5] Cf. Matt 8:5-13.
[6] Cf. Matt 15:22-28.
[7] Cf. 2 Kgs 5:15.
[8] Cf. 1 Kgs 17:24.
[9] 1 Kgs 17:2-9.
[10] Cf. Matt 10:5; Luke 10:4.
[11] Matt 4:5-7.
[12] Cf. Luke 4:29-30.
[13] Cf. Luke 10:18.
[14] Cf. Matt 4:3-4.
[15] Cf. Matt 14:13-21; 15:29-39.
[16] Cf. John 2:1-11.

The Death of John the Baptist

§28.   *Command that the head of John the Baptist be brought.*[1] Oh
Herod! See what you have done! Do not give this innocent head to the
guilty rib. He, who conquered Adam by means of the rib which was united
to him in marriage, likewise conquered Herod by means of the rib which
was his partner. The head, which was placed *on a platter,*[2] was like a light
shining for all generations, and uncovering the adultery of the slayers.
This is the mouth which they silenced, so that it could [no longer] speak.
But the preaching of his silence was much more powerful than his voice.
It was [through] the dance of Herodias' daughter that Herod and Herodias
devised the plot, the one to swear, and the other to make the request.

---

[1] Matt 14:8.
[2] Matt 14:11.

XII

Bread Multiplied and Water Changed into Wine

§1.   Our Lord made bread in plenty from just a little bread in the desert,[1] and changed water into wine at Cana.[2] He first sought to accustom their mouths to his bread and his wine, until the time would come for him to give them his blood as well as his body. He allowed them taste a superabundance of transitory bread and wine, so that he might excite them to a superabundance of his living body and blood. He gave them these lesser things without money, so that they might know that his supreme gift was free. He gave them freely those things which they would have been able to buy at a price from him. Thus, he did not sell them what they would have been able to buy, so that they might know that a price would not be required of them for that which they did not have. For they would have been able to give him the price of his bread and his wine, but they would not have been able to give him the price of his body and blood.

Thus, not only did he give us this freely, but he even allured us as well. He gave us these lesser things freely to entice us to come and receive this supreme [gift] which is priceless. These lesser realities of bread and wine which he gave were pleasing to the mouth, whereas that of his body and blood is of benefit to the spirit. He enticed us with these things which are pleasing to the palate to attract us towards that which vivifies the soul. He therefore hid sweetness in the wine which he had made, to show them what kind of treasure is hidden in his life-giving blood.

§2.   At *the beginning of his signs*[3] he made wine which rendered the wedding guests joyful to show that his blood was about to make all nations joyful. All joys that exist are bound into wine, and all the deliverances that are effected are bound into the mystery of his blood. He gave [them] an excellent wine, capable of transforming the spirit, so that they might know that the teaching he was about to give them to drink was [also] capable of transforming the spirit. What was formerly water in the

---

[1] Cf. Matt 14:13-21; 15:29-38; John 6:1-13.
[2] Cf. John 2:1-11.
[3] John 2:11.

jars he changed to wine, and he turned the former commandment into perfection. Water he brought unto excellence and the Law he brought unto perfection. The guests were drinking[1] what had been water, but they were not drinking it as water. When we listen to the former commandments we taste them as new. Wherefore the [prescription], *A blow for a blow*,[2] has been changed. When we act according to this [new] perfection, [it becomes] *whoever strikes you, offer him the other*.[3]

§3.   Take note therefore of how his [creative] activity is mixed in with everything. When our Lord took a little bread he multiplied it in the twinkling of an eye.[4] That which [people] effect and transform in ten months with toil, his ten fingers effected in an instant. For he placed his hands beneath the bread as though it were earth, and spoke over it as though thunder. The murmur of his lips sprinkled over it like rain, and the breath of his mouth [was there] in place of the sun. [Thus] did he complete in the flash of one tiny moment something which requires a whole lengthy hour. One tiny amount of bread was forgotten, and from the midst of its smallness, abundance came to birth, so that it might be like the first blessing, *Give birth and be fruitful and multiply*.[5] The loaves of bread, like barren women and women deprived [of children], became fruitful at his blessing, and many were the morsels born from them.

§4.   [The Lord] also showed the incisiveness of his word to those who were submissive, and the speed of his gift in the case of those who accepted it. He did not multiply the bread in accordance with his power to multiply it, but in accordance with what was sufficient for those eating it. His miracle therefore was not measured in accordance with his power, but was measured rather in accordance with the hunger of those who were hungry. For if his miracle were to be measured by his power, the extent to which his power is victorious could never be measured. His miracle therefore was measured by the hunger of the thousands, and it was victorious over the number of the twelve baskets. In the case of all artisans the desire of the clients surpasses the power of the artisans. They are not

---

[1] There is a scribal error in the Syriac form of this verb, which reads ܫܬ̣ܠ, "planting" instead of ܫܬ̇ܐ, "drinking."

[2] Exod 21:24.

[3] Matt 5:39.

[4] Cf. Matt 14:13-21.

[5] Gen 1:28.

able to execute according to the desires of their clients. In the case of God, however, his [creative] activity excels [the desires of] those in need. For [he said], *Gather up the fragments so that nothing may be lost*,[1] lest anyone think that he had acted [only] in imagination. Then, when the remainder would have been conserved for a day or two, they would believe that he had really done this and that it had not been just an empty vision.

§5.   When they were satisfied, therefore, they saw that he had fed them in the wilderness, as did Moses through prayer, and they cried out saying, *This is the prophet concerning whom it was said that he would come into the world.*[2] They were repeating that [word] of Moses, *The Lord will raise up a prophet for you*, not any ordinary one, but one *like me*,[3] who will feed you bread in the desert. *Like me*, he walked on the sea,[4] and appeared in the cloud.[5] He freed his Church from circumcision, and established John, who was a virgin, in place of Joshua, son of Nun. He confided Mary, his Church, to him,[6] as Moses [confided] his flock to Joshua,[7] so that this [word], *like me* might be fulfilled.

Jesus Walks on the Water

§6.   *When it was evening, his disciples arose and seated themselves in the boat, to go to Capernaum. Our Lord went up into the mountain to pray.*[8] *For behold, on the mountain are the feet of him who proclaims good news.*[9] He himself explained who this person was, *The one who announces peace.*[10] To whom, if not to the Gentiles? For, *he speaks peace to the Gentiles.*[11] *Celebrate your feasts, O Judah.*[12] It was because our Lord had performed this miracle of the bread at the time of the Azymes, the Unleavened Bread, that the prophet said, *Celebrate your feasts, O Judah.*

---

[1] John 6:12.
[2] John 6:14.
[3] Deut 18:15.
[4] Cf. Matt 14:25-31.
[5] Cf. Matt 17:5.
[6] Cf. John 19:25-27.
[7] Cf. Deut 31:7-8.
[8] John 6:16-17; cf. Matt 14:23.
[9] Nah 2:1.
[10] *Idem.*
[11] Zech 9:10.
[12] Nah 2:1.

192

For our Azymes has drawn near. *And fulfil your vows.*[1] The Lamb of truth has come and has abrogated the ancient vows and fulfilled their memorial. *Because he will no longer commit iniquity in you.*[2] What is the power of the kingdom or that of the priesthood? Why will it not continue? Because it is going to be destroyed. For all power of the kingdom and the priesthood will perish.[3]

§7.   When they were seated in the boat the wind arose upon them, and the lake was stirred up. Our Lord came and appeared to them, but they were saying, "A demon has appeared to us."[4] It was true for them that our Lord was clothed with a body that was weighty, and consequently they thought that a weighty body which could walk upon the water would be a very difficult [thing]. So, if this were indeed the case, they were not troubled for a foolish [reason]. But if, as you say, O Marcion, Jesus[5] was not clothed with a body, their being astonished at his walking on the water could not be justified. For it is not difficult for a spirit to walk on the water. Why then were they agitated? If they had known him without a body, it would have been foolish for them to have been agitated and to have cried out. But since he was corporeal, it was quite normal for them to have been afraid. They were seeing a new thing, a body that was walking on the waves but which did not sink. If [they were afraid] because it was night, it was not difficult for him, a spiritual being, who appeared on the mountain like the sun when he wished.[6] Because our Lord knew that it was quite normal for them to be agitated, he comforted them. *It is I, do not be afraid,*[7] that is, "It is I, this bodily one whom you know."

§8.   Simon, however, since he understood that it was on account of his corporality that [Jesus] had said, *It is I,* replied to him, in accordance with his word, "If this is how it is, I too am clothed with a body, and if I walk upon the waters, I will know that it is with that body which I know, that you also have walked upon them." But, when he went down to walk

---

[1] *Idem.*

[2] *Idem.*

[3] Cf. Isa 60:12.

[4] Cf. Matt 14:22-26; John 6:16-19.

[5] Ephrem uses the Marcionite form of the name here, ܢܘܣ.

[6] Cf. Matt 17:1-2.

[7] Matt 14:27.

[upon them] and *he began to sink,*[1] [the Lord] did not reject him. He did not say to him, "Without faith," but, *Little faith.*[2] Because the sea carried our Lord, the sea was revealing concerning the path that he was treading out for his apostles in the world. That [word] was fulfilled there, *You will have dominion over the splendour of the sea and you will calm its waves.*[3]

§9.   *When our Lord had arrived and had entered the boat with Simon, the wind abated.*[4] The Arian, therefore, who contradicts the birth [of the Lord], is also rejected, through the word which those who were in the boat spoke, *They came and worshipped him and they were saying to him, You are indeed the Son of God.*[5] It is he of whom it is written, *The waters saw you and trembled and the depths too were stirred up. Your pathways are upon many waters, and your footsteps are not known.*[6] So they confessed by their word that he, concerning whom these things were spoken, was indeed the Son of God.

The Bread of Life

§10.   *What sign will you do, that we may see and believe in you?*[7] For lo, a multitude of miracles had been arrayed before them. But, because they wanted only one [thing], they despised all [the others] he had performed, as if his fame had not reached their ears. What then was it that they wanted, if not that about which they had spoken openly to him, *Our fathers ate manna in the desert, as it is written, He gave them bread from heaven.*[8] As someone might say, "If you do something similiar for us, [we will believe in you], and if not, you will no longer be visible to us. For thus did Moses speak to us, *I will raise up for you a prophet like me.*"[9] So, when [the Lord] saw that they were boasting about Moses and spurning him, he withheld [the miracle], not because he was not able to grant it to them, but because he was convinced that it would not be of any avail to them. When

---

[1] Cf. Matt 14:28-30.
[2] Matt 14:31.
[3] Ps 89:10.
[4] Matt 14:25,32.
[5] Matt 14:33.
[6] Ps 77:17,20.
[7] John 6:30.
[8] John 6:31; cf. Ps 78:24.
[9] Deut 18:15.

Moses performed this [miracle] for them it was of no benefit to them. They turned away from his covenant and their deeds became depraved.

§11.   Our Lord, therefore, without spurning the gift [of manna] of [the Father] who sent him, reproved those who received it, because he knew with what kind of outcome their bitterness would receive it. Accordingly, he said to them, *This is the bread that came down from heaven, which, if anyone eats of it, will he die?*[1] Certainly not! So what kind is it? It is he, *who is given to the entire world.*[2] That [bread] of Moses was not perfect. This is why it was given to [the Israelites] only. But, in order to show his own gift was superior to that of Moses, and that the calling of the Gentiles was more perfect than that of the stiff-necked people, he said, *Whoever eats of my bread will live forever. For the bread of God has come down from heaven and is given to the entire world.*[3] *No one can come to me unless the Father who sent me draws him.*[4] [He said this] so that this teaching given by God might be awakened in them. This is like [when he said], *I am the way,*[5] and, *[I am] the gate of the sheep.*[6] Secondly, [he said this] so that each one of them would be convinced that God was drawing him, and that they would become committed through this pledge. For those who had come to [the Lord] were given their title according to the name of the Father, just as those who had perished, according to the name of Satan. *For no one perished from among them, except the son of perdition.*[7] The people [of Israel] likewise were called according to the name of Moses, even when they were sinning, because they were dependent on Moses.

Respect for Parents

§12.   *Let the one who curses his father or his mother die,*[8] and, *Whoever blasphemes against God, let him be crucified.*[9] [God] ordained that the honour due to one's parents was like that due to himself, just as

---

[1] John 6:50.
[2] John 6:51.
[3] *Idem.*
[4] John 6:44.
[5] John 14:6.
[6] John 10:7.
[7] John 17:12.
[8] Lev 20:9; Matt 15:4.
[9] Deut 21:23.

the prophet also declared, *If I am Father, where will you honour me, and if I am Lord, where will you fear me?*[1] Our Lord also confirmed this [text], *God has said, Honour your father and your mother. So, each one of you says to his father, My offering [to God] will be of use to you from me.*[2] *But this son,* upon whom you have placed these laws, *does not compel himself to honour either father or mother.*[3] For, with regard to a certain pharisee, who had stirred up his companions against him, [the Lord said], "Even [in the case of] this man, who has invited us to the banquet, I am not a respecter of persons, on account of his provisions, like you [are wont to be]. For he too, *does not honour his father or his mother. And every plantation which the Father, who is in heaven, has not planted, will be uprooted.*"[4] [This is to be understood] with regard to the commandments of their elders.

The Canaanite Woman

§13.   *She was crying out [as] she was following after him, Have mercy on me. But he did not reply to her.*[5] The silence of our Lord engendered an even deeper cry in the mouth of the Canaanite woman. He spurned her by his silence, but she did not give up. He despised her by his word, but she did not hold back. He showed honour to Israel who had spurned him, but she was not envious. On the contrary, she again humbled herself and again magnified Israel, by [her words], *Even the dogs eat from their masters' [crumbs],*[6] as though the Jews were masters of the Gentiles. His disciples therefore drew near and begged him to send her away.[7] He gave them an example of the insistent love of the Gentiles. He called them dogs, and Israel, sons. The Gentiles, symbolized as dogs, possess the daring of dogs and the love of dogs. But the Israelites, symbolized as sons, possess the frenzy of dogs. *People do not take the bread of the sons and throw it to the dogs.*[8] He poured forth and filled her ears with a great reproach, so that her faith might be revealed. Listen to her response! *Yes, indeed, My Lord.*[9]

---

[1] Mal 1:6.
[2] Matt 15:4-5.
[3] Cf. Matt 15:6.
[4] Matt 15:13.
[5] Matt 15:22-23.
[6] Matt 15:27.
[7] Cf. Matt 15:23.
[8] Matt 15:26.
[9] Matt 15:27.

But she was not ashamed, to her own benefit, of the name of dogs. Therefore [he said], *Great is your faith, O Woman.*[1] In calling the Gentiles dogs, he was comparing his gift to bread.

§14.   He performed miracles in Israel, therefore, to teach them that whoever resisted him was resisting a superior power. For Israel, who at that time had obeyed the name of Joshua, son of Nun, did not recognize the Lord of [that same] name when he came.[2] But the seed of Canaan, from the shadows which they saw at that time in Joshua, son of Nun, recognized the prototype in his images. When this impure spirit went out from the seed of Canaan, which had recognized the truth from the images, this [same] spirit entered again into Israel, who had been instructed for a long time in the images of truth. When the Lord of images arrived he was blasphemed by them. But this spirit had [already] possessed them when they returned from the exploration of the land, and they were contentious and rebellious against Moses to the point of stoning him.[3] He calmed their fury nonetheless. This name destroyed the giants before them,[4] and this [impure] spirit went off to the Canaanites, who came then to do battle against Joshua, son of Nun. But when the true Jesus came, it was by means of the faith of the Canaanites that he drove out the spirit from the young girl, who was a symbol of the race of Canaan. For, in every religion, [the impure spirits] came forth upon encountering this name [of Jesus]. If today you look at Israel, you will find that all the anger and contentiousness of the Gentiles dwell in it.

§15.   Do not, however, O Listener, focus entirely on the narrative of this spirit and its seven companions, but [rather], accept firmly the point of the comparison and the point of the parable, and do not be distracted with all the parts of the comparison or by the many garments of the parable. For, where there is an abundance of parables, [this] is a temporary clothing for the word, which takes what is of profit, so that it can appear in its truth. Just as the Canaanites who had fought against this name [of Jesus] vanished from their land, so too the Israelites were uprooted from the midst of their dwelling place.

---

[1] Matt 15:28.
[2] The names Joshua and Jesus have the same form in Syriac.
[3] Cf. Num 14:1-38.
[4] Cf. Num 13:32.

The Samaritan Woman[1]

§16. Our Lord came to the fountain of water like a hunter. He asked for water so that he might give water, under the pretext of water. He asked for a drink, like someone who was thirsty, so that the gateway to quenching thirst might be opened to him. He asked a request of [the woman] so that he might teach her, and that she in turn might make a request of him. Although rich, [the Lord] was not ashamed to make a request like a person in need, so that he might teach indigence how to make a request. He was not afraid of reproach for talking to a woman on her own, that he might teach me that whoever stands in the truth will not be upset. *They were amazed that he was standing, talking to a woman.*[2] He had sent his disciples away from him lest they chase away his prey. He cast a bait for the dove so that through it he might capture the entire flock. He made a request of her obliquely so that she might respond directly. *Give me water that I may drink.*[3] This was the beginning of the encounter. He asked for water, and [then gave] a promise concerning the water of life; he asked, and then he abandoned his request, just like she too [abandoned] her jug. He abandoned pretexts because the truth, for whose sake the pretexts had been [used], had come.

§17. *Give me water [that] I may drink. She said to him, Behold, you are a Jew. He said to her, If only you knew.*[4] He showed her [thus] that she did not know, for it was [precisely] in this regard that she was going astray, on account of [her] lack of knowledge. But he instructed her in the knowledge of the truth.[5] He wished to draw aside, little by little, the veil that was over her heart. For, if he had revealed to her in the beginning that *I am the Messiah*, she would have recoiled from him, and she would not have become a disciple of his teaching. *If only you knew who has said to you, Give me to drink, you would have asked it of him. She said to him, You do not have a vessel and the well is deep. He said to her,*[6] "My water comes down from heaven." That teaching is from on high, and that drink

---

[1] Cf. E. Beck, "Der syrische Diatessaronkommentar zu der Perikope von der Samariterin am Brunnen übersetzt und erklärt," *Oriens Christianus* 74 (1990), pp. 1-24.
[2] John 4:27.
[3] John 4:7.
[4] John 4:7,9-10.
[5] The verb in Syriac seems to be feminine, but the context favours a masculine form.
[6] John 4:10-11,13.

is heavenly. Those who drink it will not be thirsty again. Baptism is one for believers. *Whoever drinks from the water that I will give him will never thirst again. She said to him, Give me some of this water, so that I may not be thirsty, and draw water from here.*[1]

§18. *He said to her, Go, call your husband to me.*[2] He opened a door for her that he might reveal hidden things to her like a prophet. But she said, *I have no husband.*[3] [She said] this to test him as to whether he knew hidden things. He showed her two things: that which he[4] was and that which he was not; that which he was in name, but not in truth. *You have had five, and this one is not your husband. She said to him, Lord, I see that you are a prophet.*[5] He thus lifted her up onto another level. *Our fathers worshipped on this mountain. He said to her, Not on this mountain and not in Jerusalem, but true worshippers will worship in spirit and in truth.*[6] He was thus exercising her unto perfection, and instructing her with regard to the calling of the Gentiles.

To show that she was not a barren land, she was testifying, by means of the sheaf that she was offering him, that her sowing had reaped a hundredfold. *Behold the Messiah is coming and he will give us everything. He said to her, I am He, who is speaking with you.*[7] "If you are the king, why are you asking water from me?" It was not thus that he had first revealed himself to her, but rather first as a Jew, and then as a prophet, and after that as the Messiah. From degree to degree he led her and placed her on the highest degree. She first saw him as someone thirsting; and then as a Jew; then as a prophet, and after that as God. As somone thirsting, she persuaded him; as a Jew, she recoiled from him, as a learned one, she interrogated him, as a prophet she was reprimanded, and as the Messiah, she worshipped him.

§19.[8] The [Samaritan] men were afraid to espouse this Samaritan woman, for they were mindful of Judah, who had held back Shelah from

---

1 John 4:14-15.
2 John 4:16.
3 John 4:17.
4 Jesus is referring to the woman's "husband."
5 John 4:18-19.
6 John 4:20-21,23.
7 John 4:25-26.
8 Leloir notes that in this and the preceding section there are differences between the Syriac text and the Armenian translation. In §18 the Syriac text contains a number of

Tamar.[1] And to remain a widow moreover was [considered to be] shameful. Therefore, this Samaritan woman proceeded cautiously, [lest] she provide [the Lord] with the wherewithal to attack.[2] For a husband was being attributed to her, even though none had approached her. She had not therefore compelled any man lest he might die through her.[3] Anyone would have been afraid to marry her because of this, as in [the text], *Seven women will take hold of one man and say to him, We will eat our own bread and be clothed in our own garments, only let your name be called over us, and take away our shame.*[4] Accordingly, our Lord said to her, *You have had five, and the present one is not your husband.*[5] When the Samaritans perceived that they themselves had not noticed what [the Lord] had revealed concerning her, they judged wisely [as follows]: "If he is the Messiah, he is capable of showing forth his powers, not only in this [way], but in many others [also]," with the result that he showed himself glorious among them in many ways. Therefore, when they saw the miracles and the revelations that were [even] greater than the case of this Samaritan woman, they got rid of the pretext [in advance], lest she become a source of scorn to them on the part of the Jews, that they should have placed the foundation of their faith upon the revelation of a woman. Accordingly, *They said to her, It is not because of your word that we believe in him, but because we have heard his teaching and have seen his deeds; because they are from God, we know that he is the Messiah.*[6] For it is fitting that our [own] knowledge be the foundation of our faith.

§20.   *Our fathers worshipped on this mountain.*[7] This [refers] to Jacob and his sons, for they used to worship on the mountain of Shechem, or in Bethel or on Mount Gerizim. *Neither on this mountain nor in Jerusalem shall you worship*[8] means: *In every place that you make my name*

---

phrases and an allusion to the call of the Gentiles which are lacking in the Armenian. He is of the opinion that these additions are authentic and are in accord with the content of the section. However, with regard to the additional elements in the Syriac of §19, he would be inclined to give preference to the Armenian (cf. EC-CBM 8, p. 93, n. 1).

[1] Cf. Gen 38:6-30.
[2] Literally, "that she might be arms to him."
[3] An allusion to what happened to Er and Onan, Tamar's first two husbands (Gen 38:6-30).
[4] Isa 4:1.
[5] John 4:18.
[6] John 4:42.
[7] John 4:20.
[8] John 4:21.

remembered.[1] Moreover, [the woman] had said, *You say that the house of worship is in Jerusalem, but our fathers worshipped on this mountain.*[2] Therefore, to show her that God is not corporeal, he said, *Amen, I say to you! Neither on this mountain nor in Jerusalem shall you worship, but true worshippers will worship the Father in spirit and in truth. Neither on this mountain nor in Jerusalem shall [God] be worshipped.*[3] He revealed thereby that there would be worship throughout the entire world, through the excision of the fig tree which was impeding worship.[4]

The Healing of the Leper

§21.   *If you are willing, Lord, you can cleanse me.*[5] This leper had thought that he was observing the Law like Elisha, for [Elisha] had not gone forward to Naaman.[6] [The Lord] resolved this [doubt], in that *he touched him,*[7] in order to show that the Law was not an obstacle to him who had constituted the Law. Or, [the leper] was certainly thinking that [the Lord] was a stranger to the Law, and so he healed him both secretly and openly at the same time, lest he, who was healed corporeally, be wounded spiritually. *Go, show yourself.*[8] This was for the sake of the priests. For [the leper] was afraid to touch him lest he defile him. But [the Lord] touched him to show him that he would not be defiled, he, at whose rebuke the defilement fled from the defiled one.

Did not Moses carry Joseph's bones?[9] When [God] chose him, did he not indeed make him a leper when he said to him, *Put your hand into your bosom?*[10] Samson ate honey from the dead body of an impure animal,[11] and with the jawbone of a dead ass he was victorious and rescued Israel.[12] Furthermore, God gave him water from the dead

---

[1] Exod 20:24.
[2] John 4:20.
[3] John 4:21,23.
[4] Cf. Luke 13:6-9; Isa 5:1-7.
[5] Matt 8:2.
[6] Cf. 2 Kgs 5:8-12.
[7] Matt 8:3.
[8] Matt 8:4.
[9] Cf. Gen 50:23-24. This middle section of §21 as far as the end of the citation from 1 Tim 1:9 is not present in the Armenian translation.
[10] Exod 4:6.
[11] Cf. Judg 14:9.
[12] Cf. Judg 15:15-16.

201

jawbone. He gave him to drink and he was refreshed.[1] Just as [Paul] has said, *The Law was not laid down for the just.*[2]

What our Lord had showed the leper through a tangible experience, the [woman] of the haemorrhage knew through faith, before [any] experience.[3] [The need for] experience is for the stupid. Accordingly our Lord was refuting two things. If he had not touched the leper he would have been confirming [the leper] with regard to what he had conjured up in his thought, that [the Lord] was indeed afraid of leprosy. But if he had touched him, the other [thought] would have had free course in his mind, that he was a stranger to the Law. Therefore, by stretching out his hand, he showed his divinity and drove impurity away, and by the word of his mouth he showed his familiarity [with the Law] and put flight to the [possibility of] being a stranger [to it]. Because this [leper] was a Jew, and had heard it [said] by the priests that this Jesus was opposed to the Law and an enemy to the [Mosaic] precept, accordingly, he had thought that he was not positively disposed towards the healing of the Jews.

§22.   *If you are willing, you can cleanse me.*[4] The formula is one of petition and the word is one of fear. "That you are able to I know, but whether you are willing, I am not certain." Therefore our Lord showed him two things in response to this double [attitude]: reproof through his anger, and mercy through his healing. For, in response to *if you are willing*, he was angry, and in response to *you can*, he was healed. In order to cleanse the leper's soul of his [unwise] thoughts, just as [he had cleansed] his body from its defilement, he taught him, *Go!,* to those corrupt ones who taught you, *and make the offering for your purification, as Moses prescribed,*[5] and, *Do not speak of it to anyone,*[6] lest the priests think that it was because they had complained, that he was pleasing them and offering the sacrifice. "Be silent," he said, "and when you draw near to them, and they ask you how it was that you were healed, they will learn that I am concerned for the commandments of Moses, lest these be despised."

---

[1] Cf. Judg 15:18-19.
[2] 1 Tim 1:9.
[3] Cf. Mark 5:27-28,34.
[4] Matt 8:2.
[5] Luke 5:14.
[6] Matt 8:4.

§23. *If you are willing, you can cleanse me.*[1] This man was taking note that [the Lord] was not raising all dead people to life, and that he was not healing all those who were blemished. He therefore thought, "He is healing whomsoever he wishes." So he said to him, *Lord, If you are willing, you can cleanse me.* Through his anger, [the Lord] showed that he was healing without exception of persons. But, because the leper had believed that *if you are willing, you can,* he showed that he did not spurn this faith. Moreover, [the leper] had seen that the priests were not cleansing [the lepers], but [instead] were burdening them by means of the prescriptions in the Law concerning leprosy, and [thus] the service of the Law was belittled in his eyes. Wherefore, he said, *If you are willing, you can cleanse me.*[2] [The Lord] was angry with regard to this line of reasoning, and so [he ordered] secondly, *"Go, show yourself to the priests,*[3] and fulfil that Law which you are despising." [The Lord] also [commanded him thus], because [the leper] had been thinking about him in this manner, [because] he had seen him relax some elements of the Law. It is also said that [the Lord] was not angry with him, but with his leprosy.

§24. *If you are willing, you can cleanse me. So he stretched out his hand.*[4] In this stretching out of his hand was the abrogation of the Law. For [it is written] in the Law that whoever approaches a leper becomes impure. He [himself] did not approach the leper, but [rather] his right hand that was full of healing, and he extended it to him. Indeed, he did not show himself to be opposed to the Law, as the Scripture which follows narrates. He showed that nature was good in that he repaired its defect. Because he sent him to the priests, he thereby upheld the priesthood. He also ordered him to make an offering for his *cleansing.*[5] Did he not thus uphold the Law, *as Moses had commanded?*[6] There were many prescriptions concerning leprosy. But they were unable to procure any benefit. Then the Messiah came, and, with his word, bestowed healing and abolished these many precepts which the Law had reckoned should exist for leprosy. *Go,*

---

[1] Matt 8:2. In the Syriac text the personal suffix attached to the verb here, and in the next citation of this verse three sentences later, is in the first person plural form, but, in the remaining citations of the verse, it is in the singular.

[2] *Idem.*

[3] Matt 8:4.

[4] Matt 8:2-3.

[5] Luke 5:14.

[6] *Idem.*

therefore, to the priests for their testimony,[1] since it was prescribed for them that, before the cleansing, they must examine the leper, and after the cleansing, they must be witnesses. These things were the Law of Moses in the Old [Testament]. The Messiah invoked them as testimony to his teaching, [saying], *As Moses commanded,* so that these [precepts] would not take flight before him, but [instead] become his heralds before the people.

---

[1] Matt 8:4.

XIII

The Healing of a Paralytic

§1.   *There was a man there who had been ill for thirty-eight years. Our Lord said to him, Do you wish to get well?* [1] If [he had not been willing, the Lord] would not have been willing. The [sick man] said to him, *I have no one to let me down when the waters are stirred up.*[2] [The Lord] had questioned him concerning one thing, but he replied concerning another, *I have no one to let me down, for while I am still coming, another who is ahead of me goes down.*[3] So, for thirty-eight years, no one was found [to help] him. Let the Jews, who do not believe that baptism forgives sins, be put to shame. For, if they believe that an angel can heal illnesses through *the waters of Shiloah,*[4] how much more can the Lord of angels purify the stains [of sin] through baptism? Because this [sick man] thought that help could only come to him through the water, [the Lord] said to him, *Arise, take up your bed.*[5] He was a sinner, and did not believe, as these [words] testify, *Do not sin any more.*[6] Justice entered and sought faith in these porticos, but did not find it. Mercy healed him, so that grace might not go forth from there in vain.

§2.   *Arise, take up your bed and go to your house.*[7] Would it not have sufficed [to say], *Arise and go?* Would it not have been a miracle that he, who was not able to turn himself about on his bed, should arise easily and go? But to show that he had given him a complete healing, [the Lord] also made him carry his bed, not like the sick who come back to health gradually. *Take up your bed and go.* Even if he were silent, his bed would cry out. When the Jews saw him therefore, *they were saying to him, Who told you to take up your bed?* [8] They omitted to ask him, "Who cured you?" *They were saying to him, Who commanded you to carry [your bed]*

---

[1] John 5:5-6.

[2] John 5:7. The Syriac text reads a first person plural suffix, ܢܚܬܘܢ , "to let us down."

[3] *Idem.* The Syriac text reads a first person plural suffix here too.

[4] Cf. Isa 8:6; John 9:7 (Siloam); 5:4.

[5] John 5:8.

[6] John 5:14.

[7] John 5:8.

[8] John 5:12.

205

on the Sabbath? [1] O blind ones, who do not understand, and deaf ones, who do not hear! Why is it that you leave one thing aside, and interrogate concerning another? Because they had interrogated blindly, he who had been healed replied to them clearly. He was a skilled advocate, sent by the wise Physician for the correction of the perverse. *Who commanded you to carry your bed?*[2]

§3. Because they wanted to hide the miracle of his healing, and accuse him because he had carried his bed, he openly proclaimed his healing to them and refuted their denial. For, what he had said to them was not what they wanted to hear, but what they shrank from believing. *He who healed me is the one who said to me, Take up your bed. They said to him, Who is he? He said, I do not know. For our Lord had gone away from there. After a time he saw him and said to him, See, you have been made well. Do not sin any more, lest you have need of someone else.*[3] To this [he had replied], *I have no one.*[4] *This man went away then and said to the Jews, Jesus is the one who has healed me.*[5] While they were accusing him of healing on the Sabbath, *he said to them, My Father continues even until now to do deeds, wherefore I too continue to do [them]. But the Jews were seeking to persecute the Saviour on account of this, not because he was healing on the Sabbath, but because he was calling God his father, and comparing himself with God.*[6]

§4. Understand therefore that he was not making the excuse, "I have not violated it," but, "I have violated it as the Father in heaven [has]." *My Father continues to do deeds, so I too continue to do them.*[7] Do the works [of creation] and creatures, angels and luminaries, dew and rain, floods and rivers, cease [to function] on the Sabbath? Indeed the angels are not prevented from [rendering] their service on the Sabbath, nor the heavens from [giving] their dew and rain, nor the luminaries from [following] their course, nor the earth from [giving] its fruits, nor people from breathing or bearing children. But they give birth on the Sabbath, and

---

[1] Cf. John 5:10,12.
[2] John 5:10.
[3] John 5:11-14.
[4] John 5:7.
[5] John 5:15.
[6] John 5:17-18.
[7] John 5:17.

there is no command [forbidding this], and they perform circumcision on the eighth day, and the Law is thus left aside, together with the other things which they do not count. So, if created beings [can act] in this way, how much more the Creator? This is why *the Son of Man is Lord of the Sabbath.*[1]

§5.   We find in another place also that, when [the pharisees] were accusing his disciples because they were rubbing ears of corn, *he said to them, Did you not read about that which David did, that he ate the showbread, which for him was not lawful [to eat], nor for them that were with him?*[2] Understand, therefore, the meaning of the words, and see the strength that is hidden in them! *They were persecuting him because he was making himself equal with God.*[3] When they were accusing his disciples, he put the testimony of David before them, who, although a prophet, a king and a just man, was also an ordinary man, just as the apostles were ordinary men. It was fitting that the Servant should be a witness for his fellow servants. But when they wanted to accuse him, he did not bring forward the witness of David, because he was a man, nor that of the heavens, because these too were created entities, nor that of the angels, and seraphim and watchers, because all these were sent forth unto ministry.[4] He omitted all of these, both above and below, the worlds, and created entities, the heavens and all that they contain, and [instead] cited the testimony of the Lord of all nature and the God of all creatures: *My Father continues even until now to do deeds, wherefore I too continue to do [them].*[5]

§6.   The blind man was sent to go and wash himself at Siloam[6] to show [firstly] that he did not doubt that [the Lord] had healed him; and secondly, if he were interrogated, he would go and proclaim this episode, and his faith would be seen. It was likewise in the case of [the words], *Arise, take up your bed,*[7] that they might see [such a deed] on the Sabbath, and make inquiries. The Sabbath, therefore, was not constituted for God,

---

[1] Matt 12:8.
[2] Matt 12:3-4; Luke 6:3-4; Mark 2:25-26.
[3] John 5:18.
[4] Cf. Heb 1:14.
[5] John 5:18.
[6] Cf. John 9:7.
[7] John 5:8.

but for human beings.[1] Consequently, he who instituted it is its Lord.[2] Let us see [if] what was said in the words, "Whether I am the one who instituted it or not," [is verified] by the deed. For the blind man testifies [to it], and the sick proclaim [it]. Our Lord observed all the Law in its place, to show that it is to be observed, and to condemn, through his observance, those who destroy it. But he dispensed from certain [precepts] of it for higher [motives], to show that higher [motives] prevail over everything, and also to show that he was Lord of the Law through his healing. Accordingly, created beings, who have dominion over the Sabbath through the Father's will, obey him.

§7.   Through the dispensation of the Sabbath we learn that *my Father continues even until now to perform deeds.*[3] [He said this] to reproach them, for these did not dispense from the Law for higher motives. He did not reproach them for rescuing one's ox or ass [from the pit],[4] but taught them to do what was good on the Sabbath.[5] [To show] what was good, he took evidence from them. If they had been keeping it diligently, and deriving benefit, his Father's commandment would not have been impeding [them]. But, because they had not fulfilled any of the Law, he therefore removed it.

        Take note that there are strict commandments. When they are binding, they cannot be rescinded for any reason. Take note, furthermore, that there are those which their Legislator can rescind for many reasons. When a people who did the will of the Sabbath on the Sabbath came, the Sabbath was of necessity relaxed, so that the work of freedom could be seen. Examine therefore the nature of the Lord's work, so that from his observance of [the Sabbath] we can learn what is the will of him who ordained it. Is not the freedom of spirit of one who fulfils [the Sabbath] freely, without a Sabbath [constraint], better than the constraint of the Sabbath?

---

[1] Mark 2:27.
[2] Cf. Mark 2:28.
[3] John 5:17.
[4] Matt 12:11.
[5] Cf. Matt 12:12.

The Son Is Equal to the Father

§8.   *As the Father has life in himself, so too has he given [life] to the Son.*[1] If the person of the Father were something alien to life, and yet possessed life which vivifies nature, understand the same concept with regard to the Son who is like him. But, if he in his person is life, and his life is not subject to any cause, understand this also with regard to the Son, that, as in the case of the Father, *he has life in himself.* If, however, on account of what is written, *So has he given to the Son,* you are of the opinion that apart from the gift of the Father, the Son has no life in himself, you have perverted the first meaning, since the person [of the Son] appears to you as though alienated somehow from life. Place the body [of the phrase] in the middle, so that you may rest upon [the word] *he gave,* which is like that which comes after it, *he has given him power over judgement, for he is the Son of Man.*[2] The [word] *he gave* is to be understood therefore in conjunction with *he has empowered him.* For the Father has given the life which he possesses, and [he has given it] essentially to him who is. If he were not of the same essence, there would have to be supplements, and it is not likely that [such supplements] would be grafted onto him. If, however, they were grafted onto him, this would be from him [as] of the same essence, and, at the same time, alienated from his essence. It would be the same as [saying] he gave the life of his essence unto that which does not exist.

§9.   But perhaps you might say, "He did not therefore give." I have told [you] to display the body [of the phrase] well in the middle, and listen without contention: that [the Father] has given [life] to him who has received authority over judgement. The prophet too has testified to that which *he gave,* and also concerning [the words], *He has given him authority over judgement.*[3] Because he also possesses free authority through [the words], *Authority was upon his shoulders.*[4] *The Father judges no one, but he will give all judgement to his Son.*[5] Therefore, he who avenges himself is learning to spurn the Lord of all things. For he does not acknowledge that there is One who is superior to him, who will

---

[1] John 5:26.
[2] John 5:27.
[3] *Idem.*
[4] Isa 9:5.
[5] John 5:22.

bring wrongdoing before him. Accordingly, the Messiah was named Judge, so that the disciples would not judge each other individually. Moreover, it was also announced that, at the end, he himself will judge,[1] so that no one might avenge himself here below. The Messiah, therefore, is also called Head, so that his disciples would take care of each other like members.[2] For the eyes set the foot right, and the heart rebukes the stomach and corrects the other members through repentance. Take note, therefore, of what a harsh judgement there is for the one who judges himself with justice, because he has spurned the universal Judge.

§10.   *He was a lamp that was burning,*[3] which, by its increase, [was preparing for] its extinction. He was shining in the night so that he might teach that the appointed time for the sun's dominance was fading away and its rays were disappearing. *It is not from human beings that I take witness, because I have a witness that is greater than John's.*[4] If he does not take witness from human beings, why did John precede him? But, lest they be terrified by his greatness, littleness preceded him in every way, with the baptism of water before that of the Spirit. Furthermore, [it was] so that he, who knew himself to be the offsping of a priest, might testify concerning him whose conception through the Spirit was hidden, and so that they might recognize that, through that same spirit of the prophets, John was revealing concerning him who was being accused by the scribes of transgressing the Law of Moses.

§11.   If [the Lord] did not accept witness from human beings, why then did he go to John to receive witness from him? Because John was sent from God. *He who sent us said to me.*[5] The Father testified to him through John, as he said, *Moses too wrote about me.*[6] *Moses wrote about me* [in the passage], *If a prophet arises and gives a sign or a wonder, and it comes to pass, let him be received because he is a prophet. Otherwise, let him not be believed, for he is a liar.*[7] Wherefore, *Moses wrote about me,* and also, *he himself is your accuser,*[8] "because you did not take his word as true and

---

[1] Cf. John 5:22,27.
[2] Cf. 1 Cor 12:21-26.
[3] John 5:35.
[4] John 5:34,36.
[5] John 1:33.
[6] John 5:46.
[7] Deut 13:1-3.
[8] John 5:45.

you did not believe in my deeds. Also, *which of you will accuse me of sin,*[1] that I have falsely prophesized?" From whom, therefore, do the signs through which it is written that a prophet is to be accepted, no matter who he is, come? *The deeds that I do bear witness concerning me.*[2] *Moses, therefore, is your accuser,*[3] for all that he said has been fulfilled, since the deed concurs with the word. "So, if I have not preached another God to you, but [have said], *Hear, O Israel, the Lord your God is One,*[4] and that he sent me, and that I have taught you that it is to him that I pray and give thanks, why do you not believe in me?"

§12.   How then was Moses believed in Egypt by his brothers and by Pharaoh? If it was by signs, take note that even *the magicians were acting like him.*[5] How then did they believe that God had sent him, since no revelation through a prophet had been made about him, and they had heard no voice from heaven? Nevertheless, they believed him through signs and miracles, and held as true by hearsay that God their Father had sent him. The deeds testified to the truth of the word. If his signs had not withstood victoriously to the end, it would have been difficult to believe in [Moses], on account of those who were against [him], since *the magicians were acting like him.* Would he have been believed because of the fact that God had spoken to him? They had not as yet seen with their own eyes or heard with their own ears. If it was on account of the miracles [they had believed], although they did not grasp [the meaning], they should have made a defence for the Messiah, that it was fitting that he be believed on account of his signs and mighty deeds.

The Healing of a Blind Man at Bethsaida

§13.   [In the case of] that blind man, according as his faith progressed, so too did his healing. Our Lord gave him eyes that were both hidden and revealed. He believed little by little. [The Lord] gave him sight also little by little. When a little light had arisen in his eyes, a great light arose in his mind. His faith was made perfect interiorly and his sight was crowned

---

[1] John 8:46.
[2] John 5:36.
[3] John 5:45.
[4] Deut 6:4.
[5] Cf. Exod 7:11,22.

exteriorly. *He saw everything clearly.*[1] It was as though he were on the first and lowest step and our Lord strengthened his weak faith. But when it had become stronger, it jumped from the lower degree to the more perfect degree.

---

[1] Mark 8:25.

XIV

The Confession of Faith at Caesarea

§1.   *What do people say concerning me? They said to him, There are some who say, it is Elijah, and others, Jeremiah,* et cetera.[1] For those who saw his signs were not able to explain his greatness adequately, but some compared him to Elijah on account of the zeal of his father's house;[2] others to Jeremiah because of his holiness from the womb,[3] others to John because of the newness of his baptism and the wonder of his birth. For the wondrous nature of his deeds was well known. Consequently, various opinions came into being among those who saw him. *But you, what [do you say]? Simon,* first [among them], *spoke* the first [word]. *You are the Son, the Messiah, the Son of the living God. Blessed are you, Simon; the bars of Sheol will not prevail against you.*[4] In other words, that faith will not be uprooted. What he has built up, who can tear down? What he has overturned, who can restore? Assyria wished to tear down the house which [the Lord] had built, but he destroyed the throne of its kingdom.[5] So too, in the case of Nicanor.[6] Ahab also wished to rebuild Jericho [which had been] overturned, but his kingdom was uprooted.[7]

§2.   When [the Lord] built his Church, a tower was constructed whose foundations were capable of sustaining whatever was built upon them. Compare this with when one language was divided into several languages, lest they might ascend into heaven.[8] This was to constrain them, lest they put their trust in a tower rather than in righteousness. For the depths did not bring forth the flood upon them, so that they might take refuge in the heights, but rather that repentance might liberate [where] sin had suffocated. Thus did righteousness redeem. For, in the division of these [languages], the earthly tower, [which was] an ephemeral

---

[1] Matt 16:13-14. See the note above at II, § 5 for comment on this type of indication of scriptural abbreviation.
[2] Matt 16:14; John 2:17.
[3] Cf. Jer 1:5.
[4] Matt 16:15-18.
[5] Cf. 2 Kgs 18:13-19:37.
[6] Cf. 1 Macc 7:26-47.
[7] Cf. 1 Kgs 16:34.
[8] Cf. Gen 11:1-9.

construction and a perishable house of refuge, was abolished. But the Life-Giver gave them a tower from himself which reached to the heights, and a tree whose fruit was a life-giving remedy.

§3.   *You are Peter,*[1] that stone which [the Lord] established, so that Satan might stumble against it. In turn, Satan wished to set it up against our Lord, so that he might stumble against it. Hence [the words], *Be it far from you!* [2] We did not know however that Satan had thought thus, but he who knew made it known to us through [the words], *Be off with you, Satan, you are a stumbling block to me.*[3] He cast this [stone] behind him so that those adherents of Satan might stumble against it, for, *they went backwards and fell.*[4] And also this [text], *Do not say that I am the Messiah,*[5] for you will not show the truth about me by words only, but by deeds. Likewise, *he commanded them, when they came down from the mountain, Do not say anything of what you have seen until the Son of Man rises from the dead.*[6]

Jesus Foretells His Death

§4.   *See, we are going up to Jerusalem, and all that is written about me will be fulfilled. For the Son of Man is about to be crucified and die.*[7] Satan fought once again against our Lord through the mouth of Simon, head of his Church, as [he had formerly] through Eve. *Let these things be far from you, Lord.*[8] He said to him, *Get behind me, Satan.*[9] "Have you not learned the reason for my coming? Just as I became an infant and was placed in the cradle, and gave joy to those born [of women], so too it is fitting that I go down to Sheol, and console the dead, in the presence of those just ones, who for ages have been waiting to see me. *The prophets, the kings and the just have desired,*[10] and *Abraham was waiting to see my day.*[11] I will go down to see him. Who does not wish that I should ascend upon the cross

---

[1] Matt 16:18.
[2] Matt 16:22.
[3] Matt 16:23.
[4] John 18:6.
[5] Matt 16:20.
[6] Matt 17:9.
[7] Luke 18:31-33.
[8] Matt 16:22.
[9] Matt 16:23.
[10] Matt 13:17.
[11] John 8:56.

and liberate creatures, if not Satan?" *Get behind me, therefore, because you do not think that which is of God, but rather that which is of human beings.*[1] [This was] because they were fishermen and ordinary folk, whose ears were not trained in the words of the prophets.

The Transfiguration

§5. *There are men standing here in my presence who will not taste death.*[2] [He said this] to show that they would be taken up alive into the air. He summoned to him again Elijah, [who had been] taken up, and Moses [who had been] revived, and three witnesses from among the heralds.[3] These were pillars, capable of bearing witness to the kingdom. Simon, in his lack of knowledge, spoke with great knowledge, for he recognized Moses and Elijah, just like John had recognized our Lord through the Spirit as he came towards them. For he testified, *I did not know him.*[4] If the Spirit revealed to them through the mouth of Simon, this Spirit was speaking of something which [Simon] did not know. With the very [phrase] *Moses and Elijah* is linked that of the three tents. [Why is it], if not because freewill is associated with the Spirit. Or else, [it was] because of his calling [them] that the disciples recognized Moses and Elijah, for, *they appeared, talking with him.*[5]

§6. He also showed them before his death, *when his face was transfigured,*[6] that it was changed in some way or other, and that, however it was changed, they nevertheless would know that it was somehow he. He instructed them in advance, so that when he would rise from the dead, and be changed, they would not be in doubt. For, if this were the kingdom he was to receive after his resurrection, why was it not seen [then] in this image? For what reason? [He acted thus] because they were not able to gaze upon him, and so that they might know that they too would be transformed in like manner. He brought these two so that the resurrection that he was to accomplish at the end might be believed; that those who,

---

[1] Matt 16:23.
[2] Matt 16:28.
[3] Cf. Matt 17:1-3.
[4] John 1:31.
[5] Matt 17:3.
[6] Luke 9:29.

like Moses, have died would rise again, and that those who are alive would fly, like Elijah, since he is Lord of the heights and of the depths.

§7.   Therefore, when Moses and Elijah appeared Simon said, *If you wish, Lord, let us make three tents here.*[1] For he saw that the mountain was in respite from the controversy of the scribes, and that pleased him. And the odour of the kingdom breathed in his nostrils, and it was pleasant for him. He saw [the Lord's] glory instead of his shame, and he rejoiced in their sojourning with Moses and Elijah, and exulted that they had escaped from Caiphas and Herod. Just as he had had pity on him earlier [in saying], *Be it far from you*, on this occasion he said, *Let us make three tents here.* But [the evangelist said], *He did not know what he was saying,*[2] for our Lord was about to be crucified. Or else, because these tents were not those of here below, but of the world to come. *Make for yourselves friends who will receive you in their eternal tents.*[3] Also, *he did not know what he was saying*, since he counted [the Lord] in with Moses and Elijah in the numbering of the tents. Accordingly, a divine voice from heaven enlightened him, *This is my Son and my Beloved,*[4] so that our Lord might be distinguished from his servants.[5]

In his compassion, [the Lord] used our body so that we might be able to bear the sight of him and hear his voice, and not suffer what the chief disciples suffered on the mountain, those upon whom a stupor fell when his glory shone out for them through his body. For they were in amazement and stupified by his glory.[6] When it was more fitting than ever that they should have been watchful, they were asleep. This [happened] so that we might learn that this was why he appeared without glory, and why it was that he came in a body.

If then, although they did not see his divinity clearly, but [merely] a glimpse of his glory in a body which shone out for them, the apostles and the chief disciples slumbered and slept, and did not know what they were seeing and what they were saying, and if Simon spoke words altogether different, what would it have been like for us, if he had appeared to us clearly in the glory of his godhead, without a body? How

---

[1] Matt 17:4.
[2] Mark 9:6; Luke 9:33.
[3] Luke 16:9.
[4] Matt 17:5.
[5] The remainder of §7 is not found in the Armenian version.
[6] Cf. Luke 9:32.

can I say this, "If he had 'appeared to us without a body"? For how would it have been possible for him to appear without a body? How could we have been taught by means of a tongue by one who had no tongue? How could we have seen the miracles that were seen, [if performed] by one who was invisible?

§8.   Why did Moses and Elijah appear with him? [This was] because, when he asked them, *What do people say concerning me?*, *they said to him, Some say that [he is] Elijah, others, Jeremiah, and others, one of the prophets.*[1] [He questioned them] so that he might show them that he was not Elijah, nor one of the prophets. Moses and Elijah appeared beside him so that they might know that he was Lord of the prophets. He transformed his countenance on the mountain before he died,[2] so that they would not be in doubt concerning the transformation of his countenance after his death, and so that they might know that he, who changed the garments which he was wearing, [is also] he who will raise to life the body with which he was clothed. He, who gave [his body] a glory which no one can attain, is able to raise it to life from death, which everyone tastes.

§9.   If he were an alien [God], how come that Moses and Elijah were talking with him? Who resuscitated Moses, and brought forth Elijah? For see, they were brought before the Just One, before the time. If it were by force that he had gone up and brought down Elijah, this [person] could not have been the Good [God], for he would have snatched [him] from the bosom of the Just One and brought him down as a witness to himself. If, without [the Just One], he had searched out and taken Moses, he would have acted in theft, because he would have been bringing out from the graves the bones which the Just One had hidden from human eyes.[3]

So, when that voice was heard, *This is my Son and my Beloved. Listen to him,*[4] where was the Just One then? Was he terrified, and so hid himself, and did not come [in answer] to his voice? Or, was it the voice of an alien [God] passing through gently, which he did not hear? Or, perhaps he is above the third heaven, as they say, and the Just One above the second? But how could this voice have passed him by without his perceiving it? And, if he did perceive it, why would he have become silent

---

[1] Matt 16:14.
[2] Cf. Luke 9:29.
[3] Cf. Deut 34:6.
[4] Mark 9:7.

at this threat which was making little of him, "*Listen to him* and you will live"? Therefore, everyone who listens to another voice will certainly die. Or, perhaps they had entered into a pact among themselves, so that at one moment one of them would say, *I am the first and the last and there is none before or after me*,[1] and at another time the other would say, *This is my Son and my Beloved. Listen to him.*[2]

§10. *As they were coming down from the mountain, he was commanding them, You must not speak openly of what you have seen to anyone.*[3] Why so? Because he knew that [others] would not believe them, but would take them for fools, [saying], "Do you know where Elijah has come from?" and, "See, Moses is buried and no one has succeeded in finding his grave," and there would be blasphemy and scandal because of this. He said, "*Wait until you have received the power*,[4] for, when you will have recounted and they will not believe, you will raise the dead, unto their confusion and your own glory." *Wait* also [means], until the graves are rent asunder, and the just, both recent and ancient, go forth and come to Jerusalem, *the city of the great king*.[5] See, they will [then] believe that he who raised them has also [raised] Moses. *We will see whether Elijah will come and take him down.*[6] At his voice, many just ones came forth from the midst of Sheol. In the place of one [just man] many just came forth. If the dead heard him and came forth, how much more will Elijah live. Accordingly, because [the just] came forth from the tombs, let [the Jews] learn concerning [the matter] of Moses and Elijah. Wherefore [he said], *Do not make it known until the Son of Man will have arisen from the dead.*[7]

§11. The disciples, lest [the Jews] might say that [the Lord] had deceived them, proclaimed that *Moses and Elijah were speaking with him.*[8] Moses received the Law on that mountain; and Elijah came in zeal to seek vengeance for the Law, in which it is written, *If you continue hostile to*

---

[1] Rev 22:13.
[2] Mark 9:7.
[3] Matt 17:9; Mark 9:9.
[4] Acts 1:4,8.
[5] Ps 48:3.
[6] Mark 15:36.
[7] Matt 17:9.
[8] Matt 17:3.

me.[1] Moreover, because neither of them possessed anything, accordingly both of them were seen as loving each other, in the presence of him who loves everyone equally. God has fashioned equality for them too, [giving] them the same rank for their names, *Remember the Law of Moses, my servant;*[2] [and] *See, I will send you Elijah, the prophet.*[3] [The words], *After six days he led them,*[4] are a symbol of the sixth millennium.[5]

§12.   Why did he not bring all the disciples? Because Judas was among them, an alien to the kingdom, and not worthy to be brought. Nor was it fitting to leave him on his own. He was thought to be a perfect man, by reason of his having been chosen by him who chose him. His theft had not been revealed up to this point, for, if his iniquity had been known, the disciples, his companions, would have known [it]. But our Lord knew that he was a traitor, when he said, *One of you will betray me.*[6] [If the Lord had left him on his own] they would have said accordingly that he was setting him apart from his companions. But why did he choose him, and why did he hate him, and then, conversely, make him steward? To show his perfect love and his mercy.

[It was] also that our Lord might teach his Church that, even if there are false teachers in it, it is nevertheless the true seat [of authority]. For the seat of Judas did not come to naught with the traitor himself. It was also [to teach] that, even if there are evil stewards, the stewardship itself is true. He therefore *washed* his feet,[7] [those feet] by means of which he had arisen and gone to [Jesus'] slayers. *He kissed* the mouth of him who, by means of it, gave the signal for death to those who apprehended him.[8] *He reached out and gave bread* into that hand which reached out and took his price, and sold him unto slaughter.[9]

---

[1] Lev 26:21.
[2] Josh 1:13.
[3] Mal 3:23.
[4] Matt 17:1.
[5] An allusion to an interpretation of the phrase "With the Lord, one day is as a thousand years and a thousand years as one day " (cf. Ps 90:4; 2 Pet 3:8).
[6] Matt 26:21.
[7] Cf. John 13:5.
[8] Cf. Matt 26:48-49.
[9] Cf. John 13:25-26.

A Prophet Should Not Perish Outside of Jerusalem

§13. *It is not fitting that a prophet should perish outside of Jerusalem.*[1] This is [like]: *You are not permitted to offer the passover except at the place which the Lord, your God, has chosen for you, to make his name dwell there,*[2] as the apostle also attests, *Our passover is the Messiah, who has been sacrificed,*[3] to show that the types were in Israel, but the truth was through Jesus.[4]

The Epileptic Demoniac

§14. Therefore, [he said], *O perverse generation!,*[5] because they had accused his disciples that *they were not able to heal him.*[6] [These people] imagined that [the disciples] were not yet perfected in the [healing] art of their master. This [opinion] reached the disciples and raised doubts in them. They came in order to learn from him. *Why could we not heal him?*[7] *This man expels demons through Beelzebul.*[8] They were saying to this man, "These disciples of his have not learned his art. Why did they not heal him?" That is why [he replied], *O perverse generation!,* and why he chose seventy-two there and then, and sent them forth from him. They healed in a wondrous way, so that those who were thinking thus might be refuted.

§15. *How long am I to be with you?*[9] [He said this] because, after they would have killed him, they would see that his name was performing powerful deeds and wonders. Lest [his healing] be [considered as] an art, he said to him, *For the one who believes, everything is possible that it be for him.*[10] *He said to them, On account of the smallness of your faith.*[11] To lighten the burden from his disciples, he said, *I command you, dumb*

---

[1] Luke 13:33.
[2] Deut 16:5-6.
[3] 1 Cor 5:7.
[4] Cf. John 1:17.
[5] Matt 17:17.
[6] Matt 17:16.
[7] Matt 17:19.
[8] Matt 12:24.
[9] Matt 17:17.
[10] Cf. Matt 17:20.
[11] *Idem.*

spirit,[1] to show that everything was easy for him, because he was God. But how could a dumb spirit which could not hear obey them? This was not difficult for people of faith, but [it was] in order to restrain the blasphemers a little from mocking the disciples, *for, up to this, his disciples too had not believed in him*.[2] [In saying], *Go forth from him and do not come back again*,[3] he made known his freedom. Because [the spirit] had planned to go back into him again, he bound it, *Do not return there*.[4]

The Temple Tax

§16.   *He spoke first to Simon and said to him, From whom do the kings of the earth take toll or tribute? From their sons or from others?* [5] [He said this] because they had come to obtain a pretext against him, for they did not seek [this tribute] from everyone. "But your teacher, perhaps he will not give it, and [then] we will apprehend him as a rebel. But if he gives it, he will be reckoned as an alien." Although the Levites were considered as aliens, nevertheless, because *the Lord is their heritage*,[6] they are like sons and no one asks anything of them. For the king of the Jews did not exact tribute from the priests. Consequently, he made known to Simon that the scribes and the pharisees were seeking a pretext to test him. They did not consider him as a priest. But he did not give them the pretext they were seeking, that by their seeking him they would show to everyone that he was an alien. He taught [Simon], however, that the Levites do not pay [tribute] because they are free sons.

§17.   *Do not offend them.*[7] This means, "Do not throw them into confusion, when you show them that it is a pretext for conflict that they are seeking to embark upon." *Go, cast the net into the sea.*[8] "Because they think that I am an alien, let the sea teach them that I am not only a priest, but also a king." *Give unto them therefore as an alien.*[9] Because Simon had made them a promise when he took the net to go and cast it [in the

---

[1] Mark 9:25.
[2] John 7:5.
[3] Mark 9:25.
[4] *Idem*.
[5] Matt 17:25.
[6] Deut 18:2.
[7] Matt 17:27.
[8] *Idem*.
[9] Cf. Matt 17:25-27.

sea], they went off with him. When he brought out a fish which had a shekel in its mouth, [with] an image of the kingdom, the proud were confounded, because they did not think that he was a Levite, he, concerning whom the sea and the fish testified that he was both king and priest.

All creatures, however, acknowledged the coming of this high priest, and ran to present their first fruits to him, all nature in accordance with its rank. The heavenly beings sent their greetings through Gabriel, the hosts of heaven through a star, the Gentiles [through] the Magi, and the prophets, who had become silent, [through] the scribes: *He will come forth from Bethlehem*.[1] The shekel, which had been formed in the fish and had received the king's seal in the depths of the waters, provided an argument against those seeking strife and contention, because the obedience of the sea was turned towards [this] alien.

Divorce

§18.   *They came and were asking him, Is it lawful for a man to divorce his wife?*[2] He answered them and said that it was not lawful. *But they began to say, Moses allowed us*,[3] so, if Moses allowed it, why then is it not lawful? *Moses allowed you because of your hardness of heart. But, from the beginning it was not thus.*[4] It became clear, therefore, by means of this one commandment, that those things which had been established by Moses on account of the people's hardness of heart should be relaxed, since the stiff-necked people[5] had been replaced by the people who cherished Abraham's faith. These [commandments], *You shall not kill, and you shall not commit adultery*[6] and all the others, were observed even before the Law. Then they were proclaimed in the Law, and were [later] made perfect in the Gospel. All the commandments in the Law, therefore, which were introduced for any reason, have ceased, not so that the ancient [order] might be abolished, but that the new [order] might be confirmed.

---

[1] Matt 2:4-5.
[2] Mark 10:2; Matt 19:3.
[3] Mark 10:4.
[4] Matt 19:8.
[5] Cf. Exod 32:9.
[6] Exod 20:13-14; Deut 5:17-18.

The Lost Coins, the Lost Sheep and the Lost Son

§19. *Ten drachmas* and *one hundred sheep*.[1] The one who strayed did so from the perfection of righteousness. For [the Lord] composed this parable for the sons of the Law. Alternatively, the one who strayed did so from the righteousness of nature.[2] Or, he symbolized through the drachma the image of Adam. Why, therefore, is there *more joy for the sinners who repent than for the righteous who have not sinned*?[3] [Is it not] because joy comes after sorrow? For, since there was sadness in them on account of their having sinned, there was joy when they repented. *It is fitting to rejoice, because your brother was dead, and [now] he is alive,* et cetera.[4] Take note that both joy and sadness are passions of the soul. How then can there be [expressions of both] sadness and joy in heaven? [Is it not] because [some] are condemned on account of sins, that one can speak of sadness among the heavenly beings, so that we may suffer. If our sins cause the angels distress, how much more fitting is it that we do penance? This is like [the passage], *I regret that I have made human beings*.[5]

§20. [He told] another parable of two sons. *When the younger son had squandered his goods*.[6] The meaning then that he placed in this parable is as follows: *Because of the one who is converted there is joy in heaven*, cum ceteris.[7]

The Unjust Steward

§21. [He told] another parable of the steward, *who was accused in the presence of* his master.[8] But the perverse astuteness of this unjust steward was praised in the presence of his master. For he had unjustly squandered the initial treasures, and then unjustly and cunningly remitted the later debts.[9] He was praised therefore because, by means of that which was not

---

[1] Cf. Luke 15:4-10.
[2] The parable, if applied to the Gentiles, involves disobedience to the natural law.
[3] Luke 15:7.
[4] Luke 15:32. See the note above at II, § 5 for comment on this type of indication of scriptural abbreviation.
[5] Cf. Gen 6:6-7.
[6] Luke 15:13-14.
[7] Luke 15:7. See the note above at II, § 5 for comment on this type of indication of scriptural abbreviation.
[8] Cf. Luke 16:1.
[9] Luke 16:1,4-7.

his, he set about acquiring that which was to be his, namely friends and supporters.[1] Adam, through that which was not his, obtained something which [likewise] was not his, namely thorns and pains.[2] Buy for yourselves, O sons of Adam, those things which do not pass away, by means of those transitory things which are not yours!

The Forgiveness of Sins

§22.   *If someone sins against me, how many times should I forgive him? Seven times? But he said to him, More than seventy-seven times seven.*[3] [Simon] did not concede even one day to [anger], lest [sin] rule over it, by a little over much.[4] For anger injures both those who are its friends and those who are its enemies. [It is] through it that all kinds of evils are fanned into flame as though coming from an evil storehouse. In his audacity[5] the aggressor makes a sudden assault, so that he may dominate over the entire day. Consequently, the Physician first bars the way before him and submits the entire day to reconciliation, through [the words], *seventy-seven times seven.* Because [Simon] thought that there was a limit to acts of mercy and a [definite] number for graces, and that this number was measured in days and hours, he was reprimanded, since the number of remissions exceeds the number of transgressions. For who could commit all these transgressions in *one single day*?[6] It was not therefore because [Simon] was guilty in this respect that he would be justified for having been guilty, [it was lest] these remissions would make us sin because of our confidence [of being forgiven].[7] In the end, the consummation becomes visible, and at the setting of the sun the day is complete and the testimony is dissolved.

---

[1] Cf. Luke 16:4-7,9.

[2] Cf. Gen 3:17-19.

[3] Matt 18:21-22. The Peshitta reads the preposition ܥܕܡܐ "up to," whereas the text here has ܠܥܠ "above, more than."

[4] An allusion to Luke 17:4 (If he sins against you seven times in the day... you must forgive him)? Cf. Eph 4:26.

[5] The Syriac text reads ܒܪܚܡܬܗ, "in his mercy" here, whereas the Armenian attests "in his audacity" [cf. ܒܪܝܚܘܬܗ].

[6] Ephrem's commentary attests the presence of this expression, "one single day," in the Gospel text, a reading which is attested elsewhere in Ephrem, as well as in other authors, such as Aphrahat. Cf. Leloir, *Le Témoignage d'Ephrem*, pp. 183-184.

[7] The Syriac text is difficult to translate. The point that Ephrem seems to be making is that the expectation of these many remissions should not excuse one from falling into sin again.

§23. Our hidden light has thus counselled that, while the visible light lasts, we should repent of anger, lest it testify against us in the end [as] a witness, and the light, at the consummation. For our freedom, through every kind of pressure, conceives, and then in an instant aborts. How many times too does it bring to birth, and nurture fruit similar to the seed which it has received. This is why the apostle has said, *Do not let the sun set on your anger, lest you give a footing to Satan*,[1] lest the fruit he has sown in us may mature. But, while [Satan's] seed is tender, let us cut it off, and before it bears fruit, let us uproot it. For homicide does not happen in an instant, without jealousy, since the enemy cannot complete his work without his weapons.

Prayer Alone and Prayer in Common

§24. Just as the Messiah took care of his flock in every necessity, so too he offered consolation with regard to the sadness of loneliness, when he said, *Where there is one, I [am there]*, lest all those who are solitary be sad. For he is our joy, and he is with us. *Where there are two, I [am there]*.[2] His grace gives us protection. And when there are three, it is like when we are assembled in the Church, which is the perfect body, the seal of the Messiah. *Their angels in heaven see the face of my Father*,[3] that is, [through] their prayers.

The Galileans Killed by Pilate

§25. *They came and informed him concerning the men from Galilee, whose blood Pilate had mixed with their sacrifices*,[4] on the festival of Herod's birthday, when *he cut off John's head*.[5] Because [John] had been unjustly killed, and contrary to the Law, Pilate sent and killed those who were present at the feast. Since he was not able to injure Herod, he destroyed his cohort to his shame, and he parted from him in anger until the day of the Lord's judgement. There was reconciliation between them

---

[1] Eph 4:26-27.
[2] Matt 18:20.
[3] Matt 18:10.
[4] Luke 13:1.
[5] Matt 14:10.

through the pretext of [the Lord].[1] *Pilate mixed their blood with their sacrifices*, because they were forbidden by the authority of the Romans to offer sacrifice. But Pilate found them transgressing the Law and offering sacrifices, and he destroyed them in that very place and at that very time. Wherefore [the evangelist] said, *He mixed their blood with their sacrifices.* Or, they came to tempt [the Lord], as in the case of the toll-tax,[2] to see if it pleased him that these were killed because they were offering sacrifice. For, if so, he would be against the Law and in favour of the Gentiles; but, if he were in favour of the Law, they would accuse him before Pilate, that he was against the kingdom of the Romans.

The Barren Fig Tree

§26.   [He told] another parable, *A certain man had planted a fig tree in his vineyard and he said to the vinedresser.*[3] This refers to the Law, taking its point of view. *Behold, for three years I have come seeking fruit on this fig tree.*[4] [This refers] to the three captivities in which [the Israelites] were taken away as captives, so that they might be chastened, but they were not chastened. *In vain have I smitten your sons, but they have not taken correction.*[5] To show that even after these things he was still patient with it, he said to the vinedresser, *Cut it down. The vinedresser replied to him, Leave it, Lord, for another year.*[6] He agreed to be patient with them [the Israelites]. This was for the time of seventy weeks. Because, at the time of their return, the three years were completed. Thus, the one year [more] refers to the time which was before the coming of him by whose decision their sentence would be decided. The fig tree is a figure of the synagogue.[7] The fruits of faith were sought in it, but it did not have that which it could offer. The word was fulfilled in its place, *I sought among them a man who would repair the breach, but I found none.*[8]

---

[1] Cf. Luke 23:12.
[2] Cf. Matt 17:23-26.
[3] Luke 13:6-7.
[4] Luke 13:7.
[5] Jer 2:30.
[6] Luke 13:7-8.
[7] There are two words in the Syriac text here which, due to the corrupt state of the manuscript at this point, cannot be translated.
[8] Ezek 22:30.

§27. There were three years during which he showed himself among them as Saviour. When he wished that [the fig tree] be uprooted, the event was similar to that earlier one, when the Father said to Moses, *Permit me to destroy the people.*[1] He [thus] gave him a reason to intercede with him. Here too he showed the vinedresser that he wished to uproot it. The vinedresser made known his plea, and the Merciful One showed his pity, that if, in a further year, [the fig tree] did not yield fruit, it would be uprooted.[2] The vinedresser however did not pass sentence through vengeance like Moses, who, after having interceded and was heard, said, *For the day of their ruin is near and that which is about to happen them is fast approaching.*[3] Even if the burdens of the scribes were evil, their words were not [too] heavy [to bear]. Even if their words were unclean, nevertheless their fingers were clean, through one of their fingers.[4] This is similar to how the vinedresser considered it, and the owner of the vineyard was persuaded about it. If he consented to the vinedresser to learn the nature of the fig tree, he knew its nature by proof, because he came and inquired about it for three years and was testing the [vinedresser's] knowledge concerning it. We are not saying that [the Jews] are tares, for they are capable of being chosen. Nor that they are pure wheat grains, for they can be rejected.

Jesus Goes to Jerusalem for the Feast

§28. *I am not going up during this feast,*[5] that is, to the cross. He did not say, "to the feast," but, *during the feast. For, even his brothers did not believe in him.*[6] *But they were saying to him, No one does anything in secret.*[7] They were seeking him in order to hand him over. Therefore he deceived them, *I am not going up.* But he went up secretly,[8] so that it might be confirmed that they were going to hand him over.

---

[1] Exod 32:10.
[2] Cf. Luke 13:7-9.
[3] Deut 32:35.
[4] Cf. Matt 23:2-4.
[5] John 7:8.
[6] John 7:5.
[7] John 7:3-4.
[8] Cf. John 7:10.

§29.   *Why are you seeking to kill me?*[1] There were three levels [of being] in our Lord. The first was that of his unique divinity, the second was that of his divinity and humanity jointly, and the third was that of his humanity on its own. *In the beginning was the Word and God.*[2] *No one has gone up to heaven except he that has come down, the Son of Man.*[3] *Why do you seek to kill me?*[4]

[1] John 7:19.
[2] John 1:1.
[3] John 3:13.
[4] John 7:19.

XV

The Rich Man

§1.   The rich man came to the Judge in a flattering manner, with the bribe of a sweet tongue. The Judge showed him that, in his judgement, there is neither bribery nor hypocrisy. *Why do you call me good,*[1] "since in respect of that which you wish to learn from me, I am just?" The Just One was good towards the sinful woman,[2] for she had come [to him] as to one who forgives. [The rich man], however, [had come to him] as to a legislator, who had withheld his mercy the moment that he laid down the Law, and said, *Whoever kills will be killed;*[3] *What must I do in order to live?*[4] The Judge revealed the strength of his justice to him. For, when the observer of the Law showed that he had kept the observances of the Law, the Legislator thereupon rejoiced in his presence,[5] [showing] that the initial flattery was of no value, but that the observance [of the Law] was of benefit. *[If] you want to enter into [eternal] life, keep the commandments.*[6]

The flatterer knew how to call many people "good" through his hypocrisy. The Son, however, only knew One as good, one who was good [in such a way] that he did not have to learn from anyone else how to do good. This name, therefore, through which the rich man honoured the Son in a flattering manner, is the name through which the Son honours the Father in truth, not so as to please him, but in order to bear witness to him.

§2.   Moreover, the rich man called him *good,* as though favouring him, as people favour their companions with honorary titles. [The Lord] fled from that by which people favoured him, so that he might show that he had received this goodness from the Father, through nature and generation, and not [merely] in name. *One only is good,*[7] [he said], and did not remain silent, but added, *the Father,* so that he might show that the

---

[1] Mark 10:18.
[2] Cf. Luke 7:35-70.
[3] Exod 21:12.
[4] Mark 10:17.
[5] Cf. Mark 10:21.
[6] Matt 19:17.
[7] Matt 19:17.

Son he possesses is good, because he is similar to him. [The rich man] called him *Good Teacher*,[1] as though one of the [ordinary] good teachers. *No one is good*, as you think, *except one, God the Father*.[2] He said *God*, to show about whom he was speaking. [He said] *the Father*, to show that [God] could not be called Father, except on account of the Son. Because they were ready to locate many gods in heaven, he said, *There is no one good except one, the Father who is in heaven*. "I am not God and God, but God from God, and not good alongside good, but good from good." This is why he said, *Father*. For, if you hear [a judgement] about a good tree, you instantly extend the witness of goodness to its fruit also. Wherefore, just as the son of the Law had come from the Law to be instructed, he replied to him as though from the Law, *I am, and there is none besides me*.[3] So too here, *No one is good, except one*. The two [statements] are one [in meaning], just as in, *Hear, O Israel, the Lord your God is one*.[4]

§3.   He was enriched according to the blessings of the Law, and was confident in his earthly wealth, which the Law promised. So he came as one confident of receiving approbation from our Lord, both for his wealth and for his deeds. He questioned him about the Law, for he was about to question him after that with regard to what one who keeps the Law would receive in recompense here on earth. But our Lord drew back from his observance of the Law a little. So, when he came in order to say, *What further do I lack?*,[5] since he was expecting that our Lord would reply to him concerning the rest of the Law in which he was perfect like Paul, our Lord presented to him, not what he was expecting to hear, but something he did not wish [to hear], [something] which had not even entered into his heart that he might hear. For [the Lord] recited for him the truth which was in the Law, and he added to it the seal of true nourishment: "*Go!* Place this earthly wealth in heaven, and place your confidence in it, because it will be kept for you.[6] As long as it is on earth, you do wrong to trust in it. *For wherever your treasure is, there will be your heart*,[7] and not on earth."

---

[1] Mark 10:17.
[2] Mark 10:18.
[3] Deut 32:39.
[4] Deut 6:4.
[5] Matt 19:20.
[6] Cf. Matt 19:21.
[7] Matt 6:21.

So, instead of the milk and honey of infants, [the Lord was proposing to him] the nails and the cross of those who are perfect.

§4.   When [the Lord] saw from the beginning that his entire heart was buried in the earth, he startled him and shook him from the dust of the earth and made him run towards heaven. *No one is good except one, who is in heaven.*[1] Instead of the earth, he introduced him to heaven, and instead of his fathers, [he introduced] him to the one Father. If *only one is good, and he is in heaven*, lift up your love from the earth to the Good One, whom you love. But, when he turned away, our Lord said, *It is difficult for those who trust in their own riches.*[2] They trust that the earth is wealth. Consequently, he explained that it is difficult for them. For it is by means of the cross that [people] enter into the kingdom of heaven. [He said], "If you do not produce deeds for me, your judge, you will not receive [eternal] life." *You are lacking in one thing.*[3] What was lacking therefore in the old [order] has been fulfilled in the new. This is why [he said], *I have come to fulfil these.*[4] The Law blesses [in saying], *Take possession of and become rich,*[5] but you despoil us of possessions, [in saying], *You are lacking in one thing*, because your plenitude is lacking in the Law.

§5.   Know, therefore, that the one who gives his possessions, and the other who makes provision to conserve them lest any of them be stolen, are but one. For one has given the wealth on earth, and the other has prepared a treasury in heaven. Thus, the Law has given the possessions of the earth as an inheritance, but our Lord, the possessions of on high; that is, both of them [have given] of [their] possessions. While it is possible to inherit an earthly possession through killing, those who are killed, however, possess the possession of on high. God gave wealth to the patriarchs so that he might entice the Jews to become like their patriarchs, and that it might be possible for the patriarchs to take care of travellers. The sons saw the patriarchs' wealth [only], and not their righteousness. The Gentiles saw their righteousness and not their wealth. For you have said, *Do this, and you shall live.*[6] How difficult is this? It is difficult for

---

[1] Mark 10:18.
[2] Mark 10:24.
[3] Mark 10:21.
[4] Matt 5:17.
[5] Deut 28:1-16.
[6] Luke 10:28.

231

them to enter [the kingdom] through the gate of the perfect, of the crucified. Just as there is the gate of virgins, so too there is the gate of worldly people. Through their gate the worldly people can enter the kingdom. But it is difficult for them to enter by the gate of virgins. Our Lord also said, *It is difficult* to enter, but not that it was impossible.

§6. The pharisees, seekers of pretexts, were seeking to find a pretext. Accordingly, they sent one of themselves to tempt our Lord as to whether the perfection he was introducing into the Law was abrogating [it]. But our Lord closed up the mouth of the tempter in an instant through the following, *No one is good, except one,*[1] and secondly, *Do you [not] know the commandments?*[2] He restrained alienation lest it be named. For he showed that there were lifegiving commandments prior to him, and he also showed that they were [still] capable of vivifying. Thirdly, because *he looked at him lovingly,*[3] he showed how dear to him were those who kept the old Law perfectly. Therefore he said, *You lack one thing,*[4] to show him that his own coming was not in vain, and also that what was lacking [in the old Law] was not alien to the plenitude [of the new]. If then the pharisee had lied with regard to these in saying, *I have observed [these],*[5] what would have restrained him from [further] lying and saying, "I continue to observe this"? A liar is not afraid of lying [again]. If he was not ashamed when he said, "I have observed all these," would he not have been ashamed on account of those who would have known that he had not observed them?

§7. Secondly, because he was sad, and he really was sad, as is seen from [the words], *When our Lord saw that he was sad.*[6] If [the rich man] however had indeed lied he would not have been distressed, because he would not have been prepared to observe [the commandments]. But, as a man who considered himself to be perfect, he had come to display his [claim to] praise. When he saw that he was lacking [something], he was sad, for he saw that the object of his pride had forsaken him. He had toiled at his righteousness in accordance with the pride of the Law, and had

---

[1] Mark 10:18.
[2] Mark 10:19.
[3] Mark 10:21.
[4] *Idem.*
[5] Matt 19:20.
[6] Cf. Luke 18:23-24.

received good things for its sake. *He looked at him lovingly,*[1] so that he might show through this how dear to him were those who run towards perfection. While this [word], *He looked at him,* was attending to that which was inferior to it, it was also considering that which was superior to it. He loved him, in order to show how dear to him is the one who advances towards a superior degree.

§8.   [Through] that which [he said], *Good Master,*[2] he anticipated our Lord with a gift. But our Lord removed this opportunity for flattery, to show him that it is right to both speak and hear the truth. *He looked at him lovingly,*[3] so that perhaps through this he might be attracted to draw closer to perfection, through which also the former [commandments] are cultivated. But, because his righteousness was according to the Law - and because it was in the hope of the goods of here [below] that [the former commandments] were cultivated - he trusted in his wealth as the recompense for his righteousness. Wherefore, *it is difficult for the rich and for those who trust in this,*[4] for their riches are the due recompense of their activities. Indeed those who think that riches are a reward for their righteousness are not able to leave them. Lest [the rich man] say, "Even from the beginning he replied to me indignantly and rejected me with some pretext," [the Lord] said to him, *One only is good.*[5] Is he not therefore good, who is called the Son of the Good One? This is why *he looked at him lovingly,*[6] so that he might show [the rich man] that it was his own self that he was rejecting. For he is the rich man, *who was attired in purple.*[7] See, he is a son of Israel, because of what [he said], *My father, Abraham,*[8] and because of, *They have Moses and the prophets.*[9]

§9.   *No one is good, except one only.*[10] As for you, Lord, are you not good? *One is good, the Father who is in heaven.*[11] Is not your coming one

---

[1] Mark 10:21.
[2] Mark 10:17.
[3] Mark 10:21.
[4] Mark 10:23-24.
[5] Matt 19:17.
[6] Mark 10:21.
[7] Luke 16:19.
[8] *Idem.*
[9] Luke 16:29.
[10] Mark 10:18.
[11] Matt 19:17.

of grace? *I have not come of my own will.*[1] Your beautiful deeds, are these not of the Good One? *My Father, who is in me, has performed these deeds.*[2] Is not your new preaching one of grace? *He who sent me has commanded me how to speak and what to say.*[3] But, if your coming and words and deeds are from the Father, are you not also good, who are from the Good One? For the prophet has also said concerning the Spirit, *Your good Spirit will lead me.*[4] Accordingly, it was the rich man who turned himself aside. Our Lord did not give him a pretext by which he might take flight, so that his flight might be rebuked. Because he was about to give a new commandment, he confirmed the Law and gave honour to the Lord of the Law, so that [the rich man] could not say that [the Lord] was against either of them, or that he was even introducing a new alienation. For see, he showed that poverty was acceptable to him, *for the angels carried [Lazarus] to Abraham's bosom.*[5]

§10.   *Why do you call me good?* [6] This is an example of his humility, in that he honoured the Father. For in other places he called himself good, when he said, *Is your eye evil because I am good?*,[7] and also, *The good shepherd gives his life for the sake of his flock.*[8] *Why do you call me good?* [The Lord] gave a response which was contrary to the [rich man's] opinion, for he had assumed that he was from the earth, and like one of the teachers of Israel.

§11.   The [rich man] looked upon him as a man, even though calling him good, as though [he were] God. Wherefore [the Lord said], *Why do you call me good?* That is, "If it is true for you that I have come down from above and that I am Son of the Good One, you did well to call me good. But, if I am from the earth, as you think, you have wrongly called me good." If he had called God good, and then declined [from further use of this title], perhaps there might have been a place for their discussion. He had called him Teacher, however, and not God. But, how could he refuse this title, he who had said of himself, *The good shepherd gives his life for*

---

[1] John 7:28.
[2] John 14:10.
[3] John 12:49.
[4] Ps 143:10.
[5] Luke 16:22.
[6] Mark 10:18.
[7] Matt 20:15.
[8] John 10:11.

the sake of his flock,[1] since all teachers who teach sound doctrine and all those who are just and righteous are called good? *The Lord acts with goodness towards the good,*[2] and also, *The sower of the good seed is the Son of Man, and the good seed represents the sons of the kingdom.*[3] How could it be that the seed be good and its sower evil? How could he refuse the title of good, and [at the same time] participate in domination, divinity and worship? Every single evil has entered into humanity because of the love of pre-eminence. It was for this reason that our Lord abhorred pride before God, since it is this that makes humanity abhorrent before God. Accordingly, he instituted humility as a curb for humanity, so that through it humanity would be obedient to the wishes of the Law, its leader.

The Rich Man and Lazarus

§12.   Death was the same for both the rich man and Lazarus. But the retribution after death was not the same for Lazarus. He, whom not even the servants were willing to carry, was lifted up by the hands of angels. He, to whom that rich man did not give a place in his house, had Abraham's bosom as his dwelling place. For that rich man, his torture was twofold. In the first instance, his own tortures, and secondly, because he could see Lazarus, who was rejoicing.[4] [The Lord] compared the priests of the people to him who *was clothed in purple,*[5] [a clothing in comparison] to which nothing is more honourable, and he compared the disciples of the cross to Lazarus, in comparison to whom there was none more lowly. He revealed the name of his beloved ones through Lazarus, his beloved one. He also wised to reveal the name of his enemies through [the words], *If they do not listen to Moses and the prophets.*[6] It is not the case, therefore, that [all] who are living are alive, nor that [all] those who are buried are dead.

§13.   See then! The more the rich man lived sumptuously, the more [Lazarus] was humbled. The more Lazarus was made low, the greater was his crown. Why was it, therefore, that he should have seen Abraham

---

[1] John 10:11.
[2] Cf. Ps 18:26.
[3] Matt 13:37-38.
[4] Cf. Luke 16:20-23.
[5] Luke 16:19.
[6] Cf. Luke 16:31.

above all the just, and Lazarus in his bosom?[1] It was because Abraham loved the poor that he saw him, so that we might learn that we cannot hope for pardon at the end, unless the fruits of pardon can be seen in us. If then Abraham, who was friendly to strangers, and had mercy on Sodom, was not able to have mercy on the one who did not show pity to Lazarus, how can we hope that there will be pardon for us? That man called him, *My Father*[2] and Abraham called him, *My Son*,[3] but he was not able to help him. *Remember, my son, that you received good things during your life, and Lazarus evil things.*[4]

The Labourers in the Vineyard

§14.   With regard to the labourers that the master of the vineyard hired at the third, sixth and ninth [hour],[5] when he began to pay those [who came] last, *those who had been first thought that they would receive more.*[6] But he treated them equally. So, when they murmured, he said, *If I am good, why is your eye evil?* [7] For one [group] a great favour [was done], but the others were openly clamouring for their wages. Let us examine carefully the kind of words that were used. When he asked them, *Why are you standing there idle, they said to him, no one has hired us.*[8] Thus, they were ready, but no one had hired them. It is evident that one must distinguish between one who, for lack of someone to call him, sleeps, but then goes [to work], and one who, because of his idleness, sleeps. One, for the sake of his work, renders thanks to the one who calls him, whereas the other, on account of his idleness, recompenses with abuse those who call him. It is evident that the sitting down to rest of the lazy is empty in comparison to that of the industrious.

§15.   A voice hired the industrious, who, for lack of work and a patron, were idle, and a word aroused them. By reason of their diligence, they did not make an agreement with him, like those who were first [to be hired]. He evaluated their toil with discernment, and treated them equally in

---

[1] Cf. Luke 16:33.
[2] Luke 16:24.
[3] Luke 16:25.
[4] *Idem.*
[5] Matt 20:2-5.
[6] Cf. Matt 20:8-10.
[7] Matt 20:11,15.
[8] Cf. Matt 20:6-7.

their wages. He put forward this parable so that no one might say, "Since I was not called during my youth, I cannot be acceptable." He made known that, at whatever moment a person is converted, he is accepted. So he did not begin with the first, who were well assured of their wages, but he began with *the last,*[1] lest the last might think that they were going to receive less.

§16.   Also, *he went out in the morning at the third, sixth, ninth and eleventh [hour].*[2] This could be understood as referring to the beginning of his preaching, and to its unfolding thereafter, up to the cross, since it was at *the eleventh hour* that the thief entered into Eden.[3] Lest he be blamed over this, [the Lord] made known his will, that if [the thief] had been hired, he would have worked. *For, no one has hired us.*[4]

§17.   Just as we give to the divinity what is very inferior to it, it gives us that to which we are very much inferior. We are hired for a work in proportion to our potentiality, but we are invited to our recompense with a wage that exceeds our potentiality. At the end, the faithful will give him glory according to their freedom; but the rebels according to the constraint of him who is above them, of him who gave [them] freedom down here, but will constrain both good and wicked up there. The good cannot become unjust there even if they wished, nor can the wicked become just if they wish.

Furthermore, *he went out in the morning at the third, sixth, ninth and eleventh [hour],*[5] and treated the first and the last equally. They received the image of the king, *a denarius each.*[6] This is the bread of life that is the same for all people; the remedy of life is one and the same for those who take it.

With regard to the labour of the vineyard, his goodness cannot be argued against, nor can his justice be faulted. In his justice, he gave according as he had agreed, and in his goodness he took pity according as he wished. This shows that this was why our Lord composed this parable,

---

[1] Cf. Matt 20:8-9.
[2] Cf. Matt 20:1-6. This, and the following two sentences are absent from the Armenian version.
[3] Cf. Luke 23:39-43.
[4] Matt 20:7.
[5] Cf. Matt 20:1-6.
[6] Cf. Matt 20:2,9-10.

Do I not have power in my own house?[1] If [this parable applies] to all generations and to the end of the world, why did he include this [other word], *Or is your eye evil?*[2] For, who can permit the more recent just to live like the earlier just, without having to work for it? Among those who were hired in the morning, are not the young children who died included? Abel indeed was first to die as a youth. Did Seth murmur therefore about him who replaced him?

The Request of James and John

§18.   When James and John had seen Moses and Elijah with our Lord,[3] they were filled with desire to the point of saying, *Allow us to sit, one on your right and one on your left,*[4] like those who [had appeared] on the mountain. *For we wish that you would do for us that which we ask of you. He said to them, I will do it,*[5] but he did not do it. [He spoke thus], not because he did not know what they were seeking, but because he was aware that they would not become silent until he promised them, *I will do it.* Therefore he said, "I will do it," so as not to throw their request back in their face, and in order to correct all of them equally when they revealed their thoughts to him. Because they had asked publicly before their companions, and because all were saddened [by this], he rejected [their request] and did not give it to them, so that these would not be a cause of enmity between them. He saw that they had asked in simplicity, and he restrained their asking, seeing that it [their request] had already been granted. For, if the first promise was not [considered] by them to be true, then neither would a second or a third; whereas if [they considered it] true, then it had already been granted.

He replied favourably to Simon, but he refused these two. For [Simon] had asked in the name of all of them. He had said, *What will there be for us?*[6] and not, "for me." If he had asked for himself only, [the Lord] would have refused him too. Simon, therefore, had asked on behalf of all of them, and our Lord gave to all of them. None of them was distressed at Simon's request; indeed it occasioned joy for all of them. But

---

[1] Matt 20:15.
[2] *Idem.*
[3] Cf. Matt 17:3.
[4] Mark 10:37.
[5] Mark 10:35-36.
[6] Matt 19:27.

if it was not granted at the [actual] moment when they requested it, it was not fitting that they should receive it [there and then]. They had heard him say one thing but they had requested another. For he had said, *He will enter Jerusalem, and he will be apprehended and crucified.*[1] They had omitted showing their love for him, to the point of being despised and dying with him. But they displayed the love that they had for themselves, *Allow us to sit on your right and on your left.*[2]

§19.   [The Lord] recounted before them all his dishonour in order to show who would hurry forward to suffer with him. *For if we suffer with him, we will be glorified with him.*[3] If he did not give authority, because he had none, how then could he have given it to the Twelve? Did he or did he not give it? If he did not give it, his promise is not trustworthy. If it is trustworthy, then he did give it once and to them all. But, if this were not so, how could the following be realized, *All that my Father has is mine, and what is mine is my Father's?*[4] Or that other [word] which he said, *All authority that is in heaven and on earth has been given to me by my Father.*[5] For, in Greek [the evangelist] said, *All authority, as in heaven, so on earth, has been given me by my Father.*[6] He possessed the kingship of those things which were in heaven, from eternity, and those things which were on earth were given to him as of now; that is, he said, [those things which were given] to this body which he had put on.

But,[7] because they had come in order to choose places for themselves ahead of their companions, our Lord said to them, *Are you able to drink the chalice that I am about to drink?*[8] [He said this] to show that [such places] must indeed be bought at a price. *Like me:*[9] *Wherefore God has also elevated and exalted him.*[10] After they had learned that [such a place] could only be bought through deeds, he said, "Now that you have learned that it is through deeds that this [place] can be acquired, there are

---

[1] Cf. Matt 20:18-19.

[2] Mark 10:37.

[3] Rom 8:17.

[4] John 16:15. The next three sentences are absent from the Armenian version.

[5] Matt 28:18.

[6] This is the fourth of five instances in the commentary in which Ephrem refers to "the Greek." See above at II, §17 for comment on Ephrem's use of this term.

[7] The main contents of X, §1, together with the first sentence of §2, are present here in the second half of XV, §19 in a slightly shorter form.

[8] Matt 20:22.

[9] *Idem.*

[10] Phil 2:9.

perhaps those who have run, or who will run, swifter than you. However, in the Father's design, the one who excels all others in his running performance is [already] designated, and his [place] is prepared for him."

Because they had come so as to take possession of an election not accompanied by deeds, our Lord thrust it aside from him, and showed that he did not have the power to spare them from distress; just as [when he also said], *As for that hour, no one knows it,*[1] so that no one would question him concerning it. *It is not yours to know the time or the seasons.*[2] Thus did our Lord place the request of the sons of Zebedee as a crown in [their] midst, so that whoever was victorious in his combat might be crowned with it. *He will examine the thoughts of [our] hearts, and so each one of us will receive glory from God.*[3]

Zacchaeus

§20. Zacchaeus was praying in his heart as follows, "Happy the one who is worthy that this just man should enter into his dwelling." [The Lord] said to him, *Make haste, come down, Zacchaeus.*[4] He, seeing that he knew his thoughts, said, "Just as he knows this, he knows also all that I have done." Wherefore [he said], *All that I have unjustly received, I give back fourfold.*[5] *Make haste, and come down from the fig tree, because it is with you that I will be [sojourning].*[6] The former fig tree of Adam will be forgotten, on account of the latter fig tree of the chief tax collector, and the name of the guilty Adam [will be forgotten] on account of the guiltless Zacchaeus, *See, Lord, I give up half of my goods and all that I have received unjustly, I give back fourfold.*[7] Wherefore, *this day, salvation has come into this house.*[8] Let the apostate people be confused by the swift discipleship of him, who yesterday was but a thief, but today has become a benefactor; yesterday a tax collector, and today a disciple.

---

[1] Matt 24:36.

[2] Acts 1:7. There are three further sentences at this point in the parallel passage of X, §1.

[3] 1 Cor 4:5. There is an introduction to this scriptural text in X, §2, which brings the section which is paralleled in X, §§1-2 to an end.

[4] Luke 19:5.

[5] Luke 19:8.

[6] Luke 19:5.

[7] Luke 19:8.

[8] Luke 19:9.

§21. Thus, Zacchaeus left behind him the just Law, and climbed up, by way of symbol, a deaf fig tree, a symbol of the deafness of his listening. But the symbol of his salvation was depicted through his ascent. For he abandoned the depths below, and he went up into the air in the middle, to contemplate the elevated divinity. Our Lord hastened to bring him down from the deaf fig tree, as though symbolically from his way of life, lest he continue in his deafness. While the love of our Lord was becoming fervent within him, it consumed him so that his former habits might be destroyed, and that he might be fashioned into a new person through it. So that he might know that there was a new offspring there, [the Lord] said, *He too is a son of Abraham.*[1]

The Blind Man of Jericho

§22. The Light came into the world to give sight to the blind and faith to those who lacked it. When he approached the blind man, *he cried out and said, Jesus, Son of David, have mercy on me.*[2] Oh beggar, whose hand was stretched out to receive a farthing from human beings, and he found himself receiving the gift of God! *Son of David, have mercy on me.*[3] He perceived rightly that Jesus was the son of David, this [David] who spared the blind and the lame of the Jebusites.[4] What then did he reply to him? *See, your faith has saved you.*[5] He did not say to him, "It is your faith that has caused you to see," in order to show that [faith] had first given him life, and then corporeal sight. *They were trying to prevent this blind man from coming to Jesus, and that is why he increased his crying.*[6] *While he was asking who it was, they said to him, Jesus, the Nazarene.*[7] He knew that they were not saying that to him with love. He forsook that which pertained to enemies, and grasped hold of that which pertained to friends, *Son of David, have mercy on me. But they were trying to prevent him* lest his eyes be opened, lest [the Pharisees] recognize him and be vexed. *A blind man was sitting near the edge the road and his name was Timaeus, son of Timaeus, and he abandoned his cloak and came.*[8] When our Lord

---

[1] *Idem.*
[2] Mark 10:47; Luke 18:38.
[3] Mark 10:47.
[4] Cf. 2 Sam 5:6-8.
[5] Luke 18:42.
[6] Mark 10:48.
[7] Cf. Luke 18:36-37; Mark 10:47.
[8] Mark 10:46,50.

saw that the eyes of his inner self were greatly enlightened and the eyes of the outer self did not see even a little, he enlightened the eyes of the outer self like those of the inner self, so that, when [the blind man] wanted to hasten towards him again, he would be able to see him.

The Cleansing of the Temple

§23.   Those sheep and bulls which were being sold in the temple[1] were those which the priests were gathering together, on account of the sacrifices.

The Pharisee and the Publican

§24.   [In the case of] that pharisee who was praying, those things which he was saying were true. But, because he was saying them out of pride, and the [tax collector] was telling his sins with humility, the confession of sins of the latter was more pleasing to God than the acknowledgment of the former's almsgiving.[2] It is more difficult to confess one's sins than one's righteousness, and God looks on the one who carries a heavy burden. Therefore, the tax collector appeared to him to have had more to bear than [the pharisee], and *he went down more justified than he*,[3] through this fact alone, that he was humble. If this pharisee had been sinful, it was through his prayer that he would have added iniquity to iniquity, whereas [the Lord] purified the tax collector of his iniquity. And if, just by praying, [the pharisee's] prayer proved a provocation of [God's] wrath, then, as a result of that provocation, the prayer of the tax collector proved all the more potent.

---

[1] Cf. John 2:14.
[2] Cf. Luke 18:10-14.
[3] Luke 18:14.

XVI

The Fig Tree

§1.   *He cursed the fig tree.*[1] [He did this] because it is written, *Whenever you reap your harvest, leave the gleaning for the poor, and whenever you beat your olives, do likewise; thus shall you do in every instance.*[2] The owner of the fig tree did not obey the Law but spurned it. Our Lord came and found that there was [nothing] left on it so he cursed it, lest its owner eat from it again, since he had left [nothing] for the orphan and widows. It is also said that in a similar fashion the Gadarenes had made a decision not to go out to him. Therefore, [the Lord] drowned their swine so that he might attract their hearts to go out [to him], even though they were unwilling.[3] The owner of the fig tree likewise had made up his mind not to go out to him. [The Lord] dried up his fig tree so that he might go out, even though unwilling. On all [possible] occasions, therefore, [the Lord] was solicitous for the salvation of humanity.

§2.   Or, [it was] because he had said, *Destroy the temple and in three days I will raise it up. They said to him, it took forty-six years to build, and you would build it up in three days?*[4] So it was evident that they did not believe. Moreover, when they showed him its ornamentation, he said, *The days will come when it will be destroyed, and Jerusalem will be devastated.*[5]

§3.   He cursed the fig tree and it shrivelled up[6] to show them the power of his divinity, so that by means of [this] action near at hand which they could see, they might believe that which was to come. Because [Jerusalem] had not accepted the Law he cursed [the fig tree], so that there might no longer be fruit on it, according to its law. He sought fruit from the fig tree at an inopportune time,[7] that it might be a symbol of one[8] who

---

[1] Cf. Matt 21:19; Mark 11:21.
[2] Deut 24:19-20; Lev 19:9-10.
[3] Cf. Matt 8:28-34.
[4] John 2:19-20.
[5] Cf. Luke 21:5-6.
[6] Cf. Matt 21:19.
[7] Cf. Mark 11:13.

had deceitfully withheld the fruits of the Law at the opportune time. For, if he had sought fruit from it at the opportune time, no one would have known that there was a parable [in question] here. Instead of the fig tree, therefore, he showed that it was Jerusalem that he was reproaching, for he had sought love in her, but she had despised the fruit of repentance. *He was hungry and came to the fig tree, and, since he did not find [anything] on it, he cursed it.*[1] The fact that he was hungry can be attributed to the body, that is, whenever the [divine] power wished it. But, how could he, who was informed concerning the hidden things of the heart, have looked for fruit at an inopportune time? Understand therefore, that it was not because of hunger that he cursed the fig tree. For, even if it had been the opportune time, and they had not reserved [the fruit] for him beforehand, that he might find some on it, it would not have been fitting that it should have been shrivelled up and uprooted.

§4.   Some say that the fig tree was Jerusalem, which had not yielded fruit, and that by means of the fig tree he was cursing the city which was without fruit. With regard to [the words], *He was hungry,*[2] it was for penance that he was hungry. He came that he might seek [fruit] in Jerusalem, but found none. They were bringing forward that other [text], *A certain man had a fig tree in his vineyard,*[3] and referring both of these to Jerusalem. If he was seeking fruit from Jerusalem, why, therefore, when it was not the opportune time to give fruit, did he curse [the fig tree], that it be uprooted? But, if it was not the opportune time, how can the apostle's word be understood, when he said, *At the completion of times, God sent his Son?*[4] For, if the coming of the First-born occurred at the opportune time, how can the fig tree, at the inopportune time, be compared to Jersualem, for whom it was the opportune time? Let us labour then in the reading [of Scripture], so that through it we may find the solution to what we seek. For, take note that, when our Lord was entering Jerusalem, it is written that *he saw it, and he wept over it and said to it, If only you knew, even on this your day.*[5] If this was its day therefore, how much more so [was it] its time? If it was its time for Jerusalem, then it was also its day. But

---

[8] Jerusalem, personifying Israel, is probably intended here, as shown in what follows in the remainder of the paragraph.
[1] Matt 21:18-19; Mark 11:21.
[2] Matt 21:18.
[3] Luke 13:6.
[4] Gal 4:4.
[5] Luke 19:41-42.

it was not the time for the fig tree. It would appear that the fig tree is one thing, and that Jerusalem is another.

§5.   Let us examine [further] concerning this question of the fig tree, since it is not Jerusalem, as other people say. It is likely that the apostles were thinking in their simplicity, as they were wont, and then doubted. So, in order to frighten them by a miracle, he dried up this fig tree before them. *When they returned they said to him, See this fig tree that you cursed! How quickly it has dried up! He said to them, As for you too, if you had faith and did not doubt, you would speak to this mountain, and it would be transported.*[1] If this [fig tree] had [only] been a parable, he would not have been obliged to say, *If you had faith,* but, "If you had insight." This [fig tree] is a sign, therefore, and not a parable.

§6.   They were also saying with regard to [the text], *Say to this mountain*, that it was not a mountain but a demon, or something resembling one. What demon, therefore, could have been nearby when our Lord was saying these [words]? It is clear that there was a mountain near there, since he was coming towards the Mount of Olives, upon which this fig tree was [growing]. So, he said to those who were looking at the mountain, *Say to this mountain.* Let it be [supposed] then that [the mountain] was a devil, according to their words; but [if so], to whom is this [command], *Fall into the sea,*[2] addressed? For, if someone drives out a demon, why would he cast it into the sea? But perhaps such a one has as an explanation that our Lord, when he drove out demons, cast them into the sea? It is true that he drove out demons, and it is not false that they begged him to enter into the swine. But Scripture does not say that he cast them into the sea. However, the reasons as to why they entered into the swine were known: [the Lord performed] this miracle in order to bring the inhabitants of this town out to him quickly, these [people] who had decided of their own accord not [to go out to him].

§7.   If this were the reason, why then was [this word] necessary, *If you say to this mountain, fall into the sea?*[3] [It was] because he saw that they were amazed at the fig tree which had been dried up. So he said to them, *If*

---

[1] Mark 11:20-23.
[2] Matt 21:21.
[3] Matt 21:21.

you believe and do not doubt,[1] just as he had said to Nathaniel, *If you believe, you will see greater things than these.*[2] However, if *you do not doubt,* not only will you do likewise to the fig tree which is on this mountain, but the entire mountain, together with its trees, will be uprooted and cast into the midst of the sea. To show them that his word was alive and lifegiving, and that it was delivering a judgement, by means of it he dried up the fig tree that was tender,[3] and stretched out the hand that was withered.[4]

§8.   Why, therefore, did this person who was good and gentle, who everywhere revealed great things out of little things, and completion out of imperfection, why did he command the fig tree to dry up? For he healed the sufferings of everyone, changed water to wine, made an abundance from a little bread, opened the eyes of the blind, cleansed lepers, and raised the dead to life. But this fig tree alone did he cause to wither. It was because the time of his suffering was near, and, lest it be thought that he was captured because he was unable to free himself, he cursed the fig tree, that it might be a sign for his friends, and a miracle for his enemies. Thus, the disciples would be strengthened by his word, and foreigners would be amazed at his power. Because *he did all things well,*[5] and [the time] for him to suffer was near, it might be thought, as indeed it was, that he was captured because he possessed no power. He showed in advance, therefore, by means of an inanimate plant which he caused to wither, that he would have been able to destroy his crucifiers with a word. Just as he did this here, so too, lest his divine power be derided through an inferior member of the body, he likewise said to Simon, *Put back your sword in its place.*[6]

§9.   He, who came to take hidden afflictions away from humanity, imposed open afflictions on them in three places: he rent their tombs asunder and shattered them,[7] he drowned the swine in the sea,[8] and he caused the fig tree to wither from its root.[9] For, as the tombs of the

---

1 *Idem.*
2 John 1:50.
3 Cf. Matt 21:19.
4 Cf. Matt 12:10-13.
5 Mark 7:37.
6 Matt 26:52.
7 Cf. Matt 27:51-52.
8 Cf. Mark 5:13.
9 Cf. Mark 11:13-14.

believers were rent asunder, so will the hearts of non-believers be rent asunder. As the swine were drowned, so will error in the rebellious be drowned. As the fig tree was destroyed without any transgression, so will Jerusalem be destroyed because of its transgression. *He was hungry and came to the fig tree.*[1] His appearance and his word were presenting themselves before the eye of the onlookers and the ear of the listeners. *The disciples marvelled at how it had perished in an instant.*[2] The nature of the fig tree is such that when it is cut, because of its moisture, it [requires] many months for it to dry up. Our Lord chose it as a symbol, therefore, to make the quality of his power known through it. It is evident that the fig tree becomes moist and tender before the other trees, as our Lord observed concerning it in a parable, *From the fig tree learn this parable. As soon as its branch becomes tender and opens up in the outer covering of its buds, you know that summer is near.*[3] You see that he proposes it [as a symbol] because of its abundant moisture and its early buds. He marked the strength of its power thus, so that the heavenly economy might receive its seal. *He did not open his mouth*[4] before those who were apprehending him, as he opened it with regard to the fig tree. He caused it to wither thus so that the Israelites might bear fruit, but they were not willing. He was arrested *because he willed it,*[5] just as he came down from heaven because it was pleasing to him.

§10.   It was also said that, when Adam sinned and was deprived of that glory with which he was clothed, he hid his nakedness with the leaves of the fig tree.[6] Our Lord came and endured sufferings for him, to heal the wounds of Adam, and provide a garment of glory for his nakedness. Therefore, he caused the fig tree to wither, to make it known that the leaves of the fig tree were no longer required for the clothing of Adam, because he had restored him to his former glory, which, when in possession of it, he had no need of fig leaves, nor of clothing made from skins. Henceforth, there is no longer any use for the withered fig tree, whose leaves, when moist, were a garment of shame, and a clothing of mockery.

---

[1] Matt 21:18-19.
[2] Matt 21:20.
[3] Matt 24:32.
[4] Isa 53:7.
[5] *Idem.*
[6] Cf. Gen 3:7.

Jesus and Nicodemus

§11.   [Let us examine] that [text], *No one has gone up to heaven except the one who has come down from heaven, the Son of Man.*[1] Because they were asking a sign of him, he said, *If I have spoken to you about earthly things and you did not believe me, how can you believe if I tell you about heavenly things?*[2] *No one has gone up to heaven,* "to return and become a witness to me among you." Because he knew that they were about to say to him that a body does not go up, he said to them, *The one who has come down from heaven.* It was not that he came down from heaven in bodily form, but, because Mary's conception did not come about through the seed of man. Gabriel came down from heaven, however, bearing a greeting in his mouth. This was why he said, *The one who has come down from heaven.*

§12.   We should also say that it was after the word of Nicodemus, that our Lord said to him, *You are a teacher of Israel, and you do not know these things?*[3] The things he should have known were those [matters] concerning the Law and the Prophets, the cleansing of hyssop, the waters of ceremonial sprinkling, and the baptisms of purification. If types of these had not [already] been outlined before the coming of the Son, our Lord would certainly have been treating Nicodemus unjustly. But, if they were hidden in the Scriptures, and he had not discerned them, it was appropriate that [the Lord] should shake him out of his sleep, and heal his illness with his gentle voice, and remind him of the baptism of expiation, which existed in Israel. Zechariah too had doubted when it was announced to him that he was to have a son. His tongue, through which he had taught others, was bound.[4] So too, in the case of Nicodemus. These arguments were placed before him and he did not believe, so [the Lord] reproved him. But this [was done] with gentleness, because he saw that he was ill, but close to being healed. Since he did not understand the former things that were set down in the Law, our Lord revealed the baptism of complete expiation for body and soul to him.[5]

---

[1] John 3:13.
[2] John 3:12.
[3] John 3:10.
[4] Cf. Luke 1:20-22.
[5] Cf. John 3:3-7.

§13.   Did you not understand, O Nicodemus, [the story of] Jacob, who, without belly or womb, was born into the right of the first-born?[1] And [that of] Naaman, who was renewed without a womb, when Elisha spoke to him. *He went and washed himself and was cleansed, and his flesh became like that of a little child.*[2] Similarly too in the case of Miriam.[3] Is it not clear, therefore, that this was a sign of baptism given to the Gentiles, since hyssop whitens stains? For this was a wondrous thing, that Naaman believed and took some clay from the land of Israel, but Nicodemus was questioning his Lord about those things pertaining to heaven. Accordingly [he said], *If I have spoken to you about earthly things and you did not believe, how can you believe if I tell you about heavenly things?*[4] For, *with regard to the Spirit, you do not know whence it comes and whither it goes.*[5] If what is evident is not understood, who can penetrate the hidden things that are in heaven? For, *no one has gone up to heaven except the one who has come down from heaven, the Son of Man.*[6] [He said this] to show that no one has gone up, nor will go up, to the place of the divinity.

§14.   Nicodemus said to him, *Is it possible for an elderly man to enter again into the womb of his mother and be born again?*[7] For, according to the Law, the womb of one's mother, as well as her child, is rendered unclean through her giving birth. But our Lord did not abandon him in his weakness, but gave him a clear instruction, *Unless one is born of water and the Spirit, he cannot enter the kingdom of God.*[8] That is, if he had been willing, he would have understood, from those things which were before him, and from the argument [of the Lord], that baptism of water, together with the fellowship of the Spirit, was necessary for the body. *That which is born of the flesh is flesh and that which [is born] of the Spirit is Spirit.*[9] He was instructing him therefore in the faith, indicating that birth from the flesh is visible, but birth from baptism is [from] the Spirit, and this is invisible. *If you had faith in you like a grain of mustard seed, you*

---

[1] Cf. Gen 25:25.
[2] 2 Kgs 5:14.
[3] Cf. Num 12:9-15.
[4] John 3:12.
[5] John 3:8.
[6] John 3:13.
[7] John 3:4.
[8] John 3:5.
[9] John 3:6.

would say to the mountain, Remove hence, and it shall remove, and whatever you ask of God in prayer, and you believe, it shall be given to you.[1] Since this [teaching] impressed them greatly, they said to him, *Increase our faith.*[2]

§15.   The serpent struck Adam in Paradise and killed him. [It also struck] Israel in the camp and annihilated them.[3] *Just as Moses lifted up the serpent in the desert, the Son of Man will be lifted up.*[4] Just as those who looked with bodily eyes at the sign which Moses fastened on the cross lived bodily, so too, those who look with spiritual eyes at the body of the Messiah nailed and suspended on the cross, and believe in him, will live [spiritually]. Thus, it was revealed through this brazen [serpent], which by nature cannot suffer, that he who was to suffer on the cross is one who by nature cannot die.

The Unjust Judge

§16.   In what then consisted the iniquity and wickedness of that unjust judge?[5] And in what consisted the grace and justice of that Judge who was upright? The former in his iniquity was not willing to vindicate the widow, and in his wickedness he was not willing to put her mind at rest. But the justice of God knows how to vindicate, and his grace discerns how to vivify. The iniquity of this [wicked judge] was contrary to the justice of [God], and the wickedness of this rebel was in opposition to the grace of the Gentle One. His wickedness therefore was obdurate, for it dared [to go] against the fear of God. His impudence was obdurate, for it spurned the shame of humankind.

These two were obdurate, but persistent [prayer] was even more obdurate than these two. For, with regard to iniquity, which was rebelling against God, and impudence, which was behaving arrogantly towards human beings, the persistence of the widow humiliated both of these, and subjected them to her will, so that they might provide her with a vindication over her adversary. Persistence transformed these two bitter branches, and they bore sweet fruit, which was alien to their [nature]. The

---

[1] Matt 17:20; Mark 11:24.
[2] Luke 17:5.
[3] Cf. Num 21:4-6.
[4] John 3:14.
[5] Cf. Luke 18:1-8.

iniquity [of the judge] brought about an upright vindication, and a just retribution for the falsely accused [woman], and his wickedness gave peace to the afflicted one, even though iniquity does not know how to judge, nor does wickedness know how to give refreshment. If persistence constrained these two evil and bitter [branches] to give good fruit which was alien to them, how much more should we be able, if we persist in prayer, to prevail on the grace and justice of God, to give us fruit that [is in accordance] with their nature. For, let justice vindicate us, and let grace refresh us. Accordingly, the fruit of justice is the just recompense of the oppressed, while the giving of refreshment to the afflicted is the fruit of grace.

The Authority of Jesus Questioned

§17.[1]   [*While he was teaching the crowds and evangelizing them, [the chief priests and the scribes] came and said to him, By what power are you doing this?*[2] If it were a question of his teaching, how could they have called it a work? It is clear that he referred to his works as testimony to the truth of his words, according to what he said, *If you do not believe in me, believe at least in the works.*[3] *By what power are you doing this?* They interrogated him like inquisitors, but he did not reply to them, since they did not approach him out of love in order to be taught, but as rebels. He asked them in turn, *Where did the baptism of John come from?*[4] His word constrained them [in such a way] that they were forced to confess that they had not believed [in John]. He asked, *Was it from heaven or from human beings? They began to reflect on it in their minds and to say, If we say that it was from heaven, he will say, Why did you not believe in it? But if we say, From human beings, we are afraid of the crowd.*[5] When they said, *If it is from heaven,* they did not [also] say, "We are afraid of God." Thus, they were afraid of human beings but not of God.

---

[1] The beginning of §17 to the middle of §21 is missing from *Chester Beatty* MS 709, and its contents have been supplied from the Armenian translation (cf. CSCO 145, pp. 167-169).
[2] Cf. Luke 20:1-2; Mark 11:27-28.
[3] John 10:38.
[4] Matt 21:25.
[5] Matt 21:25-26.

The Two Sons

§18. {*How does it seem to you? A man had two sons.*[1] He called them "sons" to encourage them to his work. *I will go, Lord,*[2] said one. [The father] called him *son*, and he replied with *Lord*. He did not call him "father," nor did he accomplish his word. *Which of the two did the will of his father?*[3] These replied correctly and said, *The second.*[4] He did not say, "Which of them seems to you?" - since the first one had said, *I will go,* - but, *Which did the will of his father? Therefore, he said, the tax collectors and the harlots will enter the kingdom of heaven before you,*[5] because you promise with words, but they will run swifter than you. *John came to you in the way of justice,*[6] that is, he did not seize the honour of his Lord for himself, but when they thought that he was the Messiah, he said to them, *I am not worthy to undo the throng of his sandals.*[7]

The Wicked Vinedressers

§19. {[He proposed] *another parable. A certain man, a householder, planted his vineyard.*[8] This is [like] what [the psalmist] said, *You brought a vine out of Egypt, you drove out the nations and planted it.*[9] *He protected it with a hedge*, the Law, *and prepared a pit in it for the winepresses*, the altar, *and built a tower there,*[10] the temple, *and sent his servants to bring him [its] fruit.*[11] But neither the first, nor those following, nor the last were received. *Then he sent his Son,*[12] not that he was the last, for although he appeared at the end, he already existed, as John witnessed, *A man will come after me, who is before me.*[13] Thus he did, not because he was unaware that the predecessors were incapable of receiving [the produce], but to remove the detractions of [these] obstinate ones from their midst.

---

[1] Matt 21:28.
[2] Matt 21:29. Note that the order of the sons in Ephrem's text is reversed.
[3] Matt 21:31.
[4] *Idem*. Note that the order of the sons in this text is reversed.
[5] Matt 21:31.
[6] Matt 21:32.
[7] Mark 1:7; Matt 3:11.
[8] Matt 21:33.
[9] Ps 80:9.
[10] Matt 21:33.
[11] Matt 21:34; Luke 20:10.
[12] Matt 21:37.
[13] John 1:15,30.

They were saying that he was not able to direct and prepare everything that he wanted to, by the Law, so therefore he sent his Son to impose silence on them. *But when they saw his Son coming, they said, Here is the heir of the vineyard. Come! Let us kill him and the inheritance of the vineyard will be ours.*[1] They killed him, but their inheritance was taken away [from them] and given to the Gentiles, just as he had said, *To the one who has [more] will be given, and he will be in abundance. But to the one who has nothing, even that which he has seized will be taken away.*[2]

§20. {He led them to the point of judging themselves, saying, *What do the vinedressers deserve?*[3] They decreed concerning themselves, saying, *Let him destroy the evil ones with evil.*[4] Then he explained this, saying, *Have you not read that the stone which the builders rejected has become the head of the corner?*[5] What stone? That which is known to be [as hard as] lead. For see, he has said, *I am setting a plumb line in the midst of the sons of Israel.*[6] To show that he himself was this stone, he said concerning it, *Whoever knocks against that stone will be broken to pieces, but it will crush and destroy whomsoever it falls upon.*[7] The leaders of the people were gathered together against him and wanted his downfall because his teaching did not please them. But he said, *It will crush and destroy whomsoever it falls upon,* because he had gotten rid of idolatry, along with other such [things]. For, *the stone that struck the image has become a great mountain and the entire earth has been filled with it.*[8]

Tax Due to Caesar

§21. {[Let us explain] this [text] also, *They sent their disciples to him with the Herodians, [saying], Should one pay tax?* [9] These were thinking about him as follows, "He wants to take hold of the kingdom of Israel, since they are calling him, Son of David." They wanted to see}[10] whether

---

[1] Matt 21:38.
[2] Matt 13:12.
[3] Cf. Matt 21:40.
[4] Cf. Matt 21:41.
[5] Matt 21:42; Ps 118:22.
[6] Amos 7:8.
[7] Luke 20:18.
[8] Cf. Dan 2:35.
[9] Matt 22:16-17; Mark 12:13-14.
[10] *Chester Beatty* MS 709 resumes at this point.

he would permit them to pay tax. If he should say, "Do not pay it," they would find a pretext against him, [accusing him of saying] about himself that he was a king. They wanted [to interrogate him], not so as to avoid having to pay [tax], but that they might kill him. To show them that his teaching was superior to this [pretext], and that he wished [well] for the lives of human beings, he said, *Give to Caesar that which belongs to Caesar, and pay to God what you owe him.*[1]

The Resurrection of the Dead

§22.   *The Sadducees came and were saying to him, There is no resurrection of the dead.*[2] They are called Sadducees, that is "the just,"[3] because [they say], "We do not serve God for the sake of reward." They do not await the resurrection, and for this reason they call themselves "the just," since they say, "We ought to love God without a reward." *Moses commanded that if a man dies, his wife must marry his brother. One woman was [wife] to seven men. At the resurrection of the dead, to which of them will she belong?*[4] Is it right to expect that there will be marriage there too? If the Jews await marriage in the resurrection of the dead, it is not surprising that they deny marital continence in the present [world]. *You deceive yourselves greatly. The children of this world take wives,* et cetera.[5] *Those who are worthy of that [heavenly] world are like the angels.*[6] If [some] people, in their similarity with angels, do not marry, what shall we say of those who dare to revile the angels?[7]

The Great Love Commandment

§23.   *What is the greatest and first commandment of the Law? He said to him, You shall love the Lord, your God, and your neighbour as yourself.*[8] The love of God does not allow us to perish, nor does the love of humankind permit us to be offensive. For there is no one who would

---

[1] Matt 22:21.

[2] Mark 12:18.

[3] The word "Sadducee" comes from a Hebrew word, צדיק, meaning "a just one."

[4] Matt 22:24-28.

[5] See the note above at II, § 5 for comment on this type of indication of scriptural abbreviation.

[6] Matt 22:29-30; Luke 20:34-36.

[7] Ephrem is referring to the opinion of those who hold that the angels marry.

[8] Matt 22:36-37,39.

offend against one whom he loves. What heart is there that is capable of becoming a storehouse for all the love of the sons of his flesh? What mind is there capable of increasing in itself the love of all souls, which this commandment, itself the cultivator of love, has sown in it? *For you shall love your neighbour as yourself.*[1] Our faculties are too tiny to be instruments for the swift and rich desires of the divinity. The fruit [of love] which comes from [God] is sufficient, on its own, for his will. The nature of the divinity is such that it is able to accomplish whatever God wishes to do. And God indeed wishes to give life to humanity. Angels with their allotted portions, kings with their armies, and prophets with their signs make haste, but humanity was not saved until there came down from heaven the One who takes hold [of us] by the hand and raises [us] up. All this teaching is held aloft, therefore, through the two commandments, as though by means of two wings, that is, through the love of God and of humanity.

The Good Samaritan

§24.   The one who was wounded was a Jew. He became a reproach to the priests and the Levites on account of the Samaritan, because they did not take pity on the son of their people.[2] He said to him, "*And you too do likewise* [3] to this Jew, to this son of your people." He did not say, "Become a Samaritan." For this man had asked him, "*Who is my neighbour,* [4] my friend?" Our Lord showed him the Jew who was wounded. But the Samaritan is also an enemy of the Gentiles. Why then did [the Lord] not construct his parable around one of the sons of the Gentiles? Did he not put to shame thus the priests and Levites who had not taken pity on a son of their people? If he had [chosen] a son of the Gentiles, he would have been introducing an alien element, for [the Jews] do not take pity on the Gentiles. For he said to him, *Do likewise!* Let them then say to us, accordingly, "Did the Law command the priests and Levites to take pity on the wounded Jew or not? Our Lord assuredly came to vindicate the Samaritan, especially when he said to him, "Do not behave like these [people] who are without pity."

---

1 Matt 22:39.
2 Cf. Luke 10:25-37.
3 Luke 10:37.
4 Luke 10:29.

To show that it was a Jew [who had been wounded] he said, *From Jerusalem to Jericho*.[1] For the Samaritans live there because of the kings of former times, who took them into captivity and made them live there. The end of this passage shows that it has to do with mercy. *Which seems to you to have been neighbour to the one who was wounded? He said to him, The one who had mercy on him*.[2] For see, he was a Samaritan. It was clear, therefore, that [the Lord] did not say that one's neighbour was [only] the son of one's race. It may be that the Jewish people[3] and the priests, those for whom it is even more fitting that they should care for them, neglect the sons of their race. But, should you be from the Samaritans, from those who are opposed [to them], do not be contemptuous, but let this wounded one be considered as your neighbour, and care for him with diligence.

The Promise of Living Water

§25.   The [text], *Our Lord stood up and proclaimed, Let all who are thirsty come to me and drink*,[4] is like that of the prophet, *Let all who thirst come to the waters*.[5] The prophet sent [them] to the spring, but the One who fulfils the prophets' [words] invited [them] to drink. [That is] what Wisdom said, *Come and eat my bread and drink the wine I have mixed, leave folly behind you and live!*[6]

§26.   Because they were puffed up with pride in Abraham's name, and yet were doing the works of Satan, he said to them, "Do not choose the name of one and the works of the other. Either do the works of the one in whose name you boast, or take the name of him concerning whose works you are earnestly engaged." For [he said], *If you are Abraham's sons, perform his works*,[7] to show that there was a great abyss between the name of Abraham and the works they were doing. He said, *You are the sons of the Evil One, of him who from the beginning was a murderer*,[8] and, *Why*

---

[1] Luke 10:30.
[2] Luke 10:36-37.
[3] Literally, "the sons of the race."
[4] John 7:37.
[5] Isa 55:1.
[6] Prov 9:5-6.
[7] John 8:39.
[8] John 8:44.

do you seek to kill me? This is not what Abraham did.[1] He said this to
them in advance, firstly, that he might warn them against murder, and
secondly that he might receive a pledge from them, *Who is seeking to kill
you?*[2] Thus, after having killed [him], they would be found guilty. *This is
not what Abraham did.* Instead, he had great pity on evildoers, that is, on
the Sodomites. What similarity can there be between Abraham, who was
merciful to sinners, and those who were seeking to kill the Lord of the
righteous? They called our Lord "a Samaritan" because the Samaritans say
about themselves against the Jews, "We are Abraham's sons," and the
Jews say against them, *It is we who are Abraham's sons.*[3] Our Lord
however said to the Jews, *If you were Abraham's sons, you would be
doing the works of Abraham.*[4] His word appeared to the Jews to be ranged
on the side of the Samaritans, while clothed with a Jewish aspect. This is
why they said to him, *You are a Samaritan.*[5]

§27.   *Abraham hoped to see my day,*[6] he, of whom it was said, *In your
descendants shall the Gentiles be blessed.*[7] *He saw and he rejoiced,*[8] for he
recognized the redemption of all the nations through the symbol of the
lamb.[9] *You are not yet fifty years old, and you have seen Abraham? He
said to them, Before Abraham was, I am.*[10] For he existed, but in hidden
fashion, when Isaac was being redeemed, and revealed his sign through a
lamb. When the descendants of [Isaac], who was delivered through a lamb,
went down to Egypt, and remained down there for a long time, which
event was prefigured in advance through Isaac, it was likewise through a
lamb that they were delivered.[11] They used to sacrifice a lamb from that
time onwards until the coming of the true Lamb. When he drew near to
John, [the latter] proclaimed and said, *Behold the Lamb of God.*[12] Because
the true Lamb had come, these other images [of lambs] ceased.

---

[1] John 7:19; 8:40.
[2] John 7:20.
[3] Cf. John 8:39.
[4] John 8:39.
[5] John 8:48.
[6] John 8:56.
[7] Gen 22:18.
[8] John 8:56.
[9] Cf. Gen 22:13.
[10] John 8:57-58.
[11] Cf Exod 12.
[12] John 1:29,36.

The Man Born Blind

§28.   Because they had blasphemed concerning what he had said to them, *Before Abraham was, I am,*[1] he made his way towards the man who was blind from his mother's womb. *His disciples asked him, Who has sinned, this man or his parents? He said to them, Neither he nor his parents, but that God might be glorified. It is fitting for me to do the works of him who sent me, while it is yet day.*[2] That is, "While I am still with you." *For the night is coming,*[3] when the Son will be raised to his exalted place. You, who are the light of the world, will be rendered dark by it.[4] For there will be an end to signs because of the lack of faith of many. *When he had said this, he spat on the ground, and made clay from his spittle,*[5] and fashioned[6] the eyes with the clay. The light sprang forth from the dust, just as in the beginning, when the shadow of the heavens [was present]. *The darkness was spread out over everything.*[7] He commanded the light, and it was born from the darkness. Likewise here too, *he made clay from his spittle,*[8] and brought to fullness what was lacking in creation, which was from the beginning, to show that what was in his hand was bringing to completion what was lacking in [human] nature. In that hand was formed the creation which was from the beginning. Because they were unwilling to believe that he was before Abraham, he proved to them by this deed that he was the Son of him whose hand had formed the First Adam from the earth.[9] Thus, by means of the body, he restored to fullness what [the blind man] was lacking.

§29.   [He did this] to confound once more those who were saying that human beings were formed from the four elements. For see, it was from the earth and from spittle that he restored the deficiency of the members [of the body]. [He did] these things for their benefit, since miracles [were

---

[1] John 8:58.

[2] John 9:2-4.

[3] John 9:4.

[4] Literally, ܠܒܬܘܢ , "you have set." The image contained in the verb is that of evening time and the setting sun.

[5] John 9:6.

[6] The Syriac verb "to make/to do," which is used here alludes to the idea of "re-creation" in Jesus' action.

[7] Gen 1:2-3.

[8] John 9:6.

[9] Cf. Gen 2:7.

effective] in inciting them to believe. *The Jews ask for miracles.*[1] It was not [the pool of] Siloam that opened [the eyes of] the blind man, just as it was not the waters of the Jordan that purified Naaman.[2] It was [the Lord's] command which effected it. So too, it is not the water of our atonement that cleanses us. Rather, it is the names pronounced over it[3] which give us atonement. *He anointed his eyes with clay,*[4] so that other people [too] might cleanse the blindness which was in their hearts. When the blind man went among the people asking, "Where is Siloam?," they saw the clay that was spread over his eyes. They interrogated him and learned from him, as he was speaking. They went with him to see whether his eyes were opened.

§30.   Those whose [eyes] were exteriorly open were being led on by the blind man who was able to see interiorly. For the blind man was being led on in a hidden way by those whose [eyes] were open, but who were interiorly blind. The [blind man] washed the clay from his eyes, and saw himself. These others washed their blindness from their hearts, and were approved. When our Lord opened [the eyes of] one blind man publicly on that occasion, he opened [the eyes of] many blind people secretly. For that blind man was [indeed] blind. He was like a source of gain for our Lord, since he gained many blind people through him, [healing them] from blindness of heart.

§31.   There were indeed marvellous treasures hidden in [the Lord's] few words, and a symbol of the Son of the Creator of life was delineated in his work of healing. *Go, wash your face.*[5] He sent him to wash lest anyone should think that this healing was closer to [medical] skill than to a miracle. [He said this] to show that [the blind man] did not doubt that he was [in the process of] healing him. Thus, in making inquiries as he went about, he was proclaiming the event and his faith was being shown forth.

§32.   [The Lord's] saliva became thus a key for closed eyes. He healed both eye and pupil [through] the water. From the water [he made] the clay,

---

[1] 1 Cor 1:22.
[2] 2 Kgs 5:14.
[3] The water of atonement refers to the baptismal liturgy, and the names that are pronounced over it are those of the Trinity.
[4] John 9:6.
[5] John 9:7.

and brought wholeness to the deficiency. [He did thus so that], when they would spit at him in the face,[1] those eyes of the blind that he had opened with his saliva would testify against them. But [the meaning of] his reproach was not evident to them, when, on the occasion of the blind eyes that he had opened, he had said, *Let those who see become blind.*[2] [He said] this with regard to the blind, that they might see physically, and with regard to those of open [eyes], for he was not perceived by them spiritually. *He made clay on the Sabbath.*[3] They overlooked the fact that he had healed, but reproached him because he had made [clay]. Likewise, they said to him, *who had been ill for thirty-eight years, Who told you to carry your bed?',*[4] and not, "Who healed you?" Here similarly [they said], *He made clay on the Sabbath.* Even without clay, were they not jealous of him, and did they not reject him when he healed one who had dropsey on the Sabbath, one whom he healed by his voice [only]? What did he do to him in healing him? He was healed and purified by means of his word [alone]. According to their words, therefore, whoever speaks on the Sabbath breaks it. Well then, who in fact has broken it more? Our Saviour, who healed [on it], or those who spoke jealously about their Benefactor?

§33.   *All those who had come were thieves and robbers.*[5] [He said this] concerning Theudas[6] and Judas.

---

[1] Cf. Matt 26:67.
[2] John 9:39.
[3] John 9:14.
[4] John 5:5,12.
[5] John 10:8.
[6] Acts 5:36.

XVII

The Raising of Lazarus

§1. *Now Lazarus was ill, and his sisters sent [word] to our Lord, Behold, Lord, he whom you love is ill.*[1] Compare the [following] words of the Life-Giver, and learn that they are similar to each other. In the case of the blind man he said, *Neither he nor his parents have sinned, but it is so that the works of God may be seen in him.*[2] In the case of Lazarus' sickness he said, *This illness is not unto death, but for the sake of the glory of God, so that his Son may be glorified. Therefore, he said to his disciples, Come! Let us go to Judea. They said to him, The Jews are seeking to kill you and yet you are returning there?*[3] But the Physician hastens to wherever there is suffering.[4] "I am going unto those who cast stones, because instead of being stonethrowers they [are destined] to become interpreters."[5] *Many believed in him there.*[6]

§2. *Are there not twelve hours in the day? The one who walks during the day does not stumble, for he sees the light.*[7] [He said] this because he wished to teach his apostles through a parable that, until the year of his Gospel proclamation was completed,[8] that is, the twelve months,[9] the Jews would not become stumbling blocks by his murder, through which darkness was [destined] to reign over Zion. *Are there not twelve hours in the day?*, that is, "What have you to fear with regard to stoning, while I am still with you? None of you will suffer with me or instead of me, but darkness full of suffering will take hold of you when I will be lifted up from you and when I will have left you, so that you may receive crowns, just as I myself will be crowned and then lifted up." *Come then, let us go*

---

[1] John 11:1,3.

[2] John 9:3.

[3] John 11:4,7-8.

[4] While this is not a direct scriptural quote, it nevertheless picks up the sentiment of Matt 9:12.

[5] There is a striking play on words here in Syriac between the words for "stonethrowers" [ܪ̈ܓܘܡܐ], and "interpreters" [ܡܬܪ̈ܓܡܢܐ], which is not possible to render in translation.

[6] John 11:45.

[7] John 11:9.

[8] Ephrem held the view that the Lord's ministry lasted only one year.

[9] The Syriac idiom here is "the mother of months."

and die with him.[1] It was decided that, if they were going to go with him, they would be stoned too. That is why he was consoling and comforting them, and he dispelled fear from them.

§3.   *Lazarus is dead, and I rejoice for your sake.*[2] But, if he rejoiced, why was it that *he wept*[3] when he arrived [in Bethany]? Take note of just how far removed from him still were those who were near to him. As in the case of the human person, all his natural [faculties] lie hidden in him, and he causes each one of them to spring forth in its place [when required]; in similar fashion our Lord [called forth at one time] the appetite for food,[4] and [at another] tears for a friend. All physicians wear themselves out for their patient lest he die; but Lazarus' Physician was waiting for his death in order to show his victory over death. He rejoiced when he heard [that he was dead], and he wept when he came. He revealed that he was dead even before coming, and asked on arrival, *Where have you put him?*[5]

How astute is your wisdom, O our Lord! For, you revealed the death of Lazarus to your disciples from afar off, but you asked those who were seeking a pretext [against you] where his burial place was, so that, after they would have reproached you for your question, your miracle would make them wonder.

He wept, so that, in raising this man who had died, [he might show] too that people who [appear to be] alive are dead.[6] He spoke noteworthy words there, and sealed them with deeds, so that people might believe that he had truly become a human being. That is why *he wept.* He showed forth the faith of Mary and Martha. [The sisters] in fact were adoring and confessing him before these [people].[7] *They had given orders that whoever confessed him must be rejected.*[8]

§4.   *If you had been here, my Lord.*[9] [They said this] because *They had sent [word],* and he had not wished to come. They knew therefore that our Lord's will was for Lazarus to die. For he had not come and had not sent

---

[1] John 11:16.
[2] John 11:14-15.
[3] John 11:35.
[4] Cf Matt 4:2.
[5] John 11:34. The next two sentences are absent from the Armenian version.
[6] Cf. John 11:25-26.
[7] Cf. John 11:20-21,32.
[8] John 9:22.
[9] John 11:21,32.

anyone to heal him. Understand the words, *If you had been there*, as being instead of "If you had willed it." Further, because they had heard from the disciples that, [on one occasion] while he was sleeping, the waves were stirred up,[1] and that, [at another time] when he was not with them, storms had broken out.[2] [Mary and Martha] were speaking from a human perspective. For, when the Light is present, darkness cannot enter, and when Life is present, death does not dare [appear]. *He wept*, to show that [Lazarus] was dead and to give [his enemies] an opportunity[3] for saying, *He opened [the eyes of] a blind man.*[4] In seeking to put an obstacle before him from one perspective, they were confessing him in spite of themselves, from another. "O you, who raised Lazarus, raise yourself!" By this [word] they were confessing that which they had denied.

§5.   *My Lord, he gives off an odour.*[5] If you [Martha] had been sitting at his feet like Mary,[6] you would have heard him [say], as Mary did, that everything was easy for him. *I am the resurrection. Whoever believes in me, even if he dies, yet shall he live.*[7] This is clear. *And whoever lives and believes in me will never die.*[8] Such a one will not remain on forever in death, but will be raised up, and the power of death will not have dominion over him forever. There are those who refer this to the end of the world, [saying] that those whom our Lord's coming overtakes will not die, as in [the text], *Those who are still waiting for his coming will not die.*[9]

§6.   *Our Lord wept* over Lazarus, in order to show that "he could not raise him up," and while they were thinking thus, he brought their secret mockery out into the open, *Could he not have prevented him from dying?* [10] You are about to observe perhaps that they did not say, "Is he not able to raise him up?" However, they did say something against his divinity which was serious, "If he weeps to that extent, he is indeed showing that he did not want him to die, and his power therefore did not

---

[1] Cf Matt 8:23-27.
[2] Cf. Matt 14:22-33.
[3] In Syriac the expression used is: "to open a door."
[4] John 11:37.
[5] John 11:39.
[6] Luke 10:39.
[7] John 11:25.
[8] John 11:26.
[9] Cf. 1 Thess 4:15; 1 Cor 15:51.
[10] John 11:37.

prevail over death, like God, since [God] would not allow death to have dominion over him." While he was thus disclosing their mockery, he was also disclosing his divinity. This [text], *He was troubled* [1] is similar to this [other passage], *How long will I be with you and put up with you?*,[2] and also like this one, *This generation is wearing me out.*[3] *They have put me to the test ten times, but these others, twenty times.*[4]

§7.   He went forth to bring the dead man out from the tomb, and asked, *Where have you laid him? Our Lord's tears were welling forth.*[5] His tears were like the rain, and Lazarus like a grain of wheat, and the tomb like the earth. He gave forth a cry like that of thunder,[6] and death trembled at his voice. Lazarus burst forth like a grain of wheat. He came forth and adored his Lord who had raised him. [The Lord] performed his miracles by appointment and he allowed himself to be appointed by them. He went forth to meet the man who was blind from his mother's womb.[7] *And he remained two days,*[8] until Lazarus had died. But he restored Lazarus to life, and died in his stead. For, after he had drawn [Lazarus] from the tomb, and had seated himself at table with him, he was himself buried by the symbol of the ointment which Mary *poured over his head.*[9]

Here, death and greed were exposed. With regard to death, its power was exposed after four days, when [the Lord] recalled a corpse [to life], so that [death] would know that it was easy for him in his own case to leave it [there] for three days. The promise of this mouth, which had summoned and led forth *him who had been dead for four days,*[10] is trustworthy, [this promise which proclaimed] that he himself would rise on the third day. Greed was also exposed there, this [greed] through which Judas had ensnared him, and sold him for thirty pieces of silver.[11] [Greed] was reproved, since it was not because [the Lord] was presenting himself as

---

[1] John 11:33.
[2] Luke 9:41.
[3] Ps 95:10.
[4] Num 14:22.
[5] John 11:34-35.
[6] John 11:43.
[7] John 9:1.
[8] John 11:6.
[9] Cf. John 12:1-3; Matt 26:6-7.
[10] John 11:17,39.
[11] Cf. Matt 26:15.

God that [Judas] was anxious to betray him, just as it was not because of the poor that he was anxious that the ointment be sold.[1]

§8.   Thus, [the Lord] came to Bethany, raised his friend, and buried himself through the symbol of the ointment.[2] He made Mary and Martha joyful, and exposed both Sheol and greed, Sheol because it would not always be holding onto him, and greed, because it would not always be selling him. He had said, *On the third day I will rise.*[3] Whenever they would hear that this would be difficult [to believe], let them consider him who was raised on the fourth day.[4] He said something that was difficult, but then did something even more difficult, so that, through what he had done for Lazarus, one could believe what he spoke of regarding himself.

§9.   *Draw near and take away the stone.*[5] Was he, who had raised a dead man and restored life [to him], not able to open the tomb and roll back the stone? He, who said to his disciples, *If there is faith in you like the grain of mustard seed, you will say to the mountain, move, and it will move from before you,*[6] would he not have been able to move the stone which was at the mouth of the tomb by his word [alone]? He would indeed have been able to raise the stone by his word, he whose voice, when he hung on the cross, split rocks and tombs.[7] But, because he was Lazarus' friend, he said, "Open [it] and let the odour of putrefaction strike you in the face, and, *Unbind him!,*[8] you who have wrapped him up, so that you may recognize the work of your hands."

§10.   When [Lazarus] was dying, therefore, our Lord did not go to the village [of Bethany] lest [the Jews] should say, "They have made an agreement with each other."[9] He did not enter his house, nor leave the

---

[1] Cf. John 12:2-6.
[2] Cf. Matt 26:12.
[3] Cf. Matt 17:23; 20:19; 27:63.
[4] Cf. John 11:17,39.
[5] John 11:39.
[6] Matt 17:20.
[7] Cf. Matt 27:51-52.
[8] John 11:44.
[9] The material contained in the Syriac text from this point until the end of the quotation of the passage from John 11:48 some lines further on is missing in the Armenian translation. T. Baarda's study of this extra wording in the Syriac confirms Leloir's view that the Syriac text here was not a secondary insertion, but the result of an omission on the part of the Armenian translator. Cf. T. Baarda, "Mar Ephrem's Commentary on the Diatessaron, Ch.

place where he was, lest they think that this was done by means of conspiracy, and that he had heard something from [Lazarus'] sisters. He said, *Where have you put him?* [1] When he was afar off, he knew that he was dead, but he did not know where his tomb was. He also [said], *Roll back the stone,*[2] that they might understand that the door of the tomb was [acting] as a seal, so that the odour might testify concerning his death, and the deed [might testify] concerning God. He did not command his disciples to remove the stone. Nor did he, who had said to Lazarus, *Come outside!*,[3] say to the stone, "Roll yourself back," lest he provide the bitter schemings of the Jews with a pretext [for calumny]. Instead he commanded the Jews to remove the stone, so that the odour of the dead man would fill their nostrils and their eyes would see that the dead man was raised.

If we let him go, everyone will believe in him, and the Romans will come and take our country and our people.[4] [They said this] because they were subject to Roman domination. But our Lord came and reigned through his signs, and the world followed after him. Perhaps the Romans may hear that a king has been born among them, that they were calling him a son of David, and not only this, but that they were planning to seize him to make him king.[5] This is why [the Jews were saying] that he must be killed, *lest the Romans come and take our country and our people.*[6]

The Anointing at Bethany

§11.   Simon the leper[7] believed, and our Lord was good to him. From between faith and grace, leprosy, which was in the middle, was expelled. How could leprosy have continued to remain in Simon's body on seeing him, who puts leprosy to flight, reclining at table in Simon's house? While his humanity was reclining at table in Simon's house, his divinity was dwelling in Simon's heart, just as in Simon [Peter], his namesake. How could this deadly leprosy have been able to remain [in him] on seeing that Lazarus who had been dead was raised to life? *If you had been here,*

XVII:10," *Early Transmission of the Words of Jesus: Thomas, Tatian and the Text of the New Testament* (Amsterdam, 1983), pp. 289-311.

[1] John 11:34.
[2] John 11:39.
[3] John 11:43.
[4] John 11:48. The Armenian translation resumes at this point.
[5] Cf. John 6:15.
[6] John 11:48-50.
[7] Cf. Matt 26:6.

my brother would not have died.[1] How could the leprosy have continued affecting Simon while the Purifier of lepers was reclining at table in his house? How could the One with power to heal [leprosy] and the leper to be healed sit down to table together? Perhaps it was the same [as happened] to Zacchaeus the tax-collector, *Today, there is salvation in this house.*[2] He purifed him as a reward for his hospitality.

§12.   *The chief priests had planned that they would also kill Lazarus.*[3] The Law prescribed that *he who kills must be killed.*[4] But they were saying, "Let him be killed, because he has restored life, and when you will have killed him, he will not be able to raise [Lazarus] again." Should you not have feared lest the word of this mouth which raised Lazarus might kill you? Now Cain thought that he could kill a man and even deceive God. But if a man [Abel] could have been killed, because he was mortal, God cannot be deceived, since he knows all things.[5]

§13.   *Why was this ointment not sold for three hundred denarii, [which could have been] given to the poor?*[6] said Judas. Our Lord, because he saw that he was greedy for money, had placed him in charge of the money to satisfy him and to prevent him becoming a traitor for the sake of money. It would have been better for him, however, to have stolen the money rather than to have betrayed the Creator of money. But how could there have been any need for a money-box [in the case] of the five loaves,[7] or when there was wine from water,[8] or when they had been seeking to purchase remedies for the eyes of the son of Timaeus,[9] or when they were asking for two drachmas?[10] *Do not rejoice because demons are subject to you,*[11] for even the Iscariot was expelling [demons]. *But rejoice with regard to your names, for they are written in the heavens, with the angels.*[12] But

---

[1] John 11:21,32.
[2] Luke 19:9.
[3] John 12:10.
[4] Exod 21:12.
[5] Cf. Gen 4:8-10.
[6] Mark 14:5; John 12:5.
[7] Cf. Matt 14:13-21.
[8] John 2:1-11.
[9] Cf. Mark 10:46-52.
[10] Cf. Matt 17:24-27.
[11] Luke 10:20.
[12] *Idem.*

that of Judas however is written on earth with those who crucified [the Lord].

Judas expelled a demon, so that he who was our Lord's adversary might recount to the authors of the crucifixion, his companions, whether our Lord was expelling demons by Beelzebub.[1] And [it was also] so that the traitor might be confounded, since the demons, fearing the thief, had gone out [of the possessed]. Should not the thief of money fear the Creator of money? Perhaps that is what he remembered, *and he hanged himself*.[2] So, lest anyone might say that our Lord had chosen a traitor as disciple without knowing this, he said, *One of you is Satan*.[3] He did not speak the name of Judas, so as not to put him to shame in case he might be willing to repent. At the washing [of the feet],[4] he did not begin with Simon, the head of the disciples. For, since the head of the angels had abandoned for a moment his [due] honour in that [earliest] time, how could the head of the disciples have been able to remain in his level of honour? The head of the disciples learned to imitate the head of the angels. The sublime dignity of our Lord's [divine] nature was clothed with the nobility of his humble humanity at that moment of the washing [of the feet].

---

[1] Cf. Matt 12:24-28.
[2] Cf. Matt 27:5.
[3] John 6:70.
[4] John 13:1-17.

XVIII

The Messianic Entry into Jerusalem

§1.   *Untie the donkey and bring it to me.*[1] He began with a manger and finished with a donkey, in Bethlehem with a manger, in Jerusalem with a donkey.[2] This is like, *Rejoice Daughter of Zion, for behold your king is coming to you, just and lowly, and seated on a donkey.*[3] But [the daughter of Zion] saw him and was troubled. She looked at him and became sad. He, the Merciful One, and the Son of the Merciful One, had spread his benevolence over her like a father, but she conducted herself as perversely towards him as she had done towards the One who had sent him. Not being able to abuse the Father, she displayed her hatred against his Only-Begotten.

[The daughter of Zion] repaid him with evil for the immensity of his grace. The Father had washed her from her blood, but she defiled his Son with her spitting.[4] The Father had clothed her with fine linen and purple, but she clothed him with garments of mockery.[5] He had placed a crown of glory on her head, but she plaited a crown of thorns for him.[6] He had nourished her with choicest food[7] and honey, but she gave him gall.[8] He had given her pure wine, but she offered him vinegar [soaked] in a sponge.[9] The One who had introduced her into cities, she drove out into the desert. The One who had put shoes on her feet, she made hasten barefoot towards Golgotha.[10] The One who had girded her loins with saphire, she pierced in the side with a lance.[11] When she had outraged the servants [of God] and killed the prophets, she was led into captivity to Babylon, and when the time of her punishment was completed, her return [from captivity] took place.

---

[1] Mark 11:2; Matt 21:2.
[2] What follows until the end of the citation from Luke 19:41 is missing in the Armenian version.
[3] Zech 9:9.
[4] Cf. Ezek 16:9; Matt 26:67.
[5] Cf. Ezek 16:10,13; Matt 27:28.
[6] Cf. Ezek 16:12; Matt 27:29.
[7] Literally, "with fat."
[8] Cf. Ezek 16:13; Matt 27:34.
[9] Cf. John 19:29.
[10] Cf. Ezek 16:10; Matt 27:33.
[11] Cf. Ezek 16:10-11; John 19:34.

But, now that she has stretched forth her hands against the Son and crucified the Son of the living [God], her house has been uprooted and her altar overturned, just as the prophet had said, *The holy city shall be destroyed*,[1] together with the king who is to come. And she will lie there in ruins until the completion of judgements. There will be no further pact or decree for her return, as [there was] from Egypt, or from Babylon, or from the Greeks, where a fixed term [in each case] was written down. For her then the judgement is decreed: there will be no fixed term for her, and no return. No more sacrifices are needed, since the [one] great sacrifice has abolished them.[2] The fat of loins is no longer of any avail, since prudence of loins has conquered it. The mind and heart[3] are rendered vain by upright reasoning in the minds of the Gentiles, and by spiritual circumcision in faith which surpasses circumcision of the flesh.[4]

When he reached Jerusalem and saw it, he wept over it.[5] *Abraham saw [the Lord's] day and rejoiced.*[6] But [the Lord] saw Jerusalem and wept over it. He wept because it had not rejoiced. *If only on this, your day, but peace is hidden from your eyes.*[7] "Abraham your father saw my day only, and rejoiced, but, as for you, you saw both the day and the Lord of the day." This is he who wept over those who were not gladdened at the sight of him who was to help them. *He wept* also over the destruction that was to befall the city. This is like [the text], *Weep for yourselves, for the days will come when you will say to the mountains, Cover us.*[8] *Abraham saw my day and he rejoiced.*[9] He untied Isaac who was bound because of the ram caught in the bush,[10] just as our Lord loosened the bonds of the Gentiles by means of the cross. The sight of the angel was hidden from Balaam,[11] [just as] the Lord of peace was hidden from the people who had the mentality of Balaam. Peace was hidden from the former, while the Lord of peace was hidden from the latter.

---

[1] Cf. Dan 8:11-12; 9:26-27; 11:31-39.

[2] Cf. Heb 7:27.

[3] Literally, "the heart and caul." The caul [ܟܒܕܐ كبد], like the liver, is often used in Semitic imagery as a figure for the seat of passion and emotion, just as the heart was taken as the locus for intellectual reasoning.

[4] Cf. Rom 2:28-29.

[5] Luke 19:41. The Armenian version takes up here after the omission noted above.

[6] John 8:56.

[7] Luke 19:42.

[8] Luke 23:28-30.

[9] John 8:56.

[10] Cf. Gen 22:13.

[11] Cf. Num 22:22-35.

§2.   *The children were crying and saying, Hosanna to the Son of David. This displeased the chief priests and the scribes and they said to him, Do you not hear what these are saying?*[1] That is, "If these praises do not please you, make them keep silent." At his birth and at his death children were intertwined in the crown of his sufferings. *The infant* John *jumped for joy within the womb*[2] on meeting him, and children were slain at his birth.[3] They were [like] the grapes of his wedding feast. It was also children who proclaimed his praise when the time of his death drew near. *Jerusalem was in turmoil*[4] at his birth, just as it was *in turmoil* again *and trembling*[5] the day that he entered into it. When the scribes heard, *they were displeased and they were saying to him, Stop them! He said to them, If these become silent, the stones will cry out.*[6] Thus, they preferred that the children would cry out rather than the stones, lest the blind understand the clamour of creatures. This, however, was held in reserve, for the stones were crying out at the time of his crucifixion,[7] [whereas] those with words were silent. It was those things which were dumb which proclaimed his greatness.

§3.   *Now is the judgement of the world, and the prince of the world will be thrown outside.*[8] He is not, however, the prince of [all] creatures nor of all humanity. In [saying] that *he will be thrown outside,* [the Lord] was showing that he was not of [divine] essence,[9] and that he had no authority. In what way then will he be thrown out? John explains, *Behold the Lamb of God, and he takes away the sin of the world.*[10] That he is called *a ruler* is like [the text], *The gods of the nations, even though they are not,*[11] and, *Your struggle is not with flesh and blood, but against the leaders and the powers and the dominators of the world of darkness, which are beneath the heavens.*[12] It is also like, *Those whom the god of*

---

[1] Matt 21:15-16.
[2] Luke 1:41.
[3] Matt 2:16-18.
[4] Matt 2:3.
[5] Matt 21:10.
[6] Luke 19:39-40.
[7] Cf. Matt 27:51-52.
[8] John 12:31.
[9] Ephrem probably has the heresy of Bardaisan in mind here.
[10] John 1:29.
[11] Ps 96:5.
[12] Eph 6:12.

this world has rendered blind [1] {lest they believe. Likewise here, *The prince of the world has been thrown outside,*[2] and he has also said in another passage, *Those whose god is their belly and whose glory is their confusion.*[3]

§4. {We, they say, *have heard from the Law that the Messiah will live for ever.*[4] This is indeed what [Scripture] says, *It will not depart until the one to whom it belongs comes,*[5] and, *The Lord God will raise up for you a prophet like me. Listen to him!*[6] But you, they say, *you say that the Son of Man must be lifted up.*[7] They refer this to the end of the world, for they say that there is [only] one advent. Or, they have said about every prophecy, *We have heard from the Law.* [This is] just as [Scripture] says, *It is written in the Law of this [people] that they hated me unjustly.*[8] In David too it is written, *They hated me with a violent hatred,*[9] and, *Sinners, who have hated me unjustly.*[10]

"The Kingdom of God Is in Your Heart"

§5. {Where the king is, there too is the kingdom. This is why he said, *The kingdom of God is in your heart. The kingdom of God cannot be observed according to days,*[11] for they were keeping account of the times and the ages [to know] if [the Messiah] was about to appear in them. A report had circulated thirty years previously about him, and rumours had increased about his birth. In these years too there emerged Theudas and his companions, whom [the Lord] had referred to as *robbers,*[12] for they had gone before him to rob, and had begun to usurp the name of the Messiah

---

[1] 2 Cor 4:4. At this point the Syriac text is missing for approximately eighteen-nineteen folios. It resumes at XXI, §4. This is the only remaining lacuna of considerable length, since the discovery of the additional folios. It is difficult to estimate how much material the Syriac tradition actually contains since the Armenian version tends to expand at times in comparison to the Syriac towards the end of the Commentary. The translation for this lacuna is based on the Armenian tradition (cf. CSCO 145, pp. 183-224).

[2] John 12:31.

[3] Phil 3:19.

[4] John 12:34.

[5] Gen 49:10.

[6] Deut 18:15.

[7] John 12:34.

[8] John 15:25; cf. Ps 35:19; 69:5.

[9] Ps 25:19.

[10] Ps 35:19.

[11] Luke 17:21 and 20.

[12] Cf. John 10:8.

for themselves everywhere. Consequently, our Lord confounded them because they had sought to see him, not in a hidden way, but through observations.

§6. {*Rejoice, daughter of Zion, for see, your king is coming to you,*[1] and, *A star will rise out of Jacob,*[2] and, *I will make the sun of righteousness rise upon you, who honour my name,*[3] and, *He purifies many peoples.*[4] Our Lord began to confound them because they had come to him in an underhand way with traps. *These are thieves and robbers,*[5] for they do not show themselves in daylight. See, the Lord of the flock [was present], entering his sheepfold by the door, that is, [coming] into his inheritance with confidence and strength, by reason of his prodigies and miracles. See how [the kingdom] is *within your heart,*[6] not in a hidden way, but through his testimonies, lest those seeking him would need learned observations. *If I do not perform the works,* he said, *Do not believe in me.*[7] Those others were showing that they were not messiahs, since they were seeking to rob people in secret. The proud ambition which was in them was condemning them, as well as the lie which they were fabricating, and they were therefore afraid to show themselves. Theudas made himself out to be someone important. Let him prove it to them if they are to follow him. But, if he is not [what he claims to be], let it [be understood] that he was speaking of someone else, when speaking of himself. It was on account of this that they were saying, *When the Messiah comes, no one will know where he comes from.*[8]

§7. {What the [prophet] had been saying was wrongly understood and despised: *It is from the town of Bethlehem that the Messiah will come forth.*[9] Because [false] messiahs had multiplied they were perplexed in the midst of so many opinions. They were saying, *Perhaps our elders have*

---

[1] Zech 9:9; John 12:15; Matt 21:5.
[2] Num 24:17.
[3] Mal 3:20.
[4] Isa 52:15. The Armenian version (and Ephrem?) reflect the Peshitta's option in translating the difficult Hebrew text, "he sprinkles." LXX reads "many nations will be astounded at him."
[5] John 10:8.
[6] Cf. Luke 17:21.
[7] John 10:37.
[8] John 7:27.
[9] John 7:42; cf. Mic 5:1.

recognized that he is truly the Messiah,[1] the True One among all the others. This is why he said to them, *If someone were to come in his own name, you would believe in him.*[2] Because many had followed him, he said that his future coming would be with clarity, not like his birth. *If they say to you, See, he is here, Do not believe any of it, for it will be like lightning that he will shine.*[3] Just as thieves had come because of his birth, robbers will come because of his advent, and rumours will increase. Therefore, *Do not go out* [4] to seek him lest you be swept along willingly by a troublemaker or taken by force. Because he is the Lord of the kingdom, he wanted to purify simultaneously through himself the elevated and superior regions as well the inferior ones. [Understand] what he said, *He will purify the dwelling place of his kingdom of all scandal,*[5] in relation to earth and creatures, for he will renew them and cause his just ones to dwell there.[6]

Indictment of the Scribes and Pharisees

§8.   {*Woe to you, lawyers, because you have hidden the keys!* [7]That is, because they had hidden the knowledge of our Lord's manifestation which was in the prophecies. If our Lord is the door, as he has said,[8] it is clear that the keys of knowledge belong to him. The scribes and pharisees did not want to enter through this door of life, in keeping with what he had said, *See, the kingdom is in your heart.*[9] [He was referring to] himself, for he was standing in their midst. Sin had cleverly disguised its instruments and stood on the bridge which was leading to the house of life, lest souls and spirits enter into the house of life. *You have hidden the keys*, he said.

§9.   {Following this he said, *That all the blood of the just may come [upon you],*[10] because they killed the Avenger of the death of [the just], and

---

[1] John 7:26.
[2] John 5:43.
[3] Matt 24:26-27; Luke 17:23-24.
[4] Matt 24:26.
[5] Matt 13:41.
[6] 2 Pet 3:13.
[7] Luke 11:52.
[8] Cf. John 10:7,9.
[9] Luke 17:21.
[10] Matt 23:35.

so the vengeance of these latter is sought from their hands. One who kills the judge is indeed a friend of homicides, because [in killing the judge], he has suppressed vengeance and opened up the way for murderers. [The Lord] also said, *From the blood of Abel, the just one, to the blood of Zechariah,*[1] and not only until then, but even up to this day. Although still among them, he did not avenge his own blood until after they had killed him, lest they say that it had been predetermined that he do this. He pronounced the sentence of judgement in relation to [the just] who had gone before, so that they might respect [the just] who were to follow, and he gave them an opportunity to do penance for having put him to death, even though, according to the Law, there could be no [opportunity for] repentance for one who murders the prophets, for it says thus, *Let the one who kills die,*[2] and not, "See if he does penance, and [then] pardon him." But he gave them an opportunity to do penance, if they had wished, for having put him to death.

Through the murder of the more recent prophets, the people confessed that they had been participants and accomplices in the murder of the earlier ones, and through the confession of their mouth they were lacking in truth, since they had accused their ancestors of murdering the prophets, and did not blush. Since this [people] had made their unborn children participants and accomplices in the murder of the Saviour, the [Lord] made their evil will a participant and accomplice in the murder of the prophets, in spite of their lack of knowledge, since, although knowing that the Son was master of the vineyard and aware that he was an avenger,[3] they killed him.

§10.   [It was prophetic that Moses had given [the Israelites] the order to offer their sacrifices in one single place,[4] there to immolate the lamb and [there] to accomplish an image of the redemption. Herod did not kill [the Lord] with the infants of Bethlehem,[5] nor did the Nazarenes when they hurled him down from the mountain,[6] since it was not possible for him to die outside of Jerusalem. *For it cannot be that a prophet should perish outside of Jerusalem.*[7] Take note that, although it was Jerusalem that

---

[1] *Idem.*
[2] Exod 21:12.
[3] Cf. Matt 21:37-39.
[4] Cf. Deut 12:2-18.
[5] Cf. Matt 2:13-18.
[6] Cf. Luke 4:29-30.
[7] Luke 13:33.

killed him, nevertheless, Herod and Nazareth were united with regard to his death, and vengeance will be required of both for his having been killed. Learn also from this that, not only will vengeance for his blood be required of the inhabitants of Jerusalem, but also, everyone who saw and denied him will be convicted for having killed him. In saying, *Between the sanctuary and the altar*,[1] he has indeed shown their perversity, in that they did not even respect the place of expiation. The words, *How often would I have gathered you together*,[2] are similar to these, *See, these three years I have come, seeking fruit on this fig tree, and I find none*.[3]

§11.   *(If any one hears my words and does not keep them, I do not know him*.[4] Has he not said, *The Father judges no one, but has placed all judgement in the hands of his Son?*[5] But, because he is the Physican of humanity, he [also] said, *I have not come into this world to judge it, but to save the world*.[6] To show that every judgement concerns him, he taught, *Whoever does not receive my words, that word which I have spoken will judge him*.[7]

The Eschatological Discourse

§12.   {[Let us now explain] this saying, *When you will see the sign of its terrible destruction*.[8] [Jerusalem] was destroyed many times and then rebuilt, but here it is a question of its [total] upheaval and destruction and the profanation of its sanctuary, after which it will remain in ruins and fall into oblivion. The Romans placed standards representing an eagle within this temple just as [the prophet] had said, *On the wings of impurity and ruination*.[9]

     The sign of its terrible destruction, foretold by the prophet Daniel.[10] Some say that the sign of its destruction was the pig's head which the Romans gave Pilate to carry into the interior of the temple to place

---

[1] Matt 23:35.
[2] Luke 13:34.
[3] Luke 13:7.
[4] John 12:47.
[5] John 5:22.
[6] John 12:47.
[7] John 12:48.
[8] Matt 24:15.
[9] Dan 9:27.
[10] Matt 24:15.

there. [The Lord] also said, *The one who stands on the housetop*,[1] for they were not to escape in the usual way, since the concern of [God's] solicitude was not over them. He also said, *Woe to those who will be with child*.[2] [He was speaking] of those who were tortured during the siege of Jerusalem by the Romans. *There will be distress for this people*,[3] he said, such that women will eat their children.

§13. {*Keep on praying and ask that your flight may not be in winter or on the day of the Sabbath*,[4] lest you be led away [captive] at a time when it is not permitted to work. Just as winter is without fruit and the Sabbath without labour, let it not be that you be led away [captive] when you have neither fruit nor work. *In winter and the Sabbath*, one of necessity and the other willingly; winter of necessity and the Sabbath willingly. Therefore, let not the constraint of others nor your own will take you away from the work of the Lord your God. Thus, through winter and the Sabbath, he showed them once again that misfortune was going to befall them. After he had shown them his anger and had shown them that it would fall from above deservedly, he became merciful towards them again and taught them to remain in prayer, not in order [to try] to turn aside the decree of the harsh punishment hanging over them, but to change the time and the day of the great calamity that was [imminent] upon them. By his mercy [the Lord] united two things in his discourse. "It is true that distress will come and that you will have to flee; however, *Keep on praying*, lest this event and sadness come upon you *in winter*; for you cannot avoid it, even if you wanted to flee from the tribulation; or, *on account of the Sabbath*, so that the tribulation will not surprise you during your rest period."

§14. {He showed his solicitude for the Law, as a son of the Law, and made himself its guardian, lest the Law of Moses be abrogated. Lest, he said, there be found among you some who, being too innocent and simple, might keep the Sabbath in time of war as you keep it [in time of peace], and they kill you, like those who were killed in the cave.[5] *In winter and on the Sabbath*. Winter is the time of repose from all the work of the summer,

---

[1] Luke 17:31.
[2] Matt 24:19.
[3] Luke 21:23.
[4] Matt 24:20.
[5] Cf. 1 Macc 2:27-38.

and the Sabbath is [the repose] of the seven days, [the repose] for the day of the coming, according to what [the apostle] has said, *The Sabbath of God continues until now,*[1] for the Sabbath is the limit for works. As [the Lord] has said, *Remain in prayer, so that you may be worthy to escape from all that is going to take place.*[2] It is said that he was speaking of the punishment in Jerusalem, and at the same time, referring to the end of this world. You will take flight,[3] he said, because on [the day of] the resurrection, a fearful trembling will grasp hold of all those who are not perfectly prepared for it. But others hold that [this] was said only in relation to the apostles, so that if the sun were eclipsed on the sixth day,[4] they would be comforted. [He said, *on the Sabbath,* to them because] the Jews used to boast of the Sabbath, and, *in winter,* because it is the cold season. *If God had not shortened these days, no human being would have been saved.*[5] It was not the number of days or hours that was shortened, but time itself was lessened, *for the sake of the elect,*[6] in order that their tribulations would not be multiplied, but rather shortened, so that redemption might reach [them].

The Return of the Son of Man

§15.   {He also said, *But, of that hour no one knows, not even the angels, nor the Son,*[7] lest they question him as to the moment of his coming. *It is not your business to know the days and the times.*[8] He has hidden that [from us] so that we might keep watch, and that each of us might think that this coming would take place during our life. For, if the time of his coming were to be revealed, his coming would be in vain, and it would not have been desired by the nations and the ages in which it was to take place. He has indeed said that *he will come,*[9] but he did not define when, and [thus] all generations and ages thirst for him. For, although he has given [an indication of] the signs of his coming, their end cannot be understood, since they have come and gone in a constant flux and yet they

---

[1] Cf. Heb 4:9.
[2] Luke 21:36.
[3] Cf. Matt 24:16,20.
[4] The sixth day = Good Friday.
[5] Mark 13:20.
[6] Matt 24:22.
[7] Matt 24:36.
[8] Acts 1:7.
[9] Cf. Matt 24:30.

remain always. His final coming in fact is similar to the first. For the just and the prophets desired it,[1] because they thought that he would appear in their time. Likewise each of the faithful of today desires to receive it in his own time, especially since he has not clearly indicated the day of his appearance, lest any might think that he is subject to a command and an hour, he who has dominion over numbers and times.

How could that which he himself established be hidden from him, given that he has set forth the signs of his coming? Nevertheless, it is written that he knows [these things]. Why then do they take up one statement and omit the other? Or perhaps he knew the time but the moment was hidden from him? But the time is a moment, and a moment is part of time. *She is now bone of my bone.*[2] [A moment] is like the batting of an eyelid. *At that time and in that moment, Jesus exulted in his spirit,*[3] and, *Watch and remain in prayer, because you do not know the time,* et cetera.[4]

§16. {*No one knows that day, neither an angel nor the Son.*[5] This is like what he said, *Depart from me, cursed of my Father, into the eternal fire, because I do not know you.*[6] Just as he knew who were sinners, but said to them on account of their deeds, *I do not know you,*[7] so too, although he knew the moment of his coming, he declared that he did not know it, lest he be questioned [any further] about it. But, let us go further and ask, "Did he know the Father or not?" He did know him, as it is written, *No one knows the Father except the Son and no one knows the Son except the Father.*[8] How then did he not know the moment of his coming? If he knew the Father, what could he not know that would be greater than the Father? Or, for what reasons would [the Father] have hidden the moment of his coming from him? Would it have been so that he would appear to be less great than [the Father], and that his nature would be manifested as being merely that of a creature? If this were so, then, when the moment would be revealed to him and the trumpet

---

[1] Cf. Matt 13:17.

[2] Gen 2:23.

[3] Luke 10:21.

[4] Matt 24:42; Mark 13:33. See the note above at II, § 5 for comment on this type of indication of scriptural abbreviation.

[5] Matt 24:36.

[6] Matt 25:41; Luke 13:25,27.

[7] Luke 13:25,27.

[8] Matt 11:27.

would sound for him to come down from heaven,[1] he himself would become like [the Father].

The [apostle] also said, *The design of God is Christ, through whom all the secrets of wisdom and knowledge have been revealed.*[2] If all these hidden things are revealed through him, how can the moment of his coming be hidden from him? If he does not know the day of his coming, neither does he know the days when he is not coming. Some say that *the Spirit* knows what has been made by [God], because *it searches the depths of God,*[3] but does the Son not know these things [too]? They had questioned him about *the moment,* but he referred to *the day,* and declared, "I do not know," firstly to prevent them asking [any further] questions, and secondly, so that the signs [which he had announced] would be useful, such as sickness for the sick person who does not know the day of his death. He highlighted his signs so that, from the first day, all peoples and ages would think that his coming would take place in their day.

§17.   {Watch, for when the body is sleeping it is nature that holds sway over us, and our activity is directed not by our wills but by the impulse of nature. When a heavy torpor of weakness and sadness rules over the soul, it is the enemy who holds sway over it and leads it against its own desire. It is force that holds sway over nature and the enemy who holds sway over the soul. That is why our Lord spoke of vigilance of soul and of body lest the body sink into a heavy sleep and the soul into a sluggishness born of timidity; just as [Scripture] says, *Let justice awaken you,*[4] and, *When I awake I am still with you,*[5] and, *Do not lose heart.*[6] This is why *we do not lose heart* in the ministry confided to us.[7]

§18.   {He also said, *Two were in one house, on the same bed,*[8] because of the stupor which was to fall upon them at this destruction of Jerusalem, as [Scripture] says, *If ten men remain here.*[9] [He described] as *eagles*[10] the

---

[1] Cf. 1 Thess 4:16.
[2] Col 2:2-3.
[3] 1 Cor 2:10.
[4] Cf. 1 Cor 15:34.
[5] Ps 139:18.
[6] Eph 3:13.
[7] Cf. 2 Cor 4:1.
[8] Luke 17:34.
[9] Gen 18:32.

enemies who were to come against [the city], which would be their prey, according to what [Scripture] says, *His horses are swifter than eagles.*[1] Yet others apply this [number, *two*] to the body and the soul. It is also said concerning the end of the world that fear and trembling will fall upon everyone, so that they will be ready, according to what he said, *Let your belts be girded about your loins.*[2] Or, [it is said] of the just and of the sinner that neither one nor the other can save himself. He called the world a *mill,*[3] and the just, *eagles* with swift wings. He also said, *Who will be the steward, the faithful servant, a good and wise labourer?*[4] [The Lord] testified through all this, with regard to [the steward], that if he is not faithful to the affairs entrusted to him, he *will cut him in pieces, put him aside and place his lot with the hypocrites and the unfaithful, where weeping and gnashing of teeth will be [reserved] for him.*[5]

Two Matthean Parables

§19.　{*Five of them were foolish and five were prudent,*[6] said [the Lord]. It was not their virginity that he qualified as prudence, since they were all virgins, but it was their good deeds that he called prudence. If your virginity is equal to the holiness of the angels, note that [the holiness of] the angels is free from envy and all other [vice]. If you are not condemned by fornication, do not be condemned either by rage or anger.

§20.　{The reward of fruits was taken away from the one who did not cultivate his talents, as from a sterile piece of ground. He compared the mystery of this ground, in which, he said, *he hid it,*[7] to the fallow ground which does not produce any fruit. *Take his talent away from him,*[8] that is, faith, because he did not acquire for himself a life [in conformity] with his faith. Our Lord did not reprove the one [who had received] *five talents,*[9] lest they should say, "He has given us [work] beyond our strength." He

---

[10] Matt 24:28.
[1] Jer 4:13.
[2] Luke 12:35.
[3] Matt 24:41.
[4] Matt 24:45; Luke 12:42.
[5] Matt 24:51; Luke 12:46.
[6] Matt 25:2.
[7] Matt 25:18.
[8] Matt 25:28.
[9] Matt 25:20-21.

censured the one who [had only received] *one [talent]*,[1] so that he might be confounded by the one who had *five*.

§21.   *{Let your belts be girded about your loins,*[2] so that, through chastity, we may be on the alert. *And your lamps lit,*[3] because the world is like the night. It is in need of the light of the just, according to what he said, *Let your light shine before people, so that they may see your good deeds and glorify your Father who is in the heavens.*[4]

The Washing of Feet

§22.   {In his gentleness our Lord humbled his wise hands by washing the feet of his betrayer, who expressed his gratitude for the cleansing with the nails of the cross.[5] He, through whom all creatures were made, humbled himself even unto the washing of vile feet, but was hated [nonetheless] by the pharisees and tormented by the priests. Since all creatures were made by him, since he himself was mediator in their being constituted, their redemption, which came forth from him, was therefore even more abundant, because they were subjected to him by reason of their first origin. Because they were humbled, lying beneath the dominion of the curse, he humbled himself even lower than they, in order to raise them all up and exalt them. Just as he humbled them in the beginning, [so too now,] in his wisdom, he came towards them as a Physician and Peacemaker. That is why pride and arrogance could do nothing except use force. All goods are bound up in and contained in charity, and the guardian of their treasure is [also] charity.

---

[1] Matt 25:24-30.
[2] Luke 12:35.
[3] *Idem.*
[4] Matt 5:16.
[5] Cf. John 13:1-15.

XIX

"One of You Is About to Betray Me"

§1.   {*One of you, who is eating his bread with me, is he who is about to betray me. For see, the hand of my betrayer has slipped in with me at this table.*[1] *But the Son of Man goes as it is written of him.*[2] Through this [word] he was indeed weeping out of love over this evil destroyer. *It would have been better for him if he had never been born.*[3] If [the Lord] was ready to go up on the cross, how should we understand this word [concerning Judas], *It would have been better for him if he had never been born*? As foreknowledge, lack of knowledge or lie? What reasons could have prevented the repentance [of the betrayer] from being worthy of acceptance [by the Lord]?

§2.   {"If these reproaches and disparagements are yours, take the example of the serpent, and do not take issue with me. Do not blame me instead of my master. For, if Adam was prepared to sin, why accumulate reproaches against the one who filled the serpent's mouth with dust and shortened him, [thus depriving him] of the ability to walk?"[4] If Adam had not been prepared to sin without an instigator, it is with just cause that the penalty should rest on the head of [the serpent]. Even though [Adam] was prepared [to sin], it was just that the punishment should have rested firstly on him who was the cause [of sin]. But Adam, because of this weakness in temptation which we find in him, even without the occasion [presented] by the serpent, had accumulated other sins without temptation. Accordingly, the One who went up on the cross might perhaps have done so without any motive; but this is most unlikely since the Scriptures of the Hebrews and many other reasons do not permit us [to think in this way]. Love unveiled the mystery and revealed it to fear, for while love dared [to rest] on our Lord's breast, fear made a sign of interrogation.[5]

---

[1] Cf. John 13:21.
[2] Mark 14:18,20-21; Matt 26:21,23-24; Luke 22:21-22.
[3] Matt 26:24.
[4] Cf. Gen 3:14. Ephrem's line of thought here is not easy to follow. Leloir explains it as follows: "Although God foresaw the fall of Adam he did not desire it. The proof of this is that he punished him who had provoked the fall of humanity" (cf. EC-SC 121, p. 331).
[5] Cf. John 13:23-26.

§3.   [If it is truly certain that, when [the Lord] gave the bread to his disciples, he gave them the mystery of his body, one must also believe that, when he gave the bread to his slayer, he gave it to him as the mystery of his slain body. *He dipped it,*[1] to render [evident] the total participation [of Judas] in his death, for his body was destined to be dipped in his blood. Or [alternatively], he dipped it so as not to give the testament with him.[2] He moistened it and then gave it to him; moistened first because it had been prepared for [the testament] which was to follow.[3]

Judas' avarice judged and separated him from the perfect members [of the Lord], as the Life-Giver has shown in his gentle teaching.[4] [Judas] was not a member of the body of his Church, he was but the dust which clung to the feet [of the disciples].[5] That was why, on the night when [the Lord] judged and separated him from the others, he washed the mud from their feet, to teach them that he had washed Judas from the feet of the disciples with water, [like] dung fit for burning. [Judas] was considered [as] the feet of the body in as much as he was the last of the twelve. Likewise, [the Lord] separated Judas from the apostles by means of the water, when he dipped the bread in the water and gave it to him, for [Judas] was not worthy of the bread which, together with the wine, was given to the twelve. It was not permissible that, through it, he should receive the One who would save from death him, who was going to hand him over to death.

The Lord's Eucharist

§4.   [From the moment when *he broke* his body for his disciples and *gave it*[6] to his apostles, three days are numbered during which he was counted among the dead, like Adam. For, although, after having eaten of the fruit of the tree, [Adam] lived for many years afterwards,[7] he was nonetheless numbered among the dead for having transgressed the

---

[1] John 13:26.

[2] A difficult passage, which Leloir explains as follows: according to the context and the parallels in his writings, Ephrem seems to have wanted to indicate that, in dipping the bread which he was about to give to Judas, the Lord was suppressing the effect of the words of consecration and any links the action might have had with the New Testament economy (cf. EC-SC 121, p. 332).

[3] Leloir indicates that the Armenian text is difficult to translate here too.

[4] Cf. John 6:70; 13:18-19,21-30.

[5] Cf. Matt 10:14.

[6] Cf. Mark 14:22.

[7] Cf. Gen 5:5.

commandment. Thus did [God] speak to him, *The day on which you eat of it you shall die.*[1] [Scripture] also says, *Your descendants shall be for four hundred years,*[2] and the years were numbered from the day on which this word was pronounced. It was likewise for our Lord.[3] Or [alternatively], the sixth day must be counted as two and the Sabbath as one. It was because he had given them his body to eat in view of the mystery of his death that he entered into their bodies, as [afterwards he entered] into the earth. It was because Adam had not blessed [the fruit] at the time when, as a rebel, he gathered it, that *Our Lord blessed [the bread] and broke it.*[4] The bread entered [into them], making up for the avarice by which Adam had rejected [God]. Or, the three days [must be reckoned] from the descent [into hell] and the ascent: the sixth day, the Sabbath, and the first day of the week.

§5.   {He also said, *I shall not drink again of this fruit of the vine until the kingdom of my Father,*[5] to show that he foresaw his imminent departure from them. He said, *Until the kingdom of my Father,* that is, until his resurrection. Simon revealed in the Acts of the Apostles, *After his resurrection, during a period of forty days, we ate with him and we drank,*[6] on this first day of the week, according to what he had said, *They will not taste death before they see the kingdom of God,*[7] and after six days [that] was accomplished.

§6.   {He also said, *Behold Satan has received permission to sift you like wheat, but I have prayed to my Father for you that your faith may not fail.*[8] He did not say, "*I have prayed* that you might not be tempted," but, *That [your faith] may not fail.*

---

[1] Gen 2:17.
[2] Cf. Gen 15:13.
[3] That is, the three days were counted from the moment when he broke his body and gave it.
[4] Matt 26:26.
[5] Matt 26:29; Luke 22:18.
[6] Cf. Acts 10:41.
[7] Mark 9:1; Luke 9:27.
[8] Luke 22:31-32.

285

§7.　　{In saying, *Show us your Father and that will suffice us*,[1] Philip was asking him to see the Father corporeally, with bodily eyes, as formerly the just used to see the angels and archangels. This was why our Lord in his response spoke to him of the divine vision, which he could perceive with the eyes of knowledge. He did not say to him, "You have not seen me," since he was manifesting himself in his exterior aspect, but, *You have not known me*,[2] because his greatness was hidden. That is, "If you knew me in respect of what is not manifest, for the Word is not visible - you would also see my Father who is not visible." The apostle testifies to this in relation to our Lord, with this word, *He is the image of the form of God, of him who is not visible*, et cetera.[3]

§8.　　{*Whoever believes in me will also do the works which I do, and will do even greater ones*.[4] And where is this word which he said, *The disciple is not greater than his master*, [illustrated]?[5] For example, Moses killed only three kings, but Joshua killed thirty.[6] [Moses] persevered in prayer, made supplication, but did not enter [the promised land]. It was Joshua rather who entered and shared out the inheritance.[7] Likewise, Samuel was greater than Eli, and Elisha received a double portion of his master's spirit after his ascension,[8] like the Lord our Saviour, for his disciples effected twice through their signs.

§9.　　{In every person there exists an inimical element. However, this was not so with respect to our Lord. *There is nothing of his [to be found] in me*,[9] he said, and *I have overcome the world*.[10] But the disciples did participate with him in the gift of judgement which our Lord received.[11] [He said] that they will judge, not only to show that God has conquered

---

[1] John 14:8.
[2] John 14:9.
[3] Col 1:15. See the note above at II, § 5 for comment on this type of indication of scriptural abbreviation.
[4] John 14:12.
[5] Matt 10:24; John 13:16; 15:20.
[6] Cf. Josh 12:1-24.
[7] Deut 34:4-5; Josh 14:1-19:51.
[8] Cf. 2 Kgs 2:9-12.
[9] John 14:30.
[10] John 16:33.
[11] Cf. Matt 19:28.

and is judging, but also that people have conquered and are judging those who could have conquered like them, but gave way. *Just men will judge them.*[1]

§10.   {*Let the one who has no sword go and buy one.*[2] [He said that] to instruct them in humility. Simon himself had one of the two swords,[3] so that, when he would use it to show his zeal, the word which [the Lord] had spoken might instruct him, *He who strikes you in the cheek.*[4] Simon had forgotten that through love. Alternatively, [the Lord said that] to show [Simon] that it is not only the day when these things are not within our reach and when our hand cannot reach them that we must abstain from them, but also, even when they are within our reach, as, for example, "This sword which is in your hand, you must not make use of it." To make it quite clear [that he had said that] by way of reproof and not in order to propose war, he added, *Two are sufficient.*[5] If that [had been said] in view of strife, everyone would have had to take a sword. [But he said that] because they were of the Jewish people, of those who were thirsting for the sword and blood, like two of them.[6] When he saw the wrath of their ancestors breaking through, he seized the opportunity of revealing the wrath which was hidden in them to make them ashamed, and to expel it from their hearts.

§11.   {*When the days* of his ministry in Judea *were accomplished, he turned his face to go to Jerusalem. He sent* the two hot-tempered ones *ahead of him.*[7] Likewise he forewarned Judas Iscariot and said to him, *Woe to that man!*[8] If [Judas] had repented like Simon, or like the two who had accepted the admonition, he would have been freed from the curse and would have inherited his place and throne [in heaven].

§12.   {Through this occasion of the swords, let them learn that he knew the day and the hour in which he was to be handed over; let his friends learn his humility and his enemies his strength.

---

[1] Cf. Ezek 23:45.
[2] Luke 22:36.
[3] Cf. John 18:10.
[4] Luke 6:29; Matt 5:39.
[5] Cf. Luke 22:38.
[6] Cf. Luke 9:54.
[7] Luke 9:51-52.
[8] Matt 26:24.

§13. {*This is my commandment.*[1] Have you then only one precept? This is sufficient, even if it is unique and so great. Nevertheless he also said, *Do not kill*,[2] because the one who loves does not kill. He said, *Do not steal*,[3] because the one who loves does even more, he gives. He said, *Do not lie*,[4] for the one who loves speaks the truth, against falsehood. *I give you a new commandment.*[5] If you have not understood what *This is my commandment* means, let the apostle be summoned as interpreter and say, *The goal of his commandment is charity.*[6] What is its binding force? It is that of which [the Lord] spoke, *What you would that others should do to you, do you also.*[7] *Love one another,* in accordance with this measure, *as I have loved you.*[8] That is not possible, for you are our Lord, who love your servants; but we, who are equals, how can we love one another as you have loved us?

Nevertheless he has said it. Let us see, therefore, how [that can be]. *No one can have a love greater than that of one who gives his life for his friends.*[9] His love is that he has called us his friends. If we were to give our life for you, would our love be equal to yours? Even if we do not die for you we are mortal, whereas in your case, you have undergone the suffering of our death, even though you are living. How then can what he said be explained, *As I have loved you*? "Let us die for each other," he said. As for us, we do not even want to live for one another! "If I, who am your Lord and God, die for you, how much more should you die for one another."

§14. {He said, *Behold I am sending you the one who speaks good things.*[10] He showed that he too was one who speaks good things when he said, *I am sending you another who will speak good things,*[11] that is, one who will console. Just as he himself is God, the one who is sent is likewise God. If he is greater because he sends him, [the Spirit] is also greater than

---

[1] John 15:12.
[2] Matt 19:18.
[3] *Idem.*
[4] *Idem.*
[5] John 13:34.
[6] 1 Tim 1:5.
[7] Matt 7:12.
[8] John 13:34; 15:12,17.
[9] John 15:13.
[10] John 16:7.
[11] John 14:16.

he because *the Spirit led him into the wilderness so that he might be tempted there.*[1] How could he say, *It will be good for you that I should go away, for if I do not go away, he who speaks good things will not come to you*[2] and the whole truth *will not be made known to you?* Why is it good that our Lord should go away, he who was not [always] able to show the whole truth? For it is the servant who comes to give that which our Lord did not give. Why should the first who speaks good things not have exposed all the truth, which, according to his words, the second will expose to us? But he is the whole truth, and he is called Lord. [Scripture attests this], *He had received from the Holy Spirit the revelation that he would not taste death before having seen the Lord Messiah. And when he had received our Lord and held him in his arms, he said, Now, Lord, you may send your servant away in peace, according to your word.* It was from the Holy Spirit that he had received the revelation,[3] and he said, *Lord, you may send your servant away,* according to this text, *before having seen the Lord Messiah.*

§15.   {*No one knows what is in a person, except the spirit of the person which is in him. Likewise no one knows what is in God except the Spirit of God.*[4] By this comparison he did not wish to say that his Spirit is a created being, but [it was] to persuade us that our spirit is not alienated from our nature. For he said, *Except the spirit which is in him.* [He said], *Likewise, no one knows what is in God except his Spirit,* because *h e searches his depths.*[5] If one objects that [the Spirit] searches him to know him, [one could reply] that one who is searched is usually inferior to the one who searches. When he said, *Go forth into the whole world, and baptize in the name of the Father, and of the Son and of the Spirit,*[6] he did not say, "In the name of the Father, and in the name of the Son and in the name of the Spirit" to show that they were one nature only, since he referred to three persons in the one name. He said, *You are the temple of God and the Spirit of God dwells in you.*[7] If we are the temple, how can we be the dwelling of the Spirit?

---

[1] Mark 1:12; Matt 4:1.
[2] John 16:7.
[3] Luke 2:26,28-29.
[4] 1 Cor 2:11.
[5] Cf. 1 Cor 2:10.
[6] Matt 28:19; Mark 16:15.
[7] 1 Cor 3:16.

What [the apostle] has said clarifies this [text], *You are the temple of the Holy Spirit who dwells in you.*[1] Furthermore in the Acts of the Apostles he says, *Because it pleased you to tempt the Spirit of our Lord,*[2] and, *You have not lied to people but to God.*[3] Therefore the Spirit is God, because he is from God. The name of God dwells with people, for some are called gods. Moreover, through grace we have the name of the Father and the name of the Son. Therefore, the human person is called God, like Moses, who was [glorified] more than Pharaoh. But the human person has never been called the living Spirit. It was not said of Eve that she was the sister of Adam, or his daughter, but that she was taken from him. Likewise, one must not say that the Holy Spirit is his daughter or his sister, but that he proceeds from him and is consubstantial with him. If you say that he who searches is inferior to the one whom he searches, see what is written, *He who searches the hearts knows the thoughts of the Spirit.*[4] If this is the case, is [God] inferior to the Spirit?

§16.   *{Of judgements, because the ruler of this world has been condemned.*[5] It is not just recently, therefore, that Satan has received the penalty of his damnation. He was condemned forthwith.

§17.   {[The Lord] also said, *Give me glory in your presence from that which you gave me before the world was made.*[6] [This was] when the Father was fashioning creatures through his Son, according to the psalmist's account, *He is clothed with glory and magnificence,*[7] after which he drew them out of nothingness and established them as spotless creatures. *Lord God,* he said, *You are exceedingly great. You are clothed with glory and magnificence, and you have covered yourself with light as with a cloak; you have stretched out the heavens like a tent,* et cetera.[8] Following Adam's fall creatures were clothed in his humiliation, according to the apostle's word, *Creatures were subjected to futility,*[9] and

---

[1] Cf. 1 Cor 6:19.
[2] Acts 5:9.
[3] Acts 5:4.
[4] Rom 8:27.
[5] John 16:11.
[6] John 17:5.
[7] Ps 104:1.
[8] Ps 104:1-2. See the note above at II, § 5 for comment on this type of indication of scriptural abbreviation.
[9] Rom 8: 20.

the Son of the Creator came to heal them, so as to remove, at the moment of his coming, all uncleannesses through the baptism of his death, as he himself has said, *The hour has come and is at hand; glorify your Son that your Son may glorify you.*[1] He asked that, not as a beggar wishing to receive something, but, wishing to restore and accomplish the first order of creation, [he asked] for the glory with which he was clothed at the time when creatures were clothed [with glory].

For, just as he formed the first essence [of creatures] through grace so that [they would be] without stain, in the glory and magnificence with which he himself was clothed, [so] too, by the mercy of God, there will be a new creation of all things, without any stain, in the glory with which he is clothed. What he said, *Give me*, is to be understood of the glory which he possessed before creatures, with the Father and in the Father's presence, for the Greek text says clearly, *Glorify me with that glory which I possessed in your presence, before the world was made.*[2] Even more, in saying, *Glorify your Son, that your Son may glorify you,* he did not reveal a need, but a desire. The Father does not receive glory from the Son as though he had need of it, and the Son is not glorified by his Father as if he were lacking this [glory].

---

[1] John 17:1.
[2] This is the last of five instances in the commentary in which Ephrem refers to "the Greek." See above at II, §17 for further comment on Ephrem's use of this term.

XX

Jesus' Prayer at Gethsemane

§1.   {*My soul is sorrowful,*[1] he said and was not ashamed, for he was sincere, he who hid nothing beneath a deceptive appearance. [This was] to show that he had clothed himself with a weak flesh, and was united to a soul capable of suffering. He spoke the truth so that none could disfigure it, and he hid nothing so as not to be untruthful. He taught the faithful not to pride themselves in their manner of living,[2] for that would have been a denial of the truth. He also said, *I will deny the one who denies me,*[3] a [statement full of] fear and dread for apostates. Let us give praise therefore through the Only-Begotten, lest error snatch us away from his truth, and let us not acknowledge any other, lest pride wrench the advantageous wealth [of his goodness] from us.

§2.   {*If it is possible, let this chalice pass from me.*[4] It was not that he did not know that he was going to rise on the third day, but he knew well in advance the scandal of his disciples, the denial of Simon, the suicide of Judas, the destruction of Jerusalem and the dispersion of Israel. *If it is possible, let the chalice pass from me,* he said. [In view of] what he had said to Simon at the time when he took him aside, *Go behind me, Satan, for you do not think that which is of God, but rather that which is of human beings,*[5] how could he himself have abandoned *that which is of God* in order to *think of that which is of human beings*? "Why did you upbraid Simon, who was saying, *Let not this happen to you, Lord!,*[6] you, who were now saying, *If it is possible, let this chalice pass from me*?" He knew what he was saying to his Father, and was well aware that this chalice could pass from him. But he had come to drink it for everyone, in order to acquit, through this chalice, the debt of everyone, [a debt] which the prophets and martyrs could not pay with their death.

---

[1] Matt 26:38.
[2] Literally, "in their village."
[3] Matt 10:33.
[4] Matt 26:39.
[5] Matt 16:23.
[6] Matt 16:22.

§3. {*Father*, he said, *Let this chalice pass from me.* He, who had described his being slain through his prophets, and had prefigured the mystery of his death through his just ones, when [the time] came to accomplish [this death], he certainly did not refuse to drink [the chalice]. If he had not wished to drink it, but rather had wanted to reject it, he would not have compared his body to the temple in this saying, *Destroy this temple and on the third day I will rebuild it.*[1] [Nor would he have said] to the sons of Zebedee, *Can you drink the chalice which I am going to drink?*[2] [Nor would he have said], *There is a baptism for me [with which] I must be baptized,*[3] and, *As Moses lifted up the serpent in the desert, so will the Son of Man be lifted up;*[4] and, *As Jonah was in the belly of the fish, so will the Son of Man be in the bosom of the earth;*[5] and, *It is necessary that he die and that he rise again;*[6] and, *I have greatly desired to eat this Passover with you before I suffer;*[7] and, *The Son of Man goes, according as it is written about him.*[8]

Take note that, on the evening of the night when he delivered himself up, he gave his body and blood to his apostles and gave them the command to do [this] in memory of his passion. But he, who had given his apostles the command not to fear death, *Do not fear those who kill the body,*[9] how, therefore, could he himself fear death and ask that *the chalice pass from* him? He, who waited several months within the womb willingly, and several [years] within the world, having [already] spent days, months and years, with only hours left to live, how could he ask now, through the refusal of the chalice, that his entire coming be rendered void?

At the time when he was in Jerusalem, he had been proclaiming his message and wanting to show forth the richness of his gifts. He said, *If the marvels accomplished in you had been accomplished in Sodom, it would have been inhabited until now.*[10] But Sodom was destroyed, [a town] which could have continued to exist through the coming [of the

---

[1] John 2:19.
[2] Matt 20:22.
[3] Luke 12:50.
[4] John 3:14.
[5] Matt 12:40.
[6] Matt 16:21.
[7] Luke 22:15.
[8] Matt 26:24.
[9] Matt 10:28.
[10] Matt 11:23.

Lord]. But he did not change the time of his coming. Now that his coming has taken place, [how] could he have wanted to reject the gifts [flowing] from his passion, which, if they had been given in the days of Lot, Sodom and its companions *would have been inhabited until now*, according to his word? But if, for the sake of the [Jewish] people, he had wished that they would not perish through his coming, any [other] people to whom he would have come would certainly have perished, for they [too] would have handed him over to the cross.[1] Since [the Jews], however, did not heed his signs and miracles, it was not through his crucifixion that they were lost. He had already predicted their fall before his death, because they would not believe his signs.

§4.   *[If it is possible, let this chalice pass from me.* [He said this] because of the lowliness with which he had clothed himself, not in pretence, but in reality. Since he had really become unimportant and had clothed himself in lowliness, it would have been impossible for his lowliness not to have experienced fear and not to have been perturbed. Having assumed flesh, and having clothed himself with weakness, eating when hungry, becoming tired after working, being overcome by sleep when weary, it was necessary, when the time for his death arrived, that all these things that have to do with the flesh be fulfilled then. The anguish of death in fact invaded him, to render manifest his nature as a son of Adam, over whom *death reigns*,[2] according to the word of the apostle.

He said to his disciples, *Watch and pray so as not to enter into temptation. The spirit is vigilant and ready, but the flesh is weak.*[3] "In your case, when you are afraid, it is not the spirit which fears, but the weakness of your flesh. In my case however, I fear death to prove to you, through this fear of death, the truth of that same flesh with which I am clothed."

§5.   *[If Simon, whom a certain servant girl had terrified,[4] was not afraid of the Romans in their entirety, but had persuaded them with an oath to crucify him upside down, and [if] the apostle, knowing that he would not have an ordinary death, had said, *I desire my end, and the time*

---

[1] The meaning of the passage is obscure. Ephrem seems to imply that even if Christ had come to another people the crucifixion would have happened in any event, for the purposes of redemption (cf. Leloir, EC-SC 121, p. 345).

[2] Cf. Rom 5:14,17.

[3] Matt 26:41.

[4] Cf. Matt 26:69-72.

of my rest is very close to me,[1] how could [the Lord] have feared death, he, who had helped his apostles to despise death? *Do not fear those who kill the body, but who cannot kill the soul.*[2] Before the hour he was afraid, as it was thought; fear was normal at the hour when he was captured, but not at another moment. Then he healed the ear of one of his slayers.[3] He had ordered them to take swords,[4] but at the hour of using them, he said, *Put your sword back again into its place.*[5]

§6.   [Since it was through the Son that these debts were being acquitted, and the conversion of the Gentiles effected, he did not wish to appropriate for himself the grace [reserved] for the world. Similarly, *everything was created by him,*[6] but, passing over this [in silence], he spoke of another [Creator] through the mouth of Moses. He said, *God saw all that he had made, and behold it was very good.*[7] He said this so that all creatures would be indebted to his Father. Likewise, in this hour of their being re-created, he brought them back through his death, saying, *May your will be done,*[8] so that all those who would be converted by the death of the Only-Begotten would be indebted to the Father. Or alternatively, in this hour of his corporeal death, he gave to the body that which belonged to it, saying that all the sufferings of [his] body would show to the heretics and schismatics that his body was [real]. Did not this body of his appear to them, just as it was visible to everyone else? Just as he was hungry and thirsty, tired and had need of sleep, so too, he was afraid. Or, [he said that], so that it would be difficult for people in the world to say that it was without suffering and toil that our debts were remitted by him. Or, [it was] to teach his disciples to confide their life and death to God. If he, who is wise on account of the wisdom of God, asked for what was fitting for him, how much more [should] ordinary people surrender their will to the One who knows all things.

§7.   [Or, to sow consolation in his disciples through his passion, he clothed himself with their mentality so as to be an example to them, and

---

[1] 2 Tim 4:6.
[2] Matt 10:28.
[3] Cf. Luke 22:51.
[4] Cf. Luke 22:36-38.
[5] Matt 26:52.
[6] John 1:3.
[7] Gen 1:31.
[8] Matt 26:42.

took their fear on himself so that the similarity of his soul might show them not to boast of death before having experienced it. If he who is fearless was afraid [of death], and asked to be delivered from it, although he knew that it was impossible, how much more should others persevere in prayer before temptation, so that, in time of temptation, they may be delivered from it. Or, because, in the hour of our temptation, when our minds are distracted and our thoughts are wandering, he himself remained in prayer to teach us that we have need of prayer against the plots and snares [of the devil], so that through earnest prayer scattered thoughts might be recollected. Or, to comfort those who fear death, he showed that he himself was afraid, so that they might know that this [fear] would not provoke them to sin, if they did not persevere in it. *No, Father, but may your will be done.*[1] That is, "Let me die, so that I may give life to many."[2] Or, so that he might deceive death. Or, he was afraid of the passion lest it incite [death] to devour him and speedily vomit him forth.

§8.   {To gain mastery over [death], all these things which were hidden in you were mobilized against it. [Death] did not feel your divinity nor come into contact with your mysteries. Although the name of your divinity had been proclaimed, you covered it with veils, since you clothed your divine name with a human name. Every human person carrying the visible sign of the First Adam in his body became food for death, but everyone who carried the sign of the Second Adam in himself became lord and destroyer of death. The one,[3] in tasting [the fruit], loosened his will and submitted it to his body. He weakened it so that it became food for death. But the Other, through the energy of his will, hardened his body so that it would resist the mouth of death.

§9.   {*Not according to my will, but yours.*[4] [He said this word] against Adam, who had resisted the will of the Creator and followed the will of his enemy. [Consequently], he was delivered over into the mouth of his adversary. But our Lord resisted the will of the flesh to uphold that of the Creator of flesh, for he knew that all happiness depends on the will of his Father. *Not my will but yours be done.*

---

[1] Luke 22:42.
[2] Cf. Isa 53:11.
[3] That is, Adam. Cf. Gen 3:6.
[4] Luke 22:42.

Does he possess a will then other than the will of his Father? How can he say, *Not my will but yours be done* ? And again, *I have not come to do my will, but the will of him who sent me. But his will is that I should lose none of what he has given me.*[1] It might appear [from these words] that he possesses another will. Isaiah says, *The Lord wished to humiliate and afflict him,*[2] and he also said, *Because he handed over his soul to death,*[3] showing that this was his will. How should this be understood? For he has thus shown two wills, that of the Lord [God] as well as his own, even though the work [to be accomplished] was one. Although our Lord wished to convince his listeners that no other power was constraining him, those who had gone astray saw in him another will. [The same conclusion can be drawn] from his words concerning Lazarus, *I give you thanks because you have heard me and you continue to hear me, but I am doing this on account of the crowd, so that they may believe that you have sent me,*[4] so that, heard [by God], he might show that he was from God.

§10.   {This suffices [to explain] all [similar words of the Lord]. To show that he was from the Father, he attributed everything to the Father, and, although he had made everything by his will, he appeared himself as in need, for the sake of his Father's honour. It was not necessary that he should have humbled him, so that those who say that the powers of darkness have conquered him might be confounded. In fact, those same powers were indeed crying out and saying to him, *Because you are the Son of God, and they were begging him not to send them into Sheol.*[5] If they were begging him to spare them from Sheol, how could they have been triumphant over him?

§11.   {*His sweat became like drops of blood,*[6] said [the evangelist]. He sweated to heal Adam who was sick. *It is by the sweat of your brow*, said [God], *that you will eat your bread.*[7] He remained in prayer in this garden to bring [Adam] back into his own garden again.

---

[1] John 6:38-39; 18:9.
[2] Isa 53:10.
[3] Isa 53:12.
[4] John 11:41-42.
[5] Mark 3:11; Luke 4:41; 8:31.
[6] Luke 22:44.
[7] Gen 3:19.

The Arrest of Jesus

§12.   {"I called you so that you might watch with me, lest I be handed over. But now that I must be handed over, *Sleep henceforth and take your rest.*"[1] [The tribe of] Judah marked the beginning of the kingdom,[2] [the apostle] Judas marked its extinction. In deceitfully handing him over to the Romans with a kiss, he handed over to them [the responsibility of] avenging him, so that they would one day exact it from him.[3] The wicked one came to hollow out his deep abyss, and our God explained it gently to him, showing himself beneficent and a font of mercy through these words, *Judas, would you betray the Son of Man with a kiss?*[4] He showed thus that [Judas] did not have the power to hand over the Son of God. *Well then, why have you come, my friend?*[5] What is enmity [the Lord] called friendship, and turned towards him. The deceitful disciple approached the true Master to kiss him. [The Lord] withdrew from him the Spirit which he had breathed into him; he removed it from him, not wishing that the corrupting wolf might be among his sheep. He said, *That which he had has been taken away from him.*[6]

§13.   {But our Lord then said to them, *Whom do you seek?*[7] for, it seemed to them that he was not able to free himself from their hands. *They said to him, Jesus of Nazareth. Jesus replied to them, It is I. All of them, including Judas who was with them, retreated and fell backwards to the ground.*[8] In spite of themselves they were bowed down before him, to learn that he was giving himself over into their hands of his own will. But, not fearing the power which had prostrated them, they stretched out their impure hands and seized him who was purifying them. *Simon cut off the ear*[9] of one of them, but the beneficent [Lord] in his gentleness, took it and put it back in its elevated place [on the body], [as a figure of] him who had fallen into the lower abyss because of his sins. *Put your*

---

[1] Matt 26:45.
[2] Cf. Gen 49:10.
[3] The play on words is continued here: the Lord will be avenged through the fall of Judas/Judah (the kingdom, through the fall of Jerusalem in 70 A D).
[4] Luke 22:48.
[5] Matt 26:50.
[6] Cf. Matt 13:12.
[7] John 18:4,7.
[8] John 18:5-6.
[9] Cf. John 18:10; Luke 22:50-51.

sword back again into its place.[1] He had no need of a sword, he whose word was a sword. Just as he restored the ear that had been cut off back to its place, he could have separated the members that were joined. Not satisfied with showing the intensity of his power with a single example, he showed it forth on all those who *retreated and fell backwards to the ground*.[2] So that the one whose ear had been healed would not be the only one to benefit from grace, he allowed all who were about to apprehend him profit from it, so that they would indeed know whom they were going to arrest. For, it was by that same grace of him who had restored the ear to its place that those who *fell backwards to the ground* were able to get up again.

Since he had only shown a tiny fraction of his power, all those who were about to arrest him were thrown backwards and fell a second time.[3] It was by way of symbol that the sword was drawn, so that the word of Moses might be confirmed, *Everyone who does not listen to this prophet will certainly die*.[4] But, since our Lord was the term of justice and the beginning of mercy, he shut up the sword in its sheath and put justice back in its place again. Then he healed the ear through mercy. He put the ear back in its place and made good the imperfection of justice through fruitful mercy. However, he whose ear had been healed expressed his gratitude for this love with hatred. And those, who had *fallen backwards to the ground* and had been raised up again through him, thanked him for his help with chains. *They bound him*, said [the evangelist], *and led him away*.[5]

Peter's Denial

§14.   {The leader of the disciples was distressed, and was tempted to become the physician of the wounded. Perhaps it was because transgressors might be ashamed to do penance that [the Lord] exhorted, through the transgressing Simon, that they come back to him who transcends all transgressions. It was during the night that Simon denied him, but it was during the day that he bore witness. It was near a charcoal fire that he denied, and near a charcoal fire that he bore witness. The land

---

[1] Matt 26:52.
[2] John 18:6.
[3] This detail which Ephrem adds is not found in the gospel tradition (cf. John 18:7).
[4] Cf. Deut 18:19-20.
[5] John 18:12-13.

was witness to where he denied, and the sea and the dry land, each according to its nature, to where he confessed.[1] Because his tongue had gone astray and had denied, he submitted himself to the yoke and bruised his shoulders on the cross, to the point of begging and persuading that they crucify him upside down.

Jesus Handed Over to Pilate

§15.   [Hereafter, you will see the Son of Man coming with the bright clouds [and] the angels of heaven. Then the high priest lifted his hand to the neck [of his garment] and tore his tunic,[2] because he was tormented, [as] by the force of new wine. But let us mention this, that all that God was to accomplish through his unique Son, he had foreseen in advance, represented in created things, and prefigured moreover in the just. It is in the month of Areg[3] that flowers break their flower-cup and come forth, leaving them exposed so that they can become crowns of other [heads]. It was in the month of Areg that the high priest broke his priesthood and left it exposed. It came [then] and was spread over our Saviour. [The Lord] had imposed silence on the words of [the Jews], but they increased the uproar against him. He spoke because they had questioned him, and they tore their garments. They seized him and led him to the door. They gave him into the hands of Pilate, but they themselves did not enter into the tribunal, so as not to be defiled, and to be able to eat the lamb in purity.[4] O pharisees! You have heard [it said], This is the Lamb of God, this is he who, through his sacrifice, takes away the sins of the world.[5] Was it, therefore, necessary that, on the day when the lamb of your salvation was sacrificed, that too should have been [the day on which] the Lamb of our salvation was [likewise] sacrificed?

---

[1] Cf. Luke 22:54-62; John 21:9,15-17.
[2] Cf. Matt 26:64-65; Mark 14:62-63.
[3] As noted above (cf. I, §29) the Armenian months are not coterminous with the Syriac/Julian ones. Areg corresponds approximately to March/April. Cf. S. P. Brock's translation of Ephrem's Commentary on Exodus, XII. 2-3 in The Luminous Eye (Kalamazoo, 1992), pp. 108-9.
[4] Cf. Matt 27:2; John 18:28.
[5] John 1:29.

Jesus Condemned to Death

§16.   {The Lord became the defender of truth, and came in silence before Pilate, on behalf of truth which had been oppressed.[1] Others gain victory through making defences, but our Lord gained victory through his silence, because [the recompense] due to the divine silence was the victory of true teaching. He spoke in order to teach, but kept silent in the tribunal. He was not silent over that which was exalting us, and he did not struggle against those who were provoking him. The words of his calumniators, like a crown on his head, were a source of redemption. He kept silent so that his silence would make them shout even louder, and so that his crown would be made more beautiful through all this clamour. If he had spoken, his words of truth would have imposed silence on these plots which they were weaving [to plait] his crown. They condemned him because he had spoken the truth, but he was not condemned, since his very condemnation was a victory. He had no desire to persuade them; he wanted to die, and a reply would have been a shield against death. He was silent because, if he had spoken, he would have spoken the truth against which untruth could not resist. *Take him away from us, take him away from us!*,[2] they were crying out to Pilate. Replying a second and a third time, [Pilate] became the prophet of his kingdom, *Shall I crucify your king?*[3] The symbol of the blood smeared on their doors turned back the destroying angel, cause of death, from them.[4] But they used their blasphemies against this Lamb of truth, they rejected him and begged for Barabbas, a criminal.[5]

§17.   {Since *they dressed him in a purple garment*[6] he removed the kingdom of Israel. Moreover, when they had stripped him of his garments he showed that he was leaving death with them.[7] [Take note] also that they dressed him in purple because, just as they had calumniated him in relation to tax-payment, *He is preventing payment of tax to Caesar*,[8] so too, they wanted to kill him because of the purple, "See, he is making himself

---

[1] Cf. John 18:37-38.
[2] John 19:15.
[3] *Idem.*
[4] Cf. Exod 12:22-23,27.
[5] Cf. Matt 27:15-26.
[6] Mark 15:17; John 19:2.
[7] Cf. Luke 24:12; John 20:5-7.
[8] Luke 23:2.

out to be a king."[1] While they were planning for his death, they were prophesizing like Caiphus.[2] *The crown of thorns*[3] which they had used to mock him recoiled [against them] and their disdain was changed for the good. For [the Lord] condemned the enemy in removing the accursed crown of the First Adam, *The land will produce thorns and briars for you.*[4] *They spat in the face* [5]of him who had breathed the Holy Spirit into them. *They put a reed in his hand,*[6] for he was like a staff upon which the world which had grown old was leaning. It was with a reed that the sentences of judges were confirmed and approved. Likewise, it was with this reed that he wrote, and that he chased the evil ones from his house.[7]

Judas' Despair and Death

§18. {*When Judas saw that our Lord was condemned he repented. He went to return the thirty pieces of silver to the priests and said to them, I have sinned in betraying innocent blood. They said to him, What is that to us? See to it yourself! He threw the silver into the temple and went and hanged himself, and died.*[8] [The Lord] permitted this so that [Judas] would be a herald of the error which he had committed. He had thought that he might free himself from the scorn of the multitude and avoid shame. He broke his ties, as if nothing should accompany him in his departure from here below. *He put the cord round his neck and died.*[9] Lest his chastisement be discredited as mercy, there was found no peaceful or true person to kill him, but, *he hanged himself and choked,*[10] thus showing that, on the last day, the malice of the sinner will itself be killed and perish, in a similar manner.

Who then will pay the price for the shedding of the blood of him who came in human likeness, if not [Satan] who, clothing himself in a human form, betrayed him, not because he was able to condemn and betray him, but because he wished to betray him? It was not [the Lord] who

---

[1] Cf. *Idem*.
[2] Cf. John 11:49-52.
[3] Matt 27:29.
[4] Gen 3:18.
[5] Mark 15:19.
[6] Matt 27:29.
[7] Possibly an allusion to John 8:1-11.
[8] Matt 27:3-5.
[9] Matt 27:5.
[10] *Idem*.

killed malice. It killed itself through its works. Therefore [Satan] killed, in his human form, him who did not die and merited the vengeance of God. Thus, through the vengeance of God, he who was called a god[1] was killed and exterminated. If anyone shoots an arrow against his enemy which returns to strike him, he breaks the arrow and burns his bow. Likewise, Satan, seeing that the Son's death was victory for the world and that his cross freed created beings, entered into Judas, his [chosen] vessel, and the latter *went and put a cord around his neck and choked himself.* [Scripture] says that *his entrails spilled out,*[2] [indicating thus] the one on whom he relied when he put the cord on his neck. The cord broke, he fell and *burst open in the middle.*[3] Others hold that he closed the door and bolted it on the inside. Then he decomposed and all *his entrails spilled out,* and no one opened the door of the house to look inside.

§19. {*It is not permitted to receive this money into the treasury,*[4] they said. They were afraid of Scripture,[5] and wanted to prevent its [fulfilment]. But, from the moment this silver landed in the temple, it was consecrated. *They bought a tomb with it.*[6] A happy event and a great mystery, for it was for God that they were acting thus. If they gave this silver which belonged to the sanctuary, why then was it not permitted to put it into the treasury from which they had drawn it? Why was it not permitted? If they had not given it from there, they would have said so. Was this silver [more] impure than other [silver]? Was it [more] impure than Goliath's sword which was wrapped in a cloth and which was placed behind the altar to the side?[7] Or [more impure] than the gold of the Egyptians?[8] Or than the gold, consecrated by David, which came from all the kingdoms?[9] Or than the crown decorated with precious stones which he placed on his head,[10] singing in spirit? Or than the gift which the Philistines offered and which was to remain for ever?[11] Did not Nebuchadnezzar remove all the sacred

---

[1] Cf. Ezek 28:2,6,9; 2 Thess 2:3-4.
[2] Acts 1:18.
[3] *Idem.*
[4] Matt 27:6.
[5] Cf. Zech 11:12-14.
[6] Matt 27:6.
[7] Cf. 1 Sam 21:9-10.
[8] Cf. Exod 11:2-3; 12:35-36.
[9] Cf. 2 Sam 8:9-12; 1 Chr 18:9-11.
[10] Cf. 2 Sam 12:26-30; 1 Chr 20:1-2; Ps 21:4.
[11] Cf. 1 Sam 6:1-18.

vessels and place them in the temple of his gods?[1] The ark itself entered into the temple of Dagon.[2] What is it that can defile that which is holy and that which makes holy? If it was because he had made himself God that they bought [a field] with this [silver], they would have been permitted to place it on the altar. But they wished to render the prophecy vain.

Simon of Cyrene

§20.   {*After he had taken the wood of his cross and had set out, they found and stopped a man of Cyrene*, that is, from among the Gentiles, *and placed the wood of the cross on him*.[3] It was only right that they should have given the wood of the cross voluntarily to the Gentiles, [since] in their rebellion, [the Jews] had rejected the coming of him who was bringing all blessings. In rejecting it themselves, in their jealousy, they cast it away to the Gentiles. They rejected it in their jealousy and the Gentiles received it, to their [even greater] jealousy. For [the Lord] approved the welcoming Gentiles, thus provoking jealousy amongst their contemporaries through [the Gentiles'] acceptance. By carrying the wood of his cross himself he manifested the sign of his victory. He had said that it would not be another's constraint that would lead him to death. *I have power over my life, to lay it down or to take it up again*.[4] Why should another have carried [the cross], if not to show that it was for those who had rejected him that he, in whom no sin could be found, went up on the cross.

Green Wood and Dry Wood

§21.   {[The Lord] also said, *If they do that to the green wood*.[5] H e compared his divinity to *the green wood*, and those who had received his gifts to *the dry wood*. What is green bears fruit, as this [word] which he spoke testifies, *For which of my works are you stoning me?*[6] "If I [suffer to this extent], even though you have found no sin in me, *which of you will convict me of sin?*[7] And you, since you have invented a pretext [to dispose

---

[1] Cf. Dan 1:1-2; 2 Chr 36:6-7; 2 Kgs 24:10-13.
[2] Cf. 1 Sam 5:1-5.
[3] Cf. Matt 27:32; Mark 15:21; Luke 23:26; John 19:17.
[4] John 10:18.
[5] Luke 23:31.
[6] John 10:32.
[7] John 8:46.

of me], how much more will you yourselves [suffer]?" Or alternatively, [he was referring to himself] with regard to *the green wood*, because of the miracles he had done, and [he called] the just who were without virtue, *the dry wood*. They ate the fruit of this *green wood* and they rejoiced beneath its foliage. Then they took it in hatred and destroyed it. What more will they do therefore to *the dry wood*, which has not got even a sprout? That is, [what more will they do] to the ordinary just who do not work miracles?

The Two Robbers

§22.   [*When they had placed him on the cross, they also placed two other evil-doers with him, so that the prophecy, He was numbered among the wicked, would be fulfilled.*[1] One of them, concerning whom we do not know whether he was circumcised or not, was speaking like the circumcised. The other, concerning whom we also do not know whether he was circumcised or not, was speaking like the uncircumcised. One was saying, *Are you not the Messiah?*,[2] that is, the king, in accordance with the words of the circumcised crucifiers. But the other was saying, *Remember me in your kingdom*,[3] just as the uncircumcised ones who had written, *This is the Messiah, the King of the Jews.*[4] The uncircumcised were proclaiming that the Messiah was the king of the Jews, and not theirs, but the Jews were proclaiming [that their king] was Caesar, the king of the foreign nations. The people who were proclaiming a decaying kingdom had a share in its decay, but those who proclaimed the true kingdom will enter into the garden of delights, according to the promises [of the Lord]. The kingdom which [the Jews] had recognized destroyed their city, but the kingdom of our Lord, recognized by the Gentiles, gives life to their body.

§23.   [*Are you not the Messiah?* he said. *Save yourself and us with you!*[5] However, [the Lord] did not take him down from the cross, as he had asked, in order to exalt him who was on the right of the cross, and who was believing in the crucified. For it would have been easy for him to conquer anyone as a disciple by some miracle. But a more powerful

---

[1] Mark 15:27-28.
[2] Luke 23:39.
[3] Luke 23:42.
[4] Matt 27:37.
[5] Luke 23:39.

miracle [was produced], in that he constrained the scoffer of truth to adore him. That is why [the apostle] has said, *That which is the weakness of God is stronger than human beings.*[1] He submitted all peoples to the weakness of the cross.

Stretch out your arms towards the cross, so that the crucified Lord may stretch out his arms towards you. For the one who does not stretch out his hand towards the cross cannot approach his table either. He will deprive of his table the guests who should have come to him hungry, but [instead] came satiated. Do not satiate yourself before going to the table of the Son, lest he make you leave the table, while still hungry.

§24.   {Because Satan drew one of his disciples away from justice, [the Lord] rivalled with him in turn and drew one of his disciples away, so that he, who had been constrained to go up on the cross because of his sins, [the Lord] had him go up on the cross voluntarily on account of his faith. Just as Satan made Judas a voluntary outcast and a fallen man, even though grace had chosen him, and he had prepared for him a cord instead of a throne, [the Lord prepared] a garden of delights instead of the cross [for the thief]. The hands which [Adam] had stretched out toward the tree of knowledge, transgressing the commandment, were unworthy of being stretched out towards the tree of life to receive the gifts of the God which they had despised. Therefore our Lord took [these hands] and attached them to the cross, so that they might slay their slayer and arrive at his marvellous life. *You shall be with me in the garden of delights. Remember me in your kingdom.*[2] It was because he had seen, with the eyes of faith, the dignity of our Lord instead of his shame, and his glory instead of his humiliation, that he said, *Remember me.* "What is apparent now, the nails, the cross, will not make me forget what will be at the consummation and which is not yet visible, your kingdom and your glory."

§25.   {When our Lord saw that he had more faith than many others, and that he was not worried about his sufferings, but about the remission of sins, he exalted him more than many. Because he had not asked an immediate recompense for his faith - being a robber, he appeared an abject and vile person in his own eyes - our Lord hastened the arrival of his gifts

---

[1] 1 Cor 1:25.
[2] Luke 23:43,42.

and made him an immediate promise, *today*, and not, "at the end [of the world]." He thus showed the richness of his mercy, for, from the moment when this robber expressed his faith in him, he recompensed him. He gratuitously gave him great gifts, spread his treasures over him, brought him immediately into his garden and, having introduced him there, established him over his treasures, *You shall be with me in this garden of delights.*[1]

§26.   {Accordingly, Paradise was opened by means of a robber, and not by one or other of the just. It had been closed by Adam, who was just [initially], but then became a sinner. It was a sinner however who, victorious, reopened it. [The Jews] chose a robber and rejected [the Lord], but he chose a robber and rejected them. What therefore does that which he said mean, *If anyone does not eat of my flesh, he will not obtain eternal life?*[2] [Let us listen] to the apostle, *We have been baptized in Christ; it is unto his death that we have been baptized.*[3] It was through the mystery of the water and blood issuing forth from [the Lord's] side that the robber received the sprinkling which gave him the remission of sins. *You shall be with me in this garden of delights.*

Jesus on the Cross

§27.   {*They gave him vinegar and gall to drink.*[4] He had gladdened them with his delicious wine but they offered him vinegar. For the price of gall, he sweetened the bitterness of the Gentiles by the virtue of his mercy. *His tunic was not torn*[5] since it represented his divinity which was undivided, because it was not composite. *His clothing, divided into four parts*[6] symbolized his Gospel which was to go forth into the four parts of the world.

Share then, for love of him, the body of him who, for love of you, shared his garment between those who were crucifying him. Take it, all of you, absorb it in its entirety, just as he, on his own, took and absorbed your death for everyone. Open the doors of your hearts to him who opened the

---

[1] Luke 23:43.
[2] Cf. John 6:53.
[3] Rom 6:3.
[4] Matt 27:34.
[5] John 19:23.
[6] *Idem.*

doors of his kingdom to you. Mary saw our Lord in the one who had rested on his breast,[1] and John saw our Lord in the one whose womb had brought him into the world. That is why he entrusted her to him above all the other disciples.[2]

§28.   {Because the mind of those who crucified him was darkened, and they did not perceive what kind of Sun was nailed on the cross, *the sun which illumines the eyes became darkened.*[3] When their eyes had been darkened, their mind became a little enlightened, *Woe, woe to us, this was the Son of God!* [4] Do you not see that, as long as the darkness was intensified about corporeal eyes, the darkness of intimate thoughts was not removed. This was because darkness belongs naturally to the darkened. [This darkness] taught them the nature of this darkening of the Sun which they had nailed to the wood of the cross. But, when the Sun of Justice had arisen, healing lepers and opening the eyes of the blind, its light had not revealed to the blind that Jerusalem was looking at the arrival of its king. It was because the natural sun was darkened that this darkness revealed the imminence of the destruction of their city. *Behold the judgements concerning the destruction of Jerusalem have come and are here.*[5] This [city] did not receive the one who had built it. All that remains for you is to see its destruction.

§29.   {But now, you will no longer see this sight, O Jew, because you have [already] seen your city destroyed and demolished. Learn from your demolished city who he is who has planted the Church. Because the sons of Jerusalem are dispersed and scattered among all the nations of the Gentiles, learn who he is who has reunited and gathered all the nations of the Gentiles into the Church. If the womb of the spouse, deprived of her sons, does not convince you, let the sterile womb which became fruitful convince you. But if you do not see the destruction and the ruin of one, you will not see the descendants and sons of the other either. If you see the one who is destroyed and widowed, will you not see the other who is

---

[1] Cf. John 13:23,25; 21:20.
[2] Cf. John 19:27.
[3] Luke 23:44.
[4] Cf. Matt 27:54.
[5] Cf. Dan 9:2,24-27.

married? How do you understand this passage, *The sons of the desolate one are more numerous than those of the married one?*[1]

If you do not see the value of the Scriptures, why do you weary your eyes in reading the Scriptures? You know the bat; unable to bear the bright rays of the sun, it flees the day, but comes out to fly at night time, for it resembles the night. You too, if you cannot perceive the hidden light of the Scriptures, give up the toil of reading them. Every hour of night is like day for the bat, and your god for you is the calf fashioned by artisans, and spoken of by the prophets. Adore either the One whom your prophets announced or the metal cast by your fathers.[2] Joshua son of Nun declared, *Choose today whom you will serve, God or the gods,*[3] but your heart however [chose] their gods. You have the frenzy of the Gentiles for Scripture and Prophets, and dance songs for [sacred] canticles.[4] We gave you what we rejected, and what you despised has come to us. Even if the kingdom of heaven had not been promised to us all, Gehenna would suffice to contain all of you.

§30.   {*My God, my God! Why have you abandoned me?*[5] [The Lord] was condemned by death. It held him silent until he had gone up on the cross. But [the Lord] in his turn vanquished death through his great cry when he had gone up on the cross. Whereas death was binding one person on the cross, all those who had been bound in Sheol were being delivered because of the chains of one person.[6] The True One was consistent with truth in saying, *Eli, Eli, why have you abandoned me?* But the scoffers were consistent with their falsehood [in saying], *Let us see if Elijah will come to deliver him!*[7] Because they had mocked his first cry saying, "How is it that Elijah has not delivered him," he cried out a second time, but it was the dead who heard and replied to him.[8] He showed thus that if the dead who were deprived of hearing had heard him, how much more should the living hear him.

But how could the dead reply to him, since it was to his Father that he had cried out? The Father wished to show through the dead that

---

[1] Isa 54:1.
[2] Cf. Exod 32:1-4.
[3] Josh 24:15.
[4] Cf. Exod 32:6,17-19.
[5] Matt 27:46.
[6] Cf. Matt 27:52-53; Eph 4:9; 1 Pet 3:19.
[7] Mark 15:36.
[8] Cf. Matt 27:50-53.

he had heard him, in order to instruct the living, and, through the obedience of the dead, to persuade them to listen to him. They were a long way from the truth of his first cry, but his second cry forced them back to it. His first cry had provoked mockery in their mouths and scoffing in their words, but the second put "Woe" in their mouth and made them beat their breasts.[1] His first cry had been turned into derision, the second had for mission to draw vengeance on his enemies. They believed that Elijah would come to them, as it is written,[2] but they thought that it was a ridiculous illusion that Elijah should come [to the Lord]. For, when [the prophets] had been predicting their despair and the destruction of their city, they were showing that Elijah would not be coming to them.

§31.   {While his hands were being transfixed with nails, the clay, which had been formed by his hands to open the eyes of the blind, was rebuking and accusing those who were transfixing his hands.[3] For his hands, which could open the eyes of the blind so that they might see him, could indeed have blinded those who were crucifying him, so that they might not see him. And the strengthened waters which he had bound and subjected under his feet were rebuking and accusing those who were tying his strong feet with hard bonds. For his feet, which had been able to walk on the surface of the waters without their submerging him,[4] could have trampled on the backs of his enemies so that they would not have been able to crucify him.

§32.   {Since they had hung on this wood that body which contained the treasures of the salvation of the Gentiles, he looked on the land of the Gentiles which had accepted these treasures. Already Joseph had said, *Carry my bones from here*,[5] for, as long as this holy treasure continued to be located in that impure land, God had compassion on it. That is why [the Jews] came back from the land of Babylon. If this were so in the case of the just, how much more so in the case of their Lord. His hands, which delivered us from the bonds of death, were transfixed by nails, his hands which broke our chains and tied those which were binding us.

---

[1] Cf. Luke 23:48.
[2] Cf. Mal 3:23.
[3] Cf. John 9:6,11-15.
[4] Cf. Matt 14:25-31.
[5] Gen 50:25.

It was an amazing thing that the dead were killing the living one, [whereas] the slain one was raising the dead to life. They directed their fury more intensely towards heaven, whereas he humbled his greatness even further down into the depths. It was he, the dead one, whom death stole, took away and placed in the tomb. But he rose from the dead and plundered the cavern of his captivity. [Death] stole him, took him away and put him in the tomb while he was asleep, but, on awaking and standing up, he stole his stealer. This is the cross which crucifies those who crucified [the Lord], and this is the captive who leads into captivity those who had led him into captivity. The cross, through your death, has become a fountain of life for our mortal life, and those who drink of it produce fruit similar to your drink. Almost without knowing it, death used his body to taste and devour the life hidden in moral bodies. What it had hastened to gulp down while famished it was forced to restore very quickly. Death had entered through Eve's ear;[1] consequently life entered through Mary's ear. It was through the wood that humanity had contracted debts; consequently when our Lord came, it was through the wood that he acquitted them.

§33.   {[The Jews] were trying to deny his miracles, one by the other. *This is one*, they said, *who opened the eyes of the blind man. Could he not have prevented this man from dying?*[2] But, after he had raised [Lazarus], they said, *He raised him back to life, but he could not raise himself.*[3] However much they were trying to deny an earlier [miracle], [the Lord] showed forth an even greater miracle. For a blind man, [he produced the miracle of] a man dead for four days, and for this dead man, the crowds of· dead which he drew from the tombs. In mocking the second [miracle], "Why could he not do this?," they were making themselves witness to the earlier one which he had performed, *He, who opened the eyes of a blind man, is restoring others to life!*[4] [The Lord] issued them with a double wager. Firstly, he unmasked their hidden mockery, "He is not able to do this," and secondly, he led them to bear witness to what he had done, *He saved others, he cannot save himself*. In mocking him they were [actually] glorifying him. Although they had tried to prove his weakness through the fact that he did not come down from the cross, they bore witness that

---

[1] Cf. Gen 3:1-6.
[2] John 11:37.
[3] Cf. Matt 27:42.
[4] *Idem.*

311

he was giving life in saying that *he raised others*. The corpse of Elisha resuscitated a dead man,[1] prefiguring him who, through his death, opened the tombs and drew the dead out from them, so that they might accuse his slayers.

§34.   {The bones of Elisha mock them in their mockery concerning [the Lord], *He saved others and he cannot save himself*, since these bones resuscitated others, but were not resuscitated themselves. If they did not wish to be resuscitated themselves, it was because they were not truly dead. For, if they had been dead, they would not have resuscitated others. Thus, resuscitating the dead, they had need neither of life nor of the repose of the living. Moreover, how could they have desired life accompanied by all kinds of evils? If the body of that dead man, although without love or understanding, touched the bones of Elisha and received from them a new life which vanquished death, how much more will the faithful receive eternal life from the body of the Son. He, who commanded death in such a way that it gave back the spirit, would have been able to command the cross to free him [from it]. To remove from his adversaries [all possibility of] a reply, he commanded the stones and they were split in two. [He commanded] death and it did not prevent the just from going forth at his voice. He trained the lower regions to his voice to prepare them for hearing it on the last day, when this voice will empty [the lower regions].

Reflections on the Passion of Jesus

§35.   {If [the Jews] think that they were able, because of the weakness of the Son, to make a mockery of the body with which he had clothed himself, they are like the Philistines who thought that they were able to despise and mock the ark because of the [apparent] weakness of God.[2] If the Philistines were subjected to the vengeance [of God] in return, how much more should those who crucified [the Son of God be subjected to it]. In fact, the injuries of the Philistines were healed and they remained on in their land. But sufferings are renewed daily for the circumcised, [who are similar in spirit] to the uncircumcised, since they are not allowed remain in their city and can no longer enter into it. If it is because of the body

---

[1] Cf. 2 Kgs 4:8-37.
[2] Cf. 1 Sam 4:1-7:1.

312

which they killed and buried that we are filled with shame, this shame serves unto their confusion, since this body is living, rose again, went up [to heaven] and is seated at the right hand of God. But Moses broke the tablets which God had engraved, on which he had written the holy Law,[1] and for whom the holy ark had been constructed. Their fragments were not gathered up, and their parts, as necessary to each other as the parts of the body, were not joined together again, and nothing of what [is given even] to the body of sinners was given to them, neither vitality nor renewal. So, lest it be said, "No one has ever been holy in the womb," see how Jeremiah has refuted this allegation [in advance], *Before I formed you in your mother's entrails, I knew you, and before you went forth from her womb I made you holy.*[2]

§36.   {If they continue to mock his cross even more, the serpents of the desert are a reproof for them, since the faithful were healed by the serpent that was cursed.[3] Indeed, [the Jews] dare to give the cross a name that is cursed.[4] They give honour to the ram caught in the bush,[5] since the true Lamb with his cross is witness to this, he who redeemed the world which was bound in place of Isaac who was bound. Because the people were cursed, it was by a curse that [God] redeemed them, while the nations were healed by him who gives life to all. Because they were handed over to the curse of the serpent raised above them by Moses, they honoured and adored the bronze serpent, which caused souls instead of the body to be lost. Whoever refused to look at this serpent was indeed infested with its plagues. They were not worthy to look towards their God. It was the serpent which was similar to them which they looked at, and they were saved. Since [God] knew that this people would reject the Son, he instructed them through the serpent in order to confound the crucifiers, since it was a figure of our Redeemer that they were honouring.

§37.   {The place of the sanctuary was burnt and the temple destroyed,[6] that they might experience an image of [the Lord], for his body resembles that of [the temple],[7] and the Babylonians resemble the crucifiers. If you

---

[1] Cf. Exod 32:15-19; Deut 9:8-17.
[2] Jer 1:5.
[3] Cf. Num 21:4-9.
[4] Cf. Deut 21:23; Gal 3:13.
[5] Cf. Gen 22:9-13.
[6] Cf. 2 Kgs 25:9; 2 Chr 36:19.
[7] Cf. John 2:19-21.

imagine that God acted thus on account of [their] sins, how did the temple and the altar, how did Daniel and his companions sin? If it was to recompense justice that this happened, since the promised gifts were the fruit of these tribulations, justice has received its recompense through this body which went up on the cross, just as formerly [it was recompensed] through this temple that was destroyed. *He was consoled in his servants,*[1] says [Scripture].

§38.   [The [first reason] for praising the Creator is that he has created everything, and the second is that he has revealed himself through his works. Since he knew his works, he wished that they too would know him. The divine name sprung forth, went out from him, and came and rested on Moses,[2] so that the Egyptians might know the God of all things. The Word went forth from him [the Father], and came to dwell in the flesh, so that all creatures might know the Father of all things. Accordingly, the divinity [of the Son] was announced through the divine name, and the fatherhood [of God] was manifested through the name of the Son. The Egyptians did not listen to Moses, and his staff chastised them. But the cross saved those who believed in the Son. Through [Moses'] staff, a figure of the cross, the Gentiles learned about the cross in advance: the Egyptians through the signs [of the ten plagues] and the Amalekites through battle.[3] Because of their ignorance, they were directed first of all by a prefiguring of the cross only. But when the cross itself appeared above them, they were enlightened and made wise through the teaching they received. God was honouring and drawing Israel by the mystery of the cross. However, when he who had honoured them through his signs appeared, they, lashing out and recalcitrant, made him the sign of all infamous deeds. Formed, surrounded, and coddled by delicacies and pleasures since its infancy, *Israel*, in spite of the images of the cross, *grew fat, became gross and recalcitrant,*[4] so that, finally, captivity imprisoned it among the Gentiles. *The one who is pampered in his infancy will be handed over to servitude.*[5]

---

[1] Ps 135:14.
[2] Cf. Exod 3:1-4:17.
[3] Cf. Exod 7:14-12:36; 17:8-16.
[4] Deut 32:15.
[5] Prov 29:21.

314

§39.   {The true form represented by these types came to them, but their essential characteristics escaped them, although numerous figures had been prepared for them for a long time. They did not recognize this body whose shadow had covered them in the desert. The wood, image of [the cross], had sweetened their water,[1] and the serpent, a sign too, had delivered them from the plagues of the serpents,[2] whereas the Sabbath and circumcision, neither of which had been able to save them, were condemned. However, they turned away from his face whose form was constantly represented before them. His face seemed alien to them because of the indelible reflections of true beauty with which it shone. All the prophets had shown only an [imperfect] resemblance of his beauty. The aspect of [Moses]' staff is not the equivalent of the cross, and the beauty of the wood which sweetened the waters is not the equivalent of the beauty of him who sweetened the nations. Wherever the image of the Son went, created entities were shaken and stirred up: the sea before his staff,[3] the serpent before its sign, the bitterness of the waters before its type. But, wherever Truth itself appeared, all those who were covered with faults were censured. This is the source which gives happiness without envy to whose who drink without envying each other in turn. The waters came forth and were spread about on all sides, so that none could look on his neighbour's drink [with envy].

---

[1] Cf. Exod 15:22-25.
[2] Cf. Num 21:6-9.
[3] Exod 14:15-31.

XXI

Reflections on the Mystery of Jesus' Death

§1.[1] *[Into your hands I commit my spirit.*[2] His divinity committed his humanity, for it had abandoned it [and] allowed it to suffer. [His divinity] was not separated from [his humanity] so as to be cut off from it, but it was hidden in [God's] power from the slain one and from the slayers. For, if it had appeared, he who was dying would not have been afraid, and if it had been revealed, his slayers could not have slain him. Nevertheless it was indeed keeping watch over him lest he perish. He who was keeping watch was aware, but he over whom watch was being kept was not aware. Then afterwards, it was revealed and showed [something] to both of them, to the one who was slain, that he had not been abandoned,[3] and to the slayers, that they were not able to fulfil their task of keeping guard over the tomb and containing the dead one [within it].

---

[1] T. Baarda has edited, translated and commented on a Syriac fragment of Ephrem's Commentary which covers the content of XXI, §1 as far as "containing the dead one [within it]," in an article entitled "A Syriac Fragment of Mar Ephraem's Commentary on the Diatessaron," *NTS* 8 (1961-62), pp. 287-300. The manuscript in which this short portion of Ephrem's Commentary is found is *Borgia Syriaca* MS 82, of the Museo Borgiano di Propaganda in Rome. I include my rendering of the fragment in this footnote, rather than in the main text, since it is not possible to determine its relationship to *Chester Beatty* MS 709, which is missing for this section:

> "Mar Ephrem, the Teacher, from the Commentary of the Diatessaron
>
> [literally, ܕܝܐܛܣܪܘܢ, Diastaron] Gospel: *Into your hands I commit my spirit.*
>
> His humanity committed his divinity, for it had abandoned it and allowed it to suffer. He was not separated from it so as to be cut off from it, but it was hidden in [God's] power from the slain one and the slayers. For if he had appeared, not even he who had been slain would have feared, and if he had been revealed, not even the slayers would have been able to slay [him]. But he was indeed keeping watch over him lest he perish. He, who was keeping watch, was aware, but he over whom watch was being kept did not perceive. Then afterwards, he was revealed and showed [something] to both of them, to the one who was slain that he had not been abandoned in Sheol, and to the slayers, that they were not able to fulfil their task of keeping guard over the tomb and containing the corpse [within it]."

A comparison of both texts illustrates how close the Armenian version is to this particular Syriac fragment. Two points of difference are noteworthy. The Syriac reads, "his humanity committed his divinity," whereas the Armenian reads the reverse; and the Syriac attests "in Sheol" after the words, "he had not been abandoned." It would be very interesting and instructive if one could compare this Syriac fragment with the text of the missing folio of *Chester Beatty* MS 709 for XXI, §1. For fuller comments on the text of the entire fragment, cf. Baarda, *op. cit.*, pp. 293-300.

[2] Luke 23:46.

[3] Cf. Ps 16:10; Acts 2:27; 13:35.

[The Lord] confirmed his promise to mortal beings by deeds. He showed that his humanity could suffer through achieving [his goal], for it had [really] died, and he showed that even those who were dead could live [again]. He raised up [his humanity], and faith was affirmed in those who listened to him. But the enemy recognized his condemnation when *the sun was eclipsed and the curtain of the temple was torn*,[1] when the guards were overwhelmed, *and the tombs were opened and the dead were raised*.[2]

§2.   {God was born, united to human nature. It was not his person which was born, but the nature which was joined to him, and for whom it was nautral that it be born according to the flesh. It was not possible to be born in any way other than through being formed with the same members [as ours], nor to die, except through being joined together to these same [members] themselves. It was therefore in accordance with the order of things that [the Lord] brought his body from the gate of the maternal womb to the gate of the tomb. He opened the closed womb through his birth, and through his resurrection opened the tomb which was surrounded and guarded. He placed his cross in the middle [between birth and resurrection], so that those born of the womb and making their way towards death would first meet the cross, the tree of life. They would [thus] gather fruit from it and accumulate it in their body, so that when death would have assembled them into its bosom they would tear it apart and go forth from its midst.

If, therefore, at the death [of the Lord], [the divinity] was not to be found with [the humanity], it was not that it wished to be separated from it. Rather it was because death was not able to approach the place where the life that kills death was. But, at his birth [the divinity] was to be found with [the humanity] because birth and divinity are not incompatible. Birth in fact is the beginning of all beings; it unites all beings and creation participates in the power of its Creator. But death is the destruction of everything that is, whereas God is the essence which remains. This is why he cannot be in death. It was not to learn something that he came to us, but to fill our deficiencies to overflowing with his plenitude.

---

[1] Cf. Luke 23:44-45; Matt 27:51.
[2] Cf. Matt 27:52-54.

§3.   [[His] body, of its nature, suffered with his soul which was capable of suffering, for the soul experiences suffering. Therefore, his humanity suffered because of his body, and it experienced sufferings because of the soul. *The Spirit will come and his power will cover.*[1] This same body has become the bread of life and nourishment for the faithful. *The Spirit will come, together with the power of the Most High; for the one to be born of you will indeed be called Son of God.*[2] [Scripture] says of the body that it was born of [woman]. But those who claim that the body of our Saviour was but a likeness similar to that of the angels, who ate in the home of Abraham,[3] are refuted [by Scripture], for it is not written that these [angels] were attacked, tormented, slain and crucified, since it was only their form that was changed. They were not really corporeal, but had taken on a form adapted to those who saw them. Lest it be imagined that our Lord was similar to this, he was born, so that his coming forth from the womb might prevent and remove from [people's] minds the opinion that there was a similarity.

If he had been the son of an alien [god], the sun would not have been eclipsed[4] when [the Lord] was raised on his cross. But the Creator would have spread forth a more intense light, because his enemy would have been withdrawn from his sight. He would have caused his light to shine forth on the Jews, because they would have been executing his will. He would have clothed the temple with a curtain of glory, because it would have been purified of its sad [defilements] by its enemy, and the dissolver of its Law would have gone forth from it.

If [one claims] that it was the father of an alien [god] who brought about the darkness, [one could reply] that this was not part of his domain, and that if it was, he would not have brought it about, firstly, because he is beneficent, and secondly, because [the Lord] has said, *Forgive them, because they do not know what they are doing.*[5] He drew the sun back to darkness so that those who had failed to recognize him and had crucified him, although they were walking in the light, would perhaps recognize him if darkness surrounded them.

---

[1] Luke 1:35.
[2] *Idem.*
[3] Cf. Gen 18:1-8.
[4] Cf. Luke 23:45. See I, §11 above for a similar reference to this idea.
[5] Luke 23:34.

Nature's Protest at Jesus' Death

§4. {*The curtain was torn.*[1] [This was] to show that [the Lord] had taken the kingdom away from them and had given it to a people who would bear fruit.[2] Alternatively, he was indicating, through the similitude of the torn curtain, that the temple would be destroyed because his Spirit had gone forth from it. Since the high priest had wrongfully torn his robe, the Spirit tore the curtain to proclaim the audacity of the pride [of the Jews], by means of an action on the level of created beings. Because [the high priest] had torn his priesthood},[3] and had cast it from him, [the Spirit] also rent the curtain asunder,[4] came out and brought forth everything. Or [alternatively], just as the temple in which Judas had thrown down the gold[5] was dissolved and rejected, so too, [the Lord] pulled down and rent asunder the curtain of the door through which [Judas] had entered. Or, [it was] because they had stripped him of his garments that he rent the curtain in two. For the heart of the rock was burst asunder,[6] but their own hearts did not repent.

§5. [God] was victorious over the Egyptians in [the month of] Nisan, and he lit up [the way for] the Hebrews with the pillar [of fire] in Nisan.[7] *The sun became dark*[8] over them because they had rendered evil in place of the contrary [goodness]. Just as [God] had rent the sea, the Spirit rent the curtain asunder, since the King of Glory was rejected and crucified on the Skull,[9] unjustly; for this reason the curtain of the temple was rent asunder justly. Created beings suffered with [him] in his suffering. The sun hid its face so as not to see him when he was crucified. It retracted its light back into itself so as to die with him. There was darkness for three hours, then it shone [again], thus proclaiming that its Lord would rise from Sheol on the third day. *For the mountains trembled, the tombs were opened and the curtain was torn,*[10] as though lamenting in mourning over the

---

[1] Mark 15:38.

[2] Cf. Matt 21:43.

[3] The Syriac text of *Chester Beatty* MS 709 resumes at this point, after the lacuna which began at XVIII, §3 above.

[4] Cf. Matt 27:51.

[5] Cf. Matt 27:5.

[6] Cf. Matt 27:51.

[7] Cf. Exod 13:4, 21-22.

[8] Luke 23:45.

[9] I. e., Golgotha. Cf. Matt 27:33.

[10] Cf. Matt 27:51-52. The Greek text reads "earth" whereas Ephrem has "mountains."

impending destruction of the place. Or [alternatively], because a human mouth had condemned [the Lord], the mouth of created beings was acclaiming and justifiying him. These [Jews] were silent, but the stones cried out, just as he had said.[1] The curtain tore asunder their ears, which were closed up, and gave glory to [him] whom they had denied.

§6.   Or, [it was] because the Spirit, when it saw the Son, suspended and naked, lifted itself up[2] and rent in two the garment of its adornment. Or, [it was] because the symbols, when they saw the Lamb of symbols, rent the curtain asunder and went out to meet him. Or, because the spirit of prophecy, which was dwelling in the temple and had come down to herald his coming to humanity, took flight at that very instant, to announce in the heights concerning our Lord's ascent into heaven. *The tombs were rent asunder,*[3] so that he might show that he could have rent the wood of the cross asunder; but he did not rend asunder that through which the kingdom would be torn from Israel, and he did not shatter that through which sin would be routed from the midst of the Gentiles. But the Spirit rent the curtain asunder in its stead; and to show that [the Spirit] had come forth [from the temple], it summoned the just who came out of the tombs[4] as witnesses to its going forth. These two goings forth therefore were proclaiming each other mutually. Because the kingship and the priesthood were anointed and sanctified in the Spirit, the Spirit, wellspring of these two [functions], went forth from there, so that it would be known that both of them had been cut off by means of him who had assumed them both.

    We, even though we know that, through the amputation of our finger, there is healing for the person who is wholly diseased, yet we are unwilling to do what we know [we should]. However, God knew that, through the killing of his Son, there would be salvation for humanity, and so he did not turn aside from doing this.

§7.   Abraham had many servants. Why did [God] not command him to offer up one of these? It was because [Abraham's] love would not have been revealed by a servant. His son, therefore, was necessary so that

---

[1] Cf. Luke 19:40.
[2] From its dwelling in the Holy of Holies.
[3] Cf. Matt 27:51-52.
[4] Cf. Matt 27:52-53.

Abraham's love might be revealed.[1] There were likewise [other] servants of God, but he did not show his love towards his creatures through any of these, but rather through his Son, through whom his love for us might be proclaimed. *For God so loved the world that [he gave] his only Son.* [2]

§8. *Jesus' kinsfolk stood afar off,*[3] so that [the word of the psalmist] might be fulfilled, *My neighbours stood afar off.*[4] They killed him before the Sabbath, while there was opportunity[5] for death, and before the Sabbath they buried him, while there was place for mourning. For the Sabbath itself is the boundary mark for toil, and on it all distress must remain [hidden] within. There is no place for suffering on it and neither has it any share in corruption.

§9. From Abraham [onwards], the symbols of the wood and the lamb began to be delineated. For Isaac was a symbol of the lamb [caught] in the tree,[6] while Jacob showed [that] the wood can vivify water.[7] Wood therefore was worthy that he be suspended from it, since no bone in him was broken.[8] The fruits of the earth are stimulated by wood, and the treasures of the sea are grasped by means of wood. So too, in the case of the body and the soul.[9] It was this [the wood of the cross] that was hewn by the wrath of the rabid crowd. It was like a mute person in its silence, and in its agility a source of growth to the heights for humanity.

---

[1] Cf. Gen 22:1-18.

[2] John 3:16.

[3] Luke 23:49.

[4] Ps 38:12.

[5] The Syriac reading, ܐܚܝܕܘܬܐ ܒܡܘܬܐ , "intensity in death" is incomprehensible. Leloir suggests that the Armenian reading should be adopted here: "time for death" [ܠܗ ܙܒܢܐ ܕܡܘܬܐ], in place of the Syriac (cf. EC-CBM 8, p. 213). Another possibility might be "while it was yet Friday" [ܥܕ ܗܘ ܥܪܘܒܬܐ]. For this latter suggestion I am indebted to Sebastian Brock.

[6] Cf. Gen 22:1-13.

[7] Cf. Gen 30:37-42.

[8] Cf. John 19:33-36.

[9] A difficult and very condensed image; Leloir (EC-CBM 8, p. 213) suggests the following interpretation: "Just as ships are needed for the sea's treasures to be exploited, and the fruits of the earth need trees to hang from, so too the soul needs the body, its instrument." A simpler interpretation, more consonant with the passage as a whole, is that of S. P. Brock, "So too, body and soul need the wood of the cross."

Jesus Pierced by a Lance

§10.   *One of the soldiers struck him with a lance.*[1] [The Lord] honoured his friends with his dishonour, and reproached those who reproached him, so that his enemies might learn about his justice and his friends about his grace. The fountain [issuing] from his side revealed the blood which had made complaint,[2] and the waters issued forth, hastening to purify. The blood, on its appearance, roared forth against the murderers of [the Lord], and the water, through its symbol, was for the purification of his friends. [That happened] so that they would know that, after he had died, he would be [still] alive. The more they increased their torturing of him, [the more] the treasures hidden in him were revealed. The heavenly riches abounded in each one of his members, and when the destroyers drew near, they flowed in abundance to enrich his friends and accuse his crucifiers.

I have run towards all your members, I have received all [possible] gifts from them, and, through the side pierced by a lance, I have entered into Paradise enclosed by a lance.[3] Let us enter through the pierced side, since it was through the rib that was extracted [from Adam] that we were robbed of the promise.[4] Because of the fire that burned in Adam - it burned in him because of his rib - it was because of this that the side of the Second Adam was pierced, and there issued forth from it a stream of water to extinguish the fire of the First Adam.

§11.   Since all vitality is in the blood,[5] blood also issued forth in grace, the symbol of vitality for [humanity] which justly deserved mortality. Through the power of the evil mediator, fire was kindled against them, but, through the power of the [good] Mediator, extinguishing waters gushed forth for them. No one is more evil than he who deceived Adam, who had not sinned against him, and there is none comparable to him apart from the one who pierced our Lord after he had died. That evil, therefore, which had been victorious, was vanquished in turn. For, *there came forth blood,*[6] through which we were bought back from slavery, [and]

---

[1] John 19:34.
[2] Cf. Matt 26:63; John 19:9.
[3] Cf. Gen 3:24.
[4] Cf. Gen 2:21-22.
[5] Cf. Lev 17:11.
[6] John 19:34.

water too, so that everyone who approaches the redeeming blood will be washed and purified from that evil slavery which was enslaving him. *There came forth blood and water,*[1] which is his Church, and it is built on him, just as [in the case of] Adam, whose wife was taken from his side.[2] Adam's rib is his wife, and the blood of our Lord is his Church. From Adam's rib there was death, but from our Lord's rib, life. The olive tree [symbolizes] the mystery of Christ, from which spring forth milk, water and oil; milk for the children, water for the youths and oil for the sick. The olive tree gave water and blood through its death, [just as] the Messiah gave these through his death.[3]

§12.　　　Envy persecuted David, and jealousy the Son of David. David was blocked up in the depths of the cave, and the Son of David in the depths of the underworld. It was imagined that David was guilty, and that the Son of David was vanquished, [but] it was Saul who was guilty and despised, and death that was conquered and laid low. David cried out, *Where is your spear, O King?*,[4] and the Son of David, *Where is your victory, O Death?*[5] Saul hurled his spear against David, and, although it did not strike him, the wall was witness to its blow.[6] The crucifiers struck the Son of David with a lance,[7] and, although his power was not injured, his body was a witness to their blow. David was not struck, nor was the Son of David injured. The wall, the spear and the cave reprove Saul, while the body, the cross and the tomb condemn the Hebrews.[8]

§13.　　　On the day that [the Lord's] wound was [inflicted], on that [same day] the wound was closed up. The eve of the Sabbath that drove the nails into him was [the day] which removed the nails from him in the depths of Sheol. It was amongst the living that they had pierced his side, [but] it was amongst the dead that he closed up his side. But how could the wound

---

[1] *Idem.*

[2] Cf. Gen 2:21-22.

[3] There is a play here between the words for oil [ܡܫܚܐ] and the Messiah/Christ [ܡܫܝܚܐ] which are almost identical.

[4] 1 Sam 26:16.

[5] 1 Cor 15:55.

[6] Cf. 1 Sam 18:10-11.

[7] Cf. John 19:34.

[8] There is a long addition in the Armenian text at this point, a good illustration of how the Armenian text in this part of the commentary becomes the *textus longior*.

that was closed up have been broken open again after ten days, and fingers creep into it?[1]

Further Reflections on Jesus' Death

§14.   Moses' hands were spread out, and God held them stretched out until their enemies fell.[2] But these [Jews] stretched out the hands of his Son on the cross, and because they did the opposite of this,[3] [God] also effected for them this reversal, which was the opposite to their having stretched out [the Lord's] hands. They fell but did not rise up again. It will be likewise for the Gentiles who had believed in the outstretched hands, since the experience to which Moses had subjected them made them afraid. [The Gentiles] did the opposite to these [the Jews], and so the opposite was done to them.[4] The death of the cross which he died [took place] so that this [Scripture] might be fulfilled, *Like a lamb he went to the slaughter and like a sheep before the shearers.*[5] It is difficult to perceive logically[6] that he should be killed first, and then shorn. But that was said of [the Lord], because he was killed by that sentence which came forth from the judge's mouth, and after that they then came and stretched him out on the cross. Spread out [thus] over the earth, he was like a sheep before the shearers.

Or alternatively, he died the death of the cross so that, through it, there might be delineated the mystery that through his death all who die will rise. [It can be seen] from this too that, when he was crucified, he was standing erect in the centre of the cross, like the stone on the high-priest's breast.[7] Jerusalem is the centre of the earth because of the Just One who put his Law there, so that his rays might go forth to all the ends [of the earth].[8] Because, in the very same place, Grace fixed his cross so that he might extend its arms to every side, and lift up souls from every part [of the world].

---

[1] Cf. John 20:24-29.

[2] Cf. Exod 17:8-14. What follows here is a very strong anti-Jewish passage.

[3] That is, the opposite of what Moses had accomplished for the Israelites through the stretching out of hands.

[4] That is, they received the grace of conversion.

[5] Isa 53:7.

[6] Literally, "naturally."

[7] Cf. Exod 28:15-30.

[8] Cf. Ezek 38:12.

§15.   Jesus died to the world, so that none might live for the world, and he conducted himself in the flesh in a crucified way, so that none would live a life of luxury in [the flesh]. He died to our world in our body, that we might live to his world in his body. He mortified the life of the flesh, so that we would not live in a carnal way in the flesh. He became a teacher, not through the tribulations of others, but through sufferings in his own person. He himself tasted bitterness first, for he explained to us that no one could become his disciple through titles [of honour], but through sufferings.[1]

§16.[2]

§17.   There were two baptisms to be found in the case of our Lord, purifier of all. One was through water, and the other through the cross, so that he might teach about [the baptism] of water through that of suffering. For, repentance for sinners is a crucifixion for them, which nails their members secretly, lest they yield to pleasures. This is what John had proclaimed before our Lord.[3] Consequently, the two baptisms are necessary for both just and sinners. If [only] one is present, it cannot vivify without its companion.

If you say that there is no open persecution, there is [nonetheless] a secret persecution. For, should the inquiry persecute your faith, confess our Lord without [constraint from] the inquiry. Persecution by kings is not as evil as persecution by investigators. Instruments of torture are not difficult to bear like heresies,[4] nor are tortures like interrogations; nor the flaying of skin like disputation, nor decapitation like mental doubts. If hatred persecutes [you], bear witness to charity; if jealousy persecutes [you], bear witness to harmony, if lustful desire persecutes [you], be wholehearted in chastity. Thus, [if] injustice [persecutes you], bear witness to justice, and [if] wealth [persecutes you], bear witness to our Lord, the Lord of the [whole] body. All these persecutors were persecuting the confessors in [time of] peace, and it was because they were victorious through hidden persecutors that they were crowned through the external

---

[1] Cf. Matt 20:20-28.
[2] There is a long addition in the Armenian tradition here, numbered §16 in the CSCO edition.
[3] Cf. Matt 3:1-12.
[4] There is a clever play here on the words for "instruments of torture" [ܟܘܬ] and [ܟܘܬ] "heresies," which in Syriac differ only in one consonant.

persecutors. Train yourself against those which are invisible so that you may be able to withstand those which are visible. If then you are overcome by the persecutors which are within you, how can you hope to conquer the persecutors that are outside you?

§18.   The shame of the cross was greater than generations and peoples. If the death of Adam brought death on all nations, who is in a position to withstand the great shame [against] the honour [of God]? For, if justice had not been been separated from grace at that time, who would have been able to [have withstood] the force of justice? Who would have forgiven us if this grace had not forgiven us? His grace, however, took pity on us, while he was hanging on the wood, and, for the honour of his justice, it covered the wise with reproach, while it called forth unto those without knowledge, *For they know not what they are doing.*[1] His justice bears witness, and has accused us in the parable of the vineyard, *The vinedressers recognized the heir of the vineyard.*[2] It was not when the heir was near them, but while he was afar off, that they deliberated on his murder, so that the inheritance might fall to their advantage.

§19.   Lest anyone be presumptious in relation to his justice or blaspheme his grace [by saying], "Why did he come if they did not recognize him, and what use was it [to them] if they did not discern [who] he was, and why did he hide himself from the [Jewish] people and reveal [himself] to the Gentiles?", his justice has answered [for] him. So that none could accuse his justice it showed in advance that [the Jews] did know him. So that his grace might be commended because of its forgiveness and its expiation, [his justice] said concerning them that [the Jews] did not know him.

Jesus' Burial

§20.   Mary [stands] for Eve, and Joseph for [another] Joseph. For he too, *who asked for his corpse,*[3] was named Joseph. The earlier [Joseph] was *a just man, who did not denounce* Mary publicly.[4] The other one too was *a*

---

[1] Luke 23:34.
[2] Cf. Matt 21:38.
[3] Matt 27:58.
[4] Matt 1:19.

326

just man, for he did not consent to the detractors.[1] So that it might be clear that [the Lord] was entrusted at the beginning to [one bearing] this name when he was born, he further allowed one [bearing this name] to prepare him for burial when he was dead, so that [this name] might receive the full recompense for having served him at his birth in the cave, and [for having served] his corpse at the tomb.

§21.   [The fact] that *they sealed the tomb,*[2] was in [the Lord's] favour and to their disadvantage, as in [the case] of both Daniel and Lazarus.[3] [In the case] of Daniel, when [the king and his companions] saw their seal on the pit, they knew what power had liberated him who was in the pit. [In the case of Lazarus], when [his adversaries] saw their seal which was on the door of the tomb, it became clear to them that this was a power for which everything was easy. He took the body out from the tomb, although it was sealed, and the seal of the tomb witnessed in favour of the seal [of virginity] of the womb that had borne him. For it was when the virginity [of his mother] was sealed that the Son emerged alive from within her, for he was the First-Born in every way.

A stone was placed at the entrance to the tomb.[4] Thus, one stone [was placed] against another stone, so that [this] stone might be keeping guard over *the stone which the builders rejected.*[5] This [stone], lifted up by [human] hands, had to keep guard over that which was *detached, without [human] hands;*[6] this [stone], on which *the angel was sitting,*[7] [had to keep guard] over that which *Jacob had placed under his head;*[8] this [stone] with its seal [had to keep guard] over that which, through its seal, watches over the faithful. Thus did the gate of life go forth from the gate of death. *For this is the gate of our Lord, through which the just enter.*[9] When it was closed it delivered those closed in. Through its death the dead lived.[10] Through its voice the silent cried out. Through its resurrection, there was

---

[1] Luke 23:51.
[2] Cf. Matt 27:66.
[3] Cf. Dan 6:18; John 11:38.
[4] Matt 27:60.
[5] Cf. Ps 118:22; Matt 21:42.
[6] Dan 2:34,45.
[7] Cf. Matt 28:2.
[8] Gen 28:18.
[9] Ps 118:20.
[10] Cf. Matt 27:52-53.

an earthquake.[1] Its emergence forth from the tomb introduced the Gentiles into the Church.[2]

The Risen Lord and Mary Magdalen

§22.   *Mary went first to the tomb*,[3] but he was [already] risen. No one had been aware of the hour of his resurrection, but Mary announced [it] to the disciples;[4] for it was not fitting that the hour of the resurrection of him who is immortal be written down. [In order to explain why] the three days were not completed, [some] say, "Because Judas *hanged himself*,[5] many found fault with him, [saying], Why did he destroy his own life because of him who had not himself [yet] arisen?" Thus, it was to remove this idea from [their] midst that he rose before the fixed term. Moreover, [they were saying] too that the disciples had defected. For if Simon, their leader, had taken an oath and denied him,[6] there was all the more reason why those following after him [could do likewise]. That is why he first affirmed [their] weak spirit, lest it be overwhelmed. For they themselves, the sons of his right hand, did not really have confidence that he would emerge from Sheol. Because no one had ever done this before, [his] wisdom hastened to console them. Or [alternatively], from the day on which he was crucified until the day of his resurrection, one can [in fact] count three days of descent and ascent. Or again, [one can consider] that from the day on which he gave his body and blood, there are three complete days.

§23.   If he left his clothes behind in the tomb,[7] it was so that Adam could enter into Paradise without clothing, just as he had been before he had sinned.[8] In place of having had to leave it clothed, he now had to strip himself before entering there [again]. Or [alternatively], he abandoned them to symbolize the mystery of the resurrection of the dead, for just as [the Lord] rose into glory without clothes, so too, we [will rise] with our works and not with our clothes.

---

[1] Cf. Matt 27:51,54.
[2] Cf. Matt 27:54.
[3] John 20:1.
[4] Cf. John 20:17-18.
[5] Matt 27:6.
[6] Cf. Matt 26:72.
[7] Cf. Luke 24:12; John 20:5-8.
[8] Cf. Gen 2:25.

§24. [The fact] that they persuaded [them] with money [to say] that *his disciples have stolen him while we slept*[1] [shows that the Lord] had informed them through his voice that he had led the dead forth from the depths of Sheol; and it also [shows] that he had no need of robbers to be witnesses to his resurrection. For he had likewise closed the mouth of demons, since truth cannot be believed when coming from liars. If Adam had not sinned let the Jews explain to us how humanity would have lived. Likewise, if they had not killed the Messiah, God could have given life to the people and to the Gentiles by another method.

§25. Let us also say that, if Adam died because of sin, it was fitting that he who removed sin would assume death too. Just as it was said to Adam, *The day on which you eat of it you will die,*[2] - he did not die however on the day when he ate it, but [instead] received a pledge of his death through his being stripped of his glory, chased from Paradise and haunted daily by [the prospect of] death, - so too, in like manner, with regard to life in Christ, we eat his body instead of the fruit of the tree, and we have his altar in place of the garden of Eden. The curse is washed away by his innocent blood, and in the hope of the resurrection we await the life that is to come.[3] Already we walk in a new life, for these [the body of Christ and his altar] are the pledges of it for us.

§26. He said, *Do not touch me,*[4] first of all, because this body was [like] a first flowering fruit from Sheol, which our Lord, as priest, was preserving carefully from contact with any [human] hand, so as to offer it to the [only] hand capable of receiving such a gift, and capable of paying the price for an offering such as this. Secondly, [he did not want anyone to touch him] in order to show that this body was [already] glorified and magnified. Thus he showed them that, while he had been a servant, everyone had power over him, since even tax-collectors and sinners used to come and touch him.[5] But, when he was made Lord, fear of him was over everyone like [the fear of] God.[6] Even kings and nobles convince us [of this], for those who see [them] are afraid to touch them.

---

[1] Cf. Matt 28:12-13.
[2] Gen 2:17.
[3] Cf. Rom 8:23-25.
[4] John 20:17.
[5] Cf. Luke 15:1-2.
[6] The fear of God was one of the spiritual dispositions on which Syrian theologians insisted most (cf. Leloir, EC-SC 121, p. 389).

[The Lord wanted no one to touch him] to show his enemies also that they had no further power to apprehend him. But his friends have power to touch him through another means, in love and fear. For, in eating his body sacramentally, they subject him again [in a certain sense] to his passion. Let him then teach those who eat him to subject their bodies to the passion with him, so that they will give joy to him through their suffering, just as he gave them joy through his. Some say too that [the Lord did not want her to touch him] because Mary had not received the sacrament of his body and blood. [He did this] in order to give an illustration that, not only could his enemies no longer approach his sacrament - as in the case of the Isacriot - but even those of his friends like Mary, who were not marked with the seal.

[The Lord] also did not allow Mary to touch him on account of the fact that Eve, in stretching out her arm, had subjected this body to death and crowned it with all kinds of sufferings, but he reserved this [privilege] for the arm which made him sit at his right,[1] and for the hand which crowned him with all kinds of good things after his ascension.

§27.   Moreover [he did not allow her touch him] because Mary had doubted. For, having heard that he had risen, she came and, having seen him, said to him, *Is it you who have taken him away?*[2] Because she had doubted, to show her that he was truly risen, he said [to her], *I am going up to the Father.*[3] It was not that she was not to touch him before he went up to the Father, but because of her doubt [he said to her], *Before I go up to my Father, you must not touch me.*[4] This is like that [passage], *You will remove the sword, with regard to your own self,*[5] that is, a denial.[6] For if he had forbidden her to touch him because she had doubted his resurrection, take note that Thomas, who had been in doubt about him, nevertheless touched him.[7] Let us explain it as follows: just as he had predicted concerning his passion before his passion, and concerning his resurrection before his [actual] resurrection, he wished here too to foretell

---

[1] Cf. Ps 110:1.

[2] John 20:15.

[3] John 20:17.

[4] *Idem.*

[5] Luke 2:35. See II, §17 above, where this text is also quoted, with the verb likewise in the second person singular, feminine, causative form.

[6] Through the juxtaposition of these two texts Ephrem gives the impression of confusing or "fusing" Mary the Mother of Jesus with Mary Magdalen. See above, II, §17, and the explanatory note there with regard to this tradition in Syriac writings.

[7] Cf. John 20:24-29.

his ascension. By saying, *Do not touch me*, he poured forth abundantly, filling her with a new proclamation concerning his ascension, *Go! Say to my brothers, I am going up to my Father and to your Father, to my God and to your God. Do not touch me, for I have not yet gone up to my Father*.[1] He had blessed [the bread] for Cleophas' household,[2] had eaten with his disciples before he had ascended,[3] and had shown his side to Thomas. Why, therefore, did he prevent Mary from touching him? Perhaps it was because he had confided her to John in his place, *Woman, behold your son*.[4] However, just as the first sign had not been without her,[5] so too it was fitting that the first fruits [of his emergence] from Sheol should not be [without her]. Thus, although she did not touch him, she was comforted.

§28.   *I have not yet gone up to my Father*.[6] It seems that he made this response against Mary's reckoning. He had taught her, as he had the apostles, that he was about to be raised up to heaven, that he would return bodily at the end, and that he would give her the recompense that he had promised her. Having suddenly recognized him, she was transported in spirit to that other coming, and she thought she had attained the kingdom of the heavens. That is why he said to her, *I have not yet gone up to my Father*. Moreover, because [he was] a new Son, First-Born of Sheol, into which all the peoples, generations and families had perished, he had also shown by these [words] that no one would be converted by his resurrection [alone], [neither] *the fathers to their sons, nor the sons to their fathers*,[7] but that all would be converted to this, that they would become worthy of ascending through mercy towards the Father.

§29.   *I am going up to my Father and to your Father, to my God and to your God*.[8] If one understands [these words] just as they are written, the Father would be in the heavens and not on the earth. If he had also been on earth, how could the Son have gone to him in the heavens? No more than the Son was not in the heavens, the Father was not on the earth. He

---

[1] John 20:17.
[2] Cf. Luke 24:30.
[3] Cf. Luke 24:41-43; John 21:12-15.
[4] John 19:26. Note again the "fusion" of the two Marys as in §28 above.
[5] Cf. John 2:1-11.
[6] John 20:17.
[7] Cf. Mal 3:24; Luke 1:17.
[8] John 20:17.

said in reality, *I am coming to you, my Father,*[1] and not "my God." When he was speaking with him he called him, "my Father," to show that he was indeed from him. When he sent [Mary] to his disciples, saying, "I am going to him," he called him "my God" to show that he was similar to him. He also said, *I am not alone, for my Father is with me,*[2] and, *I am in my Father, and my Father is in me;*[3] and also, *We are one.*[4] *I am going up to my Father and to your Father, to my God and to your God.* He did not say, "To our Father and our God" but, "my Father" and then, "your Father"; and, "my God," and then, "your God." If he had given the response in an equal manner,[5] perhaps there would have been grounds for their objection. "My Father and your Father, my God and your God": both of these refer to his humanity. He was speaking in fact about his body which was going away, and not about the Word of God. Likewise [he said], "your Father," because they were human beings. Likewise, it was from the point of view of his humanity that it was said, *Our Father, who [is] in the heavens.*[6]

Peter's Threefold Protest of Love

§30.   [The Lord] said to Simon, *Follow me,*[7] speaking to him thus of his death. *This one returned, and seeing the other disciple, said to him, As for him, what about him, Lord? He said to him, What does it matter to you?*[8] Simon said this only because he wanted our Lord to allow this disciple to come with him. Our Lord taught thus through Simon's request that he had power over death, like his Father. He said in fact, *If I wish.*[9] But he did not wish it, however, so that they might all be crowned with the victory of his death.

---

[1] John 17:11.
[2] John 16:32.
[3] John 14:11.
[4] John 10:30.
[5] If he had not distinguished between "my God" and "your God."
[6] Matt 6:9.
[7] John 21:19.
[8] John 21:20-22. Literally, "To you, what to you?"
[9] John 21:22-23.

The Redemptive Nature of Jesus' Death

§31.   Our Lord gave the oil to his disciples, as a symbol of his name, indicating thus that he was everything to all [peoples]. Although unique, he gave the light to [all] lamps, and chased the darkness and its works away.[1]

§32   Our debt so surpassed everything in its enormity that neither the prophets nor the priests, nor the just nor kings were able to acquit it. Therefore, when the Son of the Lord of everything came, although omnipotent, he did not acquit our debt, either in the womb [of his mother], or by his birth, or by his baptism. [He did not acquit it] until he was delivered over to the cross and tasted death, so that his death might be redemption for our debt. Through it, that [debt], which all creatures were incapable of paying, would be acquitted.

§33.   Because the pledge of life was taken away from those subjected to death, death [itself] was also taken away from nature over which it was reigning,[2] and he made it sit at his right, [like] a hostage [seized] from inferior creatures.[3] He sent them a sure pledge, [issued] from his own nature, the Paraclete Spirit, pledge of life. If we have been delivered from the slavery of sin, was it by a servant that we were delivered? No, for servants are not freed by other servants. Take note then of two wonderful actions. Who divided the languages? The Father. Were those whose [language] was confused[4] sinners or just? Sinners. When the Spirit was sent, to whom did it come? To the apostles. Were not these just? Yes, assuredly. How then did the Father divide the languages of sinners, and the Spirit [that of] the just and of the apostles?[5] The work of [the Spirit] is therefore greater and more noble than that of the Father.

[The Lord] raised up our body with him, so that he would be the protector of his [human] race, and that, through him, inferior creatures would be recognized in the hall of the heavenly king, since it was through our [body] that this divinity was brought down unto us.

---

[1] There is another long addition here in the Armenian version.
[2] Cf. Rom 5:14.
[3] Cf. *De Nativitate*, 22,40. On Christ's body as a "hostage", see S. P. Brock, "Christ 'the hostage': a theme in the East Syriac liturgical tradition and its origins," forthcoming in the Festschrift for L. Abramowski (Tübingen).
[4] Cf. Gen 11:1-9.
[5] Cf. Acts 2:1-11.

XXII

The Risen Lord Commissions His Disciples

§1. *But you then, remain in Jerusalem until you receive the promise of my Father.*[1] This refers to what Joel [said], *Your sons and your daughters will prophesy; [portents of] blood and fire;*[2] *blood,* because of his crucifixion, *and fire;* that of tongues. Because the crowds which had come up for the feast went away sorrowful after the death of our Lord, he sent his builders to confirm their faith which was wavering, and he sent his steadfast pillars[3] to sustain their spirit which was weakened. [The crowds] observed in his disciples that power which seemed to them to have been extinguished with his body on the cross. When they saw that the name [of Jesus], who had been put to death,[4] was raising the dead, his death seemed to them to be of greater importance than his life. During his life he himself was restoring [people] to life; but when he was thought to have died, the name of the dead one began to work wonders with regard to death [itself]. [This was] in order to show that, if, while dead, his name was bringing death into subjection, how could death stand before his living power?

§2.[5]

Exhortation to True Insight and Wisdom[6]

§3. There are those who hang onto the fringes of the truth, and this latter does not allow them to fall on account of its vigour. You must not seek the power of words which cripple discourse outwardly. Rather you must attend to their meanings, as to how they are fulfilled, and to whom they refer. Do not seek refuge in counter arguments, but in the strength of

---

[1] Cf. Luke 24:49; Acts 1:4.
[2] Joel 3:1,3.
[3] Cf. Gal 2:9.
[4] Cf. Acts 9:36-41; 20:7-12.
[5] §2 represents a long addition in the Armenian version.
[6] What follows from this point onwards belongs more to the category of spiritual reflections and prayers, than to a commentary on the Gospel text. One could ask whether these reflections originally belonged to the Diatessaron Commentary, and whether they come directly from Ephrem.

their sound conviction, [that is], in the covenant by which the Spirit has delineated the members of Christ, to show its hidden form by means of revealed mysteries. For [the Spirit] has indicated great things by means of small things, and disclosed hidden things by means of revealed things. It has indicated the times, and shown forth the numbers. It has arranged the hours, and placed mystery in the names, and understanding in the distinctions. For those of former times, wisdom was perceived to be in deeds rather than in words. They preferred greatness of mind in silence rather than the exercise of the tongue.

§4. Have reverence for chastity as though for God himself. Know that it is good when you do good, and that you think evilly in thinking impious things. With regard to everything you think about: even if you do not accomplish it, whatever evil is [in it] is nevertheless engraven in your spirit, and the image of good things is [also] delineated in you. The good person is [like] the mind of God. The wise person, by his counsels, is a prophet for those who need him. The one who has abandoned truth, and taken refuge in its appearance, will be delivered over to death by that very refuge. Do not ask from God those riches which you cannot conserve, for the gifts of God cannot be carried off.

Stir up your soul so that, by his wisdom, you may know what is fitting, and that, by his will, what is in the commandment may come to pass. One who is pleasing to the wicked is more evil than they. Impure words are only verbiage and empty noise. *Abundance of words will not go blameless.*[1] Abundance of words is the sign of no discipline. Some disciples were asking one of their teachers what is to be preferred out of [all] good things. He replied to them, "Wisdom, for all other things can be snatched away, and each one has its opposite." [Opposite] to wealth is poverty; to love, there is death, to glory there is ignominy, to strength weakness. But greatness of soul is trustworthy wherever it is found. It comforts the rich with regard to the worries of riches, it consoles the poor with regard to the discomforts of need, it strengthens old men, it educates children and maintains youth in chastity. It is accustomed, no matter how many times familiar with shipwreck, to withstand by means of a plank. For it is the virtue which triumphs over everything.

---

[1] Prov 10:19.

335

Reflections on the Power and Mercy of God

§5.　　　Our difficulties are easy for [God], and things impossible for us are simple for him, just as [the Lord], who is from him, taught us through his first coming in humility and full of grace. He taught me that the number of our requests is greater than we [are able to make], since he inclines his ears to us and [gives] us his gifts according as our will is enlightened. For he has shown, in chastening me with [the example] of *the scribes and pharisees who were prolonging their prayers and increasing their greed*,[1] that it is not the multitude of our words that is heard, but love which surpasses all treasures.

For the Merciful One instructed me about himself silently,[2] that these [prayers] do come before him. He justified the tax collector for discretion in his words, and brought him out of the temple, accompanied by the praise of the angels who rejoiced at those who repent.[3] His voice called Zacchaeus and the sound of his voice was like rennet within him. He had him come down from the fig tree, or rather, symbolically, from his evil conduct, of which the fig tree was the symbol.[4] His voice put an end to Zacchaeus' sins, to whose iniquity there was no end. It was he too who spread his mercy over the son of Timaeus, whose repeated cries announced [not only] his distress,[5] but also the help which he was going to receive. [This was] like that sinful woman who was a physician to her wounds, because of the remedies she had taken,[6] and went to him for whom it was easy to mix into everything his forgiveness, which heals every suffering.

§6.　　　He loves the just and takes pity on sinners; he holds the good to be innocent and protects them from evil ones. He contends with the just in favour of sinners. When those who had worked continuously murmured against the unemployed, since the salary of these latter was equal, though their work was not, he made the words of those who had been rewarded, [which they uttered] against those who had been pitied, [be applied] against themselves. [He showed them] thus that, even if they had not received

---

[1] Cf. Matt 23:14.
[2] That is, by his example alone, which the author is going to illustrate.
[3] Cf. Luke 18:9-14; 15:7,10.
[4] Cf. Luke 19:1-10.
[5] Cf. Mark 10:46-52.
[6] Cf. Luke 7:36-50.

mercy, nevertheless they had not been cheated.[1] It was on account of their own glory in fact that he had not pitied them, lest he deny justice what was its right, so that those who had been rewarded through justice could be distinguished from those who had been pitied through grace.

It was fitting therefore that he who was without reproach should perform, in favour of the weak, that which surpasses justice. But it was also fitting for him who was prudent that he should perform that which could not be censured by grace. If [God] exacts and kills, does this mean that he possesses an evil nature? No! Or, if he is compassionate and merciful, does this mean that injustice moves him? When he condemns, he does not remain in doubt on the pretext that perhaps a person will do penance, as though unaware. But, if he pities and has mercy, his intention is not dissolved by fear, as to whether a person will turn back, as though [God] were unable to discern. But, since he possesses foreknowledge, this becomes an instrument at the service of his good and just will. When he judges and when he takes pity, the result of both of these shine before him. For he who has measured the world is not unmindful of this, since he suffers with each one of us; that is, with each one of us personally. But this [suffering] is through knowledge only, just as we too, in the case of someone suffering a fever. We suffer with such a one through the knowledge of it only.

---

[1] Cf. Matt 20:8-16.

337

PRAYERS[1]

Hymn to Divine Mercy

§1.   In accordance with your mercy, through which the doorway to your spiritual help is opened, the following has become clear to us, O Lord, when there is an interior conflict against ourselves within.[2] Everyone who struggles [does so] through your strength, and everyone who conquers [does so] through your will. We are instruments[3] endowed with senses, and it is in and through their rebellions that the [crown] of victory of their Creator is woven. But, apart from some kind of pact [with God], it is not possible that this be comprehended, lest we become prisoners to their caprice.[4] For we are in need of this, lest we wander about aimlessly, through the dissolution of our will. Rather, let [God's] love fall upon us [as] one, restraining us without coercion, urging us unto our spiritual benefit. For he, whose dominion is without reproach, is quite capable of forgiving our transgressions unto his glory. We are not saying these things for the sake of our own advantage, nor are we ashamed that we are seeking our spiritual help from the doorway of our Lord.

§2.   Why should you have any need to give us our treasure? Indeed [you need nothing] except that we enlarge our hearts[5] to carry your beautiful [gifts], offering you our will through the listening of our ears. All your works shine forth with the crowns which the wisdom of your mouth has woven for them, when you said, *Behold, it is very beautiful.*[6] Everything we praise you for, we also owe you.[7]

§3.   The life of Adam was a herald of your mercy, to raise up an heir who would bring his inheritance to nought. For you desired to possess a second time through repentance one who, today as formerly,[8] schemed to rebel against your providence, since he had let go of his life for your

---

[1] These paragraphs contain some prayers and a final note or appendix on the Evangelists.
[2] The opening lines of this paragraph are difficult to translate. What is offered here is an approximation of the content.
[3] Or "vessels."
[4] Literally, "their freewill" (of the inner rebellions of the senses?).
[5] Literally, "our breasts."
[6] Cf. Gen 1:31.
[7] A long addition follows here in the Armenian version.
[8] Literally, "in both [economies]."

338

kingdom. In your mercy you entrusted Abel as the first into the depths of Sheol. [This was] in order that it would be compelled in justice to cast him forth from its depths, so that, on his account, the door which had closed up everyone might be opened, and the bosom which was enfolding them might be emptied bare. For, if Adam had been the first to enter [into Sheol], which was his deservedly, it would have been meted out to him to remain there forever. You acted similarly with the sons of the house of Noah on account of [Noah], and also with the daughters of Lot because of their father.[1] For it was fitting that Abel should have become the thurible from which the blessings of the risen dead began to rise up to you, rather than that Adam should remain in Sheol, head low and shrouded in mourning, [as] first-born of Sheol and prince of darkness.

§4.   Therefore, how your mercy rejoiced in this place, for it was [like] a reins for our adversaries. It was also [similar to] when your design repented,[2] [your design] which could not repent however on account of its foreknowledge. For everything in its entirety and every achievement was revealed to it, and its ultimate achievement is of greater importance to it than its initial coming into being. [This was] so that the decree which your justice established might be rescinded, and also that we be given a remnant and a residue for the renewal[3] and leaven of humanity, as though a reward of your consolation. You opened the door to your grace so that it could enter and intercede with you on our behalf, for it had heard your voice which was accusing us. But this [accusation] was the cause of our resurrection. For, *the propensity of human beings is continually towards evil.*[4] The mouth of justice opened to exterminate us, but the tongue of grace unloosened itself to take pity on us. By this [word], justice condemned us because of our freewill, but grace confronted it and justified us on account of our nature. For [Scripture] added there, *From their youth.*[5] He, who has already chosen his friends, has shown us that we are not judged in his presence by the course of time,[6] but that all those

---

[1] Cf. Gen 6:8-19; 19:12-22.

[2] Cf. Gen 6:6.

[3] The Syriac word is ܚܘܠܦܐ , "substitute, exchange, barter."

[4] Gen 8:21.

[5] *Idem.*

[6] That is, by the length of our life.

who enter into [this] world by reason of his profound wisdom[1] are marked out, sealed and measured by their works.

§5.   For, when his Son clothed himself with our form unto our glory, we presented [him] in it to you unto the judgement of death. Although your justice appears severe, nevertheless, through our being placed under its obligation, and through the reward which [comes] from it, that fruit[2] of our deeds increases for us. For, since [the Son] has liberated our freewill from the power of the Evil One, it is an instrument which the Maker has established, through which freewill might reveal its glorious deeds; for, through it, the splendour of our victory increases in conflict. It is a furnace which, through the tribulations of its sufferings, brings us to a state of being which is full of all beauties, that we might be an adornment for the kingdom. The more we discern these things, the more we correct our soul and our discerning knowledge.

§6.   Oh mercy, sent forth and poured upon all! With whom is it to be found if not [with you], O Lord? Through your death, you take pity [on all]; you have placed [it] on all, and by your being slain [you have opened] the treasury of your mercy. Even if we say, "My Lord," as is our wont, do not snatch the name of your lordship from our mouth, but, by the testimony which is from our mouth, you are able to grasp hold of us all the more. For you are hidden from all in [their capacity] for seeing, [yet depicted] in all by reason of all their movements. His deeds depict the [Maker] for us and his created entities teach [us] about the Creator,[3] so that you may be able to touch him, [who is] hidden when one searches for him, but revealed in his {gifts}.[4] It is difficult {to gain access face to face} with him, {but it is easy} to come near {him}.

§7.   ... {We praise you}, you, who place a word in our mouth, enabling us to be pleaders on behalf of our requests. Adam acclaims you in {peace},

---

[1] Literally, ܐܘܢܝ ,"mind, intelligence"

[2] Literally, ܐܠܝ , "child/offspring."

[3] Cf. Wis 13:1; Rom 1:19-20.

[4] The overall condition of these final folios is poor. There are many lacunae for one or more words at various points. In the translation which follows, where it is possible to do so, words contained {thus} are suggested reconstructions based on the Armenian version (cf. CSCO 145, pp. 242-247). The beginning of §7 is in such poor condition that some lines cannot be translated at all and have been omitted.

340

together with his posterity, all of them are enclosed within your grace. The winds praise you when they drive the waters. The earth praises you when its tenderness is unlocked, and it hastens to give [its] fruits in their seasons. The seas praise you in their surging, when, as though with mouths, their thunderings become heralds of your lordship over them. The trees praise you when they are tossed about by the blowing of the winds, so that they may be obedient to pollination and bearing fruit. The tender grass in its variety and the flowers in their colours praise you, when they imbibe the rains, {...} together with the {vapour} of the dew. Let them {assemble} and {join} their mouths together {...}, as though {constraining} each other, {...} all your praises {...}, working for this like architects, all unto your thanksgiving. Therefore, it is for us to strain towards you with our full will, and it is for you to pour a little of your plenitude on us, so that we may possess your truth, which converts, through which you take hold of and [banish] our weakness, which, without your gift, cannot approach you, Lord of our gifts.

§8.[1]   Because we were abandoned in the desert to the wiles of the wolf,[2] beyond the reach of the peaceful staff of our merciful pastor, our state of peace was reproved by the remorse of {...}. This was not a true calm but a simulated one, despoiling the soul {in secret} but openly afflicting {...}[3] the body. {...} A vibrant remorse, which crept in after it to the innermost limit of the mind, {destroyed it}. It assuaged [the soul] in [its] thirst, inflamed it with inebriation and provoked it to repentance with chastisement. This is the medicine of our lives, in relation to which [the Lord] has made his body a breast nourishing our infancy, and his blood a font dispelling our thirst through drinking [it]. His plenitude has become [for us] a table of all good things.

§9.   Even if {our blessings} are unworthy of you, nevertheless they are {of benefit} to us, [that we may go forward] to encounter your gifts. Even if our acts of thanksgiving add [nothing] to you, nevertheless they can cause our weakness to be forgotten. Even if our prayer is [weak in its cry],

---

[1] The Syriac text here is in poor condition, which renders the task of translation difficult and approximate.

[2] The allusion here may be to certain unfortunate historical circumstances, when Barses, Bishop of Edessa, was expelled by the Emperor Valens [364-378], who installed a "wolf" in his place.

[3] There are one or two phrases missing here due to the state of the text, which renders the translation of this obscure passage even more difficult.

nevertheless [its] force is powerful. For it becomes an ascent for us towards you, and a descent for you towards us. However, it is not because it is strong that it is able to effect these things, but rather it is because you are good in your essence that you grant it its efficacy.

§10.   The cunning one approached the immature ear. In the guise of a first-fruit he gave them an [inferior] one that was later in season, and [these] foolish ones with regard to their capacity to listen surrendered to him. At rest are those who govern the heavenly beings, but those who subdue the rebellious ones are at toil. At rest also and advantaged are those who discern the good in that which is evident, but at toil and lacking are those who are brought into distress at things beautiful due to [their illegitimate] investigation into the hidden things [of God's nature]. Those who carry a glorious responsibility are more at rest than those who carry a shameful inactivity, for in the case of the latter, {their conscience} reproaches them, whereas the former are even extolled by their enemies.

Discipleship Motivated by Love Rather than Fear

Those who accomplish the Law without compulsion are chosen, but those who observe the Law under compulsion are not rejected. Even if the former are in an exalted position, the latter are nonetheless in the middle, for they are higher than others who are beneath them.

§11.   The former draw near because they are loved, while the latter do not withdraw because they are afraid. The love in which the former take refuge is not helpless and poor in [God's] presence, and the fear in which the latter seek support is not vile and despicable before him. The one [fear] casts the terrible shadow of its sceptre on all people, and whoever sees it trembles at it, with the result that such a one does not do to his companion that which is hateful to himself. The other [love] casts the shadow of its splendid crown on all people, and whoever sees it hastens to do to others what is agreeable to himself.[1] It is honourable when one does not covet that which does not belong to him, but it is a praiseworthy and godly thing when one shares what is his with many people. Those who,

---

[1] Fear induces practice of the negative form of the golden rule, whereas love induces the positive.

342

through fear, do not get involved in what is unlawful are great. They are tiny however compared to those who, through love, draw back their hands even from that which is permissible and lawful.

THE EVANGELISTS[1]

The words of the apostles are not in agreement because they did not write the Gospel at the same time. They did not receive the command like Moses, on tablets, but, as the prophet has said, *I will give them a covenant, not like this one, but my Law in their spirit, and I will write it on their heart.*[2] [Various] reasons summoned them, and they wrote.

Matthew wrote it in Hebrew, and it was then translated into Greek. Mark followed Simon Peter. When he went to Rome [the faithful] persuaded him [to write] so that they would remember the tradition, lest it be forgotten after a long time. He wrote what he had grasped. Luke began with the baptism of John. Since one had spoken of his incarnation and of his kingdom springing from David, and the other [had begun] with Abraham, John came and found that their words were proclaiming many things, for they had composed genealogies concerning his human origins.[3] Consequently he wrote that he had been not just a man, but, *In the beginning was the Word.*[4]

---

[1] This paragraph has no link with what has preceded. This fact, together with the nature and style of its contents, suggests that its authenticity should be questioned. Here too the Armenian tradition contains further material at the end of the paragraph.

[2] Cf. Jer 31:31-33.

[3] Literally, "that he was a son of man."

[4] John 1:1.

BIBLIOGRAPHY

Addai, *The Doctrine of Addai, the Apostle*, edited by G. Phillips (London, 1876).

Addai, *The Teaching of Addai*, edited by G. Howard, Texts and Translations 16 (Chico, California, 1981).

Aland, K. et al. (editors), *The Greek New Testament* (Stuttgart, 3rd corrected edition, 1983).

Aland, K. and Aland, B., *The Text of the New Testament.* Translated from the German by E. F. Rhodes (Grand Rapids/Leiden, 1987).

Aucher, J. -B. and Moesinger, G., *Evangelii Concordantis Expositio facta a Sancto Ephraemo Doctore Syro* (Venice, 1876).

Baarda, T., "A Syriac Fragment of Mar Ephraem's Commentary on the Diatessaron," *NTS* 8 (1961-1962), pp. 287-300.

Baarda, T., "Gadarenes, Gerasenes, Gergesenes and the 'Diatessaron' Traditions," *Neotestamentica et Semitica, Studies in honour of Matthew Black*, edited by E. E. Ellis (Edinburgh, 1969) pp. 181-197.

Baarda, T., "The Author of the Arabic Diatessaron," *SuppNT* 47 (1978), pp. 61-103.

Baarda, T., "In Search of the Diatessaron Text," *Early Transmission of the Words of Jesus: Thomas, Tatian and the Text of the New Testament* (Amsterdam, 1983), pp. 65-78.

Baarda, T., "Mar Ephraem's Commentary on the Diatessaron, Ch. XVII:10," *Early Transmission of the Words of Jesus: Thomas, Tatian and the Text of the New Testament* (Amsterdam, 1983), pp. 289-311.

Baarda, T., "To the Roots of the Syriac Diatessaron Tradition," *NT* 28 (1986), pp. 1-25.

Barnard, L. W., "The Origins and Emergence of the Church in Edessa during the First Two Centuries A. D.," *VigChr* 22 (1968), pp. 161-175.

Barnard, L. W., "The Heresy of Tatian - Once Again," *JEH* 19 (1968), pp. 1-10.

Barry, E., "St Ephrem's Commentary on Tatian's Diatessaron, Chapter Five," Unpublished M.A. Thesis (University College, Dublin 1990).

Beck, E., *Des Heiligen Ephraem des Syrers Carmina Nisibena*, edited and translated by E. Beck, CSCO 218-219 (Louvain, 1961).

Beck, E., "Der syrische Diatessaronkommentar zu Jo. I 1-5," *Oriens Christianus* 67 (1983), pp. 1-31.

Beck, E., "Der syrische Diatessaronkommentar zu der unvergebbaren Sünde wider den Heiligen Geist übersetzt und erklärt," *Oriens Christianus* 73 (1989), pp. 1-37.

Beck, E., "Der syrische Diatessaronkommentar zu der Perikope von der Samariterin am Brunnen übersetzt und erklärt," *Oriens Christianus* 74 (1990), pp. 1-24.

Beyer, K., *The Aramaic Language. Its Distribution and Subdivisions.* Translated from the German by John F. Healey (Göttingen, 1986).

Birdsall, J. N., "The New Testament Text," *The Cambridge History of the Bible*, Vol.1, edited by P. R. Ackroyd and C. F. Evans (Cambridge, 1970), pp. 308-377.

Birdsall, J.N., "'The Martyrdom of Eustathius of Mzhetha' and the Diatessaron: An Investigation," *NTS* 18 (1971), pp. 452-456.

Boismard, M. -E., avec la collaboration de A. Lamouille, *Le Diatessaron: De Tatien à Justin*, Etudes bibliques, nouvelle série 15 (Paris, 1992).

Brock, S. P., "An Introduction to Syriac Studies," *Horizons in Semitic Studies: Articles for the Student*, edited by J. H. Eaton. University Semitic Study Aids 8 (University of Birmingham, 1980), pp. 1-33.

Brock, S. P., "Passover, Annunciation and Epiclesis," *NT* 24 (1982), pp. 222-233.

Brock, S. P., *Syriac Perspectives on Late Antiquity* (London, 1984).

Brock, S. P., *The Harp of the Spirit. Eighteen Poems of Saint Ephrem* (Second enlarged edition, San Bernardino, California, 1984).

Brock, S. P., *The Luminous Eye. The Spiritual World Vision of St. Ephrem* (Rome, 1985, revised edition Kalamazoo, 1992).

Brock, S. P., *The Syriac Fathers on Prayer and the Spiritual Life* (Michigan, 1987).

Brock, S. P., "From Ephrem to Romanos," *Studia Patristica* 20 (Leuven, 1989), pp. 139-151.

Brock, S. P., "The Lost Old Syriac at Luke 1:35 and the earliest Syriac term for the incarnation," *Gospel Traditions in the Second Century*, edited by W. L. Petersen (Notre Dame, 1989), pp. 117-131.

Brock, S. P., "Christ 'the hostage': a theme in the East Syriac liturgical tradition and its origins," forthcoming in the Festschrift for L. Abramowski (Tübingen).

Bundy, D., "Jacob of Nisibis as a model for the episcopacy," *Le Muséon* 104 (1991), pp. 235-249.

Burkitt, F.C., *Evangelion daMepharreshe. The Curetonian Version of the Four Gospels* (Cambridge, 1904).

Cathcart, K. J., "The Biblical and Other Early Christian Manuscripts of the Chester Beatty Library," *Back to the Sources, Biblical and Near Eastern Studies in honour of Dermot Ryan*, edited by Kevin J. Cathcart and John F. Healey (Dublin, 1989), pp. 129-163.

Ciasca, A., *Tatiani Evangeliorum Harmoniae Arabice* (Rome, 1888; repr. 1930).

Clarke, G. W., "The Date of the Oration of Tatian," *HTR* 60 (1967), pp. 123-126.

Coakley, J. F., "Typology and the Birth of Christ on 6 Jan," *V Symposium Syriacum* edited by R. Lavenant, OCA 236 (Rome, 1990), pp. 247-256.

Cowley, R. W., "The 'Blood of Zechariah' (Mt 23:35) in Ethiopian Exegetical Tradition," *Studia Patristica* 18.1 (1985), pp. 293-302.

Cureton, W., *Ancient Syriac Documents relative to the Earliest Establishment of Christianity in Edessa* (London 1864; reproduced by the Oriental Press, Amsterdam, 1967).

Dols, M. W., "Syriac into Arabic: The Transmission of Greek Medicine," *Aram* 1 (1989), pp. 45-52.

Downing, F. G., "A Paradigm Perplex: Luke, Matthew and Mark," *NTS* 38 (1992), pp. 15-36.

Drijvers, H. J. W., *The Book of the Laws of Countries. Dialogue on Fate of Bardaisan of Edessa* (Assen, 1965).

Drijvers, H. J. W., *Bardaisan of Edessa*, Studia Semitica Neerlandica VI (Assen, 1966).

Drijvers, H. J. W., *East of Antioch. Studies in Early Syriac Christianity* (London, 1984).

Dungan, D. L., "Reactionary Trends in the Gospel Producing Activity of the Early Church: Marcion, Tatian, Mark," *Bibliotheca ETL* 34 (Louvain, 1974), pp. 179-202.

Edwards, O. C., "Diatessaron or Diatessara?," *Biblical Research* 18 (1973), pp. 44-56.

Egan, G. A., *St. Ephrem, An Exposition of the Gospel*, CSCO 291/292 (Louvain, 1968).

Egan, G. A., "A Reconsideration of the Authenticity of Ephrem's 'Exposition of the Gospel'," *Kyriakon: Festschrift Joannes Quasten*, edited by P. Granfield and J. A. Jungmann (Münster, 1970), pp. 128-134.

Epp, E. J., "The New Testament Papyrus Manuscripts in Historical Perspective," *To Touch the Text: Biblical and Related Studies in Honour of Joseph A. Fitzmyer, S. J.*, edited by M. P. Horgan and P. J. Kobelski (New York, 1989), pp. 261-288.

Eusebius, *The Ecclesiastical History, Books I-X*, with an English Translation by K. Lake, in two volumes. The Loeb Classical Library (London, 1926).

Eusebius, *Histoire ecclésiastique, Livres I-VI*, edited by G. Bardy. SC 31 (Paris, 1952).

Fitzmyer, J.A., "The Languages of Palestine in the First Century A.D.," *CBQ* 32 (1970), pp. 501-531.

Fitzmyer, J.A., *The Genesis Apocryphon of Qumran Cave I, A Commentary* (Rome, Second, Revised Edition, 1971).

de Halleux, A., "L'adoration des Mages dans le commentaire syriaque du Diatessaron," *Le Muséon* 104 (1991), pp. 251-264.

de Halleux, A., Review of L. Leloir, *Saint Ephrem: Commentaire de l'évangile concordant. Texte syriaque (MS Chester Beatty 709) Folios Additionnels* (Leuven/Paris, 1990), *Le Muséon* 104 (1991), pp. 392-396.

de Halleux, A., "Le comput ephrémien du cycle de la Nativité," *The Four Gospels: Festschrift F. Neirynck*, edited by F. Van Segbroeck, C. M. Tuckett, G. Van Belle, J. Verheyden, *Bibliotheca ETL* 100 (Leuven, 1992), pp. 2369-2382.

Harris, J. R., *The Diatessaron of Tatian, A Preliminary Study* (London, 1890).

Harris, J. R., *Fragments of the Commentary of Ephrem Syrus upon the Diatessaron* (London, 1895).

Hawthorne, G. F., "Tatian and His Discourse to the Greek," *HTR* 57 (1964), pp. 161-188.

Higgins, A. J. B., "The Arabic Version of Tatian's Diatessaron," *JTS* 45 (1944), pp. 187-199.

Hill, J. H., *The Earliest Life of Christ ever Compiled from the Gospels, Being the Diatessaron of Tatian* (Edinburgh, 1894).

Irenaeus, *Against Heresies*, ed. J. P. Migne, *Patrologia Graeca* 7 (Paris, 1857).

Jerome, *De Viris Illustribus*. A Select Library of Nicene and Post-Nicene Fathers of the Christian Church (Second Series), translated under the editorial supervision of H. Wace and P. Schaff, Volume III (Oxford, 1892).

Kenyon, F., *Our Bible and the Ancient Manuscripts* (London, 1958).

Kraeling, C. H., *A Greek Fragment of Tatian's Diatessaron from Dura. Edited with Facsimile, Transcription and Introduction*, Studies and Documents, Volume III, (London, 1935).

Leloir, L., *Saint Ephrem. Commentaire de l'évangile concordant* (version arménienne), CSCO 137 (Louvain, 1953).

Leloir, L., *Saint Ephrem. Commentaire de l'évangile concordant* (traduction latine), CSCO 145 (Louvain, 1954).

Leloir, L., "Le Diatessaron de Tatian," *L'Orient Syrien* 1 (1956), pp. 208-231, 313-334.

Leloir, L., *L'Evangile d'Ephrem d'après les oeuvres éditées*, CSCO 180 (Louvain, 1958).

Leloir, L., "L'original syriaque du commentaire de S. Ephrem sur le Diatessaron," *Biblica* 40 (1959), pp. 559-570.

Leloir, L., *Doctrines et Méthodes de S. Ephrem d'après son commentaire de l'évangile (original syriaque et version arménienne)*, CSCO 220 (Louvain, 1961).

Leloir, L., *Le Témoignage de S. Ephrem sur le Diatessaron*, CSCO 227 (Louvain, 1962).

Leloir, L., "Le Diatessaron de Tatien et son commentaire par Ephrem," *La Venue du Messie: Messianisme et Eschatologie*, édité par E. Massaux, Recherches Bibliques 6 (Bruges, 1962), pp. 243-260.

Leloir, L., *Saint Ephrem: Commentaire de l'évangile concordant. Texte syriaque (MS Chester Beatty 709).* Chester Beatty Monographs 8 (Dublin, 1963).

Leloir, L., "Divergences entre l'original syriaque et la version arménienne du commentaire d'Ephrem sur le Diatessaron," *Mélanges Eugène Tisserant*, 2 (Città del Vaticano, 1964), pp. 303-331.

Leloir, L., *Ephrem de Nisibe, Commentaire de l'évangile concordant ou Diatessaron, traduit du syriaque et de l'arménien.* SC 121 (Paris, 1966).

Leloir, L., "L'actualité du message d'Ephrem," *Parole de L'Orient* 4 (1973), pp. 55-72.

Leloir, L., "Le commentaire d'Ephrem sur le Diatessaron. Quarante et un folios retouvés," *RB* 94 (1987), pp. 481-518.

Leloir, L., "S. Ephrem: Le Texte de son commentaire du Sermon sur la Montagne," *Mémorial Dom Jean Gribomont (1920-1986)*, SEA 27 (Rome, 1988), pp. 361-391.

Leloir, L., *Saint Ephrem: Commentaire de l'évangile concordant. Texte syriaque (MS Chester Beatty 709), Folios Additionnels* (Leuven/Paris, 1990).

Leloir, L.,"Le Commentaire de Ephrem sur le Diatessaron. Réflexions et Suggestions," *The Four Gospels: Festschrift F. Neirynck*, edited by F. Van Segbroeck, C. M. Tuckett, G. Van Belle, J. Verheyden, *Bibliotheca ETL* 100 (Leuven, 1992), pp. 2359-2367.

Lewis, A. S., *The Old Syriac Gospels; the Text of the Sinai Palimpsest, with the Variants of the Curetonian Text* (London, 1910).

McCarthy, C., "Gospel Exegesis from a Semitic Church: Ephrem's Commentary on the Sermon on the Mount," *Tradition of the Text, Studies offered to Dominique Barthélemy in celebration of his 70th Birthday*, edited by Gerard J. Norton and Stephen Pisano, OBO 109 (Freiburg/Göttingen, 1991), pp. 103-123.

Marmardji, A.-S., *Diatessaron de Tatien. Texte arabe établi, traduit en français, collationné avec les anciennes versions syriaques, suivi d'un évangéliaire diatessarique syriaque et accompagné de quatre planches hors texte* (Beirut, 1935).

Metzger, B. M., "Tatian's Diatessaron and a Persian Harmony of the Gospels," *Chapters in the History of New Testament Textual Criticism* (Leiden, 1963), pp. 97-120.

Metzger, B. M., *The Text of the New Testament, Its Transmission, Corruption and Restoration* (Oxford, 2nd edition, 1968).

Metzger, B. M., *A Textual Commentary on the Greek New Testament* (London/ New York, Corrected Edition, 1975).

Metzger, B. M., *The Early Versions of the New Testament* (Oxford, 1977).

Migne, J. P., *Patres Graeci* 7 (Paris, 1857).

Murray, R., "Reconstructing the Diatessaron," *Heythrop Journal* 10 (1969), pp. 43-49.

Murray, R., "The Lance which Re-opened Paradise, a Mysterious Reading in the Early Syriac Fathers," *OCP* 39 (1973), pp. 224-234, 491.

Murray, R., *Symbols of Church and Kingdom, A Study in Early Syriac Tradition* (Cambridge, 1975).

Nestle, E. and Aland, K., *Greek-English New Testament* (Stuttgart, 26th Revised Edition, 1981).

Ortiz de Urbina, I. (ed.), *Vetus Evangelium Syrorum et exinde excerptum Diatessaron Tatiani*, Biblia Polyglotta Matritensia Series VI, (Madrid, 1967).

Ortiz de Urbina, I., "Una nueva reconstrucción del Diatessaron de Taciano," *Estudios Eclesiásticos* 44 (1969), pp. 519-526.

Ortiz Valdivieso, P., "Un nuevo fragmento siriaco del Comentario de san Efrén al Diatésaron (PPalau-Rib. 2)," *StPapyr* 5 (1966), pp. 7-17.

Payne Smith, R., *Thesaurus Syriacus*, 2 Volumes (Oxford, 1897 and 1901).

Payne Smith, J. (ed.), *A Compendious Syriac Dictionary* (Oxford, 1903).

Petersen, W. L., "Romanos and the Diatessaron: Readings and Method," *NTS* 29 (1983), pp. 484-507.

Petersen, W. L., "The Dependence of Romanos the Melodist upon the Syriac Ephrem: its Importance for the Origin of the Kontakion," *VigChr* 39 (1985), pp. 171-187.

Petersen, W. L., *The Diatessaron and Ephrem Syrus as Sources of Romanos the Melodist*, CSCO 475 (Leuven, 1985).

Petersen, W. L., "New Evidence for the Question of the Original Language of the Diatessaron," *Studien zum Text and zur Ethik des Neuen Testaments: Festschrift zum 80. Geburtstag von Heinrich Greeven*, edited by W. Schrage (Berlin, 1986), pp. 325-343.

Petersen, W. L., "Some Remarks on the Integrity of Ephrem's Commentary on the Diatessaron," *Studia Patristica* 20 (Leuven, 1989), pp. 197-202.

Petersen, W. L., "The Dependence of Romanos the Melodist upon the Syriac Ephrem," *Studia Patristica* 18,4 (Kalamazoo/Leuven, 1990), pp. 274-281.

Pink, K., "Die pseudo-paulinischen Briefe I," *Biblica* 6 (1925), pp. 68-91.

Preuschen, E., *Tatians Diatessaron aus den Arabischen übersetz*. Mit einer einleitenden Abhandlung und textkritischen Anmerkungen herausg. von A. Pott (Heidelberg, 1926).

Robson, P., "Ephrem as Poet," *Horizons in Semitic Studies: Articles for the Student*, edited by J. H. Eaton, University Semitic Study Aids 8 (University of Birmingham, 1980), pp. 34-38.

Segal, J. B., *Edessa, The Blessed City* (Oxford, 1970).

Tatian, *Oratio ad Graecos, and Fragments*, edited by M. Whittaker (Oxford, 1982).

Vööbus, A., *Early Versions of the New Testament, Manuscript Studies* (Stockholm, 1954).

Vööbus, A., *History of Asceticism in the Syrian Orient, A Contribution to the History of Culture in the Near East* (3 vols.) CSCO 184, 197, 500 (Louvain, 1958, 1960, 1988).

Weir, G. A., "Tatian's Diatessaron and the Old Syriac Gospels: the Evidence of MS. Chester Beatty 709," Unpublished Ph. D. Dissertation (Edinburgh 1969/70).

Wright, W., *A Short History of Syriac Literature* (London, 1894).

Yousif, P., "Exegetical Principles of St Ephraem of Nisibis," *Studia Patristica* 18,4 (Kalamazoo/Leuven, 1990), pp. 296-302.

Yousif, P., "Symbolisme christologique dans la Bible et dans la Nature chez saint Éphrem de Nisibe (De Virginitate VIII-XI et les textes parallèles)," *Parole de l'Orient* 8 (1977-1978), pp. 5-66.

Index of Biblical References

356

362

11:34-35	264	15:12	288
11:35	96, 262	15:13	288
11:37	263, 311	15:16	93
11:38	327	15:17	288
11:39	263, 264, 265, 266	15:18	161
11:41-42	297	15:19	93
11:42	154	15:20	149, 150, 286
11:43	264, 266	15:25	272
11:44	265	16:7	288, 289
11:45	261	16:11	290
11:46	142	16:15	239
11:48	265, 266	16:28	41
11:48-50	266	16:32	332
11:49-52	302	16:33	286
12:1-3	264	17:1	291
12:2-6	265	17:5	290
12:5	267	17:11	332
12:7	81	17:12	150, 195
12:10	267	18:4	298
12:15	273	18:5-6	298
12:31	271, 272	18:6	214, 299
12:34	272	18:7	298, 299
12:47	276	18:9	297
12:48	276	18:10	287, 298
12:49	234	18:12-13	299
13:1-15	160, 282	18:22	116
13:1-17	268	18:28	300
13:5	219	18:37-38	301
13:10	101	19:2	301
13:16	286	19:9	322
13:18-19	284	19:15	71, 301
13:21	283	19:17	304
13:21-30	284	19:23	307
13:23	163, 308	19:25-27	192
13:23-25	160	19:26	331
13:23-26	283	19:26-27	97
13:25	308	19:27	65, 308
13:25-26	219	19:29	269
13:26	284	19:33-36	321
13:34	288	19:34	171, 269, 322, 323
14:6	195	20:1	328
14:8	286	20:5-7	301
14:9	286	20:5-8	328
14:10	234	20:8	126
14:11	332	20:15	68, 97, 330
14:12	286	20:16-17	96
14:16	114, 288	20:17	329, 330, 331
14:30	286	20:19-23	150
15:3	101	20:24-29	324, 330

Index of Modern Authors

Pink, K.	54
Pisano, S. (ed)	17
Robson, P.	16
Sanda, A.	28
Schaff, P. (ed)	13
Segal, J. B.	10, 11, 12, 22
Vööbus, A.	4, 5, 7, 64
Wace, H. (ed)	13
Weir, G. A.	35, 36
Whittaker, M. (ed)	3, 4
Yousif, P.	13, 22, 23
Zahn, T. (ed)	23

Sequence of Topics in the Commentary